Disrupting Adult and Community Education

Disrupting Adult and Community Education

Teaching, Learning, and Working in the Periphery

Edited by

Robert C. Mizzi
Tonette S. Rocco
Sue Shore

Foreword by

John Field

Published by State University of New York Press, Albany

For information, contact State University of New York Press, Albany, NY
www.sunypress.edu

Production, Eileen Nizer
Marketing, Anne M. Valentine

Library of Congress Cataloging-in-Publication Data

Names: Mizzi, Robert C., editor of compilation. | Rocco, Tonette S.,
    editor of compilation. | Shore, Sue, editor.
Title: Disrupting adult and community education: teaching, learning, and
    working in the periphery / edited by Robert C. Mizzi, Tonette S. Rocco,
    and Sue Shore ; foreword by John Field.
Description: Albany : State University of New York Press, 2016. | Includes
    bibliographical references and index.
Identifiers: LCCN 2015026349 | ISBN 9781438460918 (hardcover : alk. paper) |
    ISBN 9781438460925 (paperback : alk. paper) | ISBN 9781438460932 (e-book)
Subjects: LCSH: Adult education—Social aspects. | Adult education—Moral and
    ethical aspects. | Community education—Social aspects. | Community
    educaton—Moral and ethical aspects.
Classification: LCC LC5225.S64 D57 2016 | DDC 374—dc23
LC record available at http://lccn.loc.gov/2015026349

10 9 8 7 6 5 4 3 2 1

Contents

IMMIGRANT EXPERIENCES OF WORK AND LEARNING
IN THE NEW WORLD ORDER

TRANSNATIONAL ADULT EDUCATION AND GLOBAL ENGAGEMENT

Foreword

Adult and community education has long survived on the periphery. This marginal status is often lamented, frequently through the much-used metaphor of "Cinderella." But it is also celebrated and enjoyed; being at the edge means that you frequently operate far from the gaze of our rulers, opening up spaces for experiment and innovation, as well as forging possibilities for new alliances and creative pedagogies. These spaces and possibilities are always bounded, of course, but they nevertheless give adult and community education an edgy quality, and allow a reworking of the balance between domesticating and emancipating practices.

For the last forty years, though, adult and community education has found its marginal status eroding. During the capitalist crisis of the 1970s, governments in a number of countries developed policies for adult skills. Until the 1990s, institutional developments focused largely on such fields as adult literacy and the expansion of higher education systems, along with increased funding for research and for development projects with specific target groups such as the adult unemployed or minority ethnic groups. From the 1990s, though, the discourse of lifelong learning and increasing concern over economic competitiveness and social cohesion in the old industrial nations started to change the rules of the game. From now on, adult and community education stands in the spotlight.

This new central position has presented opportunities, but it has also created difficult challenges. The dominant discourse of skills and employability threatens to swamp the broad and generous traditions of a learner-centered curriculum and pedagogy that had evolved in the field over decades. An emphasis on social inclusion has chimed closely with adult educators' concern for the least advantaged; but in its dominant forms it requires including the marginalized and stigmatized into the existing social and economic order, rather than working with learners in ways that can challenge and change that order.

The focus of this book is on identifying the ways in which adult and community education can support the status quo and legitimate its norms, and exploring practices that tackle stigma, explode taboos, subvert oppression and rattle the cages of the mind. On the one hand, the contributors are concerned with the ways in which the often hidden everyday practices of adult and community education can set boundaries to what learners can imagine and do—for themselves, for their families, for their communities. On the other, they seek to make visible the peripheral and subjugated practices and peoples whose learning troubles the normalizing practices of the dominant, mainstream forms of adult education. And this includes a fundamental rethinking of our basic ideas and ideals—whether this concerns easily spoken phrases like "social justice" or "learner centred," or the basic building blocks of professional identity and practice among those working in the field, or the very conception of knowledge itself.

The editors and contributors have, then, set themselves a difficult and at times a risky task. Yet, it is fair to say, it is almost certainly less risky than the marginalized learning spaces in which adult and community educators work alongside and with peripheral learners. Sustainable, just practice requires resources of hope and resilience: if we are to disrupt conventional practices and wisdoms, we need to be able to imagine ways of living otherwise. I rather suspect that editing this book also required an optimistic will to change, along with a sober appreciation of the complex ways in which multiple inequalities and oppressions must implicate us all.

I have found this a wonderful collection of perspectives on adult and community education in our times, which provides a rich resource for people working in our field. It sets out tough questions about our values, about our willingness to confront the often invisible relations of power and stigma in our field, and about our capacity to engage in just and equitable ways with learners from beyond the comfortable edge of our social world. Many people involved in adult and community education worry about the broader ethical purpose and social consequences of their work, and they try to find workable solutions to the dilemmas that poses. I hope that they share my joy in reading these chapters, and are equally inspired and challenged by this deliberately unsettling book.

John Field, University of Stirling, Scotland

Acknowledgments

Books such as this owe their emergence to many things and relationships. People who work and learn in academic and community-based institutions think about and factor work differently into daily schedules—hence it is not always possible to include writing into everyday work and we thank those who could participate and need to remain mindful of why some couldn't participate. As we worked with the 32 authors residing in seven countries, we understood just how sharp the divisions are between the academy and grassroots work. While we have known this in our various working lives, we were also reminded of the degree to which this shapes what eventually comes to be known as the written body of work. We hope that these chapters will go some way to introducing alternatives to the marginalizing and stigmatizing strategies that hold sway in so many parts of the world.

We dedicate this book to the many learners represented by the chapters in this collection and acknowledge their persistent efforts to engender cultures of respect despite a growing climate of indifference.

We also wish to extend our thanks to the many people in our lives, colleagues, friends, and students who continue to teach us, keep us grounded, and give us great joy. Thank you for understanding the importance of this work in our lives. Thanks to the Faculty of Education at the University of Manitoba (Canada) in providing financial support for the creation of the index.

Robert thanks his partner, Andrew, who walks with him every evening and listens to all sorts of ideas and questions. Andrew's mantra, "it'll be alright" always seems to be spot on. Robert acknowledges his mentors, Andre Grace and Tonette Rocco, who have taken the time to guide his interest and skills for writing and researching the lives of people historically forgotten.

Tonette wishes to dedicate this work to my granddaughter, Mason Lynne Phinney, whose mantra is "uh-oh," a feeling that I share often, and who waddles when she walks. Hopefully she will read this book one day and work with us to change the world.

Sue thanks Greg Novak and Lauren Novak who have tolerated my "occasional" preference for books and journal articles over time spent with them and are very much appreciated as friends as well as partner and daughter.

Starting Somewhere

Troubling Perspectives of Periphery and Center
in Adult and Community Education

Robert C. Mizzi
Sue Shore
Tonette S. Rocco

Adult education, as an institutionalized practice, has long been recognized as implicated in affirming *and* contesting privileged knowledge for engagement in civil society and the economic contributions expected of productive citizens around the globe. Yet affirmation practices are not always acknowledged by researchers and practitioners as problematic even when in the act of contesting privileged knowledge. Rather, affirmation practices are often justified as normative—a necessary, indeed routine, part of living, learning, and earning in the modern day world of capitalism. An exploration of the social issues associated with these routine practices of adult education, as an institutionalized practice with historical dimensions, provides the opportunity to unsettle the horizons of possibility that have structured the way educators and researchers imagine what adult education does in the name of empowerment *and also* exclusion. In recent history this has taken the form of unsettling the traditional disciplinary boundaries of the professional discipline ("adult education") by drawing on crosscutting disciplinary insights from (post)colonialism, cultural studies, feminism, conflict, labor and migration studies, and critical economics. In doing so many adult educators and adult education researchers have positioned the field of practice as an important mechanism for survival, transformation, and emancipation on multiple fronts. This work of educators and researchers has been further complicated by the extent to which neoliberal practices of transnational and institutional governance have reconfigured learning, employment, and citizenship within market discourses of progress. Such reconfigurations within the dominant discourse of the market simultaneously stigmatize, and position as peripheral to the needs of the market, collectives such as prisoners, sex workers, artisans, micro-entrepreneurs, Aboriginal and Indigenous people, immigrants, and those who contest normative sexual and gender relations. Although access and equity strategies have gained global recognition within adult education discourse, institutionalized forms of adult education are still associated with a set of mooring practices intent on normalization and reform of learners. While some Indigenous peoples have successfully disrupted skill assessments set within the logics of Western qualification frameworks (Dannenmann & Haig-Brown, 2002), immigrant populations are often caught in a paradox that currently promotes global mobility while working against recognition of their prior learning (Guo, this collection). In both instances, and indeed in the other examples provided in this book, teaching and learning practices in *alternative* forums go unrecognized. This lack of recognition reinforces a dominant meritocracy. It is the tradition of excluded groups disturbing the boundaries around adult education that we resurrect here and which shapes the spirit of this edited collection of work.

The intent of this book is to examine how people as educators, researchers, and learners take up opportunities for teaching and learning individually and collectively as they are simultaneously positioned by decisions and forces that place them, and the people with whom they work, on the periphery of social and economic decision making. This often means their lives as educators, researchers, and learners—as people—are given ad-hoc attention in "official" policy and practice. Alternatively, they are often made the *object* of those policies with little negotiation or regard for how they will live out their lives under such regimes. Consideration of the peripherality of their lives is often coupled with an expectation that they will simultaneously reconfigure their lives to align with dominant social and structural norms and practices rather than the realities of their lives being positioned as the catalyst for change.

In this book we take the position that a number of features have long defined what counts as "conduct" in adult learning settings:

appeals for self-direction, the valuing of individual experience, relevance to the immediate and everyday situations in which adults find themselves, reflective practice which will produce transparent knowledge about experience, an expectation of progress or improvement in life circumstances, a claim that such progress comes from sustained perseverance and an expectation that knowledge gained will be put to benevolent purposes. (Shore, 2004, p. 91)

Such features are at face value inherently sensible yet they are often anchored in the default assumptions of Western meritocracy. Following Grace and Rocco (2009), the significance of this collection is its focus on disturbing formalized adult education as an industrial and credentialist project and simultaneously offering examples of the kind of "conduct" that activates subversive, taboo, and clandestine theory-building work. We argue that achieving the former and ignoring the latter is a way in which adult education scholarship continues to marginalize and stigmatize the knowledge building work of "peripheral" individuals and communities. Paying attention to the practices of marginalization and listening to learners who are often sidelined is ever more urgent if we want to ensure that theorizing what might be called "adult education" continues to be relevant, respectful, and articulated with the concerns at the center of people's lives.

With this in mind, the chapters in this book challenge readers to think beyond the classroom and the credential as key pedagogical sites and resources for change. Chapters disrupt familiar notions of informal, nonformal, and post-formal schooling contexts by activating an emergent understanding of life as lived in contemporary learning spaces: urban streets, secret offices, vehicles, homes, traditional lands, and in other spaces where people gather. Keeping this paradigm shift in mind, the collection provides exemplars of emergent ways of knowing which begin from the center of lives as actually lived in places where people hold knowledge, make knowledge, "know" and produce knowing collectively. Emergent knowing shakes up how we know, how we come to know, and hence the locations from which we gain access to knowing. In turn, this surfaces examples of how peripheral and subjugated knowledges are progressively and practically removed from the privileged, the recorded, the official, and the "known."

The second purpose of this collection is to strengthen global/local conversations about how spaces of entitlement and periphery comingle. This involves rendering visible an analysis of the intersecting realities of people whose marginalization has not been embraced by educators and the extent to which this endures across transnational boundaries. As a consequence this collection troubles those marginalizing practices—heterosexism, white privilege, ableism, and racism—that have, at times, been perpetuated by some mainstream adult education programs.

In this vein we too as editors have been challenged in the process of "doing critique," to avoid reinscribing rigid binaries between official discourses—precise, prized, privileged knowledge—and unofficial discourses—exploratory, "low" valued, oppressed knowledges. The interplay of both constitutes the lifeblood of many of the communities and individuals with whom we work. Spivak's (1993, p. 58) work shaped some of our preliminary thoughts with her critique of the defensive activist claim "One must begin somewhere," in justifying the slow pace of social change:

> If the 'somewhere' that one begins from is the most privileged site of the neocolonial education system, in an Institute for the training of teachers, funded by the state, does that gesture of convenience become the normative point of departure? Does not participation in such a privileged and authoritative apparatus require the greatest vigilance?

In negotiating the contours of the chapters with authors part of our vigilance involved an understanding of our beginnings in the notion of "the periphery" as a paradoxical space of deliberate occupation (see Deer & Chlup; Grace, this volume) and of deliberate nonrecognition (see Brigham; Guo; Karim, this volume). The challenges of "doing critique" in these locations is always a matter of where one begins and is always caught in a complex web of official, institutionalized discourses which one may want to challenge as one is also caught up in reproducing them. This work is not easy work, and it includes elements of risk, uncertainty, and discomfort if troubling normative values of difference as deviance is its goal. However, as Spivak argues, where we begin, indeed who that "we" is, and where "they" begin, is always accompanied by a certain form of personal vigilance.

As the work of Freire (1984), Hart (1992), Razack (2002), and others remind us, power relations circulate in complex ways to shape how people live their lives through familial, geographic, occupational, racial, ableist, and sexualized relations. In using the term "periphery" we have endeavored to recognize the contradictions associated with the term. The decision making activated in education organizations, workplaces, and through social welfare expenditure, relies on "peripherally" named groups to conform if they are to receive recognition and resources. Herein lies one of the more difficult tensions facing educators whose goal is to change the uneven access to resources in order that people might live decent lives. During times of struggle and access to resources in particular it is not unknown for groups to take steps to demand fair treatment and inclusion in society and education when their advocacy, activism, and polite requests through policy and practice have failed them. These groups engage in acts as diverse as protests, teach-ins, clandestine acts of civil disobedience, and polite representation to have their voices included in social programs and policies. Taking up a peripheral space is not just an external act of naming. This book examines lives on the periphery through the actions and decisions of workers *and* learners who know there is something deeply unsatisfying about a world order that relies on inequality for its capitalist interests to survive. The collection examines a balance of perspectives about how people experience work and school *and* the building of education and work opportunities for people in difficult times. We present the views of chapter authors who are arguably at the core of networks with substantial resources, social power, and privilege. Yet, other chapter authors experience extreme resistance to their work, living with the threat of closure of programs, removal of resources, and peripherality within many of the university and formal systems which employ them. While traditional understandings of "adult and community education" with its primary mooring points in adult learning principles are present and obvious in some of the chapters, other chapters challenge these understandings of "adult education." They present a view of teaching and learning premised on contesting the naming practices that constitute peripherality, often through normative assumptions about what counts as adult education.

Disrupting Dominance: Introducing the Chapters

We have arranged the sections in a way that begins the work of disrupting the dominance of "adult and community education." We first ask readers to rethink the boundaries and basic tenets of adult and community education, such as "lifelong learning," "adult learning," "social justice," and "context" that often dominate adult and community education literature and research. We then explore how educators engage in work on the periphery and the challenges of working transculturally where Western "programs" and "systems" do not always mix well with living and learning on the periphery. Keeping with a critique of systems, we present the immigrant experience as a case example of where lives on the periphery become increasingly complicated through adult education and employment schemes. The final section reflects engagement with a number of transnational contexts with the intention of emphasizing how adult and community education might be an assertion of a global dominance agenda as institutions expand beyond their borders. Age-old global disparities between workers and their industrial conditions continue to exist, and historical and sociocultural practices are often excluded from the frame of reference when "beginning somewhere" in adult and community education.

In sum, we argue that, while much of the world has changed, enduring patterns of marginality and suppression of sensibilities in quite diverse corners of the globe persist. At the same time, identifiable moments come into view across these chapters that illustrate an alternative clarity about how to know complex global/local relations differently. The book comprises four sections shaped by the locations and ways in which authors have evoked, challenged, and reconfigured their "adult and community education" practices to address the enduring patterns of peripherality and marginalization they experience.

Rethinking Locations of Adult Education Practice

In this first section authors examine the dominant foundations of adult education and reconsider their utility in this era of globalism and institutionalization. **André Grace** argues that the imprints of neoliberalism and globalization, clearly evident in policy making, have placed diverse demands on public education (schooling for children and youth), adult education in institutionalized and community contexts, and higher education in colleges and universities. These diverse demands hold sway over people's learning experiences with the dominant demand arguing for career preparation, employment, and learning for new economies. The audit culture of neoliberal economies prioritizes the market as the primary metaphor for all learning across the lifespan and simultaneously activates a learner "fringe" of stigmatized and marginalized peoples. The chapter details how sexual and gender minority youth and young adults are marginalized through theory building that prepares citizens as learners for normative work and life practices. Re-conceptualizing lifelong learning as a politic and pedagogy of critique, hope, and possibility is a way to be inclusive of the learner fringe and address the marginalizing practices inherent in adult learning principles.

Naomi Nichols undertakes a similar move in illustrating how adult educators "coordinate" the lives of young people through school-based socialization practices. As such they ignore the tendency for developmental narratives to fix young people as children and neglect the in-between place between child and adult theorizing. Explanations of their experiences of living and learning based in child-focused theories are unhelpful when navigating between schooling, work, and family care experiences. Moreover, emerging adults have limited capacity to explain their experiences given the labor market conditions, lower earning potential, increased costs of housing, and other challenges faced in achieving social independence. Nichols proposes that conventional understandings of youth need to be disrupted and dominant de-contextualized developmental narratives must be substituted if youth are to turn around the deficit categories of "school-averse learners," "youth at risk," "risk to others," and students with "behavioral problems."

Institutional capture of learning and "learners" is also the focus of attention for **Joshua Collins, Lincoln Pettaway, Chaundra Whitehead**, and **Steve Rios**. This chapter examines the disciplining of bodies in a social domain that some would argue is the extreme of peripheral existence within Western liberal democracies: incarcerated people with HIV/AIDS. Collins et al. illustrate how incarceration in the United States and Jamaica facilitates the use of intimidation and power as institutionalized and legitimated practices that hamper the quality of life for those in U.S. and Jamaican prisons. As a normative theoretical framework for adult learning, situated learning is reconfigured through a Foucauldian framework of embodied (punishment and) learning experienced by prisoners. The chapter illustrates how technologies of intimidation have changed and evolved over time, yet still form the basis of unspoken educational and political oppressions despite claims of rehabilitation to better the lives of inmates.

Shannon Deer and **Dominique Chlup** provide an exemplar of adult education's engagement with beginnings and Spivak's (1993) reminder of starting points, in examining how sex work as an occupation is constituted as marginality to suit the institutional convenience of educational theorists. Deer and Chlup alert us to the polarized perspectives associated with feminist discourses of sex work and prostitution and the life realities of women engaged in such work. Mapping these perspectives and associated locations provides a frame of reference for adult educators working with the best of intentions to improve the lives of current and former sex workers and prostitutes. Deer and Chlup argue that multidisciplinary approaches to engagement with sex workers and prostitutes must begin by listening to the everyday needs for financial training and additional skills training as expressed by women working as sex workers.

Last, **Hilary Landorf** and **Eric Feldman** examine the literature on study abroad programs, international students, and global citizenship, while paying attention to the nature of knowledge and positionality inherent in these programs. Drawing on Florida International University as a center for major international trade and tourism and as gateway to South and Central America for more than 1,100 multinational corporations, the chapter outlines the Global Learning for Global Citizenship initiative. Drawing on the notion of "democratic deliberation," the global citizenship program promotes ethical and civic commitment through "democratic engagement" with evolving definitions of citizenship and interdependence. While located in the United States and hence not drawing on international travel or experiences, the democratic deliberation approach provides students with a chance to be part of a global discussion.

Educators' Work with "Peripheral" Spaces of Engagement

The second section explores how educators work with and against the objectification practices which characterize many learning theories and hence our understanding of what counts as "periphery." **Robert Mizzi**, **Robert Hill**, and **Kim Vance** argue the need to interrogate the dominance of formal schooling and other Western inventions that refuse to recognize sexual and gender minority knowledge, and subsequently renders such knowledge as "fugitive." Working in this space required them to undertake "secret" resource-building work to render more visible the informational, emotional, and social needs of sexual and gender minorities. Such resources emerge from fugitive knowledges that are necessary for existence and survival in anti-queer worlds. This clandestine work is also marked by a sense of urgency to acknowledge diverse performances of sexuality locally and globally.

Shuchi Karim's chapter addresses the issue of invisibility of women with disabilities in Bangladesh in the context of their education, employment, and citizenship practices. Due to a range of reasons, underreporting of disabilities is very common in national censuses in Bangladesh: inadequate questionnaire design; insufficient training of enumerators; and, the "forgetting" of members with disabilities. The lack of education and consequent unemployment adds to the already marginalized position of girls in the Bangladeshi system, pushing them further to the periphery of society— ultimately making them "invisible." As with Nichols, the focus on children and youth is relevant to our discussion of peripherality precisely because their experiences of access to education and employment are framed by the context of work and learning available to adult women in Bangladesh. Karim argues gender and disability are pivotal in understanding marginalization of girls in education, employment, and citizenship participation thus creating implications for when the girls become adult learners.

Carlos Albornoz and **Tonette Rocco** argue that the impact of capitalism on local places where the transnational power and resources of corporations are not shared with countries or local citizens creates conditions where localized forms of microenterprise are increasingly threatened by the dominance of multinational corporations. Yet, in Chile, adults do not have the skill sets required to participate in the modern economy and turn to microenterprise and informal businesses. Albornoz and Rocco examine how microenterprise might thrive by positioning adult education as a complementary mechanism for entrepreneurial growth and innovation. Their profile of the education system, the higher education system, and the job market locates the Chilean system in a larger context of national employment possibilities and potential false promises. Albornoz and Rocco argue that a critical question for adult educators would be to ask how they are situated when promoting entrepreneurship education "as the panacea for the poor and illiterate." Without knowing the usefulness of the impact of these programs on employment prospects, education, and training offers hope that may not translate to sustainable economic prospects.

Matthew Campbell and **Michael Christie** locate their work in the context of remote Aboriginal ranger training. The chapter outlines the interconnecting work spaces of Australia's national training system: a violent history of invasion and subsequent settlement, a national training system anchored in Western knowledges; elective units as diverse as animal and vehicle management, recording and reporting plants and animals, and contemporary Indigenous practices of caring for country. While their approach appears to draw from conventional adult learning principles, Campbell and Christie argue it is in the generative process of "delivery" that they navigate tensions associated with both-ways teaching as an espoused pedagogy for working with Aboriginal learners, groups, and communities. "Cognitive authority" emerges as a pivotal point in their practice of both-ways pedagogy and marks its difference from normative adult learning theories.

Last, **Sue Shore's** chapter picks up the elision of knowledges and erasure practices noted in Grace's chapter and connects them to the university work associated with preparing educators to teach in the Australian national training system. As elsewhere, Australian education and training organizations have been subject to a highly regulated policy environment anchored in neoliberal market reforms. These reforms have positioned strategies of inclusion, access, and equity within increasingly neoliberal policy contexts that promote market discourses, flexibility in learning content, and seamless pathways between sectors. Yet many of these reforms are disconnected from long histories of racialized employability. Shore's chapter illustrates the possibilities and limits of preparing vocational educators for living in these racialized worlds by invoking a contrapuntal pedagogy that prompts educators to re-read their racialized histories through the lens of contemporary studies of whiteness and privilege.

Immigrant Experiences of Work and Learning in the New World Order

The third section takes up experiences of learning for work and life as the contemporary practices of mobility shape opportunities for recognition even as they also impact on labor practices across borders. **Susan Brigham**'s chapter draws on the extended history of labor relations between Jamaica and Canada to illustrate some of the challenges of unauthorized migrant laborers in Canada. This particular group is under-represented in adult education literature on work and Brigham argues their migration experiences are more complicated and more precarious than authorized workers. Brigham's contribution raises questions about the extent to which neoliberal discourse positions the inequalities the women experience, both in their home and host countries, as outside normative work experience. Brigham argues this provides an important crossover for adult education practitioners and researchers particularly with the rise of workplace studies in adult education which seem to pay limited attention to gendered roles of family work.

Continuing a theme of absences and exclusions in the adult education literature, **Aziz Choudry** argues that social movement activists and scholars alike have downplayed incidental learning and informal education in activist milieus. Learning from the ground up is one way of problematizing dominant understandings of "margin" and "center" in Canada's labor market. Choudry explores the processes of learning and knowledge production in campaigns for immigrant and migrant workers' rights. Choudry's analysis of precarious worker organizing through and within temp agencies provides a base for understanding the effects of precarious work practices in a globalizing world and has implications for recognition of prior learning and work experiences which are, in large part, poorly implemented in this sector.

Shibao Guo draws on three barriers to the process of integration of qualifications: the glass gate denying immigrants' entrance to guarded professional communities; the glass door blocking immigrants' access to professional employment at high-wage firms; the glass ceiling preventing immigrants from moving into management positions, often because of their ethnic and cultural differences (Guo, 2013). The chapter argues that PLAR in Canada must embrace cultural difference and diversity as underpinning assets of a recognition system that enables migrant professionals to promote the validity and usefulness of their own knowledge and practices.

Labor studies and workplace research has documented the effects of physical and emotional violence in the workplace and illustrated how apparently benign behaviors morph into deliberate acts of harm. **Fabiana Brunetta** and **Thomas Reio** argue that workplace incivility obscures deep-seated behaviors that foster conditions of aggression, blame, and harm in a workplace. Pronounced changes in immigration appear to exacerbate this potential for increased harm by opening up a wider range of interpretations of interpersonal conflict, rude behavior, and incivility. Brunetta and Reio argue that workplace design might be an issue where marked instances of stereotypes, biases, and discrimination occur.

Transnational Adult Education and Global Engagement

In this section **Peter Kell** and **Marilyn Kell** draw attention to the tensions between liberal views about education and the economic priorities of industry and business activated during the Sputnik crisis of the late 1950s. They argue the need to understand the constitution of this crisis in the context of the school effectiveness movement, and subsequent "backlash politics" which push into adult, vocational, and workplace education and training via discourses of declining national standards and competitive country rankings. The core of Kell and Kell's argument is the constitution of a perpetual crisis created out of the struggle between science as the master narrative and its domination over a more liberal education paradigm. The implications are substantial for many training, workplace, and adult education programs that are ostensibly about preparing a future workforce through mobility for integration and cooperation rather than mobility for competition.

Bob Boughton offers a critical view of the internal elision of knowledges associated with the field of adult education by drawing on the Cuban Literacy Campaign to illustrate how adult education theory building has its own built-in selectivities and practices of erasure. Internationally linked and networked socialist and communist political parties and movements have committed to educating their members and supporters to change the world for over a century. Boughton argues that increasing professionalization and specialization of the field has instantiated a periphery by arguing (incorrectly in his view) of the decline in socialist movement activism over recent times.

Mark Webber and **Michael Brown** further argue the need for historical and intergenerational perspectives on learning about antiracism. With a focus on personal learning in the context of global and intergenerational experience, students in an undergraduate program participate in a global exchange program which assists future educators to "know" racism differently. Students learn about antiracism through conversations and debates underpinned by recursivity. The approach models how controversial opinions can be exchanged openly and respectfully with progressive development of a student's self-awareness. The intergenerational component of the program is an important feature in activating recursivity—no matter where one starts a particular discussion, it will turn out to have precedents.

Korbla Puplampu and **Lindsay Wodinski** face similar issues as they work in a North American context to build internationalization of off-shore and on-shore students through a university globalization program that is cognizant of its location within colonizer/colonized relations. Puplampu and Wodinski foreground the importance of entrepreneurial spirit in university goals to maintain a competitive reputation and maintain a healthy bottom line in funding formulae. Internationalization initiatives meet the above goals as they also grow competencies for knowing the world through a developing global citizenship agenda within the university curriculum. However, the authors argue such programs can reinforce a Euro-American curriculum and experience which for some students reinscribe the very structures and curriculum of their home university and thus challenge the notion of learning underpinning the programs.

In the final chapter **Sue Shore**, **Robert Mizzi**, and **Tonette Rocco** return to some of the central issues that have been raised in working with authors to produce this book. We draw attention to the "structures of feeling" (Williams, 1977) that have played such an important role in shaping adult education as a field, a professional discipline, and a social movement. Not least is the way in which the work of adult education has been drawn center stage in complex and problematic relations between global, national, and individual productivity and empowerment. In the final chapter of the book we offer three provocations for educators and researchers who aim to continue the work of disrupting the normative ontologies of periphery as ever deficit.

Closing Comments

Being adults that occupy the social margins in any learning situation carries a great deal of risk. Being educators who work with adults in these spaces prompts reflexive engagement with the transformative agendas that drive this work as well as a potential for professional marginalization. Our goal in this book has been to call into question the normative assumptions of adult learning principles and the presumed locations of practice repeatedly mentioned in adult education texts.

In this collection we have tracked processes of marginalization and in doing so have noted a continuing theme of resilience associated with working and learning in complex situations of oppression. Such activity requires a sense of hope and optimism for change and simultaneously an awareness of the extent to which educators and learners are implicated in the very oppressions they seek to unsettle. Some chapters reveal that although learners are often the primary focus of studies to understand marginalizing practices, aligning with marginalized communities also impacts on educators' lives. Their "secret work" (Mizzi, Hill, & Vance, this volume) aligns with what Campbell and Christie (this volume) argue is morally responsible work. As such, educators may also be disenfranchised, disavowed, arrested, or worse for the clandestine work in which they engage.

Disruption is a central theme in this collection, as authors seek to unsettle the articulations between professional norms, pedagogical rules, policies, and curriculum mandates that convey the assumptions of western meritocracies. Disruptions to the accepted canons, or indeed rendering visible localized practices that reinscribe those canons, will generate fresh understandings of the particular social realities in which learners, educators, and researchers engage in a world of increasingly mobile knowledges and people. This has consequences for the interventions and intrusions "adult education" makes into people's lives and the extent to which it will be experienced as facilitation or meddling.

References

Dannenmann, K., & Haig-Brown, C. (2002). A pedagogy of the land: Dreams of respectful relations. *McGill Journal of Education/Revue des sciences de l'éducation de McGill, 37*(3), 451–468.

Freire, P. (1984). *Pedagogy of the oppressed.* (Myra Bergman Ramos, Trans.). New York, NY: Continuum.

Grace, A. P., & Rocco, T. S. (Eds.) (2009). *Challenging the professionalization of adult education: John Ohliger and contradictions in modern practice.* San Francisco, CA: Jossey-Bass.

Guo, S. (2013). Economic integration of recent Chinese immigrants in Canada's second-tier cities: The triple glass effect and immigrants' downward social mobility. *Canadian Ethnic Studies, 45*(3), 95–115.

Hart, M. (1992). *Working and educating for life: Feminist and international perspectives on adult education.* New York, NY: Routledge.

Razack, S. (Ed.). (2002). *Race, space and the law: Unmapping a white settler society.* Toronto, ON: Between the Lines.

Shore, S. (2004). Reflexive theory building "after" colonialism: Challenges for adult education. In P. Kell, S. Shore, & M. Singh (Eds.), *Adult education @ 21st century* (pp. 107–120). New York, NY: Peter Lang.

Spivak, G. C. (1993). *Outside in the teaching machine.* New York, NY & London, UK: Routledge.

Williams, R. (1977). *Marxism and literature.* New York, NY: Oxford University Press.

RETHINKING LOCATIONS OF ADULT EDUCATION PRACTICE

1

Lifelong Learning as Critical Action for Sexual and Gender Minorities as a Constituency of the Learner Fringe

André P. Grace

Neoliberalism and globalization have driven a change culture of crisis and challenge that has altered life, learning, and work since the 1970s (Barros, 2012; Giroux, 2004; Harvey, 2005; Jarvis, 2007; Schuller & Watson, 2009). As I emphasize in my book *Lifelong Learning as Critical Action* (Grace, 2013a), the upshot of globalization and the neoliberal tendency to prioritize instrumental learning over social and cultural learning is a contemporary lifelong-learning paradigm that is limited in scope. As synchronous and omnipresent forces, neoliberalism and globalization have narrowed our view of education and what it ought to encompass, setting and shrinking parameters to how we envision lifelong learning as a way forward and a way out of difficulties we face in life, learning, and work contexts (Grace, 2013a). Indeed the contemporary politics shaping this paradigm contravene the notion of *lifelong learning for all*, which has been the buzz phrase of the Organization for Economic Cooperation and Development (OECD) since the mid-1990s (Grace, 2013a). While lifelong learning has certainly become a large-scale international policy-and-practice phenomenon over the past twenty years, thanks in large part to the increasing fervor with which the OECD has spearheaded various educational policymaking initiatives, there is still much missing in its design (Field, 2006; Grace, 2006a, 2013a). With imprints of neoliberalism and globalization clearly evident,

these policymaking initiatives have placed diverse demands on public education (schooling for children and youth), adult education (both in institutionalized and community contexts), and higher education (in colleges and
universities). In higher education there has been a shift toward reducing
learning to such extrinsic purposes as career preparation and learning for
new economies from local to global contexts (Grace, 2013a; Greenspan,
2008; Holmwood, 2014). The OECD, in tandem with multinational corporate interests, national governments, and an array of educational interests, has ardently linked lifelong learning to the demands of neoliberalism,
globalization, individualism, privatization, corporatism, competition, and
progress as it is defined within a burgeoning knowledge economy (Grace,
2013a). Today lifelong learning linked primarily to economistic concerns is
the usual purview of formal education as an institutional and predominantly
instrumental endeavor. It is commonly the purview of education in many
nonformal and informal learning contexts as well. From this perspective,
instrumentalized lifelong learning can be viewed as the common link and
thread that connects learning across the diverse spaces and contexts in which
it now occurs. In this milieu, the tendency is to sideline learning for social
and cultural purposes.

Amid the dynamics of neoliberalism, globalization, and other inter-
locking change forces, tensions abound in lifelong learning, which ought to
be a lifewide educational formation that emphasizes more than learning that
enhances worker performance and productivity (Burke & Jackson, 2007;
Grace, 2012, 2013a). For learners, especially those in vulnerable categories who need lifelong learning to be something more, there are persistent
and unresolved issues of recognition, access, and accommodation as they
confront social, cultural, and political as well as economic challenges and
calamities (Grace, 2013a). These learners constitute the learner fringe. They
struggle to experience the rights and privileges of full citizenship in societal
contexts where access to, and accommodation in, worthwhile learning and
quality work remain substantive issues to address (Grace, 2009a, 2013a).
They tend to matter little as learners in the neoliberal milieu, and their
concerns are largely ignored or treated peripherally in mainstream lifelong
learning. Those occupying the learner fringe are seen neither as contributors to the neoliberal world nor are they seen as valuable commodities in
instrumental contexts where learning is geared to efficient economistic purposes. Moreover, educators who foster social and cultural forms of education
that could improve their lot generally comprise a lesser tier compared to
those educators who prioritize instrumental learning for middle-class learners (Grace, 2012, 2013a). These already educated learners are expected to

return periodically to the learning treadmill to keep up with the demands of navigating a neoliberal work world (Grace, 2013a).

Clearly then, there is vital political and pedagogical work to do to recast lifelong learning as an encompassing project enveloping *all* learners. In order for lifelong learning to be an inclusive and meaningful discourse for today and tomorrow, I have suggested framing *lifelong learning as critical action* that prepares citizens as learners for work *and* for the rest of life (Grace, 2013a). This formation of lifelong learning emphasizing holistic development has this modus operandi: to nurture social engagement, political and economic understanding, and cultural work to benefit learners as citizens and workers. Here learners need to feel confident that lifelong learning is a wide-ranging paradigm involving principles and practices that can help them to make good choices as they question what constitutes worthwhile learning, quality work, and the good life. For example, in this chapter I consider how lifelong learning as critical action engages sexual and gender minority (SGM) youth and young adults in useful, sensible ways that flesh out a politics and pedagogy of critique, hope, and possibility aimed at nurturing and supporting them. In the end, these young learners build assets and functional toolsets needed to grow into resilience as a process and outcome. SGM youth and young adults deliberately and deliberatively engage in critical action and become change agents in personal contexts as well as in an array of institutional and community contexts. Lifelong learning framed as critical action is especially important for these individuals as well as for others occupying the learner fringe. These learners are mediating life, learning, and work in peripheral spaces where they deal with social, cultural, economic, and political exclusion. For them, lifelong learning, especially as it has evolved under neoliberalism and globalization, has been bounded and exclusionary, with responsibility for lifelong learning shifting from the public to the private domain (Grace, 2013a). In this milieu, learners are expected to take individual responsibility for their own learning and the blame when lifelong learning fails. The historically valorized concept of lifelong learning has become highly politicized, leaving many citizens to question the meanings and values associated with the construct within increasingly instrumental paradigms of work and life (Grace, 2012, 2013b).

The learner fringe has become even more disenfranchised in recent years. Social upheaval and a politics of dislocation continue to mark their lives indelibly (Grace, 2006a, 2013a). Since the profound panic that first engulfed the global financial market from October 6–10, 2008 (Krugman, 2009), the plight of the learner fringe has worsened amid the faulty logic of neoliberalism that suggests if you improve economic output, then social advances will flow in tandem (Grace, 2013a). In this milieu, the vast economic debacle has implications for lifelong learning and subsequent responses to meet learner needs now and into the future. In this regard, lifelong learning as critical action has two objectives: (1) to interrogate the neoliberal formation of lifelong learning as a predominantly economistic venture, examining social, cultural, and political change forces that demand lifewide policymaking in governmental, educational, and other institutional contexts; and, in critical counter measure, and (2) to implement inclusive, holistic, and engaged forms of lifelong learning that attend to matters of ethics, democratic learning, learner freedom, and justice in civil and economic contexts (Grace, 2013a). With regard to the latter, as I demonstrate in my book *Lifelong Learning as Critical Action*, there are pockets of hope and activity in learning for social and cultural purposes (Grace, 2013a). This more holistic learning often involves the learner fringe. It is driven by their individual and social needs that extend beyond the need for instrumental learning focused on economic advancement. In this regard, I explore constituent groups comprising the learner fringe who navigate diverse social and cultural contexts in Canada, Australia, Ireland, South Africa, New Zealand, the United Kingdom, and the United States. Within this exploration, I consider the politics and realities of locating such constituencies as youth and young adults, older women, learners with disabilities, Aboriginal learners, and SGM learners. These groups are often considered to be vulnerable learners running social and educational deficits, at least from neoliberal perspectives. Such narrow characterization requires that we interrogate how neoliberal institutions define learners; how communities define them; how educators define them; and how learners define themselves.

In this chapter I take up this analysis with particular attention to sexual and gender minorities as a constituency of the learner fringe. First, I consider the dynamics of constructing lifelong learning as critical action, with some consideration of the utility of the social history of adult education in framing its formation. Then, after considering sexual and gender minorities and their holistic learning plans, I conclude by calling on caring professionals—understood in this chapter as schoolteachers, adult educators, social workers, counselors, and other significant adults with the disciplinary knowledge associated with the caring professions—to engage in lifelong learning as critical action that makes the lives of the learner fringe better *now*. Such critical action involves engaged professional practices soaked in findings emanating from researching resilience and further framed using critical perspectives emphasizing democracy, freedom, ethics, social justice, and equity.

Constructing Lifelong Learning as Critical Action

I have been an educator for over three decades, and I have worked in public schooling (for children and youth), adult, and higher education (Grace, 2007a). As a lifelong educator, I advocate that learners need to be recognized, respected, and accommodated across power relationships and the contexts that locate them in everyday life, learning, and work. This involves holistic learning as a lifelong and lifewide venture incorporating instrumental, social, *and* cultural purposes. I have recently explored the achievement of these educational priorities in the face of neoliberalism and globalization as powerful change forces that prioritize learning linked to the economy over learning linked to the whole of life (Grace, 2013a). In doing this work five principles apprise my philosophy of "teaching and learning as resistance," in order to make life better *now* for the learner fringe (Grace, 2007a): (1) teaching is a political engagement that builds an inclusive practice guided by an ethic of mutual respect; (2) teaching is enhanced as a social construct and process when it emerges in the intersection of social theorizing and practice; (3) teaching as a social process has to be interdisciplinary, mining history, philosophy, psychology, and other disciplines for insights, and intra-disciplinary, mining public, adult, and higher education for further insights; (4) the teaching-learning interaction has to be dynamically staged as a critically reflective, interactive, and collective engagement where educators and learners both contribute; and (5) learning has to be a holistic and lifelong endeavor, addressing the instrumental, social, and cultural needs of learners across life, learning, and work domains. For me, these five principles are embodied and embedded in lifelong learning as critical action that attends to ethical, political, psychosocial, and cultural aspects of an ecological educational practice that is integral to sustaining democratic citizenship. This practice incorporates the intellectual, the organic, the pragmatic, and the ideal in weighing realities and desires for living a full and satisfying life (Grace, 2013a). It interrogates survivalist approaches to lifelong learning that primarily engage learners in skill pruning to abet workplace performance. It critically questions what is included or excluded as well as gained or lost in developing learners as human resources.

Mining the History of Adult Education as Social Education

In designing lifelong learning as critical action from policy and practice perspectives, it is useful to turn to the history of adult education for inspiration (Grace, 2012, 2013a, 2013b). In Canada, this history demonstrates a collectivist orientation to learning, especially as it is linked to social action and social progress (Welton, 2011). In a nod to Canadian adult education constructed as social education historically grounded in "collective orientations to the world" (p. 4), Welton (2011) challenges adult educators to involve adults in lifelong, lifewide, and democratic learning. He sees such learning as integral to a critical sociality in which the "concept of civil society subsume[s] local action and individual social movements into an idea of representation, resistance, and action that incorporates a vast array of ordinary communal activities" (p. 3). This understanding of civil society reflects a history of Canadian adult education as community-based and critically oriented (Grace, 2006b). However, in today's world sociality is twisted by an individuality that burdens citizens as learners and workers who are held captive by, as well as accountable to, systems and structures that are the sources of problems and ties that bind individuals in a neoliberal world (Grace, 2013a). Welton describes this world as it emerged during the late twentieth century: "We became conscious of ourselves as persons who were constantly adapting to new learning challenges—in our bodies, minds, and spirits; at work; in civil society's many domains; in cultural expression and play" (p. 7). This self-consciousness caught up in individualism and accountability tended to work against possibilities for a cohesive, integrated social. Moreover, it demonstrated neoliberalism at work, shifting the blame to individuals for failures in learning, work, and life contexts (Grace, 2013a). While this state of affairs can be construed as a bombardment of lifelong learning and constituent adult education with challenge after challenge, it can also be conceived as a contemporary impetus to construct lifelong learning as critical action. Here we can mine the tensions emanating from juxtaposing identity politics and the contemporary dynamics of sociality. We can engage learners in holistic learning that transforms the politics of education, transgressing binary thinking that pits the individuality of instrumental learning against the collectivity of psychosocial and wider social learning. Here learners can focus on the sum of instrumental and social learning within a culture of learning that emphasizes lifelong learning for all and for all of life (Grace, 2014). This would require keeping practice in dynamic equilibrium with research and social policymaking in work to locate lifelong learning as critical action (Grace, 2012, 2013a).

Lifelong learning as critical action honors the social history of critical forms of education by keeping the political ideals of modernity—democracy, freedom, and social justice—at the heart of learning for all and for all of life (Grace, 2013a, 2014). As a critical formation, this paradigm is about engaging in instrumental, social, *and* cultural forms of learning that sustain the learner fringe in the quest to live full and satisfying lives (Grace, 2013a). It is also about shaping learning as a democratic and just engagement for the learner fringe so vulnerable populations can engage in educational and cultural work to improve their lives and build better everyday worlds. Here learners consider matters of context (social, cultural, economic, historical, and political factors that impact policymaking and implementation); disposition (the attitudes, values, and beliefs of educators and learners that moderate lifelong learning); and relationship (interactions among learners variously positioned in demographic and geographic terms that impact learner access and accommodation) (Grace, 2013a). This immerses learners in strategic teaching-learning interactions where their knowledge and experiences matter. In this political and pedagogical engagement, in-tune lifelong educators bring the instrumental, social, *and* cultural to bear on both pragmatic and exploratory work aimed at helping learners to become change agents able to navigate life, learning, and work contexts successfully.

Sexual and Gender Minorities as a Constituency of the Learner Fringe

Sexual and gender minorities, including lesbian, gay, bisexual, trans-spectrum, queer Indigenous (or, more commonly, Two-Spirit Aboriginal), and intersexual individuals, comprise a historically disenfranchised and defiled constituency of the learner fringe, jettisoned to the social periphery not only by the learning mainstream but also by other learner-fringe groups. In Canada, in keeping with the *Canadian Charter of Rights and Freedoms*, sexual and gender minorities have legal and legislative protections just like linguistic and ethno-cultural minorities (Grace, 2007b, 2013c). Since our sexual orientations and gender identities fall outside normative understandings of sexuality and gender as well as outside the either/or categories of the heterosexual/homosexual and male/female binaries, sexual and gender minorities have needed these protections as matters of survival and accommodation (Grace, 2013c, 2013d).

Within SGM populations, SGM youth and young adults—a multivariate population across race, ethno-cultural location, class, and other relational differences—remain a particularly vulnerable group (Brill & Pepper, 2008; Fassinger & Arseneau, 2007; Saewyc, 2011; Tolman & McClelland, 2011). As a growing body of transdisciplinary research indicates, most SGM youth and young adults know the daily distress caused by marginalization that entrenches fear, mistrust, helplessness, and a sense of being alone.

They continue to be involved in a paradoxical struggle to be cared about in education, healthcare, and other purportedly caring institutions (Chief Public Health Officer [CPHO], 2011, 2012). Indeed they often experience education and healthcare services, as well as government and legal services, as fragmentary and insufficient to address the stressors and risks associated with living with the adversity and trauma induced by homophobia and transphobia, which are ignorance- and fear-induced responses to sexual and gender differences respectively (Bowleg, Huang, Brooks, Black, & Burkholder, 2003; Grace, 2015). For SGM youth and young adults, key stressors can include (1) neglect by such significant adults as parents, educators, counselors, and family doctors and other healthcare professionals; and (2) abuse and victimization through symbolic violence (such as anti-gay name calling and graffiti) and physical violence (such as bullying that can include assault and battery) (Shelley, 2008; Trotter, 2009; Wells, 2008). Key risks can include truancy, quitting school, and running away; developing alcohol and drug addictions, emotional problems, and mental illness; and suicide ideation, attempts, and completions (D'Augelli, 2006a, 2006b; Grace, 2013d; Grossman & D'Augelli, 2006, 2007; Savage & Miller, 2012). These dire realities indicate the urgent need for greater synchronicity in research, policy, and practice arenas so stakeholders in education and other caring institutions like health care can collectively help these youth and young adults to build capacity (a solutions approach), moving away from unconstructive strategies focused on stigmatizing or fixing SGM youth and young adults as a source of social disorder (a problems approach) (Grace, in press; Liebenberg & Ungar, 2009; Marshall & Leadbeater, 2008; Wells, Roberts, & Allan, 2012).

To realize a solutions approach, more inclusive and critical lifelong-learning initiatives are needed to address personal, social, cultural, and environmental issues that variously disenfranchise SGM youth and young adults in life, learning, and institutional contexts (Grace, 2009b, 2013d, 2013e). Recognizing this, in my practice of lifelong learning as critical action there has been an increasing focus on this constituency and their issues and concerns in relation to recognition, access, and accommodation in education, health care, and other caring institutions. This work as advocacy requires conducting research and using findings to inform policymaking and its implementation in caring practices. Currently, there is a lack of transdisciplinary research focused on studying sexual and gender minorities and the effects of limitations on access and accommodation in institutional contexts (Grace, in press; Haas, Eliason, Mays, Mathy, & Associates, 2011). In Canada, three national reports profoundly demonstrate the need for this research. I served as an external reviewer and contributor for two of these reports: the Chief Public Health Officer's 2011 and 2012 annual reports on the state of public health in Canada. The 2011 report—*Youth and Young Adults: Life in Transition*—draws a disturbing conclusion: While, in general, Canadian youth and young adults comprise a healthy and resilient population, SGM individuals are disproportionately represented among those who are not thriving. In sum, the report indicates that these youth and young adults are commonly at inordinate risk of experiencing physical and electronic bullying, verbal and sexual harassment, and physical violence at home and in educational and community settings. SGM youth and young adults are also more likely to ideate about, attempt, or complete suicide. In the face of these stressors and risks, they also experience more health and adjustment problems, which the report states are exacerbated by a lack of adequate and appropriate educational policies, supportive health and social services, protective measures, and educational and community programs. Linking education to comprehensive health and well-being, the report accentuates the importance of comprehensive health education and interventions, which need to start early in schooling and consider the histories, social and cultural attributes, and sexual and gender differences depicting SGM students. With regard to SGM youth and young adults, the 2012 report—*Influencing Health: The Importance of Sex and Gender*—is clear on a key point: With sex and gender traditionally expected to function within the parameters of heterosexuality and the male/female binary, individuals have problems adjusting to heteronormative and genderist boundaries and expectations associated with parenting, schooling, and healthcare provision. With respect to schooling, not adjusting can impact their success in learning as well as their overall well-being. The report states that sex and gender should be considered in all research areas. In its focus on educational research, the report stresses the need to study how both sex and gender affect the development of young people, their learning experiences and outcomes, and the kinds of educational policies and initiatives needed to create SGM-inclusive schools.

Complementing these transdisciplinary reports, in 2011 Egale Canada—our national organization committed to SGM inclusion—released the results of *Every Class in Every School: Final Report on the First National Climate Survey on Homophobia, Biphobia, and Transphobia in Canadian Schools* (Taylor, Peter, et al., 2011). The Egale Canada report provides evidence of significant homophobic and transphobic bullying and harassment—verbal, physical, and sexual—substantiating the vital need to address these stressors in schooling. The report also notes the magnified discrimination that students experience if they are transgender or gender-nonconforming individuals. Of importance, the report points to the need for educator in-service and sex-and-gender diversity and sensitivity training. Setting directions for policymaking, the climate survey found: (1) generic safe school policies that do not include anti-homophobia guidelines are ineffective in providing safer climates for sexual-minority students; (2) having specific anti-homophobia policies reduces incidents of harassment and bullying based on non-heterosexual orientation; and (3) specific anti-homophobia policies, however, do not appear to reduce harassment and bullying based on gender identity, thus signaling the need for schools to develop anti-transphobia policies to advance gender-minority inclusion. There is a need for similar policymaking and its implementation in caring practices in colleges and universities (Hill & Grace, 2009).

Institute for Sexual Minority Studies and Services (http://www.ismss.ualberta.ca)

At the Institute for Sexual Minority Studies and Services (iSMSS), which I had the support of the University of Alberta to establish in the Faculty of Education in 2008, I employ lifelong learning as critical action as a holistic model that brings to bear the strengths of research, advocacy, policymaking, teaching, and community outreach in developing programs to protect and meet the needs of SGM youth, young adults, and their families as they construct them. To meet their needs, iSMSS uses the synergy of research, policymaking, and outreach programming initiatives to help this constituency of the learner fringe to focus on building and nurturing their personal resilience and leadership potential within an environment that fosters individual development, positive socialization, and enhanced self-esteem. In this regard, iSMSS works to achieve the following objectives:

✓ to help SGM youth and young adults to grow into resilience by building assets in ways that attend to their individual, social, cultural, and material needs;

✓ to advocate for SGM youth and young adults and to use research and professional supports to help improve their comprehensive—physical, mental, sexual, and social—health, educational attainment, safety, and emotional well-being;

✓ to create safe spaces for parents and SGM youth and young adults to network with peers in efforts to help them effectively navigate processes of affirming SGM identities;

✓ to empower SGM youth and young adults to address bullying, harassment, hate incidents and crimes, and to know their rights;

✓ to engage SGM youth and young adults in social and cultural learning through art, music, writing, performing arts, games, and digital media creations including zines, videos, and digital comics;

✓ to assist SGM youth and young adults with self and social development;

✓ to educate all youth and significant adults about sexual and gender minorities and our issues and concerns so everyone contributes to creating a safe and caring environment free from discrimination based on personal characteristics;

✓ to identify and strengthen resilience-based protective factors so families, as SGM youth and young adults construct them, can support their children;

✓ to reduce youth homelessness and street involvement by helping parents and caregivers to provide nurturing home and in-care environments that effectively support SGM youth and young adults; and

✓ to inform public policy and community advocacy.

These objectives are subsumed under iSMSS's overarching goal: to help SGM youth and young adults to grow into resilience by building the assets they need to be stronger, hopeful individuals who have the potential to be change agents in the social settings they navigate (Grace, 2009b, 2013d, 2013e). To achieve this goal, my colleagues and I use research findings (1) to inform social policymaking in education and health care and (2) to develop and implement inclusive, ethical, and engaged educational and cultural programming that makes the world better *now* for those we serve. This work is an engagement in critically progressive social education and community outreach that focuses on (1) designing programs to assist youth and young adults directly, and (2) training educators, healthcare providers, youth workers, and other caring professionals.

In this work, I use the notion of *growing into resilience* to indicate the dynamic nature of how SGM youth and young adults develop resilience as capacity building, successful adaptation, and sustained perseverance in the face of stressors and risk factors (Grace, 2009b, 2013d, 2013e). Importantly, contemporary research on resilience is exploring how youth and young adults develop self-confidence, social competence, and problem-solving abilities by building assets that include a strong internal locus of control, access to healthy mentors and social resources, and a sense of value and support in community settings (Goldstein & Brooks, 2005; Grace, 2015). While there is not a common definition of resilience, most contemporary researchers agree that it is a complex biopsychosocial process (Goldstein & Brooks, 2005). This process can be viewed as ecological since growing into resilience means an individual can increase the ability and capacity to deal with biopsychosocial aspects of development, situational barriers, and climate and cultural contexts (Brill & Pepper, 2008; Saewyc, 2011; Tolman & McClelland, 2011). Growing into resilience is complicated by living context (such as family, group home, or street environments) (D'Augelli, 2006a, 2006b; Grace, 2015; Hatzenbuehler, 2011). For SGM youth and young adults, it is further complicated when sexual orientation and gender identity are considered alongside other characteristics including Aboriginality, ethnocultural location, ability, class, age, and geography (Bowleg et al., 2003; CPHO, 2011; Grace, 2013d). Importantly, certain SGM youth and young adults show signs of thriving, growing up to be healthy and productive despite the effects of stressors and risk taking (Cagle, 2007; Goldstein & Brooks, 2005; Liebenberg & Ungar, 2008). More research is needed to help us understand this process and outcome as well as to study how resilience may be different in the academic, personal, social, emotional, and other spheres of an individual's life (Herrenkohl, Herrenkohl, & Egolf, 1994; Luthar, 1993).

Growing into resilience is an everyday preoccupation in our work at iSMSS. Through our intervention and outreach programming, iSMSS helps hundreds of SGM youth and young adults annually to overcome challenges and thrive through our research-informed and university-and-community-based programming. This engagement in lifelong learning as critical action includes such key programs as Camp fYrefly (http://www.fyrefly.ualberta.ca), our summer residential, community-based leadership camp for SGM youth and young adults, and the Family Resilience Project (http://www.ismss.ualberta.ca/FamilyResilience), which provides families with professional supports, resources, and peer support groups in which parents and other significant adults can meet others who can relate to their experiences of navigating life with an SGM child (Grace, 2013d, 2013e; Grace & Wells, 2007a, 2007b). When SGM youth and young adults need mentoring; counseling; medical, legal, or police assistance; housing; or help to mediate schooling or work, iSMSS is there to provide the supports they need. As iSMSS research clearly demonstrates, SGM youth and young adults who set realistic goals and engage in problem solving with people who are supportive become self-reliant, happier, and healthier, even in cases of complete family and societal rejection (Grace, 2013d). With mentors, resources, and supports, SGM youth and young adults are better able to survive and thrive despite the daily stressors, risks, and barriers they encounter in their social lives. This constituency is growing into resilience. By helping them to develop a resilience toolset, SGM youth and young adults can become self-respecting and self-confident individuals who actively participate in creating change for themselves and others.

Calling on Caring Professionals: Engage with Lifelong Learning as Critical Action

Currently, many researchers, policymakers, and caring professionals in education, health care, and other domains are concerned about limited and even declining efforts to intervene in the lives of SGM youth and young adults, especially those living with adversity and trauma (CPHO, 2011, 2012). There is a recognized need to educate and connect caring professionals working in education, health care, and other caring institutions so they can work collaboratively to help SGM youth and young adults (Cagle, 2007; CPHO, 2011, 2012; Grace, 2015; The Lancet, 2011; Weber & Poster, 2010). For example, it is vital (1) to address the lack of knowledge that educators (including health educators) and other caring professionals have about SGM youth and young adults and their needs in terms of access and accommodation in institutional contexts, and (2) to address the unequal status and adjustment of SGM youth and young adults in relation to social factors, including family, educational, and street violence, and medical factors, including the lack of youth knowledge of sexually transmitted infections (including HIV) and clinician misunderstanding, bias, and even homophobia and transphobia (CPHO, 2011, 2012; Dysart-Gale, 2010; Grace, 2008a; Grace, 2015; Hatzenbuehler, 2011; Weber & Poster, 2010).

Addressing these absences ought to be embodied in a call for caring professionals to engage in lifelong learning as critical action. Through my research and political and pedagogical work, I assist caring professionals to be inclusive educators who engage in lifelong and lifewide learning as social learning that advocates for and accommodates sexual and gender minorities within a politics of recognition and respect (Grace, 2008b). I work to increase caring professionals' awareness of this constituency of the learner fringe by educating caring professionals about the identities, needs, and concerns of SGM youth and young adults. I also educate caring professionals about the process of growing into resilience whereby youth and young adults deal with stressors and risk taking, develop assets, and show signs of thriving (Grace, 2013d, 2013e; Grace, 2015). In researching resilience as a process and outcome and sharing findings with caring professionals, I want them to link knowledge building to advocating for SGM youth and young adults and helping them to develop skills as problem solvers. This reflects my history of using research to locate policy as protection for minorities and to inform programming so SGM youth and young adults become thrivers and change agents in their lives and in the lives of peers whom they support (Grace, 2013a). This involves helping this constituency of the learner fringe to deal with homophobia and transphobia, manage conflict, and build strong relationships in family, educational, and community contexts (CPHO, 2011, 2012).

References

Barros, R. (2012). From lifelong education to lifelong learning: Discussion of some effects of today's neoliberal policies. *European Journal for Research on the Education and Learning of Adults, 3*(2), 119–134.

Bowleg, L., Huang, J., Brooks, K., Black, A., & Burkholder, G. (2003). Triple jeopardy and beyond: Multiple minority stress and resilience among Black lesbians. *Journal of Lesbian Studies, 7*(4), 87–108.

Brill, S., & Pepper, R. (2008). *The transgender child: A handbook for families and professionals.* San Francisco, CA: Cleis Press.

Burke, P. J., & Jackson, S. (2007). *Reconceptualising lifelong learning: Feminist Interventions.* New York, NY: Routledge.

Cagle, B. E. (2007). *Gay young men transitioning to adulthood: Resilience, resources, and the larger social environment.* (Doctoral dissertation). Retrieved from ProQuest (AAT 3280304).

Chief Public Health Officer (CPHO). (2011). *The Chief Public Health Officer's report on the state of public health in Canada 2011: Youth and young adults—life in transition.* Ottawa: Office of the CPHO. (Available at http://www.phac-aspc. gc.ca/cphorsphc-respcacsp/2011/index-eng.php.)

Chief Public Health Officer (CPHO). (2012). *The Chief Public Health Officer's report on the state of public health in Canada 2012: Influencing health—the importance of sex and gender.* Ottawa: Office of the CPHO. (Available at http://www. phac-aspc.gc.ca/cphorsphc-respcacsp/2012/index-eng.php.)

D'Augelli, A. R. (2006a). Developmental and contextual factors and mental health among lesbian, gay, and bisexual youths. In A. M. Omoto & H. S. Kurtzman

(Eds.), *Sexual orientation and mental health: Examining identity and development in lesbian, gay, and bisexual people* (pp. 37–53). Washington, DC: American Psychological Association.

———. (2006b). Stress and adaptation among families of lesbian, gay, and bisexual youth: Research challenges. In J. J. Bigner (Ed.), *An introduction to GLBT family studies* (pp. 135–157). New York, NY: Haworth Press.

Dysart-Gale, D. (2010). Social justice and social determinants of health: Lesbian, gay, bisexual, transgendered, intersexed, and queer youth in Canada. *Journal of Child and Adolescent Psychiatric Nursing, 23*(1), 23–28.

Fassinger, R. E., & Arseneau, J. R. (2007). "I'd rather get wet than be under that umbrella:" Differentiating the experiences and identities of lesbian, gay, bisexual, and transgender people. In K. J. Bieschke, R. M. Perez, & K. A. DeBord (Eds.), *Handbook of counseling and psychotherapy with lesbian, gay, bisexual, and transgender clients* (2nd ed., pp. 19–49). Washington, DC: American Psychological Association.

Field, J. (2006). *Lifelong learning and the new educational order* (2nd ed.). Stoke-on-Trent, UK: Trentham Books.

Goldstein, S., & Brooks, R. B. (Eds.). (2005). *Handbook of resilience in children.* New York: Kluwer.

Giroux, H. A. (2004). *The terror of neoliberalism.* Boulder, CO: Paradigm Publishers.

Grace, A. P. (2006a). Reflecting critically on lifelong learning in an era of neoliberal pragmatism: Instrumental, social, and cultural perspectives. Keynote address in D. Orr, F. Nouwens, C. Macpherson, R. E. Harreveld, & P. A. Danaher (Eds.), *Proceedings of the 4th International Lifelong Learning Conference, Central Queensland University* (pp. 1–16). *Rockhampton, Australia: Central Queensland University Press.* (Also available online at http://lifelonglearning.cqu.edu.au/2006/papers-ft/keynote-grace.pdf.)

———. (2006b). Critical adult education: Engaging the social in theory and practice. In T. Fenwick, T. Nesbit, & B. Spencer (Eds.), *Contexts of adult education: Canadian perspectives* (pp. 128–139). Toronto, ON: Thompson Educational Publishing.

———. (2007a). André P. Grace: An autobiography. In K. B. Armstrong & L. W. Nabb (Eds.), *North American adult educators: Phyllis M. Cunningham archive of quintessential autobiographies for the twenty-first century* (pp. 123–128). Chicago, IL: Discovery Association Publishing House.

———. (2007b). In your care: School administrators and their ethical and professional responsibility toward students across sexual-minority differences. In W. Smale & K. Young (Eds.), *Approaches to educational leadership and practice* (pp. 16–40). Calgary, AB: Detselig Enterprises/Temeron Books.

———. (2008a). The charisma and deception of reparative therapies: When medical science beds religion. *Journal of Homosexuality, 55*(4), 545–580.

———. (2008b). Respondent's text: Situating contemporary educational research as a traversing and transformative practice. In R. Henderson & P. A. Danaher (Eds.), *Troubling terrains: Tactics for traversing and transforming contemporary educational research* (pp. 223–229). Teneriffe, Queensland, Australia: Post Pressed.

———. (2009a). A view of Canadian lifelong-learning policy culture through a critical lens. In J. Field, J. Gallacher, & R. Ingram (Eds.), *Researching transitions in lifelong learning* (pp. 28–39). London, UK: Routledge.

———. (2009b). Resilient sexual-minority youth as fugitive lifelong learners: Engaging in a strategic, asset-creating, community-based learning process to counter exclusion and trauma in formal schooling. In J. Field (Ed.), *Proceedings of the Lifelong Learning Revisited: What Next? Conference of the Scottish Centre for Research in Lifelong Learning, University of Stirling, Stirling, UK* (CD format, 4,041 words).

———. (2012). The emergence of North American adult education (1947–1970): With a reflection on creating critically progressive education. *Studies in the Education of Adults, 44*(2), 225–244.

———. (2013a). *Lifelong learning as critical action: International perspectives on people, politics, policy, and practice.* Toronto, ON: Canadian Scholars' Press.

———. (2013b). A periodization of North American adult education (1919–1970): A critical sociological analysis of trends and perspectives. *International Journal of Lifelong Education, 33*(2), 183–206.

———. (2013c). Gay rights as human and civil rights: Matters of degree in culture, society, and adult education. In T. Nesbit, S. Brigham, T. Gibb, & N. Taber (Eds.), *Building on critical traditions: Adult education and learning in Canada* (pp. 72–81). Toronto, ON: Thompson Educational Publishing.

———. (2013d). Researching sexual minority and gender variant youth and their growth into resilience. In W. Midgley, P. A. Danaher, & M. Baguley (Eds.), *The role of participants in education research: Ethics, epistemologies, and methods* (pp. 15–28). New York, NY: Routledge.

———. (2013e). Camp fYrefly: Linking research to advocacy in community work with sexual and gender minority youth. In W. Pearce & J. Hillabold (Eds.), *OUT SPOKEN: Perspectives on queer identities* (pp. 127–142). Regina, SK: University of Regina Press.

———. (2014). It's about adult education and more: It's about lifelong learning for all and for all of life. *Canadian Journal for the Study of Adult Education, 26*(2), 33–46.

———. (2015). Part II with Wells, K. *Growing into Resilience: Sexual and gender minority youth in Canada.* Toronto, ON: University of Toronto Press.

Grace, A. P., & Wells, K. (2007a). Using Freirean pedagogy of just ire to inform critical social learning in arts-informed community education for sexual minorities. *Adult Education Quarterly, 57*(2), 95–114.

———. (2007b). Everyone performs, everyone has a place: Camp fYrefly and arts-informed, community-based education, cultural work, and inquiry. In D. Clover & J. Stalker (Eds.), *The art of social justice: Re-crafting activist adult education and community leadership* (pp. 61–82). Leicester, UK: NIACE.

Greenspan, A. (2008). *The age of turbulence: Adventures in a new world.* New York, NY: Penguin Books.

Grossman, A. H., & D'Augelli, A. R. (2006). Transgender youth: Invisible and vulnerable. *Journal of Homosexuality, 51*(1), 111–128.

———. (2007). Transgender youth and life-threatening behaviors. *Suicide and Life-Threatening Behavior, 37*(5), 527–537.

Haas, A. P., Eliason, M., Mays, V. M., Mathy, R. M., Cochran, S. D., D'Augelli, A. R., Silverman, M. M., & Associates. (2011). Suicide and suicide risk in lesbian, gay, bisexual, and transgender populations: Review and recommendations. *Journal of Homosexuality, 58*(1), 10–51.

Harvey, D. (2005). *A brief history of neoliberalism.* New York, NY: Oxford University Press.

Hatzenbuehler, M. L. (2011). The social environment and suicide attempts in lesbian, gay, and bisexual youth. *Pediatrics, 127*(5), 896–903.

Herrenkohl, E. C., Herrenkohl, R. C., & Egolf, B. (1994). Resilient early school-age children from maltreating homes: Outcomes in late adolescence. *American Journal of Orthopsychiatry, 64*(2), 301–309.

Hill, R. J., & Grace, A. P. (Eds.). (2009). *Adult and higher education in queer contexts: Power, politics, and pedagogy.* Chicago, IL: Discovery Association Publishing House.

Holmwood, J. (2014). From social rights to the market: Neoliberalism and the knowledge economy. *International Journal of Lifelong Education, 33*(1), 62–76.

Jarvis, P. (2007). *Globalisation, lifelong learning and the learning society: Sociological perspectives.* New York: Routledge.

Krugman, P. (2009). *The return of depression economics and the crisis of 2008.* New York, NY: W. W. Norton & Company.

Liebenberg, L., & Ungar, M. (2008). Introduction: Understanding youth resilience in action: The way forward. In L. Liebenberg & M. Ungar (Eds.), *Resilience in action* (pp. 3–16). Toronto, ON: University of Toronto Press.

———. (2009). Introduction: The challenges in researching resilience. In L. Liebenberg & M. Ungar (Eds.), *Researching resilience* (pp. 3–25). Toronto, ON: University of Toronto Press.

Luthar, S. S. (1993). Methodological and conceptual issues in research on childhood resilience. *Journal of Child Psychology and Psychiatry, 34*, 441–453.

Marshall, E. A., & Leadbeater, B. L. (2008). Policy responses to youth in adversity: An integrated, strengths-based approach. In L. Liebenberg & M. Ungar (Eds.), *Resilience in action* (pp. 380–399). Toronto, ON: University of Toronto Press.

Saewyc, E. M. (2011). Research on adolescent sexual orientation: Development, health disparities, stigma, and resilience. *Journal of Research on Adolescence, 21*(1), 256–272.

Savage, D., & Miller, T. (Eds.). (2012). *It gets better: Coming out, overcoming bullying, and creating a life worth living.* New York, NY: A Plume Book, Penguin Group.

Schuller, T., & Watson, D. (2009). *Learning through life: Inquiry into the future for lifelong learning.* Leicester, UK: NIACE.

Shelley, C. A. (2008). *Transpeople: Repudiation, trauma, healing.* Toronto, ON: University of Toronto Press.

Taylor, C., & Peter, T., with McMinn, T. L., Schachter, K., Beldom, S., Ferry, A., Gross, Z., & Paquin, S. (2011). *Every class in every school: The first national climate survey on homophobia, biphobia, and transphobia in Canadian schools. Final report.* Toronto, ON: Egale Canada Human Rights Trust.

The Lancet. (2011). Health concerns of adolescents who are in a sexual minority. *The Lancet, 377*(9783), 2056. (Available at www.thelancet.com.)

Tolman, D. L., & McClelland, S. I. (2011). Normative sexuality development in adolescence: A decade review, 2000–2009. *Journal of Research on Adolescence, 21*(1), 242–255.

Trotter, J. (2009). Ambiguities around sexuality: An approach to understanding harassment and bullying of young people in British schools. *Journal of LGBT Youth, 6*(1), 7–23.

Weber, S., & Poster, E. C. (2010). Guest editorial: Special issue on mental health nursing care of LGBT adolescents and young adults. *Journal of Child and Adolescent Psychiatric Nursing, 23*(1), 1–2.

Wells, K. (2008, Winter). *Homophobic bullying* [Fact Sheet]. Government of Alberta. Edmonton, AB.

Wells, K., Roberts, G., & Allan, C. (2012). *Supporting transsexual and transgender students in K–12 schools: A guide for educators.* Ottawa: ON: Canadian Teachers' Federation.

Welton, M. R. (2011). Falling into the company of adult educators: Travels with CASAE. *Canadian Journal for the Study of Adult Education, 23*(2), 1–10.

2

Youth Development in Context

Housing Instability, Homelessness, and Youth "Work"

Naomi Nichols

Schools rely on families to coordinate between the routines and relevancies of the home and those of the public school system (Dodson & Luttrell, 2011; Griffith & Smith, 2005). School staff expect and depend on families' support for school-based socialization practices (e.g., learned deference to authority, academic literacy development, sleeping and eating routines) and developmental outcomes (e.g., impulse control, processing and memory skills, self-regulation, planning, and focus) that align with and support youth's participation in school. Schools and other mainstream institutions operate in relation to, and substantiate, dominant decontextualized narratives of development—for example, that adolescence is a transitional phase between childhood and adulthood, where one focuses on development of self and identity. Embedded in the delivery of public education is the assumption that human development represents a universal set of age-based stages. In this context, the impacts of socialization on development remain insufficiently acknowledged. As such, schools interpret as deficient the skills and conduct of children and youth whose developmental pathways do not conform to age-based expectations. Youth who fail to align their conduct with the expectations for behavior that schools require end up categorized as "behavioral students," "school-averse learners," "youth at risk," or youth who pose "a risk to others." The contexts shaping diverse developmental trajectories among youth as well as the school systems' expectations for particular age-based developmental outcomes remain unacknowledged and un-interrogated.

Changing labor market conditions, lower earning potential, and an increased cost of housing all make it increasingly challenging for youth to achieve economic and social independence (Gaetz, 2014). Youth who live in economically disadvantaged and racialized communities report that these socioeconomic trends are exacerbated (Nichols, Anucha, Houwer, & Wood, 2013). My use of the term racialized in this chapter emphasizes the social processes through which race is constructed, imposed on, and contested by particular individuals and groups. The rising cost of housing also impacts families that are struggling to make ends meet (Gaetz, Donaldson, Richter, & Gulliver, 2013) and disadvantages youth who leave familial or state care environments as soon as they are legally allowed to do so (e.g., once a youth is 16 years of age) or prior to achieving material and social stability. Given the above and in the context of this chapter I argue for a definition of youth as the time of life between 15 and 29 years of age (Gaetz, 2014; Nichols et al., 2013). This expansive definition of youth reflects the recent socioeconomic shifts in societies where youth has emerged as a distinctive period of life between childhood and adulthood. It also resonates with the sociology of generous work (Smith, 2005) informing this chapter.

In the remaining sections, I consider what an approach to education and community development for youth would look like, if it acknowledged the sociocultural contexts of development and the work organization of homes, institutional settings, and public spaces where youth are active and where adults work to manage their lives. My analysis privileges the experiential knowledge of youth whose developmental trajectories are "out-of-sync" with expectations for age-based development held by mainstream institutions, particularly schools. I include the voices of youth who have been unable to get what they want and need from their interactions with the mainstream system. These voices from the margins reveal the limitations of educational and social programs aligned with conventional understandings of age- and stage-based youth development. I conclude this chapter with a discussion of principles of adult education that may improve access to education for youth whose developmental trajectories do not conform to expectations for development held by mainstream schools.

The Social Age of Youth and Youth Work

While policies, programs, and services often reflect chronological age-based distinctions between children, youth, and adults, human development is a function of the complex interplay between biological, social, environmental, and cultural factors (Almeida, Wood, Messineio, 1998; Brent, & Silverstein, 2013; Halfon, Larson, & Russ, 2010; Gupta, deWit, & McKeown, 2007; Luby et al., 2013). Contrary to traditional human development theories that espouse a homogenous developmental trajectory, it is increasingly clear that developmental pathways reflect the diverse environmental, social, cultural, and political conditions in which people live (Clark-Kazak, 2009; Gee, 2004; Lave & Wenger, 2003; Rogoff, 2003; Sen, 2004; Super & Harkness, 2002). As our understanding of human development evolves, it is time to re-think the organization of social policy and practice framed according to age-based social and educational interventions and complement these with locally situated programming that builds on participants' prior knowledge and experiences.

Clark-Kazak's (2009) notion of *social age* may be useful here. Social age refers to the situated meanings, roles, and relationships that people link to particular biological developmental milestones (Clark-Kazak, 2009). Drawing on the use of gender analysis in development work, Clark-Kazak advocates social-age "mainstreaming" as a way to systematically attend to "localized, socially constructed definitions and roles of children and young people" and the significance of their intergenerational relationships (p. 1312). The recognition of development as a relational phenomenon is where the theory and analysis of social age mainstreaming intersects usefully with the theory and analysis of youth work, as I have conceptualized it elsewhere (Nichols, 2014).

Traditionally the term "youth work" conveys a particular set of work activities conducted by adults who hold a professional title, such as Child and Youth Worker (or CYW). CYWs support the work of institutions (e.g., schools or child protective services) by helping youth bring their work in line with particular institutional expectations or processes. The activities of CYWs and the institutions that employ them typically reflect dominant age-based developmental frameworks. In contrast, I use the term youth work to direct analytic attention to *all of the things youth do* in institutional settings (whether they are deemed institutionally effective or not), as well as the activities of any adult who works with youth. I focus analysis on the co-ordering of relations between people in particular organizational contexts, rather than generalizing universal frames that cannot sufficiently attend to diversity. Used in this way, the term directs our attention to the processes of coordination (Smith, 2005) that shape educational and social outcomes for youth who are the subjects of policy and/or practice interventions.

Data explored in this chapter were gathered through qualitative research strategies (e.g., in-depth open-ended interviews and focus groups as well as document analysis). Interviews and focus groups were conducted with youth and the adults with whom youth interact across organizational contexts. Pseudonyms are used in this paper and ethical clearance was secured through a university committee (2007, 107). I use the alternative sociology, institutional ethnography or IE (Smith, 1990a; 1990b; 1999; 2002; 2005; 2006) as my guiding sociological approach. The research proceeds from the standpoint of youth, but the foci of investigation are the organizations and organizational processes that youth engage in their efforts to seek and maintain housing, take care of their physical and mental health, interact with the justice system, schools, child welfare, social assistance, and immigration. IE is attentive to the lived experiences of individual participants *and* the generalizing/able relations that give shape to these experiences.

By focusing analytic attention on the social organization of youth's interinstitutional work—with emphasis on their work in school—this chapter demonstrates how relations between youth and the adult professionals they encounter (a) are shaped by naturalized age-based developmental narratives, embedded in ordinary institutional processes and knowledge, and (b) influence the subject positions/possibilities for action afforded to youth in institutional settings.

Youth Development in Context: Organizational Practices

North American schools are organized by and perpetuate a framing of childhood and adolescence as periods in the life course characterized by learning and play. In this context, active participation in academic and extracurricular activities is understood to be the central task of youth. This assumption is out-of-sync with the expectation some youth experience to contribute to the material well-being of the family, take care of their own needs and/ or those of siblings, or live independently in the community. It also fails to acknowledge the other institutional work some youth must do, relative to their interactions with the youth justice, mental health, or housing and homelessness systems.

Work Organization Practices of Homes, Streets, and Schools

Structured school-led opportunities to responsibilize youth (e.g., through homework and participation in extracurricular programs like student government) assume that fostering academic and social capacities is a young person's primary developmental task. Such singular, decontextualized notions of childhood and adolescence do not take into account the diversity of human experiences or the interrelated effects of class, race, culture, and gender (Burton, 2007; Jarett, 2003; Nebbitt & Lombe, 2010). When children and youth actions in schools do not correspond with expectations of a "homogeneous and naturally occurring group of individuals at a certain stage of human development" (Ferguson, 2001; p. 81 in Burton, 2007), some youth—for example, those who can be described as adultified—are systematically disadvantaged during their interactions with school.

As a researcher and a former educator, I have interacted with many youth for whom adolescence has been characterized by considerable work within and outside the home. Xavier was one young man that I met while conducting research for a community-based organization in an economically disadvantaged and racialized community. He explains how his teachers' presumptions about the work of adolescence made him feel "under-estimated" and "hushed" in school. Xavier observes how the mainstream school system's inability to recognize his care-giving work in the home meant that his teachers did not interpret these experiences as strengths. Xavier felt that his maturity and responsibilities were not acknowledged and his contributions were not valued:

> [some youth] have to go and do on their own, like you know what I mean? From young! . . . The teachers in schools don't understand that a twelve year old kid is doing what *you* do at *your* home—like cooking dinner, giving his younger siblings food to eat, and you know what I mean? And that his brain is more mature. They [mainstream school teachers] try to like under-estimate youth, like "oh you don't know what you are saying." Like, they start to hush you.

Xavier's extensive work in the home is out-of-sync (Burton, 2007, p. 331) with expectations for youth development held by contemporary institutions like schools. As Burton notes, there is a disjuncture "between what social institutions, such as schools, expect of children and what families with severe economic needs require of them" (p. 331). As such, youth like Xavier end up feeling like their experiential knowledge is incompatible with, and incomprehensible to, the mainstream system.

Homelessness and Housing Instability

Other youth I have known left their familial homes or foster care settings shortly after their 16th birthdays and went to live on the streets and in emergency shelters, bouncing between independent housing, justice facilities, mental health institutions, and the shelter system throughout adolescence. These youth describe themselves as having been "rushed into being responsible" and explain that they simply don't have "the head for school." The preoccupation with social and academic development that is characteristic of mainstream school is insignificant when compared with the exigencies of street-involved youth who are unsure where they will sleep, what they will eat, or how they will keep themselves safe from harm on the street, in a "trap-house" (i.e., a building people occupy for the purpose of using drugs), or in a shelter. Contextualized notions of development are necessary in order to effectively work with the strengths of diverse children and youth.

For homeless youth, schooling represents a singular aspect of their institutional work—and in many instances, schooling is overshadowed by the primacy of their mental health or street work. The assumption that adolescence is a time for school-based learning and supported entry into public spaces (e.g., through student government, youth councils or volunteerism) is misaligned with their realities. Many of the youth who I met while working on this study were placed in a homeless shelter by child welfare services because of a lack of suitable housing options for adolescent youth "in care." Their experiences suggest that housing precarity—not simply absolute homelessness—contributes to school failure.

It is not uncommon for youth involved with child welfare to experience multiple housing placements (including the use of emergency shelters) throughout their tenure with the agency. Packing up one's belongings, familiarizing oneself with a new neighborhood, and establishing new social relationships, take work. All of this work on the part of the youth is mediated by adult social workers who must ascertain the reason for a housing breakdown, communicate with their own managers or directors, find another suitable housing placement, and document these efforts in their own case notes. If a youth is found to be unsafe or has been evicted, the child welfare worker may have to coordinate an interim housing placement, often at a youth shelter or motel. As a legal guardian, the Children's Aid Society (CAS) must know where a youth "in care" is at all times. When a youth in care is missing, it is a legal issue. The police are called and requested to locate the individual and bring him or her back. For privacy reasons, educators are not generally privy to any of these changes. Malachi was 17 years old when I met him. By this time, he had experienced numerous familial and community housing placements:

> I went to a group home . . . I was in some other places before
> then too: at my uncle's house. I was in some hospitals and

stuff [for mental health concerns] . . . So then I went in a
group home, which was kind of abusive or whatever. And then
I went back to my mom's, and then I went to a foster home.
Then I went to the shelter, and then I went to a foster home,
and then another foster home. And then now I'm at Pritchard
House [a congregate housing environment for youth with an
on-site youth worker].

Like other youth, Malachi's housing instability was interspersed with time
spent in institutional care for mental health issues. He experienced multiple
placements throughout adolescence, living at the youth shelter intermittently
throughout his teenage years while his child welfare worker endeavored to
find something more permanent for him. He also attended a mainstream
high school, but it was difficult to keep up with the standardized curriculum when he was missing school due to frequent changes in his living
environment. Eventually he enrolled in an alternative school for homeless
youth. He was making progress toward credit accumulation while he was
living in the youth shelter, but began experiencing attendance issues once
he was living outside the direct supervision of shelter or group home staff.

Madeleine experienced a similar housing trajectory during adolescence.
Although she lived in a stable foster care environment for most of her
childhood, she was transitioned into a group home when she began high
school. In the three years that followed, Madeleine had five different housing placements arranged for her by her CAS worker. During this time,
she was placed at the youth shelter more than once. In the spring of her
grade 11 year, she "AWOLed"—was absent without leave—from the shelter
and was ultimately expelled for truancy from the second mainstream high
school she had attended. When she received the written expulsion notice,
she immediately registered at the Loft—the alternative school for homeless
and precariously housed youth—but by the following autumn, she had been
de-registered by staff for failing to attend her co-op placement. Between
May and October of this same year, Madeleine moved in with two different
male partners, both of whom physically abused her.

During a focus group conversation, Neil told me that, including
respite homes, he'd had 57 different placements throughout his tenure with
child welfare as a child and youth. Most recently, he was living at Pritchard
House with Malachi and a number of other youth between 16 and 24 years
of age. Due to a change in child welfare workers and some logistical issues
with enrolling at a school within walking distance from his latest housing
placement, Neil missed an entire month of classes during this transition.

With a chuckle, Dmitri told me that the longest he'd lived anywhere since coming into care was nine months. During this period of his life, he had actually run away from care and was living in another city with his girlfriend while working at a call center, rather than attending school.

Seven of the 31 youth I interviewed for this study described experiences where they were institutionalized for mental health concerns throughout their adolescence. Instances of therapy, prescribed and/or illegal drug use to manage mental health concerns, stays in youth justice facilities and homeless or precarious housing all disrupted their participation in school. Asked to tell me how she ended up in that shelter, Stella began by speaking with me about the onset of her mental health concerns and her interactions with school, child welfare, mental health, and youth justice organizations. Stella's story captures the disruptive effects of mental health interventions and involvement in the youth justice system on a young person's schooling experiences. As she tells it, her disengagement from school began during middle school when she began to experience depression:

> When I first went through depressions and shit in grade 7, I kept on getting kicked out of class—and my teacher would ask me "what's wrong with you? You're always angry all the time— why are you failing your tests and shit?" I was a really good student—and then when I was depressed, I got yelled at in class. I remember my teacher saying, "You're the smartest kid in the class but you're the only one who failed the test."

Prior to the seventh grade, Stella had been engaged in school and had done well. She participated in extracurricular activities as a dancer and a singer. In developmental terms, expectations, and aspirations, Stella was the student that schools anticipate: school-based learning and participation in pro-social extracurricular activities were her primary developmental tasks. When she began to experience depression in grade seven, however, the focus of her own developmental work changed. Her free time was spent participating in assessments and therapy, and she felt angry all the time.

Stella's teacher interpreted her drastic drop in grades and unprecedented acting out in class as a discipline issue. Teachers are accountable for student learning, and Stella was disrupting the learning of the group. The teacher's response was to kick her out of class. She was also moved from her family home. First she went to stay with an aunt and uncle, but later she was forcibly hospitalized by the police, and then moved into a treatment-focused group home. Between the ages of 12 and 15, Stella was institutionalized in

five different mental health treatment facilities and hospitals, often returning to the same psychiatric wards on numerous occasions. Intermittently
throughout her adolescence Stella also spent time in various youth justice
facilities. She explains how this impacted her schooling:

> I was on 5 different medications at a time. . . . I was completely
> knocked out, but also when you move around a lot, it's just that
> you tune out. It was really hard for me to do schooling because
> when I lived in the group home it just wasn't what I was focus-
> ing on. I had more important issues to deal with than school.
> Like when your head isn't in the right space, you can't really do
> schooling because your focus is somewhere else.

Stella went on to become a Ward of the Crown, living in a homeless shelter for youth for much of her adolescence. Periodically during this time
(between 15 and 18 years of age), she was also re-institutionalized in youth
justice and mental health facilities. Throughout adolescence, Stella continued
to find it difficult to participate in mainstream school. She explains that she
had "more important issues to deal with than school." Like the other youth
whose stories I share in this chapter, Stella experienced multiple disruptions
to her housing and social relationships. Her adolescence was punctuated
by repeated periods of incarceration in youth justice facilities, institutionalization in mental health treatment facilities, and a series of child welfare
housing placements that undermined her efforts to establish relationships
with adults and other young people.

Other youth experience homelessness as the result of family breakdown during adolescence. These youth are more likely to experience absolute
homelessness and street involvement, which contribute to sleeplessness, hunger, and stress. Darcy was 16 when he left home. It was February and very
cold and his friends' parents were unwilling to have him stay with them.
He didn't know about the city's youth shelter, so Darcy spent the first two
weeks after leaving home alternating between walking the streets all night
and sleeping in an Automated Teller Machine (ATM):

> I made the idiot decision to see how I would fare outside on
> the street. It is the worst feeling possible. You feel like the world
> has turned its back on you. You don't know where to go. All the
> people you thought—it's almost like a sense of betrayal. I don't
> know. Cold, hungry . . . along with feeling homeless, there are
> a lot other negative thing that you feel.

Without "a dollar to [his] name," Darcy was not worried that he would be robbed, but he describes being constantly harassed by security guards and others. As such, he maintained a "state of constant alert and readiness" that undermined his ability to sleep: "You'll pass out for about two hours and then a noise—a car driving by or something—will kind of jolt you." During the day, chronic sleep deprivation, stress, and lack of food undermined his ability to participate effectively in class. Aware that he needed some help to find housing, Darcy sought the support of his school's guidance department. He discovered that they were ill-prepared to help him access the services he would need to remain in school:

> Some guidance counsellors will try to persuade you towards the Ontario Works [social assistance] program, but a lot of them are uninformed as well. They don't have any information to give you. The bottom line is that they are kind of useless in that way too. Because, as I said, you live in a time where if you don't need it and you haven't used it before, you probably don't even know that it exists.

The obvious material consequences of the guidance department's ignorance are Darcy's continued lack of knowledge about the youth shelter, local food cupboards designed particularly for youth, or how to apply for Ontario Works (OW) social assistance as a minor. Less obvious, but perhaps more profound, are the social and emotional consequences of the school staff's inability to recognize and effectively mediate Darcy's experiences of homelessness. Staff's inability to productively support Darcy at this time of profound vulnerability and need contributed to his sense of isolation and disconnection—what he described as feeling like "the world has turned its back on you." For Darcy, experiences of homelessness—and the invisibility of this reality among mainstream school staff—prompted feelings of loneliness and depression that ultimately led to his disengagement from school.

The experiences of housing instability and interactions with street life described by adolescent youth in care make it difficult for them to participate actively and consistently in school. Books and homework are lost. Deadlines are missed. Tests need to be rescheduled, and youth fall further and further behind. From the perspective of their adult teachers—most of whom will be unaware of the changes in a youth's housing situation—it appears as though the youth is having difficulty with time management or commitment. Day planners and calendars are recommended to help a youth be more organized and attentive to deadlines. Pep-talks and stern lectures are given. Ultimately, a lack of housing stability manifests as poor attendance, disengagement, and/or an inability to complete credits. Schools treat the manifestations of housing instability as a disciplinary issue. Youth are expelled, unenrolled, and charged with truancy for failing to attend schools. An expulsion or truancy charge reflects expectations for stability during adolescence that cannot be met by youth who are precariously housed and/or highly systems-involved. As such, a school's response (particularly as it intersects with other institutions such as youth criminal justice) may actual magnify instability and experiences of social isolation, and hinder pro-social development.

Developmental narratives that frame adolescence as a period of concerted learning and emergence into the public sphere underestimate (a) the primacy of social relationships and the urgency of day-to-day life occurrences for youth who are street involved; (b) the burden of learning and work born by these youth on a daily basis; and (c) the degree to which youth development is influenced by a person's institutional involvements. By and large, interventions targeting youth are not designed to take into account a young person's other social and institutional relationships nor do they adequately leverage their prior learning and experience as resources.

Adult Education, Youth Development, and Participatory Reflection

Critical reflections on my institutional ethnographic work in the area of youth homelessness shape my current program of research. Most of the youth engaged in my current research project (an extension of the one described in this chapter) are involved with Youth Justice and Safe Schools alternative learning programs. Many are also involved with child welfare, mental health, homelessness (e.g., emergency shelters), Ontario Works (social assistance), and/or social and community-based services (e.g., youth advocates, youth workers, and youth engagement initiatives). Most live in poverty, would be categorized institutionally as having visible minority status, and have experienced racism in their neighbourhoods and in their schools. The research acknowledges youth's institutional work (i.e., their youth work) as taking time and energy. Youth who participate as research subjects are considered to be experts on the inter-institutional organization of services for "youth at risk." They are compensated, economically, for their time and provided with ongoing opportunities to guide the direction of the project and speak to emerging project findings.

Youth also participate in the project as paid research assistants. These youth receive training and mentorship from project leads (academics and community leaders), age-based peers engaged in graduate work, and front-line social service professionals. Youth are provided with opportunities to integrate/contrast their experiential knowledge with the theoretical ideas we are exploring together as a project team, and contribute their insights to our collective analytic work. As this research continues these research assistants are helping to hire, train, and mentor a team of younger youth in a youth-led community-based research initiative that operates within the larger project structure. Learning and mentorship occurs across the project, as people interact across difference. From a research point of view, the opportunity to engage in team-based ethnography with people who are diversely positioned relative to the research problematic is invaluable.

The inclusion and education of youth researchers on this project reflects the principles of adult education—training and mentorship revolve around opportunities for experiential learning and merging of youth's tacit knowledge of the community with an analysis of structural forms of oppression that influence how young people come to know and act in particular settings (Freire, 1974). The project aims to develop their capacity to think critically and communicate effectively, but also to capitalize on their evolving knowledge and experience as we co-design and implement a paid summer cooperative education initiative for younger youth in the community to participate in the project as research assistants. This multidirectional approach to learning acknowledges and builds on people's prior knowledge and experiences. By taking a community- and team-based approach to the research, there is significantly more economic and human resources to invest in this second project. We employ a multilayered training and mentorship model which capitalizes on critical dialogue and learning across age-based and other differences (e.g., race, class, gender).

Conclusion

This chapter advocates re-visiting the developmental assumptions that underpin age-based educational and community development programming for youth. The mainstream education system works reasonable well when youth can rely on adult caregivers to take care of their material and emotional needs, and ensure that the work organization of the home fits with and supports the work organization expectations of schools, health, social service, and justice system facilities. The education system is less effective when youth live independently of parents or guardians or have otherwise been unable to depend on caregivers to do the work that schooling requires (e.g., ensuring youth attend school and on time, promoting literacy development and stimulating pro-social activities during holidays). As this chapter suggests, the system is also less effective when schooling represents only one of a youth's institutional relationships or when he or she must engage in considerable unpaid work in the home and community (e.g., caring for young siblings, shopping for and preparing food, finding and maintaining housing).

Even within a single urban setting, different developmental trajectories shape the degree and manner in which youth engage educational and social services. Increasingly, large urban cities reflect considerable economic, racial, ethnic, linguistic, and sexual diversity. Increased diversity, coupled with the use of expansive definitions of youth, requires the development of educational and social programs that are attentive to, and leverage, difference.

References

Almeida, R. V., Woods, R., & Messineo, T. (1998). Child development: Intersectionality of race, gender, class, and culture. *Journal of Feminist Family Therapy, 10*(1), 23–47.

Arendt, H. (1968). *Between past and future: Eight exercises in political thought.* New York, NY: Viking Press.

———. (2003). *Responsibility and judgement.* Toronto, ON: Schocken Books, Random House.

Brent, D. A., & Silverstein, M. (2013). Shedding light on the long shadow of childhood adversity. *JAMA Pediatrics, 309*(17), 1777–1779.

Burton, L. M. (2007). Childhood adultification in economically disadvantaged families: An ethnographic perspective. *Family Relations, 56*(4), 329–345.

Clark-Kazak, C. R. (2009). Towards a working definition and application of social age in international development studies. *The Journal of Development Studies, 45*(8), 1307–1324.

Dodson, L. & Luttrell, W. (2011). Families facing untenable choices. *Contexts, 10*, 38–42.

Dodson, L., & Dickert, J. (2004). Girls' family labor in low-income households: A decade of qualitative research. *Journal of Marriage and Family, 66*, 318–332.

Freire, P. (1974). *Pedagogy of the oppressed.* New York, NY: Seabury Press.

Fuller, B. & Garcia-Coll, C. (2010). Learning from Latinos: Contexts, families, and child development in motion. *Developmental Psychology, 46*(3), 559–565.

Gaetz, S. (2014). Coming of age: *Reimagining the response to youth homelessness in Canada.* Toronto, ON: The Canadian Homelessness Research Network Press.

Gaetz, S., Donaldson, J., Richter, T., & Gulliver, T. (2013). *The state of homelessness in Canada, 2013.* Toronto, ON: The Canadian Homelessness Research Network Press.

Gee, J. P. (2004). *Situated language and learning: A critique of traditional schooling*. New York, NY: Routledge.

Griffith, A. I., & Smith, D. E. (2005). *Mothering for schooling*. New York, NY: Routledge.

Gupta, R. P. S., deWit, M., & McKeown, D. (2007). The impact of poverty on the current and future health status of children. *Paediatric Child Health, 12(8)*, 667–674.

Halfon, N., Larson, K., & Russ, S. (2010). Why social determinants? *Healthcare Quarterly, 14.*

Jarrett, R. L. (2003). Worlds of development: The experiences of low-income African-American youth. *Journal of Children & Poverty, 9*(2), 157–188.

Lave, J., & Wenger, E. (2003/1991). *Situated learning: Legitimate peripheral participation*. Cambridge, MA: Cambridge University Press.

Luby, J., Belden, A., Botteron, K., Marrus, N., Harms, M. P., Babb, C., Nishino, T., & Barch, D. (2013). The effects of poverty on childhood brain development: The mediating effect of caregiving and stressful life events. *JAMA Pediatrics, 167*(12), 1135–1143.

Nebbitt, V. E., & Lombe, M. (2010). Urban African American adolescents and adultification. *Families in Society: The Journal of Contemporary Social Services, 91*(3), 233–240.

Nichols, N. (2014.) *Youth work: An institutional ethnography of youth homelessness*. Toronto, ON: University of Toronto Press.

Nichols, N., Anucha, U., Houwer, R., & Wood, M. (2013). Facilitating equitable community: Academic research collaborations. *Gateways, International Journal of Community Research and Engagement, 6,* 57–76.

Province of Ontario. (2000). *Bill 81: An act to increase respect and responsibility, to set standards for safe learning and safe teaching in schools and to amend the teaching profession act*. Retrieved from http://www.ontla.on.ca/bills/bills-files/37_Parliament/Session1/b081ra.pdf.

Rogoff, B. (2003). *The cultural nature of human development*. Toronto, ON: Oxford University Press.

Sen, A. (2004). Dialogue: Capabilities, lists, and public reason: Continuing the conversation. *Feminist Economics, 10*(3), 77–80.

Smith, D. E. (1990a). *Texts, facts, and femininity: Exploring the relations ruling*. New York: Routledge, NY.

———. (1990b). *The conceptual practices of power: A feminist sociology of knowledge*. Boston, USA: North Eastern University Press.

———. (1999). *Writing the social: Critique, theory, and investigations*. Toronto, ON: University of Toronto Press.

———. (2002). Institutional Ethnography. In T. May (Ed.), *Qualitative research: An international guide to issues in practice* (pp. 36–65). London, UK: Sage.

———. (2005). *Institutional ethnography: A sociology for people*. Toronto, ON: Altamira Press.

————. (2006). Introduction. In D. E. Smith (Ed.), *Institutional ethnography as practice* (pp. 1–12). Toronto, ON: Rowman and Littlefield.

Super, C. M., & Harkness, S. (2002). Culture structures the environment for development. *Human Development, 45,* 270–274.

3

A Synergy of Understanding

Intimidation Technologies and Situated Learning in United States and Jamaican Prisons

Joshua C. Collins
Lincoln D. Pettaway
Chaundra L. Whitehead
Steve J. Rios

> Prisons provide the perfect breeding ground for transmission of the HIV . . . drug use and unprotected sex, including coerced sex, are common in prisons around the world.
>
> —The Human Rights Watch Prison Report

In 2006, the United Nations Office on Drugs and Crime, the World Health Organization, and the Joint United Nations Programme on HIV/AIDS, produced a new framework for responding to the international health crisis of HIV/AIDS in prisons (United Nations, 2006). The framework promoted the idea that prisoners should have the same access to prevention information, care, treatment, and support for HIV/AIDS as is available to people outside prisons. To date, this powerful call to action has not been met by many nations, including the United States and Jamaica.

The prevalence of HIV/AIDS among U.S. prisoners is four times the rate among the general U.S. population (Maruschak & Beavers, 2010). In Jamaica, pervasive cultural norms of homophobia have led to riots and the death of inmates even at the mere suggestion of condom distribution in prisons (Andrinopoulos, Figueroa, Kerrigan, & Ellen, 2011). In fact, the distribution of condoms, a preventative measure that can curtail the spread of HIV/AIDS, is not practiced in many prisons throughout the world. This is in direct contradiction of safe sex practice policies and, we argue, an intentional policy aimed at making a public example of the incarcerated.

Male inmates are often required to negotiate safe sex practices and awareness with limited reliable sexual health education available. With scant sexual health information, inmates face a high risk of HIV infection (World Health Organization, 2007). Opportunities for learning and making use of knowledge are extremely limited. Male inmates are often incarcerated for long periods of time and told that they have to stop functioning as sexual beings for the entirety of their incarceration, even if that happens to be for life (Ristroph, 2006). This mandate presumes that situational sexual contact between inmates can be regulated out of existence. Many inmates report that they are not able to maintain a practice of celibacy due to pressures from other inmates to engage in sexual activity and threats if they do not comply.

This chapter will discuss current realities related to HIV/AIDS for male inmates in U.S. and Jamaican prisons. These two settings illustrate the lack of dialogue about HIV/AIDS in prisons. This chapter then attempts to address the challenges that are both situated in intentional educational and policy choices designed to create examples of the incarcerated. These individuals, already physically isolated from society, are frequently pushed to the periphery of society's care and left to learn, negotiate, and manage safe sex practices without readily available educational resources. However, this chapter is not simply a comparison of HIV/AIDS statistics and practices across these settings. Rather, the chapter focusses on how intimidation and power have become institutionalized and rationalized through specific policy choices that inhibit and diminish the experiences and quality of life for those living in peripheral circumstances in U.S. and Jamaican prisons. To address this issue, policies and practices must promote effective situated learning experiences and help inmates understand and handle, in their own minds and bodies, complex contradictions of sexual practices in prison settings. We discuss the role of this type of situated learning in the lives of the incarcerated and imagine a future in which health educators and incarcerated people work together to address the internationally systemic problem of HIV/AIDS behind bars.

An Overview of the Regulation of
Sexual Practices in U.S. and Jamaican Prisons

Policy related to health education in U.S. prisons is guided by the Correctional Officers Health and Safety Act of 1998, requiring high standards for infectious disease detection and prevention for both correctional officers and inmates (House of Representatives, 1997). Regarding HIV/ AIDS, however, this mandate is often not met. While not openly advocating condom distribution, the National HIV/AIDS Strategy emphasizes sexual health education "in communities where HIV is concentrated [so] we can have the biggest impact in lowering all communities' collective risk of acquiring HIV" (The White House Office of National AIDS Policy, 2010, p. viii). It is difficult to realize this potential in prisons because the millions of intermittently incarcerated U.S. prisoners are among the most difficult people to reach with vital health information, management, and treatment. While admittedly a captive population, much of the literature is only available in printed form and written in English, yet Kantor (2006) argues that as many as 50 percent of U.S. prisoners are functionally illiterate or non-native English speakers. For these reasons, the available literature is usually of little value to them.

Although the primary goal of HIV/AIDS education in U.S. prisons is prevention, other critical objectives include promoting rational and humane treatment of inmates. However, the dynamics of correctional settings suggests that information provided by people who are not prisoners—from general facts to specific medical advice—often is not trusted. HIV/AIDS education programs in prisons have to provide information in a manner that addresses and bridges not only language, culture, and literacy gaps, but also manages the distrust of people on the other side of the bars. Individual and peer counseling, support groups, and special programs for women, designed by and for prisoners, have been successful in a number of institutions and seem to be the best educational tools. But these tools are not always encouraged, supported, or funded because of pervasive cultural norms that presume inmates "chose" their "lifestyle" and therefore deserve to be punished, however that punishment may manifest itself.

In Jamaican prisons, condoms are considered as contraband and the powerful stigma associated with same-sex practices regulates against the integration of safer sexual practices and sex education behind bars. Independent research into the prevalence of HIV among males incarcerated in Jamaica concluded not only that HIV testing and education should be instituted across the island, but that "special attention should be given to inmates labeled as homosexual, as the prevalence of HIV was higher among this group" (Andrinopoulos, 2008, p. 17). Jamaican prison officials indicate that one major way they promote health and safety among their homosexual inmates is to house them separately. Inmates who are known to have been charged with buggery (anal sexual intercourse) are in great danger from other inmates. Efforts to educate prisoners about HIV/AIDS in Jamaica have focused on using peers to pass out prevention information and to inform inmates about behaviors and practices that place them at risk (Panos Institute Caribbean, 2007).

While condom distribution is forbidden in Jamaican prisons, perhaps even more potent is the reluctance of high-level government officials to acknowledge that sex among prisoners occurs. In 2008, the (now former) Commissioner of Corrections Major Richard Reese said that prisoners "do not engage in sexual intercourse with each other" (Panos Institute Caribbean, 2007, p. 7). The reluctance of one of Jamaica's highest-ranking corrections officials to recognize what UN, U.S. and Jamaican researchers have already documented is alarming for a number of reasons, not least that such ignorance directly impacts the lives of the incarcerated—people who, as the word "corrections" implies, *should be* receiving knowledge and tools for development while behind bars, but in actuality are not always on the receiving end of educative processes. This "shroud of secrecy regarding HIV diagnosis and treatment" (Ibid., p. 12) is a major issue to be overcome.

A Glimpse of the Past and Present and a Vision of the Future

In the sections that follow, we explain how HIV/AIDS is leveraged as an intimidation technology (Foucault, 1977) in the incarcerated populations of the United States and Jamaica. We examine the potential role of situated learning (Lave & Wenger, 1991) in prisons and imagine a future in which health educators and inmates are empowered to break the cycle of intimidation and lower the prevalence of HIV/AIDS behind bars.

Intimidation Technologies

Foucault (1977) posited knowledge attainment within the prison systems is administered strategically and tacitly, rather than being intentionally influenced and acquired by the prisoners. Foucault attested that the bodies of prisoners are vehicles for learning, as throughout history the bodies of the punished have been disciplined publicly as a caution to onlookers. It is understood that if and when rules, policies, or laws are broken, there will be consequences. Thus, public displays of disciplinary power may be understood as a measure aimed at controlling the bodies of the punished and a prospective warning to those who challenge the authority of the state, government, and/or other ruling powers. The spectacle of torturing rule-breakers and outlaws is a compulsory technology for education of the masses through intimidation. Although the visibility of technologies of intimidation have changed and evolved over time, and varied in their cruelty, oppression of the body is still a part of this unspoken educative and political process.

In the early history of the United States, public executions for White citizens were uncommon. However, Black slaves were frequently and publicly murdered (Christian & Bennett, 1998). Hangings were a form of intimidation to remind Blacks of their vulnerability. Intense racial tension contributed to similar events in Jamaica, where Black slaves frequently engaged in uprisings that were publicly squelched and punished by the White slave and plantation owners, some records indicating that at times as many as 400 slaves would be killed in an exhibition of dominance (King's College London, n.d.). In the same actions, White onlookers were reminded of their elevated status. As a form of spectacle, public murders of Blacks were akin to terrorism, reinforcing the punishers' dominance through the destruction of the Black body (or bodies). Black men were most often the victims of heinous punishment tactics such as cutting off their penises and then placing them in the mouths of the hanging dead (Abu-Lughod, 2007). The body was the technology which many early White settlers used to affirm their superiority and control large masses of Black slaves through fear mongering. Yet central to this educative process were not the odious methods of display, but the messages tacitly inscribed therein. The ability to redefine the body without fear of recourse was assumed to rest within the hands of Whites at the expense of Black slaves. Black slaves were branded, whipped, and their bodies deconstructed over a lifetime of inhumane and brutal working conditions. Their bodies were destroyed through lynching and dismantling reproductive organs, which might have been used to bring other Black bodies into existence. Hence, these technologies of intimidation operated in educative *and* actual ways to reduce the likelihood of future Black bodies gaining a proper education and (to the dread of White slave owners) eventually coming to question the system.

Our argument in this chapter is that similar intimidation technologies, if perhaps less obvious, but nonetheless just as serious, are in operation today. Prison populations continue to consist of primarily minorities who are leveraged as examples of what will happen if one does not follow the law. These minorities are kept from educational, health, and other opportunities and resources in morally questionable, and yet often legally permissible, acts of institutionalized prejudice and violence.

The Politics of Bodies and Education: The Role of Situated Learning

When public schooling within the United States was first established in Massachusetts, the settlers' primary motivation was to ensure that citizens had the requisite skills to understand and follow the Christian Bible, as well as the laws of the community (Race Forward, 2006). Part of the rationale was that individuals with basic reading and writing skills could be held liable for any legal violations of the written law. This ensured a rudimentary level of protection and safety for landowners, employers, and the general public. Similar phenomena emerged in Jamaica, where, at the advent of their education system, the children of White slave and plantation owners were sent back to Great Britain to receive an education, but education for Black slaves and Indigenous people was primarily directed toward learning the virtue and value of submission through religion texts (Wilkins & Gamble, 2000). In both the United States and Jamaica there is a history of using intimidation technologies (Foucault, 1977) to educate people about society and "their place" in it. In the United States, there was a growing awareness of the need to provide basic education to individuals who *had already* violated their place in society by breaking the law. Thus, prison education became part of the U.S. prison system in 1798, seven years after the first U.S. prison began operating (Coley & Barton, 2006). However, in the United States, Jamaica, and in other areas of the world, the purported focus of prisons on rehabilitating and bettering the lives of inmates remains ambiguous.

In this chapter, we link educating people about their place in society to the concept of situated learning, or "learning knowledge and skills in contexts that reflect the way the knowledge will be useful in real life" (Collins, 1991, p. 122). Situated learning places the learner at the center of an instructional process in which it is difficult to separate the learning process from the situation in which the learning is occurring (Merriam, Caffarella, & Baumgartner, 2007; Stein, 1998). A core aspect of situated learning is that the practice of interest—in this case, learning to do something (a sexual act) or be someone (a person who has same-sex partners)—is considered legitimate peripheral participation, a "particular model of engagement of a learner who participates in the actual practice of an expert, but only to a limited degree and with limited responsibility for the ultimate product as a whole" (Lave & Wenger, 1991, p. 14).

Sexual intercourse in prisons is a good example of situated learning because, while it is technically illegal to have sex while in prison, it continues (Lave & Wenger, 1991), positioning the context of prison as an important learning site of both learning and resistance. Sex is elicited as a form of resistance to mitigate and assuage the exposure to prolonged strain behind bars and to send a message that the constraints of prison cannot fully control those within. As a community of practice, incarcerated people recognize and obey the tacit rules and requirements of the community, which must also be learned by new community members—newcomers—in order to be accepted. This implicit activity is a form of situated learning akin to Lave and Wenger's (1991) notion of legitimate peripheral participation. With regard to sexual practices in prison, learning is often reduced to implied and unstated knowledge, passed to learners in a multilayered, complex, environmental-based, community of practice. In this context the community of practice has such strong influence it successfully urges many heterosexual male prisoners to relinquish aspects of their heterosexual identities for homosexual behaviors.

Situated learning is especially relevant to the issue of HIV/AIDS and prison, where it is common for incarcerated males to encounter complicated contradictions regarding communication about HIV/AIDS, health, and wellness, and where policies regarding sex (and especially safe sex) are incongruent with the situations in which inmates often find themselves. Situated learning can be a central component of a system of intimidation or conversely encourage health educators and inmates to acquire and use the knowledge necessary to change the situation. It may be beneficial for prisons to incorporate comprehensive and regular health and HIV/AIDS programs into the curriculum and opportunities offered to inmates, treating the relationship less as that of a trainer and a trainee and more as that of a mentor and apprentice, working toward the common goal of safer and smarter health practices in prisons.

Incarcerated men's sexual identities and sexual practices are also learning processes transmitted, experienced, and reinforced by others and articulated through filters, inscribed by the community and understood as codes articulated as communal practice. Among incarcerated males, the performance of masculinity and/or femininity is a more prominent concern than actual sexual practices such as oral or anal sex (Hartley, 2012). While men in prisons may engage in a variety of sexual behaviors with other men, variances and convergences of gender norms and expressions are often punished. Although never directly spoken within the prison context, most members of the community hold a clear understanding of the codes of expected behaviors, as determined by the necessities perceived by the community as a whole—for example, developing prison "families" or assigning more feminized roles to certain men and expecting them to adhere to those roles. However, such informal codes, when considered alongside the formal codes, expectations of government agencies and prisons, and their day-to-day management practices contribute to escalating difficulties and inconsistencies regarding HIV/AIDS in both U.S. and Jamaican prisons.

HIV/AIDS as Intimidation in U.S. and Jamaican Prisons

Prisons in the United States are operated mostly by state governments or the Federal Bureau of Prisons and generally detain people who have been convicted of state or federal felonies and are sentenced to terms of longer than one year (Harrison & Beck, 2006). In contrast, jails are often run by counties and house inmates with generally shorter sentences. Mass incarceration has health consequences as many offenders circulate through the correctional system. All chronic illnesses and communicable diseases are over-represented in the incarcerated population. It is estimated that the overall rate of HIV/AIDS among prison inmates is 2.5 times that of the rate in the U.S. general population. In 2008, 20,231 (1.5%) of male inmates and 1,913 (1.9%) of female inmates in state or federal prisons were HIV-positive or had AIDS (Zoukis, 2012). Such high prevalence has been attributed to the dramatic increase in drug offenders, many of whom engage in intravenous drug use, share needles, and/or trade sex for drugs (Mauer, 2006). In Jamaica, similar issues exist with regard to HIV/AIDS and are compounded by deep-seated stigma and prejudice related to homosexuality (Andrinopoulos, Figuero, Kerrigan, & Ellen, 2011). Jamaican inmates "[labeled] as 'homosexual' continue to face stigma and discrimination and suffer a disproportionate burden of infection without access to effective methods of HIV prevention" (para. 4).

These statistics and assertions support the view that the spread of HIV through prisons is further facilitated by intimidation technologies and failure to manage the induction of newcomers within the system (Foucault, 1977). This includes the lack of andragogical curriculum addressing condom use, modes of transmission of HIV, and condom distribution. The bodies of inmates who are infected with HIV while incarcerated are often transformed as a result of the articulation of power within the context of the prison system. HIV/AIDS becomes the dominating technology that re-inscribes the body of the prisoner. The prisoner, who is required to not have sexual intercourse while incarcerated, and usually not allowed condoms nor given any sexual health education upon entering the prison system, is unprepared for the unspoken communal rules and expectations that govern the situated learning occurring in the prison. To defy the stated rules of the prison, however, is to chance HIV infection. Hence, one understands, as a result of the regulatory restrictions placed on the bodies of those incarcerated by the prison system, the prisoners' contraction of HIV, which traditionally results in a lifetime of medical dependency by the inmate. This is the ultimate punishment, which is to re-inscribe the body on the cellular level for life. This is the result of the dominating power, not because of the HIV infection, nor is this to suggest that HIV infection is a death sentence. However, the failure to provide choices to those incarcerated persons regarding HIV/AIDS is the primary way the prison system implements the intimidation technologies which are considered a means to make inmates a spectacle of punishment.

A Synergy of Understanding

However, the body can also be an object of rehabilitation when combined in a synergic fashion with health education, which may also provide opportunities to facilitate inmates' empowerment in the context of their bodies (Ross, 2011). We envision the relationship between intimidation technologies, situated learning, and HIV/AIDS in prison as a synergistic cycle (figure 3.1) wherein intimidation technologies are taken up as part of a cycle of situated learning in prisons.

Under these conditions situated learning may operate to (a) create better practices for dealing with HIV/AIDS in prison, or (b) continue to intimidate the incarcerated population through the specter and reality of HIV/AIDS. We argue that current standards encourage high HIV/AIDS prevalence in prison by being under-equipped (i.e., not having condoms available) and by promoting a culture of under-education (i.e., poor understanding of how HIV/AIDS is spread). We argue further that this current reality is *intentional*, a form of public punishment, propagating intimidation technologies to remind the public and incarcerated people of what happens when you break the rules. We imagine a future where intimidation technologies are used to fuel positive experiences of situated learning in prisons, where health educators and the incarcerated population work together to develop and encourage preventative knowledge and tools aimed at lowering HIV/AIDS prevalence.

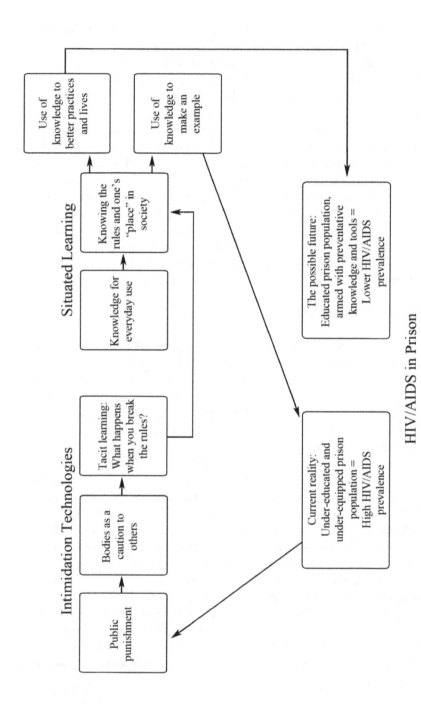

Figure 3.1. A Synergy of Understanding: Current Realities and a Possible Future of HIV/AIDS in U.S. and Jamaican Prisons.

Implications and Conclusion

Addressing the issue of the spread of HIV/AIDS in prisons is not a simple issue. A one-time brief workshop or providing an informational pamphlet is not effective for several reasons: (a) many inmates have low levels of literacy and may not comprehend the materials, (b) the stigma attached to HIV/AIDS may cause the learner to detach from the presentation in order to disassociate himself from the population addressed, and/or (c) inmates often miss one-time workshops for a variety of reasons including visitation and court dates. Providing regularly scheduled HIV/AIDS workshops and routinely requiring that inmates repeat the workshops may ensure that they are exposed to the information several times. Repeated measures are needed in order to disseminate correct information to the incarcerated and overcome the stereotypes and misconceptions people have associated with HIV/AIDS. But breaking the cycle of intimidation with regard to HIV/AIDS will require integration of resources and information about HIV/AIDS into the situated learning environment of inmates and into general health education programs.

Community-based health programs can serve the incarcerated population as well as those previously incarcerated once they return to society. Educators who work in these programs are usually focused on social action which resonates with some of the key principles of situated learning, and such educators understand that training can provide powerful tools for helping learners take control of their own lives (Merriam, Caffarella, & Baumgartner, 2007). Simply knowing this and acting on it would be a tremendous solution to the complex problems faced—if the onus of responsibility belonged only to inmates themselves. Not only should outside educational organizations work closely with facilities to be aware of the formal and informal rules established by the correctional community, but more importantly they need to work in collaboration with the policymakers and government officials who remain complicit in the marginalization of inmates' needs. The view that inmates do not deserve care and health education is dated, inhumane, and nothing more than a form of continued punishment for crimes.

Peer educators can be valuable assets in a more holistic approach to addressing this pervasive issue. As Ross (2011) proposed:

> an approach to prison health education that is minimally related
> to direct reduction in recidivism, occupying inmates' time, or
> vocational skills training, but rather addresses the health disparities

associated with the disadvantaged in general and prisoners in particular. It is emancipatory from a personal health and community health perspective and situates the participants as a peer educator both inside and outside the correctional environment. (p. 9)

This type of peer health education program creates peer educators who "develop skills" and are "empowered" with information they can also take to their communities. The current structure of correctional facilities as total institutions presents barriers to creating dynamic changes in the procedures. However, to meet the broader meaning of "correction" embedded in their role correctional facilities need to develop a culture of concern for HIV/AIDS awareness among the staff and the communities in which facilities are situated.

Prisons' attempts to regulate sexual contact between inmates often fail. Fundamental to this conversation pertaining to the policies of incarcerated persons' regulated condom usage are the effects these policies have on the rate of HIV infection experienced by the prisoners and the communities to which they are later released. Providing condoms for use in correctional facilities would be the most progressive and direct intervention. Nevertheless, discussing this option is not possible at many correctional facilities and would be illegal in the Jamaican prison system, where even being found with a condom would result in being labeled "homosexual" and lead to condemnation by other inmates as well as by the prison administrators. Even in a prison system where secrecy about anal sex is rampant, in a country where homophobia is widespread, the availability of reliable and accurate HIV/AIDS information is imperative to protecting the health and well-being of all inmates.

References

Abu-Lugghod, J. (2007). *Race, space, and riots in Chicago, New York, and Los Angeles.* Oxford, UK: Oxford University Press.

Andrinopoulos, K. (2008). *Examining HIV/AIDS within the context of incarceration in Jamaica.* Unpublished dissertation. Baltimore, MD: The Johns Hopkins University.

Andrinopoulos, K., Figueroa, J. P., Kerrigan, D., & Ellen, J. M. (2011). Homophobia, stigma and HIV in Jamaican prisons. *Cultural Health and Sexuality Journal, 13*(2), 187–200.

Christian, C. M., & Bennett, S. (1998). *Black saga: The African American experience: A chronology.* New York, NY: Basic Civitas Books.

Coley, R. J., & Barton, P. E. (2006). *Locked up and locked out: An educational perspective on the U.S. prison population*. Princeton, NJ: Educational Testing Services.

Collins, A. (1991). Cognitive apprenticeship and instructional technology. In L. Idol & B. F. Jones (Eds.), *Educational values and cognitive instruction: Implications for reform* (pp. 121–138). Hillsdale, NJ: Lawrence Erlbaum.

Foucault, M. (1977). *Discipline and punishment: The birth of the prison*. New York, NY: Random House.

Harrison, P. M., & Beck, A. J. (2006). *Prisoners in 2005*. U.S. Department of Justice, Bureau of Justice Statistics. Retrieved from http://www.ojp.usdoj.gov/bjs/pub/pdf/p05.pdf.

Hartley, H. (2012). *When the lights go out: The truth about black male prison sexuality*. Chicago, IL: Brother Hassan's Publishing, LLC.

House of Representatives H.R. 2070, 105th Congress. (1997). *Correction Officers Health and Safety Act of 1998*. Retrieved from http://www.govtrack.us/congress/bills/105/hr2070.

Kantor, E. (2006). *HIV transmission and prevention in prison*. HIV InSite. Retrieved from http://hivinsite.ucsf.edu/InSite?page=kb-07-04-13#S1X.

King's College London. (n.d.). *Uprising in Jamaica*. Retrieved from http://www.kingscollections.org/exhibitions/specialcollections/caribbean/emancipation/uprisinginjamaica.

Lave, J., & Wenger, E. (1991). *Situated learning: Legitimate peripheral participation*. New York, NY: Cambridge University.

Maruschak, L. M., & Beavers, R. (2010). *HIV in Prisons, 2007–08*. U.S. Department of Justice, Bureau of Justice Statistics. Retrieved from http://www.bjs.gov/content/pub/pdf/hivp08.pdf.

Mauer, M. (2006). *Race to incarcerate*. New York, NY: The New Press.

Merriam, S. B., Caffarella, R. S., & Baumgartner, L.M. (2007). *Learning in adulthood: A comprehensive guide*. (3rd ed.) San Francisco, CA: John Wiley & Sons.

Panos Institute Caribbean. (2007). *No sex or condoms here: HIV prevention, treatment, and care in Jamaican prisons*. Retrieved from http://issuu.com/ampwritersclub/docs/no_sex_or_condoms_here.

Race Forward (2006). *Historical timeline of public education in the U.S.* Retrieved from https://www.raceforward.org/research/reports/historical-timeline-public-education-us.

Ristroph, A. (2006). Sexual punishments. *Columbia Journal of Gender and Law*, *15*, 163–165.

Ross, M. W. (2011). Pedagogy for prisoners: An approach to peer health education for inmates. *Journal of Correctional Health Care, 17*(1). 6–18.

Stein, D. (1998). *Situated learning in adult education*. ERIC Digest No. 195. Columbus, OH: ERIC Clearinghouse on Adult Career and Vocational Education. Retrieved from http://ericae.net/edo/ed418250.htm.

United Nations. (2006). *International guidelines on HIV/AIDS and human rights*. Retrieved from http://data.unaids.org/publications/irc-pub07/jc1252-intern guidelines_en.pdf.

White House Office of National AIDS Policy. (2010). *National HIV/AIDS Strategy for the United States.* Retrieved from http://www.whitehouse.gov/sites/default/files/uploads/NHAS.pdf.

World Health Organization. (2007). *Effectiveness of interventions to manage HIV in prisons—Provision of condoms and other measures to decrease sexual transmission.* Retrieved from http://www.who.int/hiv/idu/Prisons_condoms.pdf.

Wilkins, J., & Gamble, R. J. (2000). An examination of gender differences among teachers in Jamaican schools. *Multicultural Education, 7*(4), 18–20.

Zoukis, C. (2012). *Education behind bars: A win-win for maximum security.* Camp Hill, PA: Sunbury.

4

Listen Carefully, Act Thoughtfully

Exploring Sex Work as an Adult Education Context

Shannon Deer
Dominique T. Chlup

While attending a conference in Ghana on sex trafficking, renowned author, journalist, and activist Gloria Steinem made a trip to Zambia (Steinem, 2014). She found herself sitting among 30 village women mourning two female tribe members who had disappeared after going to Lusaka to trade sex for money to support their families. Steinem learned the women's husbands worked in the tourism industry at nearby wildlife lodges. These lodges did not hire women, which meant the women had to find work elsewhere to cover basic living costs and their children's school fees. Many of the women contributed to the village farming, but just as the vegetable crops neared harvest, the elephants would eat them to the ground. Seeing no other option for income available, some women engaged in prostitution.

When Steinem asked, "What would help?" the women's answer was surprisingly simple, "Find a way to keep elephants out of their gardens" (Steinem, 2014, p. 117). Steinem refers to this story as the "parable of the fence," and its lessons are simple: "Helping begins with listening. Context is everything. People who experience a problem know best how to solve it. Big problems often have small solutions. And, finally, do whatever you can" (p. 117).

All these lessons served as the impetus for writing this chapter, but perhaps the last lesson—do whatever you can—underscored our reason for writing a chapter focused on the potential roles adult educators can play in improving the women's lives who remain in or choose to exit sex work or prostitution. Steinem's experience is specifically about African women, but prostitution is global. This chapter primarily focuses on sex work and prostitution in the United States (U.S.). We adopt a common definition of sex work and prostitution as exchanging sex for money or "other material benefit" (Davidson, 1998, p. 8). The sex industry also includes exotic dancers, pornographers, phone sex operators, and other occupations. These workspaces are important to discussions about the diversity of the sex trade (Beloso, 2012), but are beyond this chapter's scope and deserve a comprehensive inquiry. Furthermore, even though seemingly interchangeable to some, we use both terms—sex work and prostitution—to capture feminist debates about how to define, indeed even what to call, the sex trade (Weatherall & Priestley, 2001). The scope of our definitions therefore have limitations (Phoenix, 1995) and these become evident as we develop our locally situated framework for sex work in the context of women's global mobility. Before exploring how educators might position themselves within this terrain, further understanding is needed about the polarized perspectives framing feminist discourse and the diverse realities lived by women engaged in sex work and prostitution.

On one end of the spectrum, radical feminists use the term "prostitution" and argue that women cannot choose prostitution, because prostitution violates a woman's human rights and results from women's subordination to men (Barry, 1995; Hughes, 2008; Jeffreys, 2009; MacKinnon, 1983). In contrast, liberal feminists (informed by Marxism), use the term "sex work," which they consider a profession much like any other job. Liberal feminists recognize an individual's agency, or ability to choose sex work as an income source (Desyllas, 2007; Pheterson, 1996; McElroy, 1999).

Our position aligns more closely with postmodern feminists (Bell, 1994; O'Neill, 2001; Shrage, 1994) who recognize the diverse experiences in sex work and prostitution (Scoular, 2005). We use this positioning to challenge the dichotomous nature of modern theories. Postmodern feminists consider prostitution neither inherently liberating nor oppressive, but recognize both possibilities by allowing for multiple realities along a continuum of feminist perspectives (Scoular, 2005). For example, in the U.S., oppressive conditions, such as low pay, unsafe working conditions, and little access to resources may be more common for minorities based on race and class (Beloso, 2012). Postmodern feminism also considers the perspectives of transgender individuals (Kulick, 1998), male-to-male, male-to-female (Morse, Simon, & Burchfiel, 1999), and female-to-female providers (Jeffreys, 1993). We recognize prostitution is a complicated topic often wrapped in the cloak of morality, legality, feminism, sexual taboos, religion, and cultural differences (Bullough & Bullough, 1998). These complexities may be contributing to the marginalization of women often working, learning, and living underground and on the periphery. All the more reason therefore that caring professionals, such as adult educators and health workers, identify the touchstones of their personal biases and address how those biases are engaged as they become involved in developing learning opportunities with sex workers and prostitutes. By exploring differences among sex workers and prostitutes, we hope adult educators will be able to better understand and evaluate their beliefs in the context of the marginalization experienced and perceived by sex workers and prostitutes.

The purpose of this chapter is to first evaluate the existing academic literature on sex work and prostitution using a postmodern feminist lens as a way to illustrate variety in women's experiences in the profession and how they engage differentially with discourses of empowerment and oppression. Although we appreciate the diversity postmodern feminism brings to light, this chapter focuses specifically on "cisgender" women's experiences with sex work and prostitution. Cisgender refers to someone whose gender identity corresponds with their biological sex. Second, this chapter evaluates current interventions and offers suggestions for adult educators' involvement.

Stratifying Sex Workers' and Prostitutes' Experiences

Consistent with postmodern feminist theory, this section explores the heterogeneity in sex workers' and prostitutes' experiences. Different sex work and prostitution categories are commonly discussed throughout scholarly literature. Specifically, five forms of sex work and prostitution emerge from the literature and are discussed in detail below: (1) high-end sex workers, (2) brothel workers, (3) street prostitutes over age 18, (4) involuntarily trafficked, and (5) under 18 years of age, each described below. Factors such as satisfaction with their experiences in the profession, control over working conditions, and the quality of alternative employment options often vary across these forms of work. Additionally, how a woman aligns with that work may influence her biases toward sex workers or prostitutes in the other categories. These variations may contribute to women's marginalization (by women and men) within and across categories. A high-end sex worker may have more earning potential and a higher status than control than a street worker. A street worker who abuses drugs may be most marginalized (Chapkis, 1997). To assist adult educators, each sex worker and prostitution category will be described below.

High-End Sex Workers

Escorts, call girls, and private sex workers are sometimes grouped together as high-end sex workers or "elite prostitutes" (Lucas, 2005, p. 513) and positioned highest in the sex-work hierarchy (Beloso, 2012; Wahab, 2004). Typically, high-end sex workers completed more education, were born with higher socioeconomic status (Seib, Dunne, Fischer, & Najman, 2012), made more money (Bernstein, 1999), and exercised more control over client selection, working conditions, and sexual boundaries than women who undertook other forms of work (Lucas, 2005; Wahab, 2004).

The 30 elite American sex workers Lucas (2005) interviewed commonly viewed sex work "not as a last-ditch alternative to destitution, but as a preferred choice" (p. 523). Women in this category may describe trading sex as a business, a service profession, and/or a career (Lucas, 2005). They may possess skills necessary to succeed in many legal careers based on their experiences negotiating with clients, managing logistics, and deciding which services to provide and where (Lucas, 2005). The current skills, agency, and earning potential differ among high-end sex workers based on women's experiences and perspectives (Lucas, 2005) with great differentiation found between high-end sex workers and women in other categories.

Brothel Workers

Brothels within and across countries differ in organizational structure and working conditions for women. The famous Moonlight Bunny Ranch, depicted in the reality television series *Cathouse*, is a legal, regulated brothel in the American state of Nevada, which is housed indoors on a secure property (Dunn, 2012). In contrast, women in Amsterdam's well-known red-light districts, where prostitution is legal and regulated, can be seen on public display in windows along the street (Harcourt & Donovan, 2005). In Sonagachi, in Kolkata's red-light area, three different brothel categories define the employment conditions under which women work: *chhukri* are women working as bonded sex workers; an *adhiya* works as a contractor; and there are also self-employed workers (Kotiswaran, 2011). Chhukri are sold (bonded) to a madam in exchange for money paid to family members or an agent and do not decide which services they will provide, to whom, or at what price and frequently start working as young girls (Kotiswaran, 2011). We consider chhukri in the involuntarily trafficked category discussed later. An adhiya could be a chhukri once her debt is paid off or a woman entering sex work directly under the adhiya mode. An adhiya splits her earnings with the brothel and typically has better working conditions than chhukris. Finally, a self-employed sex worker in Sonagachi shares similarities with a high-end escort, maintaining all earnings and controlling client selection and boundaries. Adhiya and self-employed workers' conditions and pay differ based on each brothel's size and profitability (Kotiswaran, 2011).

Women working illegally in unregulated brothels may have less control over client selection and boundaries—the acts they are required to perform and those they may refuse (Harcourt & Donovan, 2005; Kotiswaran, 2011). Even in legal, regulated brothels compliance with regulations may vary impacting women's working conditions (Dunn, 2012).

Street Prostitutes Starting Over Age 18

This chapter differentiates between street prostitutes who enter the profession before and after the age of 18 based on U.S. regulation (U.S. Department of State, 2000) and differences found in women's experiences based on entrance age (Seib et al., 2012). We discuss street prostitutes who enter the profession prior to 18 years of age as a separate form of work later in this chapter.

Street workers reported less control and power in interactions with customers than women in other categories (Wahab, 2004). Pimps are much more common in street work and, like madams in some brothels, may control women's client selection and pay (Bernstein, 1999; Dalla, 2000; Exner, Wylie, Leura, & Parrill, 1977). Additionally, street prostitutes more frequently demonstrated drug addiction (Bernstein, 1999), personality disorders, psychopathy, antisocial tendencies, and lower skill levels compared to sex workers in other categories and peers who are not prostitutes even more so than high-end sex workers (Exner et al., 1997). These differences may result in fewer or less appealing employment options outside of prostitution for street workers than for high-end prostitutes (Wahab, 2004). Alternative employment is especially limited for drug addicts desperate to sustain their habit, making them especially vulnerable (Bernstein, 1999) and less confident in their ability to secure employment (Sherman, German, Cheng, Marks, & Bailey-Kloche, 2006). Addicts have been described by researchers as having to experience the lowest class among prostitutes (Exner et al., 1977), contributing to their further marginalization. Scholars have identified unique challenges for racial minorities and women in a lower socioeconomic status, such as less social support from a network of peers, lower pay, and higher susceptibility to arrest and violence than white or more socioeconomically advantaged street prostitutes (Bernstein, 1999; Wahab, 2004).

Involuntarily Trafficked

Influenced by feminist debates about voluntary versus involuntary trafficking (Agustín, 2003a & 2003b; Doezema, 2001; Desyllas, 2007), this chapter includes women who voluntarily migrate for sex work in another category based on where they work, such as in brothels or on the street. By definition, women included in this category are involuntarily trafficked into prostitution, meaning through force or coercion they enter prostitution against their will and without choice or alternatives. The U.S., in the Trafficking Victims Protection Act of 2000 (TVPA 2000), defines "severe forms of trafficking" as "sex trafficking in which a commercial sex act is induced by force, fraud, or coercion, or in which the person induced to perform such act has not attained 18 years of age" (U.S. Department of State, 2000, section 103-8). The wording adopted by the United Nations (UN) is similar to TVPA 2000.

　　Involuntarily trafficked women are unlikely to control client selection, the boundaries of sexual acts required of them, or pay rate, which are decided by their owner or captor (Kotiswaran, 2011). They may have been sold into prostitution by a family member or bonded to absolve a debt (Kotiswaran, 2011; Kristof & WuDunn, 2009). They are typically given shelter and food, and may only receive payment once any debt owed is recovered, often at exploitative interest rates (Kristof & WuDunn, 2009). Women in this category are often more like slaves than sex workers.

　　Organizations such as the International Labor Organization (ILO) estimate 4.5 million victims of forced sexual exploitation (International Labour Organization, n.d.). However, quantifying involuntary trafficking is challenging due to the industry's underground nature (Okech, Morreau, & Benson, 2011; U.S. Department of State, 2013), and how trafficking is defined. Trafficking is typically defined as the "movement of people across national and international borders" (Desyllas, 2007, p. 57). Therefore, individuals trafficked or enslaved within their own nation may be excluded from trafficking statistics and programs designed to help and rescue women involuntarily trafficked. Differentiating between women who have been trafficked by force or coercion and women in the other categories is also challenging (Kristof & WuDunn, 2009). Once broken by their captors or madams, trafficked women can be seen smiling and soliciting business (Kristof & WuDunn, 2009) and may not leave sex work even when given the opportunity (Kotiswaran, 2011), possibly due to shame, addiction, or perceiving sex work as a better employment option than more oppressive working conditions or unemployment (Kristof & WuDunn, 2009).

Under 18 Years of Age

The age at which young girls and young women's are considered responsible for their decision making, behavior and consequence comprehension varies, thus limiting the extent to which young girls actually *choose* sex work as an occupation (Annitto, 2011). As a result, trafficking individuals under 18 years of age does not have to involve force, fraud, or coercion to be considered a severe form of trafficking in the U.S. (TVPA 2000).

Many young girls who enter prostitution are runaways, making them particularly vulnerable (Annitto, 2011; Bernstein, 1999). Qualitative accounts describing young girls' experiences uncovered girls lured by men promising love, money, and/or protection (Annitto, 2011). A pimp may seem like a boyfriend until he convinces a girl to sell sex to meet her financial needs, which is a more likely scenario when girls start prostitution before the age of 18 and allows them very little control over their labor and very few employment alternatives (Annitto, 2011).

Other complications compound struggles to end child prostitution. For example, the marriage of child brides is considered in some quarters to be prostitution or sex trafficking, because young girls lack the ability to choose marriage or their partner (Ghosh, 2009). In addition, such marriages commonly involve a financial exchange where the girls are traded for a dowry or bride price to a husband with sexual expectations (Ghosh, 2009). Additionally, premiums may be placed on young prostitutes who meet pedophiles' demands or preferences for virgins (Kristof & WuDunn, 2009). In some areas of Africa, folklore claiming sex with a virgin will cure a man of AIDS makes young girls more desirable (Kristof, 1996). The demand for young girls and high prices obtained for them make them more vulnerable to forced prostitution and trafficking. These factors make the contrast between underage girls' experiences on one extreme and high-end escorts on another very pronounced, and have implications for how educators would explore, engage or intervene. These issues are considered in the next section.

Implications for Adult Education

While the potential for adult educators to work with women and girls remaining in or exiting sex work and prostitution is substantial, little work appears to have documented how adult educators might approach this field of practice. Adult education's learner-centered focus requires us, as Steinem did in Zambia, to ask "what would help," then make space for people's voices to be heard, and then support them in the context in which they live. Attempting to address problems without such consideration can have unintended negative consequences.

As a result, in the broader field of adult education, questions might commonly be asked about participation: who participates in formal and nonformal education programs, what motivates participation, are existing programs meeting women's needs, what efforts can be taken to increase voluntary participation in education programs, how can programs increase engagement from marginalized women (Ginsberg & Wlodkowski, 2010)? Adult educators may also be able to collaborate with non-governmental organizations (NGOs) and sex worker organizations to provide determine what kind of training will be most useful for women and girls. In the following section we show that organizations may disagree on appropriate approaches to resolve challenges and injustices facing current and former sex workers and prostitutes. However we argue such questions might be explored by combining a systems approach with critical adult learning theory (Elias & Merriam, 2005) and human resource development (Bierema, 2010). Some of this literature reflects our concern that learners are experts in their own lives and able to identify problems and guide their own education (Attwood, 2006; Maruatona, 2006).

Adult education scholars, such as Monaghan (2010) and Nsteane (2006) recommended applying feminist theory to education issues and programs, such as adult education leadership and management and HIV education, respectively. Using a feminist lens, we propose a systems approach for planning current and former sex worker and prostitute education, provide examples of sex worker engagement in adult education, and offer some models for enhancing participants' involvement in such education. Taking a lead from the village woman whose story opened this chapter, the following discussion is intended to question if current forms of adult education provision and structures are the only way for adult educators to engage with sex workers and prostitutes to disrupt the current structures under which they work. Feminist debates about the nature of systems interventions in women's lives provide some insights into associated questions of leadership, management and funding approaches.

Feminist Debates and Their Impact on Interventions

In the U.S., the Bush administration favored radical feminist philosophies when establishing trafficking laws (Desyllas, 2007), does not subscribe to the view that prostitution is a form of employment and hence prevents support organizations from receiving funding (Desyllas, 2007; TVPRA, 2003). As a result organizations that promote HIV prevention programs (Desyllas, 2007, p. 70) have limited access to funding while programs adopting a rescue mentality, such as International Justice Mission (IJM), are supported to undertake brothel raids. Following a recent raid conducted with a Thai NGO and law enforcement, sex workers were involuntarily detained, lost their personal goods, and were deported back to their home country, which was Burma in this case (Cavalieri, 2011). Some women caught up in the raid claimed to work in Thailand to avoid rape, hunger, and oppression inflicted on them as Burmese Shan—Burma's Indigenous group (Cavalieri, 2011).

The brothel raid highlights several opportunities for adult educators' involvement. First, according to this account, the U.S. NGO's actions contradict their goal to place victims in facilities and reeducation programs, since the women were deported back to the oppressive conditions they left in Burma (Desyllas, 2007). Second, adult educators may design programs to increase understanding between NGOs with opposing views so problems can be solved more effectively. For example, some Thai NGOs opposed IJM's approach and viewed sex work as a rational alternative to avoid oppression, hunger, poverty, and rape the women experienced in Burma (Cavalieri, 2011). The conflict created a stalemate *between NGOs* with conflicting ideologies and approaches and prevented them from reaching a shared understanding of their differences for the benefit of the women.

A Systems Approach and Critical Adult Education

Without better alternatives the Burmese women preferred sex work in a different country to avoid oppression. Without a solution to elephants eating their crops, women from Zambia in the introductory story turned to sex work. These narratives illustrate how the structures influencing women's lives lead to particular preferences for work. We believe adult educators may be able to play a role in adjusting such structures to provide women with other options or improve their existing working conditions and human resource development (HRD), critical adult education, and feminist theories provide them with some alternatives.

Bierema (2010) recommends adult education adopt a systems approach, which is a tenant of both critical adult education theory and HRD. A systems approach requires understanding the micro and macro influences on women's lives, including the structures oppressing them and that this requires multidisciplinary thinking *and* collaboration (Chadibe, 2006; Hill, 2006; Nsteane, 2006; Mohasi, 2006). Specifically, adult educators addressing the injustices facing current and former sex workers and prostitutes would benefit from collaboration with experts in economics, politics, business, psychology, health, and gender issues. For example, adult educators should consider how globalization and economic challenges work together to encourage migration to increase income (Stromquist & Monkman, 2014). Such factors can make women more susceptible to forced trafficking and unfavorable working conditions in an unfamiliar country.

Additionally, the systems approach warrants considering unique interventions for the specific structural barriers and challenges faced by women taking up different forms of sex worker or prostitution. Brothel workers and managers may benefit from learning about fair working conditions and increasing brothel profitability, which could improve working conditions (Kotiswaran, 2011). Street prostitutes may benefit from comprehensive programs addressing drug addiction and psychological disorders (Wahab, 2004), along with opportunities for further education. Minors rescued from prostitution may need education designed for reintegration back into their families or the education system (Baker, Wilson, & Winebarger, 2008). Using a systems approach would provide adult educators a better understanding of learners' constraints, motivations, and specific needs.

Feminist Theory—Meeting Women's Practical versus Strategic Needs

Similar to the systems approach used in critical adult education theory and HRD, feminist theory is concerned with adjusting the structures oppressive to women (Monaghan, 2010). Moser (1989) offered a specific feminist theory for altering gender bias, which we use to analyze existing education programs. Moser argued an important consideration in economic development is meeting women's strategic needs rather than just their practical needs. Moser defined women's practical needs as basic survival needs common to all humans such as food, clothing, and shelter. Related to job training, practical needs can be met by teaching women exiting the profession to make jewelry, bags, soap, bind books, or sew, which some NGOs do (e.g., see http://www.thistlefarms.org/). These skills are traditionally used in professions dominated by women, which may not provide sufficient income. Many studies have found sex workers and prostitutes make more money than women with comparable skills in other professions (Bernstein, 1999;

Bilardi et al., 2011; Dunn, 2012; Exner et al., 1997; Lucas, 2005). From a systems perspective, there needs to be caution in moving women into low-paying positions, which may not eliminate the need for sex work, or may leave women susceptible to oppressive working conditions. Additionally, acquiring feminine skills may perpetuate gender biases about women's work-place roles, which can be harmful to all women (Moser, 1989).

In order to address women's strategic needs, gender biases must be disrupted. Moser proposed training women in traditionally masculine job skills, such as masonry and carpentry, to challenge labor division based on gender and provide women with greater economic independence. Very few programs are designed to meet women's strategic needs by training them in masculine job skills. One example is Prajwala (http://www.prajwalain-dia.com), started by Sunitha Krishnan, which teaches former sex workers and trafficking victims welding and carpentry skills, which may change people's perceptions about women's role in the workplace. Considering the macro-level operation of systems enables educators to see the economy as a whole and patterns of jobs demand. Some believe the U.S. is experiencing shortages in skilled laborers, which will only worsen as aging workers retire (Wright, 2013). Women exiting sex work could fill the demand with adult educators' help. With the infrastructure already in place, existing programs meeting women's practical needs could be modified to incorporate strategic interventions fitting Moser's framework.

JEWEL is a pilot program adult educators might use as a model for new or expanded programs. JEWEL is not a job-training program, but was designed to empower women economically through jewelry making in order to reduce HIV risk behaviors for women who continue in sex work (Sherman et al., 2006). Women were simultaneously taught HIV prevention and how to make and sell jewelry. Using practical interventions, JEWEL resulted in reduced HIV risk behaviors and increased confidence in participants' ability to maintain a legal job compared to a control group only receiving HIV prevention education. Sherman conducted a similar pilot study with similar results in Chennai, India, where women made bags rather than jewelry (Sherman et al., 2010). The pilot programs incorporated economic empowerment into sex worker education. Adult educators can add a strategic dimension to these programs by supplementing jewelry making and bag making with training in carpentry, welding, construction, electrical, and plumbing to change attitudes toward the capability of women.

However there are also implications for disrupting gender biases. For example, microlending has disrupted gender biases and empowered many women across the world. Studies have shown microlending reduces domestic violence in the long term, but can increase domestic violence when domestic power relations are also disrupted (Bellessa, 1997). Similar consequences could occur as sex workers and prostitutes are economically empowered and could be subverted by implementing domestic violence prevention programs.

Another possible consequence of training women in traditionally masculine jobs is the potential for sexual harassment in the workplace. However, several women included in Lucas's (2005) study claimed their experiences in sex work made them better equipped to address sexual harassment than most women. Sex workers and prostitutes have learned strategies to set boundaries with men to avoid sexual harassment, thus providing adult educators with exemplars of a knowledge and skills base of value to other women.

Learner Involvement—"Who holds the Power?"

Lucas's (2005) work demonstrated other professional skills possessed by some sex workers, such as negotiating pay and working conditions, managing clients, and running a business. Sex workers across the world are acting as adult educators by teaching each other such skills through formal and informal networks for learning and support (Kotiswaran, 2011; Sutherland, 2004).

SEX WORKER RIGHTS GROUPS AND LABOR UNIONS

Sex workers have served a more formal role as educators through sex workers' rights organizations, which started emerging in the mid-1970s (Sutherland, 2004) and are now established in areas as diverse as the International Union of Sex Workers based in the UK, (http://www.iusw.org/), the Karnataka Sex Workers Union (http://sexworkersunion.in/), and the Dubar Mahila Samanwaya Committee (DMSC or Dubar—http://www.durbar.org/) in India. DMSC members advocate for better working conditions and have made progress in reducing the number of chhukri and bonded, sex workers in India (Kotiswaran, 2011).

Call Off Your Old Tired Ethics (COYOTE) is a U.S.-based sex workers' rights organization which has garnered attention from feminists and policymakers (Bernstein, 1999). COYOTE members have worked in adult education for many years, educating the general public and policymakers on sex workers' rights, and sex workers and prostitutes about safe sex and their legal rights (Jenness, 1990).

Some individuals reference these organizations as evidence for sex worker's choice, control, and power. However, to be relevant to all sex workers, these organizations may need to incorporate more diversity (Chapkis, 1997), especially as critics claim such organizations do not embody all women's experiences, may disproportionately represent white, middle-class privilege, or may not be fit "spokeswomen for the majority of prostitutes—whose 'choice of profession' is made under far greater constraints" (Bernstein, 1999, p. 110). Bernstein's research indicated little diversity in sex workers' rights groups. Perhaps adult educators can draw on social movement and labor strategies to assist in increasing representation from all sex workers and prostitutes.

RELEVANT ADULT LEARNING MODELS

Two existing models successfully utilized in adult education may be useful in efforts to increase inclusion and resolve challenges and injustices sex workers and prostitutes face. REFLECT (Regenerated Freirean Literacy Through Empowerment) (Attwood, 2006; Maruatona, 2006) works with participants to "develop a more critical consciousness as they collectively begin to untangle the relationship between structural and social factors, such as poverty and gender inequality, and their own life situations" (Attwood, 2006, p. 299). REFLECT processes have been used in adult education programs as diverse as HIV prevention education and literacy education. This and other community development approaches allow communities to identify and prioritize problems and then develop their own solutions (Ceballos, 2006). In collaboration adult educators could facilitate approaches for former and current sex workers as a community of learners. The adult educator would serve not as an expert, but as a facilitator attempting to promote the diversity of voices in the community of learners.

Importantly, these education efforts in collaboration with current and former sex workers and prostitutes cannot be assumed by adult educators alone. We advocate a multidisciplinary, systems approach incorporating critical adult education and thoughtful consideration of feminist theories and debates to evaluate potential structural adjustments in the lives of sex workers and prostitutes. We call for increased awareness about this issue by all disciplines through more mainstream discussions and action. Following the lessons Steinem learned from the Zambian women (2014), start by listening to those seeking help, make a space for all their voices and not just a privileged few, then "do whatever you can" (p. 117). Through this approach, we may see improvement in the lives of sex workers and prostitutes, whether they choose to remain in and exit the profession.

References

Agustín, L. M. (2003a). A migrant world of services. *Social Politics, 10*(3), 377–396. doi: 10.1093/sp/jxg020.

———. (2003b). Sex, gender, and migrations: Facing up to ambiguous realities. *Soundings, 23,* 1–13. Retrieved from http://www.nswp.org/sites/nswp.org/files/Sex%20Gender%20and%20Migrations%20-%20Facing%20up%20to%20Ambiguous%20Realities.pdf.

Annitto, M. (2011). Consent, coercion, and compassion: Emerging legal responses to commercial sexual exploitation of minors. *Yale Law & Policy Review, 3*(1), 1–70. Retrieved from http://web.ebscohost.com.

Attwood, G. (2006). Adult education and social capital: Supporting communities in the context of HIV/AIDS. In S. Merriam, B. C. Courtenay, & R. M. Cervero (Eds.), *Global issues and adult education: Perspectives from Latin America, Southern Africa, and the United States* (pp. 219–230). San Francisco, CA: Jossey Bass.

Baker, L. M., Wilson, F. L., Winebarger, A. L. (2008). An exploratory study of the health problems, stigmatization, life satisfaction, and literacy skills of urban, street-level sex workers. *Women & Health, 39*(2), 83–96. doi: 10.1300/J013v39n02_06.

Barry, K. (1995). *The prostitution of sexuality.* Retrieved from http://muse.jhu.edu/books/9780814786086/.

Bell, S. (1994). *Reading, writing, and rewriting the prostitute body.* Bloomington, IN: Indiana University Press.

Bellessa, M. (1997). Effects of microlending on women's empowerment in Bangladesh. In W. Woodruff (Ed.), *Small really is beautiful: Micro approaches to third world development microentrepreneurship, microenterprise, and microfinance* (pp. 3–29). Ann Arbor, MI: Third World Thinktank.

Beloso, B. M. (2012). Sex, work, and the feminist erasure of class. *Signs: Journal of Women in Culture and Society, 38*(1), 47–70. doi: 10.1086/665808.

Bernstein, E. (1999). What's wrong with prostitution? What's right with sex work? Comparing markets in female sexual labor. *Hastings Women's Law Journal, 10,* 91–117. Retrieved from http://heinonline.org/HOL/Page?handle=hein.journals/haswo10&div=11&g_sent=1&collection=journals#99.

Bierema, L. L. (2010). Professional identity. In C. E. Kasworm, A. D. Rose, & J. M. Ross-Gordon (Eds.), *Handbook of adult and continuing education (2010 ed.)* (pp. 125–134). Thousand Oaks, CA: Sage Publications, Inc.

Bilardi, J. E., Miller, A., Hocking, J. S., Koegh, L., Cummings, R., Chen, M. Y., Fairley, C. K. (2011). The job satisfaction of female sex workers working in licensed brothels in Victoria, Australia. *International Society for Sexual Medicine, 8,* 116–122. doi: 10.1111/j.1743-6109.2010.01967.x.

Bullough, B., & Bullough, V. L. (1998). Introduction: Female prostitution: Current research and changing interpretations. In J. E. Elias, V. L. Bullough, V. Elias, & G. Brewer (Ed.), *Prostitution: On whores, hustlers, and johns* (pp. 420–434). New York, NY: Prometheus Books.

Cavalieri, S. (2011). Being victim and agent: A third-way feminist account of trafficking for sex work. *Indiana Law Journal, 86*, 1409–1458. Retrieved from http://ilj.law.indiana.edu/articles/86/86_4_cavalieri.pdf.

Ceballos, R. M. (2006). Adult education for community empowerment: Toward the possibility of another world. In S. Merriam, B. C. Courtenay, & R. M. Cervero (Eds.), *Global issues and adult education: Perspectives from Latin America, Southern Africa, and the United States* (pp. 219–230). San Francisco, CA: Jossey Bass.

Chadibe, I. E. (2006). The role of the church in combatting HIV/AIDS. In S. Merriam, B. C. Courtenay, & R. M. Cervero (Eds.), *Global issues and adult education: Perspectives from Latin America, Southern Africa, and the United States* (pp. 209–218). San Francisco, CA: Jossey Bass.

Chapkis, W. (1997). *Live sex acts: Women performing erotic labor.* New York, NY: Routledge.

Dalla, R. L. (2000). Exposing the "Pretty Woman" myth: A qualitative examination of the lives of female streetwalking prostitutes. *The Journal of Sex Research, 37*(4), 344–353. Retrieved from http://web.ebscohost.com.

Davidson, J. C. (1998). *Prostitution, power, and freedom.* Oxford, UK: Polity Press.

Desyllas, M. C. (2007). A critique of the global trafficking discourse and U.S. policy. *Journal of Sociology & Social Welfare, 34*(4), 57–79. Retrieved from http://web.ebscohost.com.

Doezema, J. (2001). Ouch! Western feminists' "wounded attachment" to the third world prostitute.' *Feminist Review, 67*, 16–38. Retrieved from http://www.jstor.org/stable/1395529.

Dunn, J. C. (2012). "It's not just sex, it's a profession": Reframing prostitution through text and context. *Communication Studies, 63*(3), 345–363. doi: 10.1080/10510974.2012.678924.

Elias, J. L. & Merriam, S. B. (2005). Philosophical foundations of adult education (3rd ed.). Malabar, FL: Krieger Publishing Company

Exner, J. E., Wylie, J., Leura, A., & Parrill, T. (1977). Some psychological characteristics of prostitutes. *Journal of Personality Assessment, 41*, 474–485. Retrieved from http://web.ebscohost.com.

Ghosh, B. (2009). Trafficking in women and children in India: nature, dimensions and strategies for prevention. *The International Journal for Human Rights, 13*(5), 716–738. doi: 10.1080/13642980802533109.

Ginsberg, M. B., & Wlodkowski, R. J., 2010). Access and participation. In C. E. Kasworm, A. D. Rose, & J. M. Ross-Gordon (Eds.), *Handbook of adult and continuing education* (2010 ed.) (pp. 13–24). Thousand Oaks, CA: Sage Publications, Inc.

Harcourt, C., & Donovan, B. (2005). The many faces of sex work. *Sexually Transmitted Infections, 81*, 201–206. doi: 10.1136/sti.2004.012468.

Hill, R. J. (2006). Environmental adult education: Producing polychromatic spaces for a sustainable world. In S. Merriam, B. C. Courtenay, & R. M. Cervero (Eds.), *Global issues and adult education: Perspectives from Latin America,*

Southern Africa, and the United States (pp. 265–277). San Francisco, CA: Jossey Bass.

Hughes, D. (2008). Combating sex trafficking: A perpetrator-focused approach. *University of St. Thomas Law Journal, 6*(1), 28–53. Retrieved from http:// www.wunrn.com/news/2009/07_09/07_06_09/070609_trafficking2_files/ Traffickng-Combating-Perpetrator%20Focused%20Approach-D.Hughes.pdf.

International Labour Organization. (n.d.). *Forced labor: Facts and figures.* Retrieved from http://www.ilo.org/global/topics/forced-labour/lang--en/index.htm. (November 4, 2013).

Jeffreys, S. (1993). *Lesbian heresy: A feminist perspective on the lesbian sexual revolution.* North Melbourne, VIC: Spinifex Press.

———. (2009). Prostitution, trafficking and feminism: An update on the debate. *Women's Studies International Forum, 32,* 316–320. doi:10.1016/j. wsif.2009.07.002.

Jenness, V. (1990). From sex as sin to sex as work: COYOTE and the reorganization of prostitution as a social problem. *Social Problems, 37*(3), 403–420. Retrieved from http://heinonline.org/HOL/Page?handle=hein.journals/ socprob37&div=36&g_sent=1&collection=journals#413.

Kotiswaran, P. (2011). *Dangerous sex, invisible labor: Sex work and the law in India.* Princeton, NJ: Princeton University Press.

Kristof, N. D. (1996, April 14). Asian childhoods sacrificed to prosperity's lust. *New York Times.* Retrieved from http://www.nytimes.com/1996/04/14/ world/children-for-sale-special-report-asian-childhoods-sacrificed-prosperity-s-lust.html?scp=1&sq=kristof%20asian%20childhoods%20sacrificed& st=cse.

Kristof, N. D., & WuDunn, S. (2009). *Half the sky: Turning oppression into opportunity for women worldwide.* New York, NY: Vintage Books (Random House).

Kulick, D. (1998). *Travesti: Sex, gender, and culture among Brazilian transgendered prostitutes.* Chicago, IL: The University of Chicago Press.

Lucas, A. M. (2005). The work of sex work: Elite prostitute's vocational orientations and experiences. *Deviant Behavior, 26,* 513–546. doi: 10.1080/01639620500218252.

MacKinnon, C. A. (1983). Feminism, Marxism method, and the state: Toward feminist jurisprudence. *Signs: Journal of Women in Culture and Society, 8*(4), 635–658. Retrieved from http://www.jstor.org/stable/3173687.

Maruatona, T. (2006). Adult literacy education and empowerment in Africa. In S. Merriam, B. C. Courtenay, & R. M. Cervero (Eds.), *Global issues and adult education: Perspectives from Latin America, Southern Africa, and the United States* (pp. 344–355). San Francisco, CA: Jossey Bass.

McElroy, W. (1999, November 12). Prostitution: Reconsidering research. *Spintech.* Retrieved from http://www.zetetics.com/mac/articles/spin1199.html.

Mohasi, M. V. (2006). Mainstreaming marginalized populations through adult education programs: The Herdboys of Lethoso. In S. Merriam, B. C. Courtenay, & R. M. Cervero (Eds.), *Global issues and adult education: Perspectives from*

Latin America, Southern Africa, and the United States (pp. 53–63). San Francisco, CA: Jossey Bass.

Monaghan, C. H. (2010). Management and leadership. In C. E. Kasworm, A. D. Rose, & J. M. Ross-Gordon (Eds.), *Handbook of adult and continuing education (2010 ed.)* (pp. 177–186). Thousand Oaks, CA: Sage Publications, Inc.

Morse, E. V., Simon, P. M., & Burchfiel, K. E. (1999). Social environments and male sex work in the United States. In P. Aggleton (Ed.), *Men who sell sex: International perspectives on male prostitution and HIV/AIDS* (pp. 83–102). Padstow, UK: UCL Press.

Moser, C. O. (1989). Gender planning in the third world: Meeting practical and strategic needs. *World Development, 17*(11), 1799–1825. doi: 10.1016/0305-750X(89)90201-5.

Ntseane, P. G. (2006). Western and indigenous African knowledge systems affecting gender and HIV/AIDS prevention in Botswana. In S. Merriam, B. C. Courtenay, & R. M. Cervero (Eds.), *Global issues and adult education: Perspectives from Latin America, Southern Africa, and the United States* (pp. 219–230). San Francisco, CA: Jossey Bass.

Okech, D., Morreau, W., & Benson, K. (2011). Human trafficking: Improving victim identification and service provision. *International Social Work, 55*(4), 488–503. doi: 10.1177/0020872811425805.

O'Neill, M. (2001). *Prostitution & feminism: Towards a politics of feeling*. Malden, MA: Blackwell Publishers, Inc.

Pheterson, G. (1996). *The prostitution prism*. Amsterdam, Netherlands: Amsterdam University Press.

Phoenix, J. (1995). Prostitution: Problematizing the definition. In M. Maynard & J. Purvis (Eds.), *(Hetero)sexual politics* (pp. 69–81). London, UK: Taylor & Francis.

Scoular, J. (2005). The 'subject' of prostitution: Interpreting the discursive, symbolic and material position of sex/work in feminist theory. *Feminist Theory, 5*, 343–355. doi: 10.1177/1464700104046983.

Seib, C., Dunne, M. P., Fischer, J., Najman, J. M. (2012). Predicting job satisfaction of female sex workers in Queensland, Australia. *International Journal of Sexual Health, 24*, 99–111. doi: 10.1080/19317611.2011.632073.

Sherman, S. G., German, D., Cheng, Y., Marks, M., & Bailey-Kloche, M. (2006). The evaluation of the JEWEL project: An innovative economic enhancement and HIV prevention intervention study targeting drug using women involved in prostitution. *Aids Care, 18*(1), 1–11. doi: 10.1080/09540120500101625.

Sherman, S. G., Srikrishnan, A. K., Rivett, K. A., Liu, S-H., Solomon, S., Celentano, D. D. (2010). Acceptability of a microenterprise intervention among female sex workers in Chennai, India. *Aids Behavior, 14*, 649–657. doi: 10.1007/s10461-010-9686-z.

Shrage, L. (1994). *Moral dilemmas of feminism: Prostitution, adultery, and abortion*. New York, NY: Routledge.

Steinem, G. (2014). Am I helpful? *O Magazine, 15*(4), 117.

Stromquist, N. P., & Monkman, K. (2014). Defining globalization and assessing its implications on knowledge and education, revisited. In N. P. Stromquist & K. Monkman (Eds.),*Globalization and education: integration and contestation across cultures* (pp. 1–20). Lanham, MD: Rowan & Littlefield Education.

Sutherland, K. (2004). Work, sex, and sex-work: Competing feminist discourse on the international sex trade. *Osgoode Hall Law Journal, 42*, 139–167. Retrieved from http://web.ebscohost.com.

US Department of State. (2000). Victims of trafficking and violence protection act of 2000. (October 28). Retrieved from http://www.state.gov/j/tip/laws/61124. htm (accessed November 5, 2013).

US Department of State. (2013). Trafficking in persons report June 2013. Retrieved from http://www.state.gov/j/tip/rls/tiprpt/2013/index.htm (accessed November 4, 2013).

Wahab, S. (2004). Tricks of the trade: What social workers can learn about female sex workers through dialogue. *Qualitative Social Work, 3*, 139–160. doi: 10.1177/1473325004043378.

Weatherall, A. & Priestley, A. (2001). A feminist discourse analysis of sex 'work.' *Feminism & Psychology, 11*, 323–340. doi: 10.1177/0959353501011003005.

Wright, J. (2013, March 7). America's skilled trade dilemma: Shortages loom as most-in-demand group of workers age. *Forbes.* Retrieved from http://www. forbes.com/sites/emsi/2013/03/07/americas-skilled-trades-dilemma-shortages-loom-as-most-in-demandgroup-of-workers-ages/.

5

Using Democratic Deliberation in an Internationalization Effort in Higher Education

Hilary Landorf
Eric Feldman

Florida International University (FIU) and its global learning initiative present an example of the importance and possibility of creating spaces for discussion where no member is on the periphery. We define the term *periphery* as those people and communities on the edges, those who are without power or the ability to voice and influence opinion. The concept of periphery is such that it is always reliant on a context depending on the perspectives of the observers and definers of that periphery. The definition and composition of the periphery can shift over time as well as show the importance of a current context to defining any particular periphery. Likewise, those on the periphery have their own unique view or perspective relative to their place in the defined community or situation, welcome or not. When voices remain on the periphery, they are lost from the conversation, and perpetuate the disenfranchisement of groups of people who hold an equal stake in the institutions and communities to which they belong. The sidelining of these voices prevents their ideas and insights from potentially addressing and solving problems.

FIU is a relatively new North American public research institution located in the vibrant, diverse, and globally connected city of Miami, Florida.

Miami is home to the highest concentration (58.1 percent) of foreign-born residents in the United States (U.S.). (United States Census Bureau, n.d.). It is a center for major international trade and tourism, and serves as a gateway to South and Central America for more than 1,100 multinational corporations (The Beacon Council, n.d.). FIU's location at this global crossroads imbues it with a special responsibility to prepare all undergraduates to live and work successfully in highly diverse and fluid settings.

Since its founding in 1965, FIU has always aspired to respond to the needs of its diverse community and has been on the forefront of providing a quality education to minorities and working, adult learners. When FIU opened its doors in 1972 to 5,667 students, it was an upper-division-only institution that served a nontraditional college population. The typical student was 25 years old and attended school full time while holding down a full-time job. Today FIU is the fourth largest institution of higher education in the U.S. in terms of student enrollment, with over 54,000 students, of which 63 percent are Hispanic (Florida International University, 2014; National Center for Education Statistics, n.d.). The typical FIU undergraduate is Hispanic, an older student, a first- or second-generation American citizen, has a full course load and a full-time job, and is usually the first of his or her family to attend an institution of higher education.

In Miami there is a hierarchy within the Hispanic community itself, defined by country of origin and wealth, with Cubans perceived to be the most powerful and influential in politics and the economy (Moreno, n.d.). Bishin, Kaufmann, and Stevens (2012) describe a first generation Hispanic community in Miami–Dade County in which members hold "nationality-based affinities" such that "some groups are perceived as unfairly dominant over other groups." Specifically, they say that, "Cuban-Americans hold a dominant group position, and are often perceived as unduly privileged in the local power structure" (p. 112–113).

To illustrate the privileged position of Cubans in Miami, and the peripheral position of Haitians, who are also from the Caribbean, consider this true set of events: On October 29, 2002, more than 200 Haitian refugees jumped off a 50-foot wooden boat near Miami and swam to shore after spending eight days at sea. Under U.S. immigration law, refugees captured at sea are immediately sent back to their homeland. If the refugees reach land, unless they can show a well-founded fear of persecution, they are also sent back. Knowing that they would most likely be deported, several of the Haitians who had made it ashore "jumped in the back of a black pickup truck and others appeared to try to get rides from motorists on the bridge. Local police rounded up dozens of the Haitians, seating them on the side of the highway. One man was wrestled to the ground by authorities and handcuffed" (Potter, 2002). Two weeks later, a group of eight Cubans, forced to land their stolen plane in Key West, Florida, were released in four days and allowed to stay legally in the United States and apply for permanent residency under the 1966 Cuban Adjustment Act, known as the "wet-foot, dry-foot" policy (Associated Press, 2002). Inequities that are reinforced by policies like "wet-foot, dry-foot" can extend to the campus. The periphery in FIU's student body, administration, and faculty includes African-Americans, Asians, and Haitians. Yet in certain academic areas, such as African Diaspora Studies, or graduate Engineering, Cuban students are on the periphery for different reasons relating to interest, culture, and experience.

How can a large minority-serving public university located in the global crossroads of Miami, Florida, prepare students for success in a fast changing globalized world? How can it enact large-scale curriculum and co-curriculum reform and include the voices of all sectors and communities? This chapter explores these questions in a case study of *Global Learning for Global Citizenship*, a university-wide curriculum and co-curriculum initiative at FIU which used democratic deliberation in its development and implementation. First, we show how we designed and implemented *Global Learning for Global Citizenship* using democratic deliberation and how we have embodied its principles and practices in teaching and learning, both in the curriculum and the co-curriculum. We then describe a number of ways in which democratic deliberation is being used to maintain the fidelity and strengthen *Global Learning for Global Citizenship*. Finally, we discuss some of the challenges of using democratic deliberation and show how we are addressing them.

Periphery in Education

In education, the concept of periphery is embodied in teaching practices and a learning environment which seeks to serve *all* students. Good teaching practice seeks to give those on the margins a voice in their learning and the opportunity to perform to their fullest potential. At an even higher level the recognition of the periphery, the contextuality of the periphery, and the inclusion of the different perspectives of the periphery are integral to the teaching and learning experience.

The importance of context in education is expressed by Landorf and Lowenstein (2010), who state that "the core of teaching practice is a relational process in which teachers and students with specific personal, cultural, and social configurations interact and make meaning with each other, particular subject matter, and curriculum materials" (p. 129). They refer to McDonald (1992) who describes this process as a "wild triangle of relations" where *the points of a triangle shift continuously* between teacher, student, and subject since what teachers actually teach and what students actually learn depends on the ever-shifting nature of who teachers and students are and the specific curriculum materials with which they are working. This applies not only to the subject matter but also to the dynamism, elasticity, and shifting dimensions in which the educational process occurs and which come from the social, cultural, temporal, and historical communities of the institutions, teachers, and students. Outside of the classroom, educational institutions that are closely connected to their local community also typically use and support opportunities to include the periphery in the greater community connected with that institution. However, there are limits to how an educational system that has international ambitions can include the periphery. We explore this point in the next section of this chapter.

Internationalizing/Globalizing Education

Internationalization is now an essential goal of institutions of higher education around the world. The most common definition for the internationalization of higher education is "the process of integrating an international, intercultural, or global dimension into the purpose, functions, or delivery of postsecondary education" (Knight, 2004, p. 11). Knight's definition is intentionally a neutral one. Depending on an institution's purpose for internationalizing, the definition it chooses to use may vary, as will the target areas of the internationalization endeavor which depend on the purpose being pursued. Currently almost all institutions of higher education use "global" or "international" in their mission statement, goals, and/or objectives. Not only do Northern American, European, and Pacific universities now embrace an international agenda, but emerging economies in Asia, Latin America, the Middle East, and Africa have also become proactive in internationalizing their institutions of higher education (Brandenburg & de Wit, 2012). Recent developments like this one have led to global learning as a necessary element in higher education.

We define global learning as the process by which students are prepared to fulfill their civic responsibilities in an increasingly diverse and interconnected world. As an educational process, global learning provides the conditions for students to gain this preparation by explicitly focusing on interconnections between disciplines, perspectives, people, problems, trends, and systems. The "global" in global learning includes the concepts of international (between and among nations), global (transcending national borders), and intercultural (referring to cultural differences at home and around the world). "Global" also emphasizes the complexity of our lives, implying expansiveness in thought and attitude. Moreover, "global" implies an ethical call to action. The American Association of Colleges of Universities (AAC&U) argues that liberal education "has the strongest impact when studies reach beyond the classroom to the larger community, asking students to apply their developing analytical skills and ethical judgment to concrete problems in the world around them and to connect theory with the insights gained from practice" (AAC&U, 2002, pp. 25–26). Closely related to the ethical imperative is a civic commitment—a sense of global ethics that emerges in the context of evolving definitions of citizenship and interdependence.

Global learning explicitly recognizes the "wild triangle" (McDonald, 1992) of context and relativity in the teaching process as it seeks to bring context and contributions to problem solving by instructional strategies such as cooperative learning, responsive improvisation, and simulations. Global learning is by its very nature an educational process which recognizes and involves the periphery at all levels and stages and seeks to include all communities. In order to bring multiple perspectives to problem solving, a student must be able to see all aspects of a situation, not the least of which are the perspectives of those people on the periphery. FIU emphasizes attention to issues of culture, diversity, perspective, power and privilege as a hallmark of global learning.

Global Learning at FIU

Global Learning for Global Citizenship was developed over three years and formally launched in fall 2010. It is focused on the educative process of developing specific student learning outcomes through global learning, rather than on the number of international activities in which students and faculty are involved. Regardless of where students take global learning courses, and most do so in Miami, the aim is for students to take responsibility for solving problems in an increasingly globalized world. As the "global" is literally local in Miami, students use their local community as their problem-solving laboratory.

On a basic level, *Global Learning for Global Citizenship* is a two-course global learning requirement for all undergraduates. All undergraduates also participate in globally focused co-curricular activities prior to graduation. Students take a global learning foundations course as part of their general education sequence and a second, discipline-specific global learning course in the context of their major program of study. Foundations courses are thematic, problem-centered, and interdisciplinary; include an integrated co-curricular learning experience; and are placed in categories throughout the general education curriculum. Courses such as "Artistic Expression in a Global Society," "International Nutrition, Public Health, and Economic Development," and "The Global Scientific Revolution and its Impact on Quality of Life" set the stage for students to make multi-perspective connections throughout their university career. Discipline-specific global learning courses provide students with a global view of their major program of study. Through active learning strategies, these courses give students multiple opportunities to apply the knowledge, skills, and attitudes they gain in the foundations courses. Discipline-specific global learning courses range from "Hurricane Engineering for Global Sustainability" to "Geography of the Global Food System," and "World Nutrition." To date, there are over 160 global learning courses in 69 of the 70 FIU undergraduate programs.

Democratic Deliberation

One of the most important concepts and tools used in *Global Learning for Global Citizenship* is that of democratic deliberation. Democratic deliberation is a strategy and process for including those students positioned such that their voice, influence, and opinion are often marginal to the decision making around them. Hence democratic deliberation aims to bring their values, opinions, and perspectives to problem solving and decision making in a community. It is defined by De Vries, Stanczyk, Wall, Uhlmann, Damschroder, and Kim (2010) as a process that has "equal participation, respect for the opinions of others, the adoption of a societal perspective on the issue, and reasoned justifications of one's opinions" (p. 1891). In another view, Halpern and Gibbs (2013) summarize Habermas's conceptualization of democratic deliberation as an "interchange of rational-critical arguments among a group of individuals, triggered by a common or public problem, whose main focus or topic of discussion is to find a solution acceptable to all who have a stake in the issue" (p. 1160). This definition, despite criticism from some that it is too idealistic (Johnson, 1989; Rienstra & Hook, 2006) still serves as a solid basis for the common and necessary components of the concept.

Case Study

As will be discussed below, democratic deliberation was used to develop the overall framework of the global learning initiative at FIU, in the design of its key components, as an integral learning strategy in global learning courses and activities, and as a tool in maintaining the fidelity of the initiative and allowing it to grow. In all of these respects, democratic deliberation has been a keystone to giving the changing and evolving periphery a voice and place at the table.

When Drs. Hilary Landorf and Stephanie Doscher began their work as leaders of the Office of Global Learning Initiatives (OGLI), an interdepartmental development committee was grappling with complex questions such as: What do our students need to know and be able to do in order to be successful in a globalized world? What kinds of classes and activities will prepare students for these outcomes? Do these classes and activities already exist or will we have to create new ones? These were important issues to consider, yet Landorf and Doscher saw a larger, more critical issue at hand: the committee was wrestling with these questions in isolation. As experienced educators, Landorf and Doscher ascertained that successful large-scale curriculum change could only be achieved through democratic deliberation. In adopting democratic deliberation as the mechanism and process for leading this institutional change, they quickly discovered that the university's stakeholders wanted, in Landorf and Doscher's (2013) words, "curriculum reform rather than reinvigoration," and instead of minor changes, "a paradigm shift would be required to achieve our goals" (p. 164). This disconnect implied another issue: was the university prepared to educate students for the knowledge, skills, and attitudes they needed as twenty-first-century citizens? Landorf and Doscher felt that democratic deliberation could be used to great effect to not only help FIU find overlapping consensus concerning student learning, but also to help the organization develop the capabilities it needed in order to educate students for these outcomes.

When Landorf and Doscher began this work, the development committee had tentatively titled the initiative, "Adding an International Component to the Curriculum." Several subcommittees were researching ways to make an FIU education more international. Missing from this process was essential input from the vast array of people affected by the initiative, namely, students, academics, administrators, staff, alumni, parents, local businesses, and community members. Despite the use of the term "international" in the title of the initiative, when Landorf and Doscher analyzed the subcommittee's working documents and meeting minutes, they noted the frequent use of "global." They brought this to committees' attention and facilitated an open dialogue concerning the meanings of the two terms and their relevance to FIU. Members agreed that while *international* commonly refers to a relationship between nation-states, *global* encompasses global, international, intercultural, and local interconnections. For the committees, global was a broader term and more descriptive of FIU's present character and activities.

To establish consensus on the meaning of global and international, and the direction and focus of the initiative, Landorf and Doscher conducted focus groups, open forum discussions, open-ended interviews, meetings, and surveys. Stakeholders from every corner of the university community were involved in this collective conversation. At each meeting, after an initial brainstorming period they shared responses from other groups in order to facilitate conversation across groups. In this way they were able to identify growing consensus around themes that would eventually become global learning outcomes. At the end of a full year of dialogue, democratic deliberation, and over 75 iterations, the university molded three developmentally cohesive, interdependent global learning outcomes:

- Global Awareness—knowledge of the interrelatedness of local, global, international, and intercultural issues, trends, and systems;

- Global Perspective—the ability to conduct a multi-perspective analysis of local, global, international, and intercultural problems;

- Global Engagement—a willingness to engage in local, global, international, and intercultural problem solving.

In large part because all university members had a stake in developing these outcomes, they have proven to be dynamic enough to be used in courses in almost all academic departments, and robust enough to have become an exemplary model for global learning initiatives throughout the U.S. and the world (Green, 2012).

Global Learning Courses

Having utilized democratic deliberation to develop the global learning outcomes of *Global Learning for Global Citizenship*, Landorf and Doscher were faced with the challenge of incorporating those outcomes in the curriculum. This depended on providing global learning courses within the curriculum and recruiting and training faculty to develop new courses or infuse existing courses with global learning components.

It was determined that global learning courses include four required components: global learning course outcomes; diverse global, international, and intercultural content; active learning strategies; and authentic assessments. A process was set up to create courses and bring them into the curriculum to be approved for global learning designation. The courses are proposed, developed, and, once approved by the Faculty Senate, they are taught by faculty members who have undertaken global learning professional development.

Since Fall 2009, the OGLI has facilitated monthly workshops for over 450 faculty and staff redesigning or developing new global learning courses and associated activities. A significant part of the workshops is devoted to drafting course and activity outcomes and assessments. These address content that is specific to the discipline, and aligned with FIU's global learning outcomes. Each semester additional courses are developed and/or revised, and approved for global learning. These interdisciplinary, interdepartmental workshops engage participants in active, problem-based learning strategies that can also be implemented with students, moving them toward new perspectives on effective content and pedagogy.

Every workshop begins with a reiteration of the democratic deliberative process in which the university engaged to determine FIU's definition of global citizenship and the global learning outcomes, and the open-ended questions, "What is global citizenship? What must global citizens know, and be able to do?" Participants take some time to consider the answer to these questions on their own, gather in small groups to discuss their thoughts, and then discuss findings with the group at large. Discussions are animated and sometimes controversial and contentious. The facilitator records all responses on a large poster and together the group identifies common, overlapping themes. Knowledge themes addressing complexity, interconnectedness, and diversity emerge, as well as skills such as critical thinking and problem solving, and attitudes associated with mutual responsibility and commitment. Since the groups are interdisciplinary, different terms are used to describe these ideas, but invariably, when facilitators code for themes with the group, they are able to demonstrate how they cluster around FIU's three global learning outcomes. The process supports the freedom of individuals to simultaneously articulate their visions and aspirations for global citizenship, while at the same time identifying overlapping consensus that lies beneath differences in language, discipline, and outlook. For many, this begins a paradigm shift in their conception of teaching and learning.

Using Democratic Deliberation as a Learning Strategy

The same deliberative process that was used to develop the global learning outcomes through the consideration of all voices and perspectives is used at FIU as a pedagogical strategy to advance global learning in the curriculum and co-curriculum. Democratic deliberation exposes students to the full spectrum of perspectives that exist on a social issue, ensuring that those on the periphery are not excluded. By virtue of discussion the process of deliberation transforms preferences to "other regarding, not just self-regarding" (McAfee, 2012, p. 24).

In global learning courses, students often work with case studies. They are assigned roles in specific social, political, or economic groups and then asked to advocate for their group. These groups include examples of dominant groups and marginalized groups that will be found on the periphery. Issues arising in advocacy for groups and stakeholders can be economic, environmental, social, political, ethical, and/or historical in nature. They are usually complex and comprehensive in application to the case at hand and present no obvious or easy solution if all issues are to be fairly and democratically addressed through democratic dialogue.

For example, in Global Supply Chains and Logistics, an interdisciplinary, global learning foundations course team-taught by a faculty member in the College of Business and a faculty member in the College of Engineering, students participate in a semester-long simulation of supply chain operations and logistics. Students are divided into teams that represent companies throughout the levels of the supply chain. Throughout the course, each team must make decisions in every part of the chain from location of production to inventory tracking, competing with one another for vital resources and economic interests. At the same time, within each team, and as a collective supply chain, collaboration and consensus are key elements to a successful supply chain.

The use of simulation explicitly helps students to consider how a person in his or her assigned role would be affected by decisions that the group makes. This gives each student the experience and appreciation of different perspectives and particularly those on the periphery. A facilitator ensures that every group gets a fair hearing and no one group is allowed to dominate. Students are encouraged to come to a consensus on the best solution to the problem for all groups.

Democratic Dialogue in the Co-Curriculum

Credit-bearing academic courses are one-half of the global learning initiative at FIU. The other half is a robust global co-curriculum, the programs which extend and enhance students' scholarship. These can include everything from moderated discussions, to film series, to issues-centered clubs, to international service trips. In the co-curriculum, democratic deliberation plays a key role in global learning activities and outside-of-the-classroom programing. McAfee (2012) writes that democratic deliberation achieves its goals through access to "balanced briefing materials and expert knowledge" (p. 24), and that is exactly the *modus operandi* for many of FIU's global learning activities. Our signature Tuesday Times Roundtable and National Issues Forums series center on the technique. In particular, the Issues Forums are intentionally designed to introduce students to the concept of democratic deliberation. According to the website for the National Issues Forum Institute (n.d.), the forums are "rooted in the simple notion that people need to come together to reason and talk. Indeed, democracy requires an ongoing deliberative public dialogue." The topics of the individual forums range from American foreign policy to the role of higher education in society, and act as vehicles for learning about and practicing the concepts and procedures of democratic deliberation.

Challenges in the Concept and Implementation of Democratic Deliberation

While democratic deliberation lends itself to being perceived as an ideal form of democratic and inclusive decision making, it also brings dialogic and participatory challenges and has been criticized for being unrealistic. Rienstra and Hook (2006) discuss Habermas's belief that participants in democratic deliberation must be "free, equal, and rational" (p. 3). They add that such a person, in their words, would "need to possess some remarkable qualities, not the least of which is an uncanny ability to scrutinize with great accuracy and humility, the complex relationships between a multitude of values and means-end relationships" (p. 316). Abdel-Monem, Bingham, Marincic, & Tomkins (2010) point out that deliberation has been criticized for subscribing to dominant-group communication norms, such as favoring rational arguments over emotional claims.

At FIU we have focused our attention to the challenges of the process of democratic deliberation, particularly in the classroom and professional development workshops. We use the learning experience to elucidate and examine the process itself as well as to discover and examine other challenges inherent to democratic deliberation. Our goal is to model the best practices of democratic deliberation so that students and faculty can take these practices to other learning situations or incorporate them in problem solving in their own lives. Consequently, it is a real concern for us that the use of democratic deliberation does not perpetuate or magnify any of the dominant-group norms that we are trying to avoid through our intentional efforts to include those on the periphery.

For example, moderators of deliberative forums typically encounter situations that stall the process of consensus. In one issue forum held at FIU on American foreign policy, a participant refused to move in the conversation, repeatedly bringing up one alleged fact regarding a specific dollar amount that was being spent by the United States government to maintain a fleet of Army tanks in the Afghan desert. While deliberation values facts in its pursuit of rationality, it is not set up to verify such specific and obscure claims during a group session. A facilitator will help the group through this process by putting aside unverifiable facts and continuing the dialogue.

Sometimes consensus will not be reached because participants have different cultural orientations or opposing values. This ensuing disagreement, or agreement to disagree, is an important part of the process of democratic deliberation. From the viewpoint of Gaus (1997), parties involved in democratic deliberation need not give up their beliefs in order to honor their participation in the deliberative system. A facilitator can assist the participants in understanding it is acceptable to agree to disagree. The facilitator can also illustrate that in some cases argument is futile and unproductive. As James Johnson (1989) says, "it is unreasonable to anticipate that deliberation will massively transform the preferences, capacities, or character of participants in normatively attractive ways, and that in any case, such a transformation would, at best, emerge as a by-product of deliberation aimed at attaining some tangible outcome" (p. 174).

Another example of the role of the moderator in a democratic deliberation is to provide a safe environment in which participants feel they can freely express their opinions and advocate their position. At FIU Cuban-Americans often represent the dominant group in global learning courses. Faculty members teaching these courses often find it difficult to facilitate a thoughtful discussion regarding subjects that include the Cuban missile crisis, Fidel Castro, or even President John F. Kennedy because of knee-jerk hostile reactions from Cuban-American students. Global learning professional development workshops show faculty how to step in and establish an environment in which differing opinions can be freely expressed.

Now that global learning has been institutionalized at FIU, one of the biggest challenges for the initiative is in maintaining and reinvigorating its components and in sustaining the democratic deliberation which supports and nurtures the involvement of all. One of the ways we respond to this challenge is by conducting frequent, rigorous, and comprehensive assessment and review of all aspects of the initiative.

A specific example of our commitment to maintaining the quality of global learning is in the continuous improvement in the development and teaching of global learning courses. Having overcome the initial obstacle of instituting undergraduate curriculum reform, one of FIU's foremost challenges for the global learning initiative now concerns the long-term fidelity of its growing suite of global learning courses which has a direct impact on student learning. Faculty members who designed the courses engaged in extensive professional development and coaching through the OGLI, and these courses were approved through a comprehensive Faculty Senate vetting process. The question for the University now is how can it ensure that students continue to benefit over the long term from the substantial global learning components built into course syllabi?

To address this question, the OGLI has expanded its professional development offerings to include workshops targeting instructors inheriting courses from first-generation global learning faculty. It is essential that differentiated professional development continue for the duration of the initiative to allow for reflection and continuous improvement.

Another example of our process of maintaining the quality of the global learning initiative relates to students. The OGLI keeps its finger on the pulse of what students are learning, the circumstances that facilitate learning, and the incremental and cumulative impacts of the initiative on students' global capacities. This is done through continual multi-method assessment of FIU's global learning efforts and includes direct and indirect assessment of course level and university level global learning outcomes. These examples show how the OGLI is able to maintain the veracity of the process of democratic deliberation in the global learning initiative at FIU and to develop and expand the skills to facilitate democratic deliberation

Conclusion

Global learning uses democratic deliberation to recognize and include the periphery through a multiple perspective approach to dialogue and problem solving. Democratic deliberation has been an integral part of FIU's *Global Learning for Global Citizenship* initiative in all facets—in determining the framework of the initiative, in administrative decision making, as pedagogy in the curriculum and co-curriculum, and in reflective assessment. Democratic deliberation has been a critical process in bringing together members of our FIU community, including learners from traditionally marginalized populations and adult learners, in order to learn about and take action on a wide variety of issues inside and outside of the classroom. The initiative has been in place now for five years and has received national attention for the depth and breadth of its curriculum, the seriousness of its assessment, and the early success stories of students who have been immersed in the "new global" FIU.

We acknowledge that continuous review and improvement is essential in an institutionalized initiative where the periphery in the community is ever changing and evolving. Only with continuous review can democratic deliberation be inclusive and democratic, and give recognition and effect to the outcomes of the democratic deliberative process. Democratic deliberation is a powerful way to include the periphery and give everyone a voice at the table.

References

Abdel-Monem, T., Bingham, S., Marincic, J., & Tomkins, A. (2010). Deliberation and diversity: Perceptions of small group discussions by race and ethnicity. *Small Group Research, 41*(6), 746–776. doi: 10.1177/1046496410377359.

Associated Press (2002). Eight Cubans in 2-Seat plane land in Key West seeking asylum. *New York Times,* November 12, 2002. Retrieved from http://www.nytimes.com/2002/11/12/us/8-cubans-in-2-seat-plane-land-in-key-west-seeking-asylum.html.

Association of American Colleges and Universities. (2002). *Greater expectations: A new vision for learning as a nation goes to college.* Washington, DC: American Council on Education.

Beacon Council (n.d.). *International data.* Retrieved from http://www.beaconcouncil.com/web/Content.aspx?Page=internationalData.

Bishin, B. G., Kaufmann, K. M., & Stevens, D. (2012). Turf wars: Local context and Latino Political Development. *Urban Affairs Review, 48*(1), 111–137.

Brandenburg, U., & de Wit, H. (2012). Higher education is losing sight of what internationalisation is all about. *The Guardian,* April 2, 2012. Retrieved from http://www.theguardian.com/higher-education-network/blog/2012/apr/02/internationalisation-labeling-learning-outcomes.

De Vries, R., Stanczyk, A., Wall, I. F., Uhlmann, R., Damschroder, L. J., & Kim, S. Y. (2010). Assessing the quality of democratic deliberation: A case study of public deliberation on the ethics of surrogate consent for research. *Social Science & Medicine, 70*, 1896–1903. doi:10.1016/j.socscimied.2010.02.031.

Florida International University. (2012). *Full-time instructional faculty by rank and ethnicity* [table]. Miami, FL: Florida International University Office of Planning and Institutional Research.

Florida International University. (2014). *Birth country of FIU students by academic career* [table]. Miami, FL: Florida International University Office of Retention & Graduation Success.

Florida International University. (2014). *Quick facts* [table]. Miami, FL: Florida International University Office of Planning and Institutional Research.

Gaus, G. (1997). Reason, justification, and consensus: Why democracy can't have it all. In J. Bohman & W. Rheg (Eds.), *Deliberative democracy* (pp. 205–242). Cambridge, MA: MIT Press.

Green, M. F. (2012). *Measuring and assessing internationalization*. Washington, DC: NAFSA, Association of International Educators. Retrieved from http://www.nafsa.org/uploadedFiles/NAFSA_Home/Resource_Library_Assets/Publications_Library/Measuring%20and%20Assessing%20Internationalization.pdf.

Halpern, D., & Gibbs, J. (2012). Social media as a catalyst for online deliberation? Exploring the affordance of Facebook and YouTube for political expression. *Computers in Human Behavior, 29*, 1159–1168. doi: 10.1016/j.chb.2012.10.008.

Johnson, J. (1989). Arguing for deliberation: Some skeptical considerations. In J. Elster (Ed.), *Deliberative democracy* (pp. 161–185). New York, NY: Cambridge University Press.

Knight, J. (2004). Internationalization remodeled: Definition, approaches, and rationales. *Journal of Studies in International Education, 8*(1), 5–31.

Landorf, H., & Doscher, S. P. (2013). Global learning for global citizenship. In M. Walker & A. Boni (Eds.), *Universities and human development: A sustainable imaginary for the XXI century* (pp. 162–177). New York, NY: Routledge Press.

Landorf, H., & Lowenstein, E. (2010). Designing an interactive learning center museum in the school context. In E. E. Heilman, (Ed.). *Social Studies and diversity education: What we do and why we do it* (pp.129–132). New York, NY: Routledge Press.

McAfee, N. (2012). Three models of democratic deliberation. In W. M. Barker, N. McAfee, & D. W. McIvor (Eds.), *Democratizing deliberation: A political theory anthology* (pp. 21–37). Dayton, OH: Kettering Foundation Press.

McDonald, J. P. (1992). *Teaching: Making sense of an uncertain craft*. New York, NY: Teacher's College Press.

Moreno, D. (n.d.). *Cuban-American political empowerment*. Retrieved from http://www2.fiu.edu/~morenod/scholar/empower.htm.

National Center for Education Statistics. (n.d.). *College navigator*. Retrieved from http://nces.ed.gov/collegenavigator/?s=FL&zc=33199&zd=0&of=3&id=133951#enrolmt.

National Issues Forum Institute. (n.d.). *About NIF forums.* Retrieved from http://nifi.org/forums/about.aspx.

Planas, R. (2014). The most Latino Congress ever is coming in 2015. *Huffington Post*, November 5, 2014. Retrieved from http://www.huffingtonpost.com/2014/11/05/latinos-in-congress_n_6111410.html.

Potter, M. (2002). Boatload of Haitians swarms ashore in Florida. CNN.com, October 30, 2002. Retrieved from http://edition.cnn.com/2002/US/South/10/29/haitians.ashore/index.html?_s=PM:US.

Rienstra, B., & Hook, D. (2006). Weakening Habermas: The undoing of communicative rationality. *Politikon: South African Journal of Political Studies, 33*(3), 313–339. doi: 10.1080/02589340601122950.

United States Census Bureau. (n.d.). *State & county quickfacts: Miami (city), Florida.* Retrieved from http://quickfacts.census.gov/qfd/states/12/1245000.html.

EDUCATORS' WORK WITH "PERIPHERAL" SPACES OF ENGAGEMENT

6

Beyond Death Threats, Hard Times, and Clandestine Work

Illuminating Sexual and Gender Minority Resources in a Global Context

Robert C. Mizzi
Robert Hill
Kim Vance

Fictive lives are those narratives that, we tell ourselves and others, are always shifting; the self-narrator is an inscribed figure who responds to experiences, in large measure, in the continual retelling of life events. Fictive lives are neither myth nor fiction but simply the constant re/membering and re/storying of selves. They are not "fictional" in the sense of arbitrarily made up or consciously designed to fool ourselves or others. Benjamin reminds us that "it is not the object of the story to convey a happening per se, which is the purpose of information; rather, it embeds it in the life of the storyteller in order to pass it on as experience to those listening" (cited in Gengenbach, 2003, para. 1). With this in mind, we tell a version/vision of our lives below; small windows into, and escape hatches out of the autographed memories we hold. What we have elected to reveal has been designed to illustrate our thesis that queer transformative and pedagogical efforts are occurring in complex and contradictory ways—at times transparent and open, and in other moments, clandestine and subterranean. We see ourselves as having the capacity to transverse the arbitrary but very consequential locations of "center" and "margin"; we are non-unitary beings with multiple subjectivities (Mizzi, 2010). At times the result is community building; at times it is fraught with fragmentation and dissolution. Our struggle in writing this chapter is to avoid monolithic narratives and to work against the appropriation of knowledge of others on the margins, and finally to not reproduce that which we hope to critique. As all self-telling, it is both imperfect and incomplete.

Our objectives through this chapter are threefold. Through the act of storytelling we first raise awareness of "secret" resource-building work being done in various cultural spaces (acknowledging also that much action occurs overtly). Second, we call into question the dominance of "formal" schooling and other Western inventions that do not recognize this secret work nor seek ways that alleviate some of the challenges. Last, we put forth some considerations for community workers, consisting of educators, facilitators, and activists, when it comes to sexual and gender minority communities. In this contribution, we employ the term "sexual minorities" to refer to people who possess same-sex sexual attractions and may or may not identify as lesbian, gay, or bisexual. The term "gender minorities" is defined as people who have gender identities, expressions, or behaviors that are not associated with their birth sex (Mayer et al., 2008). We will focus more on the consolations than the desolations of these three objectives; however, we are cognizant that our fictive retellings are much more complex, convoluted, and at times contradictory than can possibly be related here. The chapter is thus more a heuristic device to point to learning that has historically been intentionally held close to the vest by sexual and gender minorities and yet ostracized by formal systems. The work of this chapter is therefore informed by three sexual minority educators who have lengthy careers pursuing activist agendas through community development in both local and global settings. Together, yet in separate circles, we engage in both covert and clandestine work with colleagues in hopes of addressing the informational, emotional, and social needs of sexual and gender minorities in the various spaces around the globe. This clandestine work is also marked by a sense of uncovering the shifting realities that shape the lives of our colleagues and learners, given that sexuality is often understood differently everywhere (Herdt, 1997; Mizzi, 2008). In this chapter, we explore some of this work, highlight power dynamics, and describe recent efforts relating to policy and practice changes that acknowledge and support sexual and gender minority issues. We offer suggestions for navigating the resources available to community workers in our conclusion.

Narratives of Community Building

The following three stories characterize some of the tensions that render our work clandestine and controversial. Through these vignettes we hope to highlight where, why, and how clandestine, community-building work is being done to include sexual and gender minority issues. We aim to show practicalities, while keeping in mind some of the realities that shape sexual and gender minority informational, emotional, and social resource building in a global context.

Robert M.'s Experience

Delivering capacity-building seminars to community educators is a common form of community work. In one instance, I was invited to work with two grassroots, sexual and gender minority rights organizations in Central Asia. The mandate was to co-facilitate with a Canadian lesbian colleague a series of skills-building workshops that relate to working with media, strategic planning, and volunteer mobilization. We managed to plan this event together with the organizations, and with great care because the police had stepped up their efforts to stop such educational events from taking place. Without warning they may demand entrance into the "secret" office and remove the learners and facilitators in order to shut down the educational experience. While homosexuality is legal in Central Asian countries, police still feel rather uncomfortable with social organizing efforts taking place. Coupled with recent homo/transphobic attacks against the sexual and gender minority community and a public denouncement of homosexuality by politicians, there is just cause to keep this work on the "down-low."

During the session on media, a provocative question was asked by Maria, who was one of the adult learners: "Robert, how do we productively work with media representatives that continually give us bad press?" I seriously thought about this question because my response needed to be sensitive to the political environment that excludes this organization and respect efforts made in the past to "bridge the cultural gap" between media and human rights. This question also exposes my "foreignness" in the learning scenario, which is not an uncommon occurrence in international development practice.

"I think that there could be a variety of responses, Maria. One response stems from Lebanon when a similar organization was experiencing some of the same problems with their media. They opened up a food bank and won over the hearts of community members that were so adamantly against them. What are your thoughts about this idea? Would it work here, be adapted or generate other ideas?"

"Interesting idea! Then I suggest that we learn from the Lebanese and try to work with our community rather than trying to strategize around them. I have some ideas . . . ," replied Maria.

Robert H.'s Experience

I love the quote by Kevin Yoshino (2006), "Only after I came out broadly did this pressure ease. Once I was irrevocably gay, the fight for my soul was over—angels and demons alike looked for other quarry" (p. 44). It fits my journey particularly well. In writing an invited autobiography (Hill, 2007a), many of my experiences—the consolations and desolations of a Queer, activist academic—have been told. They not only include death threats, hard times, and subversive work, but also how these experiences intersect with, inform, and are informed by multiple oppressions of others. In particular, my Queer work activism has included efforts to fashion a space for voice and praxis by developing ground-breaking initiatives.

I coordinated the first policy statement to include sexual minority rights in an International Council for Adult Education (ICAE) declaration tabled at its 6th World Assembly in Jamaica, 2001. This Jamaica experience was particularly important since it brought to light, in a very palpable way, the consequences of queer activism. Prior to the World Assembly, ICAE requested the North American Alliance for Popular and Adult Education (NAAPAE) to arrange a "Banner/Mural Making Project." Local community artists were invited to participate in the mural project, collaboratively working with World Assembly participants inscribing the mural with meaning. As a queer activist, I sketched graphics for the mural that included signs and signifiers linked to sexual-minority communities, and penned the phrase, "Difference Is A Human Right" resulting in a significant controversy, documented by me (Hill, 2001). This "art-attack" and other tensions surrounding sexual-minority rights were an opportunity for workshop participants to raise the issue of organizational intolerance on the basis of sexual orientation and gender presentation. Jamaica taught me the serious consequences of queer work; my life was threatened and the President of the Caribbean Island Adult Education Association informed me that I was in danger and that I should consider leaving the island. I remained . . . we organized . . . and we won recognition at this important assembly!

In another pivotal moment I never imagined I ended up in the "cross-hairs" of several state legislators. In February 2009, Georgia State legislators called for my firing. I was remonstrated by one legislator, who reported that I taught, "special interest classes . . . on . . . Queer Theory" saying, "Yes . . . you haven't misread. In this current economy, our taxpayer's dollars are being used by the Board of Regents to research and inform students about such social topics. In fact, there is a professor at UGA [the University of Georgia] that has confirmed and verified courses in 'Queer Theory' among other things. . . . This in itself is very disturbing news" (Byrd's Eye View, 2009). She then provided my official College of Education website to illustrate my heinous educational agenda. This opened a full in-depth investigation of my academic activities by the university. The attack was carried on national commercial media, and promulgated by Christian media in particular. Later that month, after intensive inquiry and scrutiny including searching all archived emails and listserv postings, syllabi, and discussions with current and former students, the university Provost issued a public announcement titled, "Statement Clearing Allegations of Impropriety Against Professor Robert Hill" wherein he wrote, in part, that my "body of scholarship [is] designed to study . . . aspects of society and to inform public policy decisions. We have found nothing in our very thorough investigation to indicate any inappropriate activity on his behalf. Professor Hill is a nationally and internationally recognized scholar" (Peterson, 2009, n.p.).

Kim's Experience

In March 2008, ARC International began initial planning for its next International Dialogue, a quasi-annual opportunity for organizations from various movements to discuss issues and strategies pertaining to human rights from a gender and sexuality perspective. A respected colleague from the NGO Mulabi started a dialogue with me about whether it might be time to move the event back to Latin America, where the first such dialogue had been held in Brazil in 2003 (in response to Brazil's announcement that it was tabling a resolution on sexual orientation at the United Nations Commission on Human Rights—now reformed as the UN Human Rights Council). Mulabi brings together activists from the Global South to work on issues related to sexualities and rights from critical and celebratory perspectives, as well as to circulate Latin American perspectives on these issues.

The option of Latin America had already been considered by ARC International, but because one of the goals of previous Dialogues was "realizing organizational capacity," we questioned the need for such an event in Latin America at the time, as there seemed to be so many success stories and strong movement work within the region. While agreeing with this analysis, my colleague commented, "why not view this year's Dialogue as an opportunity to highlight what organizations, especially some of those in the Global North and the rest of the world, can learn from US about best practice?" She was right, of course, "best practice" was not the exclusive domain of the Global North, and we had known that. The shift in thinking for us, however, was the idea that "best practice" experiences from the Global South can and should inform and assist the development of movements in the Global North and across the world, and that we could work collaboratively to create a platform for that learning to happen.

Negotiated Meaning

Human engagement in the world is primarily about negotiating mean-ing-making and constructing subjective knowledge (Wenger, 1998). Such negotiation of meaning, for some, entails achieving rights and respect for sexual and gender minorities which seems to be a never-ending battle nearly everywhere. As Hill (2013) and Merriam and Brocket (1997) point out, there is a long history of conscious or benign neglect of the input that many people, including "homosexuals," have had regarding what counts as adult education. Baird (2007) adds that sexual orientation remained taboo terrain in most technologically developing nations, and we would argue also in those nation states that are technologically developed. In a world that focusses on knowledge resources the majoritarian view has omitted or erased the need for informational, emotional, and social resources, across temporal and geographic dimensions, related to sexual orientation, gender identity, and gender expression. This has made full and effective community services, and educational needs-attainment, difficult or impossible for sexual and gender minorities.

Even with moderate gains in areas of same-sex marriage, same-sex parent adoptions, and protection within anti-discrimination policies in some countries, human rights are barely making advances when it comes to unconditional and comprehensive inclusion of sexual and gender minori-ties (Hill, 2013). The act of positioning sexual and gender minorities on the social periphery is one largely rooted in the "cross (Christian) and sword (power)" of colonialism, where colonists criminalized homosexuality as means to assert a *moral dominance* as a boundary marker of right/wrong, good/bad, well/sick, and so forth. The effects of this dominance are still felt around the world among sexual and gender minorities, resulting in greater challenges facing community workers whose work must involve a wider array of perspectives.

On one hand, the desire for community workers to be inclusive of sexual and gender minorities' informational, emotional, and social needs in their practices and policies is more pressing now than ever before. Discussions about sexual and gender minorities are taking place worldwide with sharp divisions being drawn and violence remaining a pervasive aspect of life for many sexual and gender minorities. On the other hand, community workers are often ill-equipped to effectively handle the needs of sexual and gender minority citizens due to the legal, social, and religious barriers that legislate and normalize hate, injustice, and prejudice. Contexts vary from one region to the next, and with those variances come new sets of politics, problems, and policies that shape the lives of sexual and gender minorities, especially in such a globalized society as ours. For example, the 2014 Olympic Games in Sochi, Russia, became a site of controversy because the Russian parliament has criminalized sexual and gender minority expression. Global activists called for a boycott of the Olympic Games in an effort to draw global attention to the oppression that continues to exist in Russia. Clearly, just as promising developments emerge, such as the United States Supreme Court striking down a portion of the Defense of Marriage Act as unconstitutional—one that defined marriage in federal law as between an opposite-sex couple (Lord, 2013)—dangerous battlegrounds, such as those depicted in our stories still exist.

Sometimes the brave work of being inclusive becomes too risky for the professional and personal lives of community workers working in the margins, regardless of their sexual or gender orientation. Death threats, violent acts, imprisonment, police intimidation, and other fear tactics often characterize the community work of sexual and gender minority inclusion. Nevertheless, there is a vast amount of historical and contemporary literature, drawing on the experiences and perspectives of activists who support informational, emotional, and social needs for sexual and gender minorities (e.g., Adam, Duyvendak, & Krouwel, 1999; Pinar, 1998). Some of the transformative and pedagogical efforts that are occurring are transparent and open, while others are subterranean. Although we cannot highlight all of this work in this chapter, we can discuss why this work is clandestine in nature, why we position it as producing "fugitive knowledge" (Hill, 1997; Hill, 2004a), and what may occur if this work becomes visible.

Fugitive knowledge in lesbian, gay, bisexual, transgender, and queer discourse is a prerequisite of existence and survival in an anti-queer world filled with hate and violence but it also is ludic and erotic in nature. It is constructed by and for us, sometimes shared, and also appropriated (stolen from us) without permission. Such appropriation is a form of neo-colonialism premised on heteronormative assumptions and we believe it is our responsibility to engage in overt and covert decolonization. Here we draw on Smith (1999) who argues that decolonization is not merely postcolonial, but is rather the critical engagement of colonialism and sociocultural imperialism "at all levels" (p. xiv). Queer fugitive knowledge is radical knowledge that is based on every day experience as queer folks. It is outside of the control of knowledge-elites or professional knowledge makers, as well as of heterosexual, or straight, popular constructions of knowledge. Queer knowledge is fugitive in the sense that it has escaped their control and is on the run from oppressive regimes. Based in the concepts of the Gramscian organic intellectual, fugitive knowledge is the "common sense knowledge belonging to the people at the grassroots and constituting part of their heritage" (Fals-Borda, 1982, p. 27).

We engage this concept in terms of defining queer heritage as articulated through community development work. This work is also informed by Hill's (2007a) writings on "space travellers" working the interstitial zones—traveling along intellectual and activist locations in public and private spheres—and at times blurring the boundaries of these spheres. He writes, "My vocation has been to join the 'space makers' in the field, to carve out and travel in an ideological space where we put into practice a comprehensive vision of justice. This is revolutionary pedagogical work" (2007a, p. 156). This "space traveller" metaphor often characterizes our transnational work, as we move between borders and boundaries, defy authority figures and other gatekeepers, and claim a place and presence at the table with other community builders working on improving sexual and gender minority lives. In a real sense we hold dual "passports" since those who are members of "out-groups" typically have learned to navigate the intricacies of the majoritarian (and often dominating) group. We know our lifeworld, the lifeworld of "the Other," and inhabit a tension belt that constitutes a "third space" (Bhabha, 1995). This tension surfaces when, for instance, there has been no guarantee made by organizations that embrace sexual and gender diversity that they can prevent homo/transphobic practices from taking place (Colgan et al., 2008; Hill, 2008). Organizations still operate in heteronormative ways. Workplaces still possess, almost uncompromisingly, male and heteromasculine values of "competiveness," "control," and "instrumentality" (Rumens & Kerfoot, 2009; Whitehead, 2003) and "heteroprofessionalism" (Mizzi, 2013). Sexual and gender minorities are not cushioned from the effects of such dominant norms when organizations sever learning and sexuality.

Acknowledging Privilege in Transnational Community Work

Being researchers, activists, and educators that focus on international issues, we are connected with several opportunities that attract and appeal to

Western interests. As people with Western (North America) origins, we receive opportunities to travel, meet people, and exchange customs and different ways of thinking. Despite our good intentions, we risk worsening conditions for the local population that we work with if our interventions are not respectful and participatory. Indeed, there has been a pattern of Western colonial encounters that manage colonized people according to new scripts and rules that makes "normal" one group of people, and casts another group as being "abnormal" because of their differences in race, sexual orientation, gender, class, or ability (Smith, 1999). In a sexual and gender minority context, this may mean the (re)production of a "gay community" in the image of a Western "gay rights" movement, something that has been criticized as the "McPinking of the World" (Hill, 2004b).

Even though our community work is often done in secret places and in the shadows, we still have a responsibility to focus on engaging with appropriate cultural "protocols, values and behaviours" (Smith, 1999), especially since oftentimes we work with Indigenous populations. It cannot be assumed that this responsibility is absolved simply because social justice goals and visions for social emancipation appear to be shared. In our work greater emphasis is placed on "people whose bodies, territories, beliefs and values that have been traveled *through* [original italics]" (Smith, p. 78) in order to understand the complexities of current issues facing oppressed peoples, such as sexual and gender minorities.

Given the Western genealogy of disenfranchising sexual and gender minorities as a conduit of colonialism (Wekker, 2004), there is valid concern that similar practices of disenfranchisement are being repeated in various global spaces. As Wekker explains "in hegemonic versions of sexual globalization ahistoricism and an overlooking of continuing imbalances of power have shaped the definition of Euro-American sexualities as normative and non-Western sexualities as deviant" (p. 226). Ways that this hetero/homo (and male/female) binary plays out need to be challenged and critiqued in community work. In order to "fix" social problems, Western educators have inadvertently invalidated Indigenous knowledge, worsened the already impoverished material conditions, and classified Indigenous identities according to Western knowledge theories and systems (Smith, 1999).

Since we (as chapter authors) are a part of Western genealogy, our work with sexual and gender minorities organizing and teaching in secret spaces may require the development of trust first before participating in any kind of community development activities (Mizzi, 2009). Additionally, such communities may refuse to work with us and insist that only local community workers facilitate the learning experience. Reclaiming local power over the learning deepens the story being shared, promotes commitment and engagement, and develops a "participatory connectedness" with other learners (Mizzi & Hamm, 2013). Sexual and gender minorities become a social group excluded from being considered "normal." Heteronormativity primarily destabilizes same-sex desire, and paralyzes its fluidity, causing binary positions that are "non-heterosexual" (Horswell, 2005). Introducing Western morally charged terms such as "sodomite" or "homosexual" blocks learning on how people interpret their sexual experiences and feelings (Altman, 2001; Horswell, 2005; Wekker, 2006). The global "gay rights" movement contributes to this practice with its use of classifying identities, such as "lesbian" and "gay," which complicates Indigenous practices of identity-formation and community development. The situation is indeed messy and involves risky work, but respectful inclusion into social programs is not an unattainable or impossible task.

A Framework for Sexuality and Gender Inclusion

In a presentation at the *51st Annual Adult Education Research Conference*, Hill (2010) espoused principles for a critical Indigenous methodology—one that offers insights transferable to sexual and gender minorities. Lessons are numerous including: the survival value of learning by observation and doing; learning through situated experiences; learning through enjoyment and through protest; the essentiality of culturally based education; learning for continued existence; narratives/story-telling as central to the adult education enterprise; the centrality of affective (emotional), kinesthetic/embodiment/somatic, relational/social, spiritual, and environmental domains in learning; and how to join the post-imperialist discourses of groups taking place outside of hegemonic systems of power (i.e., subaltern social movements, see Abdi & Kapoor, 2009). It is based on these principles that we suggest the following practical, yet risky, steps as part of a framework for sexual and gender minority inclusion. We acknowledge that doing so can be viewed as one more example of appropriation from the marginalized—in this instance by one marginalized group from another. On the other hand, we argue with Denzin and Lincoln (2008) that hybrid discourses emerge when critical theory and action theory interact. In our view this generates liberatory praxis that aims to emancipate and decolonize rather than appropriate and enslave.

In consideration of acknowledging and promoting the emotional, social, and informational needs of sexual and gender minorities, we argue that it is first important to question the dominance of educational institutions and how they "gatekeep" what kinds of training and education are considered (in)valid. This step seeks to reveal troubling patterns of exclusion and hold some accountability as to why these patterns exist in the first place—and how to disturb them.

A second step is to trouble formal education or training, since not everyone can openly describe their education on, say, democratic leadership if this training was done in secret. Once trust is gained, perhaps a more flexible model of "accreditation" can welcome forms of education that would have otherwise placed the sexual and gender minority in danger.

A third aspect of the framework encourages community workers to join the conversations, be informed of the debates, discussions and thoughts, and then begin to teach and act in inclusive ways. This approach addresses the historical relationships between people and land, deconstructs the Western categorizations that have entrapped people, and engages a cultural hybridity between the community workers and learners. Hill's primary message is to be "Out" when possible and safe, seek allies, be open to the transformative properties of collective action, culture jam, educate, subvert, advocate, confront, organize in "cells" to mobilize actions, and avoid dangerous situations when necessary. Activism is indeed the practice of adult and community education (Hill, 2011a).

Finally, Hill (2007b) offers some "ways out" for oppressed sexual minorities that can be adapted to community work(ers). They include, deploying fugitive knowledge with civil and human rights education as anti-oppression tools to build skills and capacity for queer advocacy; exploiting "globalization" by joining in solidarity with the work of sexual and gender minority freedom fighters in all parts of the world, especially where they have had to work underground and under guard; work to broaden the definitions of "intercultural competence" and "diversity" to include sexual minorities and "Indigenous and fugitive wisdom"; organize to call attention to and to resist violence in all of its forms, against sexual and gender minority communities; work to change policies at the governmental, religious, legal, and judicial levels; where resistance to our liberation is great, and the consequences of being who we are could lead to opprobrium, violence, imprisonment or death, meet in clandestine "cells" that are spontaneous and have multiple leadership roles so that should one trailblazer "disappear" another is in the wings to carry on; use technology such as social media to organize, inform, educate and resist on our behalf; where possible, engage in culture jamming—activities that disrupt or subvert the media, cultural venues, or public events (for a review of techniques that are context dependent, see Dery, 1993); and offer asylum from oppression to those who hail from communities or countries that oppress sexual and gender minorities.

Concluding Thoughts

Writers in the *Handbook of Critical and Indigenous Methodologies* (Denzin & Lincoln, 2008) have pointed out that emancipation and liberation will only be possible by employing the techniques and methods from marginalized groups, drawn from local traditions and knowledge (and we would add that fugitive knowledge is at the heart of the process). It is only through the intersection of critical methodologies, in concert with the wisdom of the Out-group that an anti-colonial praxis will emerge to lift the injustices experienced by "women, women of color, Third World women, African American women, Black women, Chicana and other minority group women, *queer, lesbian, and transgendered* [emphasis added], Aboriginal, First Nation, Native American, South African, Latin American, and Pacific and Asian Islander persons" (Denzin & Lincoln, 2008, p. x). This work must be explicitly political, utopian in scope, activate critique and criticism, and constantly reflexive in seeking subversive, transgressive, multivocal, and fully participatory methodologies, methods, and epistemologies (Lather, 2007).

Community work when it comes to sexual and gender minority communities must include a politics of liberation. Heywood (1989), several decades ago asserted that the liberation theology of sexual minorities had to "critique the dualistic and heterosexist charter of . . . theological tradition . . . while developing a constructive theological and moral alternative, grounded in reclaiming our embodied experiences of the erotic in relations of mutuality as a central experience of God" (p. 267). In essence, our way forward is predicated upon the confluence of critical praxis, sexual and gender minority experiences, and migration from an apologetic effort to "fit in" to one of Queering (radically questioning normative epistemologies) patterns of justice and relationships. We must realize that it is always already spiritual (Spencer, 2004), political, pedagogical, cultural, and revolutionary. At times our work will be in the public sphere (Hill, 2006) and at times fugitive, by stealth, through manufactured dissent, insubordination, and civil disobedience, but always done with the notion that another world is possible. Of significance is the notion that sexual and gender minorities deserve human rights and recognition, similar to what is proposed through the *Yogyakarta Principles on the Application of International Human Rights*

Law in Relation to Sexual Orientation and Gender Identity (2006). Our most radical response and most sanguine pedagogical venue is to abandon the closet and be visible, when safe to do so; it is activism as the practice of community education. When we do these things, we too believe that angels and demons alike will look for other quarry.

References

Abdi, A., & Kapoor, D. (Eds.). (2009). *Global perspectives on adult education.* New York, NY: Palgrave.

Adam, B., Duyvendak, J., & Krouwel, A. (Eds.). (1999). *The global emergence of gay and lesbian politics: National imprints of a worldwide movement.* Philadelphia, PA: Temple University Press.

Altman, D. (2001). Rupture or continuity?: The internationalization of gay identities. In J. Hawley (Ed.). *Post-colonial, queer: Theoretical Intersections* (pp. 19–41). Albany, NY: SUNY Press.

Baird, V. (2007). *The no-nonsense guide to sexual diversity* (rev. ed.). Toronto, ON: New Internationalist.

Bhabha, H. (1995). Cultural diversity and cultural differences. In B. Ashcroft, G. Griffiths, & H. Tiffin (Eds.), *The Post-Colonial Studies Reader* (pp. 206–209). London, UK: Routledge.

Byrd's Eye View. (2009, February 15). *Untitled.* Retrieved from file:///Users/bob-hill/Documents/powerpoint%20presentations/International%20Gay%20RIghts/Charlice%20Byrd%20-%20Georgia%20State%20House%20Representative%20-%20District%2020.webarchive.

Colgan, F., Creegan, C., McKearney, A., & Wright, T. (2008). Lesbian workers: Personal strategies amid changing organizational responses to sexual minorities in UK workplaces. *Journal of Lesbian Studies, 12,* 65–86.

Denzin, N., & Lincoln, Y. (2008). Preface. In N. Denzin & Y. Lincoln (Eds.), *Handbook of critical and Indigenous methodologies* (pp. ix–xv). Los Angeles, CA: Sage.

Dery, M. (1993). *Culture jamming: Hacking, slashing, and sniping in the Empire of the signs.* Retrieved at http://project.cyberpunk.ru/idb/culture_jamming.html.

Fals-Borda, O. (1982). Participatory research and rural social change. *Journal of Rural Co-operation, 10*(1), 27–35.

Gengenbach, H. (2003, December). Binding memories: "Everyone has her own hand." In *Binding memories: Women as makers and tellers of history in Magude, Mozambique.* Columbia University Press eBook. Retrieved from http://www.gutenberg-e.org/geh01/frames/fgeh11.html.

Heywood, C. (1989). *Touching our strength: The erotic as power and the love of God.* San Francisco, CA: Harper and Row.

Herdt, G. (1997). *Same sex, different cultures: Gays and lesbians across cultures.* New York, NY: Westview Press

Hill, R. J. (1997). *Growing grassroots: Environmental conflict, adult education and the quest for cultural authority* (unpublished doctoral dissertation). The Pennsylvania State University, Pennsylvania, USA.

———. (2001). Contesting discrimination based on sexual orientation at the ICAE Sixth World Assembly: "Difference" is a fundamental human right. *Convergence, 34*(2–3), 100–116.

———. (2004a). Fugitive and codified knowledge: Implications for communities struggling to control the meaning of local environmental hazards. *International Journal of Lifelong Learning, 23*(3), 221–242.

———. (2004b). Going global: Internationalizing LGBTQ resilience and inclusion. In A. Grace, K. Wells, & M. Holcroft (Eds.), *The Second Annual LGBTQ&Allies Pre-Conference of the 45th Annual Adult Education Research Conference—Canadian Association for the Study of Adult Education (CASAE)/ ACÉÉA,* (pp. 16–30). Victoria, BC: University of Victoria.

———. (Ed.). (2006, Winter). *Challenging homophobia and heterosexism: Lesbian, gay, bisexual, transgender and queer issues in organizational settings. New Directions for Adult and Continuing Education #112.* San Francisco, CA: Jossey-Bass.

———. (2007a). Breaking open our times (and other liberatory acts). In K. Armstrong & L. Nabb (Eds.), *American adult educators: Quintessential autobiographies by educators of the 21st century* (pp. 153–158). Chicago, IL: Discovery Association Publishing House.

———. (2007b). Finding a voice for sexual minority rights (lesbian, gay, bisexual, transgender, Indigenous/Two-Spirit, and Queer): Some comprehensive policy considerations. *Convergence 40*(3/4), 169–180.

———. (2008). Que(e)rying intimacy: Challenges to lifelong learning. In R. Hill & A. Grace (Eds.), *Adult education in queer contexts: Power, politics, and pedagogy* (pp. 45–68). Chicago, IL: Discovery Association Publishing House.

———. (2011a). Activism as practice: Some Queer considerations. In S. Merriam & A. Grace (Eds.), *A reader on contemporary issues in adult education* (pp. 424–435). San Francisco, CA: Jossey-Bass.

———. (2013). Queering the discourse: International adult education and learning. In P. Mayo (Ed.), *Learning with adults: A reader* (pp. 87–98). Rotterdam, Holland: Sense.

Horswell, M. (2005). *Decolonizing the sodomite: Queer tropes of sexuality in colonial Andean culture.* Austin, TX: University of Texas Press.

Lather, P. (2007). *Getting lost.* Albany, NY: SUNY Press.

Lord, R. S. (2013, July 17). Supreme Court strikes down Defense of Marriage Act, creating new rights for same-sex spouses and new obligations for employers. Association of Corporate Council. Retrieved from http://www.lexology.com/ library/detail.aspx?g=1aa47c7b-16b7-48cd-94c8-975c05965834.

Mayer, K., Bradford, J., Makadan, H., Stall, R., Goldhammer, H., & Landers, S. (2008). Sexual and gender minority health: What we need to know and what needs to be done. *American Journal of Public Health, 98*(6), 969–995.

Merriam, S., & Brockett, R. (1997) *The Profession and Practice of Adult Education.* San Francisco, CA: Jossey-Bass

Mizzi, R. (Ed.). (2008). *Breaking free: Sexual diversity and change in emerging nations.* Toronto, ON: QPI Publishing.

———. (2009). When the down-low becomes the new high: Integrating sexual dissidence into community education programs in Kosovo. In R. Hill & A. Grace (Eds.), *Adult education in queer contexts: Power, politics, and pedagogy* (pp. 241–253). Chicago, IL: Discovery Association Publishing House.

———. (2010). Unravelling researcher subjectivity through multivocality in auto-ethnography. *Journal of Research Practice, 6*(1), Article M3. Retrieved from http://jrp.icaap.org/index.php/jrp/article/view/201/185.

Mizzi, R., & Hamm, Z. (2013). Canadian community development organizations, adult education and the internationalization of a pedagogical practice. In T. Nesbit, S. Brigham, N. Taber & T. Gibb (Eds.), *Building on critical traditions: Adult education and learning in Canada* (pp. 342–352). Toronto, Canada: Thompson Educational Publishing.

Mizzi, R. (2013). "There aren't any gays here": Encountering heteroprofessionalism in an international development workplace. *Journal of Homosexuality, 60*(11), 1602–1624.

Peterson, H. (2009, February 17). *Professor cleared of allegations.* Retrieved from http://www.redandblack.com/news/professor-cleared-of-allegations/article_3619a2a2-ca7b-5ae1-81b1-cb5d0e346cdd.html?mode=jqm.

Pinar, W. (Ed.). (1998). *Queer theory in education.* New York, NY: Routledge.

Rumens, N., & Kerfoot, D. (2009). Gay men at work: (Re)constructing the self as professional. *Human Relations, 62*(5), 763–786.

Smith, L. (1999). *Decolonizing methodologies: Research and Indigenous peoples.* London, UK: Zed Books.

Spencer, D. (2004). Lesbian and gay theologies. In M. De La Torre (Ed.), *Handbook of U.S. theologies of liberation* (pp. 264–273). St. Louis, MO: Chalice Press.

Wekker, G. (2004). *The politics of passion: Women's sexual culture in the Afro-Surinamese diaspora.* New York, NY: Columbia University Press.

Wenger, E. (1998). *Communities of practice, learning, meaning and identity.* New York, NY: Cambridge University Press.

Whitehead, S. (2003). Identifying the professional 'man'ager: Masculinity, professionalism and the search for legitimacy. In J. Barry, M. Dent, & M. O'Neill (Eds.), *Gender and the public sector: Professionals and managerial change* (pp. 85–103). New York, NY: Routledge.

Yoshino, K. (2006). *Covering: The hidden assault on our civil rights.* New York, NY: Random House.

7

Invisible Women

Education, Employment, and Citizenship of Women with Disabilities in Bangladesh

Shuchi Karim

Bangladesh is a South Asian developing country, with a total population of 152.25 million as of July 2012 (Bangladesh Bureau of Statistics, 2013). Available figures for developing countries from the World Health Organization and World Bank suggest "an overall disability prevalence of about 10% of the population is a valid working estimate" (World Bank, 2004, p. 15). This makes tentative numbers of persons with disabilities in Bangladesh much higher than government projections, in part because underreporting of disabilities is common, questionnaire design is complicated, family members may "forget" to report relatives with disabilities, and enumerators receive limited training for such a sensitive data collection exercise (World Bank, 2004, p. 13). The United Nations' Convention on the Rights of Persons with Disabilities (2006) states that disability is an evolving concept resulting from interaction between persons with impairments and attitudinal and environmental barriers that hinder their full and effective participation in society. It is

> the disadvantage or restriction of activity caused by the way
> society is organized which takes little account of people who have
> physical, sensory or mental impairments. This results in people

with disabilities being excluded and prevented from participating fully and equally in mainstream society. (Naidu, Haffejee, Vetten, & Hargreaves, 2005, p. 8)

With these reference points in mind, persons with disabilities are one of the most vulnerable social groups as they receive little or no assistance accessing services and opportunities related to education, health, and other services in a country like Bangladesh (Japan International Corporation Agency [JICA], 2002). To ameliorate their situation, the government of Bangladesh has disability-specific laws and regulations, such as the Bangladesh Persons with Disability Welfare Act, which adopt a multisector development approach inclusive of education, employment, health, and so forth (UNESCAP, 2014). As a primary or basic right of citizens, the government argues that Bangladesh has made significant progress in the education sector, especially in regard to increasing access and gender equity, both at primary and secondary levels (Bangladesh Ministry of Education, 2014). More specifically, gross primary school enrollment rates rose from 90 percent in the late 1990s to 98 percent in 2003, while a corresponding increase in enrollment rates (between the 1990s and 2003) at the secondary level rose to 44 percent. The same report also notes gender parity has been achieved for access to primary and secondary education. Even though Bangladesh has witnessed a remarkable progress in girls' education through its universal primary education policy and a steady rise of girls' net enrollment, there has been insufficient attention to "inclusive education" to ensure better education opportunities for children with disabilities (UNICEF, 2013a). Education for children with disabilities was less than 4 percent in 2003 (DRRA, 2003).

In general, children with disabilities are among the most vulnerable to violence, abuse, exploitation, and neglect. This is particularly so where they are hidden or institutionalized because of social stigma associated with sin, bad karma, or character and/or the much higher economic cost of educating children with a disability. Even though primary education in Bangladesh is free and compulsory, the cost of additional resources often associated with education (clothing, shoes, food, transport, etc.) can still be a burden for a large part of a poor population. Household survey data from 13 low- and middle-income countries (in Africa, East Asia, and the Pacific) show that children with disabilities aged 6 to 17 years are significantly less likely to be enrolled in school in comparison to their peers without disabilities (UNICEF, 2013b). The intersecting effects of gender and disability indicate that girls with disabilities face greater hardship and social barriers when it comes to achieving access and rights to education. Lack of education and consequent unemployment adds to the already marginalized position of children and young people with disabilities, and especially girls who are positioned on the periphery of economic access in a patriarchal system.

An educational system which has exclusion built into its structures and the extent of demand for access to education and consequent employment opportunities for persons with disabilities, suggests disenfranchisement from formal education may be only part of the struggle girls face. This chapter uses empirical research to shed light on the lifespan realities of girls and adult women with disabilities in Bangladesh. Through this ontological approach, I disturb the silo-like approach to researching the lives of adults which begins with their entry to adulthood. Drawing on the notion of "lifespan" as a point of information and inquiry for the development of adults I consider the following questions:

a) In what ways do existing education systems exclude girls and adult women with disabilities from accessing their basic rights to education?

b) What are the gendered consequences of limited access to education for girls and adult women with disabilities, especially in terms of employment?

c) How do limited opportunities of education and subsequent impact on employment contribute to limited participation in citizenship?

This chapter first explores the gender, disabilities, and education nexus in the context of Bangladesh. It then introduces data from a qualitative research study conducted with young Bangladeshi girls, women, and their families and discusses the findings of the study in the context of guidance for policymakers, educators, and activists concerned with the lives of girls and women with disabilities.

Gender, Disabilities, and Education in the Context of Bangladesh

Like other South Asian countries, Bangladesh has patriarchal roots that dominate both private and public discussions (Azim, 2010; Azim & Sultan, 2010; Baden, Green, Goetz, & Guhathakurata, 1994; Karim, 2012a; Karim,

2012b). Male dominance and privilege occupies much of everyday life, including household affairs, politics, labor and employment, sexuality, marital choice, access to and ownership of income/assets, and so forth. Despite the growing visibility of women's political leadership, gender equity is still a problematic issue in Bangladesh (United Nations Development Program, 2005). The country continues to have low levels of female representation in the civil service, in parliament as elected officials, in leadership positions, and in ownership of assets, such as land.

Discussions of poverty and education crosscut discussions about gender equity. Even though Bangladesh has seen an impressive growth in gender-parity in formal education, especially in enrollment in primary schools, the dropout rate of 37 percent for girls in the later primary and lower secondary years remains very high (UNICEF, 2014). UNICEF also reports that there are approximately 1.5 million primary school girls not enrolled in school and limited options for girls and women within greater society aggravates the problems of inadequate schooling for girls. The key barriers to girls' education are: (1) social perceptions of girls as subservient to boys, (2) reduced opportunity to develop sufficient life skills and understandings to participate and advance in economic sphere, (3) early marriage, and (4) lack of social security (Chowdhury, Nath, & Chowdhury, 2001; Ferdaush, 2011; Habib, 2012; UNICEF, 2014). There are significant groups of children who never attend school, such as working children, children from urban slums, children located in hard-to-reach (often rural) geographical areas, and children with disabilities. Habib (2012), Hussain (2008), Khan, and Anisuzzaman (2011) and Sabates, Hossain, and Lewin (2010) agree that a vast majority of children with disabilities never attend school and the dropout rate is assumed to be high mainly because most schools do not offer significant support for students with disabilities after the primary level. Inaccessible infrastructure, teaching practices of exclusion, and unfriendly learning environments are reasons cited by these researchers.

People with disabilities in developing countries tend to come from poorer economic backgrounds and face additional socioeconomic barriers. The World Bank estimates that disabled people make up 15 to 20 percent of the lower class in developing countries (JICA, 2002). This sizeable percentage means that women with disabilities are especially invisible because they are less vocal and apparent in public spheres, and are always sidelined, ignored, and devalued by the majority and within the disability movement (Karim & Chowdhury, 2010; World Bank Report, 2004). As Lonsdale (1990) says, it is men, and I argue, *able* men, who comprise the powerful and the majority in the public discourse.

Young (1990) explains that the above processes of marginalization construct people as "dependents," and therefore also position them as subordinate and subjugated to authority regimes. Being disabled can reduce one's power position in social institutions such as school settings and some families. While it is difficult not to raise the issue of gender in these discussions, it is unfair to cast vulnerable populations with a broad stroke of marginalization, as oppression based on bodily ability has different causes, meanings, and effects. Disability is not an experience only confined to women; it is important to conceptualize how men and women experience disability differently on the basis of their gender. That said, in a society where being female is perceived as being "dependent" and of lesser value than males, the customary laws that men take for granted and also favor them, such as the inability to own property or receive inheritance rights, further disadvantage women with disabilities. An exploration of male experiences with disability falls outside the scope of this chapter, but would be a worthwhile comparative study for the future.

Research Design

The purpose of the research project was to explore the experiences of a small cohort of women with disabilities in hopes of understanding what kinds of changes are necessary in order to promote inclusion. The study had three field sites in Bangladesh: Chittagong, Faridpur, and Dhaka. These sites were chosen because of important nongovernmental program intervention taking place in those areas, which facilitated access to participants (Karim & Chowdhury, 2010) and because each area represents rural (Faridpur), peri-urban (Chittagong), and urban/metropolis (Dhaka) perspectives. Since the project aimed to develop an approach to understanding the lifespan realities of girls and women with disabilities in Bangladesh, informants belonged to two age groups: youth aged 11 to 24; and matured adults aged 24 and above. Nevertheless, age in a Bangladeshi context, especially in rural areas, is mostly a matter of assumption because birth registration is not a common practice and social conventions do not always permit young girls to reveal their actual age.

A multi-modal approach using four forms of data collection—interviews, focus groups participatory observations, and informal discussions—generated a fulsome understanding of the struggles facing girls and women with disabilities. Over a period of three months, I conducted 18 in-depth interviews with 18 key female informants, 12 focus group discussions (which included some of the 18 key female informants as well as local women with disabilities who were beneficiaries of specific interventional programs), participatory observation with two specific stakeholder groups (mothers of children with disabilities who attended parenting discussion sessions and girls/women with disabilities who joined cooperative group discussions) and, informal discussions with local social development workers, parents, and caregivers of girls/women with disabilities and other related workers. Thematic analysis was used to analyze the data (Denzin & Lincoln, 2003; Somekh & Lewin, 2005) and pseudonyms have been use for all participants.

Women with Disabilities and Education: Life Realities of Invisibility

Participants in this study narrated difficult journeys through education systems in Bangladesh, which is an indication of how families devoted little time and money to the education of women with disabilities at a young age. Gaining unconditional support from *both* parents was a common struggle across all three study sites. Girls often detailed how their mothers' relentless care gave support for their daughters with disabilities to have an education. In contrast, adult participants in the study indicated that fathers and other family members offered support gradually and eventually over time.

The invisibility of women with disabilities in the public sphere may start as early as their exclusion from elementary school and a participatory role of parents is key to ensuring their access and continuation with studies. Girls with disabilities would find it more than difficult to start education and/or continue with it for long enough if support from both parents is not at the forefront. Moreover, special provisions at schools that cater to different types and levels of disabilities, ongoing caregiver supports and logistical support that extends beyond the rare occasions when a disability friendly ramp is installed, are minimal if girls with disabilities are to have a meaningful start to their adult lives.

In addition, there was evidence of how education is determined by others without consultation with participants. An adolescent participant from Faridpur narrated her experiences at a reputable girl's school. At the start of school she was not asked any questions by teachers, was ignored and isolated in the lessons and, as a result, made no friends. After the class exams, and in informal settings, she excelled and proved to be an excellent student and peer. The teachers' gradual acceptance enhanced her academic performance, and this eventually allowed her to have a less restricted and marginalized placement in a mainstream classroom:

> When you find a good school, where you are appreciated for being a good student. A lot of love, affection from teachers and friends—you feel wonderful, you feel really good—it makes you want to go ahead in life . . . really ahead!

The above narrative does not stand alone in the data. Samira also talked about insensitivity within classrooms:

> Although I had the right to education, as soon as I stepped into the field of education, many of my teachers posed that common question: "So why do you study?" I feel strange even today when I think about it. However, as a child I kept silent though I wanted to be like other children and therefore I cannot alienate myself from the mainstream. Therefore, despite being visually impaired, I immediately made up my mind that no matter what happens, how miserable I became, I ought to survive in this school.

An important observation in Samira's case (and for others in the research) is that hostility comes in the form of intimidation, violence, rejection, and exclusion. A college student shares her point of view on gender and the education system:

> Girls need an all-girls' school after a particular age because in the co-education system boys are the majority and the teasing and physical discomfort cannot always be ignored or tolerated. I left a co-education school and shifted to all girls' school out of anger and frustration because they [the school authority] initially refused to re-admit me after I fell ill, became disabled, and had a 2 year gap.

The Government of Bangladesh has introduced an "inclusive" education policy to cater to children with special needs in mainstream schools. This study, along with others (Ahsan, Sharma & Deppeler, 2011; Mullik & Sheesh, 2013; Rahman & Sutherland, 2011), indicates major gaps in policy implementation. Lack of appropriate and modern teacher education programs, assistance during sports practice, additional teaching materials and tools, and pre-service teachers' motivation are among the most significant gaps that teachers and schools suffer from in accommodating children with disabilities in general. The presence of an "inclusive education" policy without the appropriate classroom logistics and adequately trained teachers only results in more mismatches between the expectations of students with disabilities and teachers' inability to cater to specific educational needs.

Barriers to education for this marginalized group of people are not limited to the classroom or school premises. They can start with the journey from home to school on a daily basis. In one of the informal discussions in mixed gender groups of young boys and girls with disabilities, participants explain that commuting to school is layered with gendered assumptions and expectations among school authority. Young boys described difficulties in commuting to schools and colleges, but because of their gender (and depending on the extent or severity of disability), they enjoy relative freedom to ride their bike to schools, and/or share rides with others (by rickshaw or bicycle) and, as a result, are able to continue with their education for longer periods of time. These commutes often involve long distances and strenuous effort, especially in rural and peri-urban setups, but being male allows some privileges and opportunities to "push forward" one's determination to pursue education. Even when parents cannot afford to buy a bike or pay for regular rickshaw rides for their son who has a disability, they can still request of others a "pillion" ride to school (i.e., riding as the passenger behind the bike-rider). This is not possible for girls. As study participants pointed out, she has to have enough money to pay for a ride and look for whatever school is willing to take her within close proximity to her house. Her parents, especially mothers, have to be extra-vigilant about their daughters' safety when they are in school or participating in after-school activities. Gender-based violence against girls and women is highly prevalent in Bangladesh and adolescent girls are five times more likely to be abused compared to women aged 40 to 49. Young women aged 20 to 24 were four times more likely to be exposed to violence compared to the same reference category (Amin, Khan, Rahman, & Naved, 2013, p. 34). Violence and sexual harassment threats are a major cause for adolescent girls' dropout rates in secondary school (Karim, 2007). In the light of such gender-based violence and threats to a girl's physical safety and security, it becomes clear how parents of daughters with disabilities are reluctant to risk their daughter's lives for the sake of education. These discussions of everyday activities, such as commuting to school, shed light on complicating social and economic difficulties facing girls with disabilities. The structural and social disenfranchisement of participants from an early age may be an indication of a trend that follows through to their adult life.

Education Leading to Employment: Aspirations for Dignified, Independent, Adult Life

Two of the most important areas that enable one to participate in society are access to education and employment. Having a disability often means extra time and support is required for personal care, travel, health, studies, and other occupational needs. Extra money is needed to cover the cost of special equipment (if available) and participants also raised the issue that Bangladeshi women receive less pay and less access to stable careers. These challenges make it difficult to access higher levels of education and employment as well as sustaining that employment.

One participant, a 16-year-old girl with autism, explained it this way: "I save the money I get from my disability welfare benefit, and I don't spend any of it, not even for myself . . . I keep it for my future. Don't you think I have a future?" She understands the significant relation between economic independence, gender, and dignified existence for girls with disabilities in Bangladesh. If girls in general are perceived as "burdens," then it is not difficult to conceive how she struggles to find a place for herself in society at large.

The ability to live a dignified and independent life comes with education, information, decision-making power, and employment and, as one female college student with disabilities suggested, such independence and decision-making power means having control over one's life:

> When my parents look at other "healthy" (able-bodied) girls, and watch them get married they feel bad, they feel pain . . . but it is difficult for a girl with disability to be married, to set her own household and just live an otherwise regular life . . . don't I think of marriage, or what happens in a marriage? . . . I won't lie to you . . . I am curious, I am intrigued . . . I do think about all these once a while . . . but I am still happy. I am studying, I dream of a future . . . I will get some kind of job, right? Won't I get a job or the other . . . ? A simple life with a simple job.

As much as benefits from the state are required to ensure a minimum running of households or personal expenditure for women with disabilities, women require access to different options for income-generating activities as well as social security. For example, when study participants described how they formed support groups and income-generating groups (such as paper cutting, packet making, small shops, embroidery work, and so forth), it was clear that such involvement provides an opportunity to earn at least some money to bear their basic living costs, personal expenditures, and contribute to the family's household expenditure.

Aside from generating income, employment opportunities structure the everyday lives of women and provide them with a sense of purpose and a chance to collaborate along similar interest lines and form friendships. One woman shop owner in her 40s with no education behind her explained her journey:

> I run my own shop. It started very small, it still is small . . . but I received a loan. I have a husband now, which is good, but I need to earn my own money. He helps me out through purchasing supplies for the shop, but I run the shop. I stay here most of the day, keep a (sic) track of transactions. In the evening, after sunset, I go home, which is very near this shop . . . and I hope to do better.

Maya from Chittagong and Dhaka and Rekha from Faridpur expressed similar thoughts. Despite a severe disability, including being paralyzed below her chest, Maya proved to be a very successful activist, fundraiser, and career-driven woman who now owns her own organization that focuses on disability awareness. She travels the world, owns property, and is considered the head of her family. She credits much of her success to her family support, but there is also her own determination and eagerness to obtain access to professional opportunities that also shaped her future:

> I have worked hard for years, and have built this house with courtyard, modern amenities . . . all through years of hard work. I am independent and happy. My mother and brother's family live with me, and it works well. When my other siblings come from abroad, they stay in my house. Look at the courtyard, I have kept it spacious, clean and natural . . . there is a space for tea and adda (get together) as well.

Rekha, on the other hand, is an entrepreneur who suffers from a polio-related disability. She generates income from sewing and embroidery work, supplies her products to large fashion houses, and trains other girls to become leaders and entrepreneurs. Rekha lives in her father's house where she runs the household as a single mother.

What is striking about these women is that both Maya and Rekha present as confident, dignified women at ease with their respective disabilities. Neither polio nor severe paralysis come across as a hindrance in their pursuit of a better life. Having a disability matters, but it does not define their interaction with the outside world, their involvement with different organizations, or their ability to make a decent and substantial living. While their stories do not reflect the dominant experience of women and girls in the study, they do suggest ways forward in light of the struggles identified earlier in this chapter.

Aside from these success stories, in the rural or peri-urban areas study participants are generally not perceived as being capable of work and/or of contributing economically to the household. In rural areas (like in Faridpur and Chittagong) study participants, often with the help of parents (mostly mothers), work from home making packets, sewing, and tailoring or work in various income-generating groups as part of the informal economy. Only five of the 18 in-depth interview participants had achieved what might be called a successful regular mainstream career. Their stories indicate long hardship, but notably these women came from highly educated, middle-class and urban backgrounds, and, as a result, had access to resources and information unavailable to the study participants with peri-urban and rural backgrounds. Above all, the data in this study suggests that being able to earn and have sense of self-worth is important for girls/women with disabilities because with economic independence or support they can better negotiate discriminating and prejudicial encounters.

Conclusion

Based on the literature and this empirical study, girls and women with disabilities face social marginalization from multiple sources: parents, teachers, classmates, strangers, and agencies. They are often viewed as dependents to larger regimes and stripped of their agency and autonomy as persons. Women with disabilities are more vulnerable to discrimination and violence than women in general in the socioeconomic context of Bangladesh, thus making them more powerless to address the systematic institutional exclusion processes within the country. Barriers such as lack of independence, unequal opportunities to participate in education and employment, and discriminatory attitudes toward rehabilitation push women with disabilities toward the periphery of the society and deprive them of enjoying the rights and dignity of fully integrated citizenship. Without the opportunity for full participation in quality education, women with disabilities will have a much harder time becoming educated and economically independent in the broader context of exclusion.

This research project aims to understand the relationship between gender, education, and employment for women with disabilities in Bangladesh from a perspective across the lifespan. Future intervention work that includes adult education and training programs needs to acknowledge the difficult socio-economic-cultural context for women with disabilities and recognize that education may have provided a "disservice" rather than a "service" to women and girls. Girls/women with disabilities need assistance that promotes emancipation and social change, and is shaped by a deep understanding of gender relations. Commitment to improve gender equity and empowerment of women is a common goal shared among many governmental and non-governmental development agendas. These goals may have good intentions, but may also fail in their scope to consider gender inequity and its impact on everyday lives. In the case of women with disabilities, adult education may mean starting at a young age to reconstruct education systems to be inclusive and respectful of difference. Significantly, when young girls with disabilities become adult women, they would then know how to engage adult education as an ally to their situations.

The government's "inclusive" education policy for children with special needs must address gender-specific needs of girls with disabilities in terms of infrastructure (commutes, facilities, services), health and safety, parent education and support, and teacher education in order to strengthen the journey toward achieving a successful adulthood. Lack of attention to and interest in vulnerable groups result in further marginalization from the development process and reinforce an inferior position in a hierarchical society. Through the voices of girls/women with disabilities this research illustrates how one can become socially, economically, culturally, and systematically isolated and too easily situated on the periphery. Study participants indicated that girls/women with disabilities can be either neglected or denied their needs, aspirations, and interests. The multi-modal approach adopted in this study drew on a wide range of community experiences to provide intervention perspectives aimed at informing all stakeholders about how to build social inclusion and more visible education and employment participation for girls/women with disabilities.

References

Ahsan, T., Sharma, U., & Deppeler, M. (2011). Beliefs of pre-service teacher education institutional heads about inclusive education in Bangladesh. *Bangladesh Education Journal, 10*(1), 9–29.

Amin, S., Khan, T. F., Rahman, L., & Naved, R. T. (2014) *Mapping violence against women in Bangladesh: A multilevel analysis of demographic and health survey data*. Retrieved from http://r4d.dfid.gov.uk/pdf/outputs/ORIE/VAWG_Bangladesh_Final_Report.pdf.

Azim, F. (2010). The new 21st century women. In F. Azim & M. Sultan (Eds.), *Mapping women's empowerment: Experiences from Bangladesh, India and Pakistan* (pp. 261–278). Dhaka, Bangladesh: The University Press.

Azim, F., & Sultan, M. (2010). (Eds.). *Mapping women's empowerment: Experiences from Bangladesh, India and Pakistan*. Dhaka, Bangladesh: The University Press.

Baden, S., Green, C., Goetz, A. M., & Guhathakurta, M. (1994). *Background report on gender issues in Bangladesh*, BRIDGE Report 26, Brighton, UK: Institute of Development Studies. Retrieved from http://www.bridge.ids.ac.uk/sites/bridge.ids.ac.uk/files/reports/re26c.pdf.

Bangladesh Bureau of Statistics (December 2013) *Health and morbidity status survey—2012*, Bangladesh: Statistics and Informatics Division, Ministry of Planning, Government of the People's Republic of Bangladesh. Retrieved from http://www.bbs.gov.bd/WebTestApplication/userfiles/Image/Health_Demo/HMSS.pdf.

Bangladesh Ministry of Education. (2014). *Education Statistics—2012*. Retrieved from http://www.moedu.gov.bd/index.php?option=com_content&task=view&id=300&Itemid=301.

Chowdhury, A. M. R., Nath, S. R., & Choudhury, R. K. (2003). Equity gains in Bangladesh primary education. *International review of education, 49*(6), 601–619. Retrieved from http://202.116.42.39/xxjy/xxjy2/content/wenjian/ckwx/y/2/3.pdf.

Danish Bilharziasis Laboratory for the World Bank. (2004). *Disability in Bangladesh: A situation analysis*, Bangladesh: The Danish Bilharziasis Laboratory for the World Bank. Retrieved from http://siteresources.worldbank.org/DISABILITY/Resources/Regions/South%20Asia/DisabilityinBangladesh.pdf.

Denzin, N., & Lincoln, Y. (2003) *Collecting and interpreting qualitative materials*. London, UK: Sage.

Disabled Rehabilitation & Research Association (DRRA). (2003). "Bangladesh: Towards right-base approaches for the persons with disabilities," paper presented at the Expert Group Meeting and Seminar on an International Convention to Protect and Promote the Rights and Dignity of Persons with Disabilities, Bangkok. Retrieved from www.worldenable.net/bangkok2003/paperbangladesh2.htm.

Ferdaush, J. (2011). *Inequalities in primary education in Bangladesh*. Dhaka, Bangladesh: Social Policy Unit of Unnayan Onneshan—The Innovators. Retrieved from http://www.unnayan.org/reports/Inequality%20in%20Primary%20Education%20of%20Bangladesh.pdf.

Habib, A. (2012). Education right of the disabled children in Bangladesh: A sociological review. *ASA University Review, 6*(1), 21–31. Retrieved from http://www.asaub.edu.bd/data/asaubreview/v6n1sl3.pdf.

Hussain, A. (2008). *Report on women with disabilities in Bangladesh, social assistance and rehabilitation for the physically vulnerable.* Dhaka, Bangladesh: Social Assistance and Rehabilitation for the Physically Vulnerable. Retrieved from http://www.dpiap.org/resources/pdf/WWDs_Bangladesh_11_02_07.pdf.

Japan International Corporation Agency (JICA). (2002). *Country profile on disability people's republic of Bangladesh.* Tokyo, Japan: Planning and Evaluation Department, Japan International Corporation Agency. Retrieved from http://siteresources.worldbank.org/DISABILITY/Resources/Regions/South%20Asia/JICA_Bangladesh.pdf.

Karim, S. (2007). *Gendered violence in education: Realities for adolescent girls in Bangladesh.* Bangladesh: Action Aid.

Karim, S., & Chowdhury, M. (2010). *Right situation of women with disabilities in Bangladesh.* Bangladesh: Action Aid.

Karim, S. (2012a). Living sexualities: Non heterosexual women and sexuality in urban middle class Bangladesh. In A. Helic & H. Hoodfar (Eds.), *Gender and sexuality and Muslim countries* (pp. 269–293). London, UK: Zed Books.

Karim, S. (2012) Sexualities: Practices: Bangladesh. In J. Suad (Ed.), *Encyclopedia of women & Islamic cultures.* Retrieved from http://referenceworks.brillonline.com/entries/encyclopedia-of-women-and-islamic-cultures/sexualities-practices-bangladesh-EWICCOM_001441.

Lonsdale, S. (1990). *Women and disability: The experience of physical disability among women.* London, UK: Macmillan Press.

Khan, N. & Anisuzzaman, Md. (2011). *The status of un-served children in education: Children with disability in Bangladesh: A situation analysis.* Dhaka, Bangladesh: Campaign for Popular Education.

Mullik, U., & Sheesh, S. K. (2013). Perspectives of students and parents about mainstreaming education for children with special needs in Bangladesh. *Asian Journal of Inclusive Education, 1*(1), 17–30.

Naidu, E., Haffejee, S., Vetten, L., & Hargreaves, S. (2005). *On the margins: Violence against women with disabilities.* South Africa: Centre for the Study of Violence and Reconciliation. Retrieved from http://www.csvr.org.za/old/wits/papers/papdisab.htm.

National Forum of Organizations Working with the Disabled (NFOWD). (2005). *Community based rehabilitation practices and alleviation of poverty of people with disabilities in Bangladesh.* Paper presented at the Workshop on Community-Based Rehabilitation and Poverty Alleviation of Persons with Disabilities Bangkok. Retrieved from www.worldenable.net/cbr2005/paperbangladesh.htm#_ftn1.

Rahman M., & Sutherland, D. (2011). Teachers' struggles in applying inclusive education practices for students with disabilities at secondary schools in Bangladesh. *Bangladesh Education Journal, 10*(1), 31–46.

Sabates, R., Hossain, A., & Lewin, K. (2010) School drop out in Bangladesh: New insights from longitudinal evidence. CREATE Research Monograph 49, Brighton, UK: University of Sussex.

Somekh, B., & Lewin, C. (Eds.). (2005). *Research methods in the social sciences.* London, UK: Sage.

United Nations. (2006). *United Nations convention on the rights of persons with disabilities.* Retrieved from http://www.un.org/disabilities/convention/conventionfull.shtml.

United Nations Development Program (UNDP). (2005). *Bangladesh common country assessment.* Retrieved from http://www.un-bd.org/docs/CCA_Jan_2005.pdf.

UNICEF. (2013a). *Bangladesh.* Retrieved from http://www.unicef.org/bangladesh/education.html.

———. (2013b). *State of the world children: Disability.* Retrieved from http://www.unicef.org/sowc2013/.

———. (2014). *Girls' education: Key issues.* Retrieved from http://www.unicef.org/bangladesh/education_463.htm.

United Nations Economic and Social Commission for Asia and the Pacific (UNESCAP). (2014). *Disability policy central for Asia and the Pacific: Bangladesh.* Retrieved from http://www.unescapsdd.org/files/documents/DPC_Bangladesh.doc.

Young, I. M. (1990). *Justice and the politics of difference.* New Jersey, NJ: Princeton University Press.

8

Moving Beyond Employability Risks and Redundancies

New Microenterprise and Entrepreneurial Possibilities in Chile

Carlos A. Albornoz
Tonette S. Rocco

"Globalization . . . is a phenomenon. It has political, economic, sociocultural, and technological dimensions, and refers to integration and interconnectedness across national boundaries along these dimensions" (Gans, 2005, p. 1). Gans describes how current globalization differs from past forms such as colonization because of the spread of capitalism, internationalization of production, communications technology, and the speed of travel. Globalization differs from colonization in the sheer magnitude "of interconnectedness of goods, services, people and ideas" (Gans, p. 1) and that power is held by corporations and not shared with countries or local citizens. During colonization the colonizing country generally invested in the country by creating infrastructure and a market for goods. Multinational corporations do not invest in the host country, instead they negotiate for the lowest tax burden and other benefits the country will provide (Morisset, Pirnia, Allen, & Wells, 2000). In the current context of globalization, localized forms of microenterprise are becoming increasingly threatened by the dominance of multinational corporations. At a first glance, multinational corporations earn the affection of governments and policymakers because they seem to bring large investments into the country. But large businesses also compete with local businesses for consumers, raw materials, labor, and government resources. Multinational corporations lure capable Latin and South American entrepreneurs into the complex web of competition and capitalism. Local enterprise, although under fire, has not entirely become extinct. Small entrepreneurs and local governments make an effort to help local businesses, in the formal and informal economies, to survive. This support usually consists of training programs in addition to some seed capital. However, to achieve the expected effect of training programs, entrepreneurs require a minimum level of education that allows them to develop entrepreneurial skills. Many adults involved in microenterprise in Chile do not have the minimal skill set to take advantage of entrepreneurial programs (Bravo, 2013). This chapter explores ways that microenterprise continues to thrive amidst globalization in spite of adult education practices which fail to meet the needs of learners. It also provides a general understanding of the Chilean context in terms of microenterprise, publicly funded microenterprise programs, current challenges for the Chilean public education system and the effects on adult education. Practical suggestions to advance possibilities conclude the chapter.

Microenterprise

Schumpeter's classical approach (1912 [1934]) describes business-entrepreneurs as revolutionary innovators motivated by pull factors, such as economic motives like increased income, but also independence, status, or merely recognition. These entrepreneurs are motivated by opportunities and are self-directed learners. Many theoretical and empirical studies have shown that most entrepreneurial activity in developed countries results from opportunities (Bosma, Jones, Autio, & Levie, 2008). In contrast, necessity-motivated entrepreneurship is significant in most developing nations.

The informal economy is far from being marginal. The International Labor Organization (2002) found that some 48 percent of non-agricultural employment in North Africa is in the informal economy, 51 percent in Latin America, and 65 percent in Asia. The informal economy is defined as the production and sale of goods and services that are legitimate in all respects aside from the fact that they are not registered with or are hidden from the state. A lack of registration means that there is no governmental oversight to ensure quality and taxes are not paid. Even though entrepreneurs in the informal economy can be employed in the formal economy, individuals excluded from the formal labor market are more likely to engage in informal entrepreneurship (Williams & Round, 2009). Necessity-based entrepreneurs are individuals who are *pushed* into entrepreneurship because they do not have better job options. Reynolds et al. (2005) defined them as individuals who "cannot find a suitable role in the world of work" and for whom "creating a new business is their best available option" (p. 217). The assumption is that entrepreneurs with low levels of education, resources, and social capital are generally involved in low productivity activities. Many of these entrepreneurs operate in the informal sector and are survival entrepreneurs (Naudé, 2009).

The survival of new businesses is a complex endeavor. Money, networks, and technical knowledge are just some of the critical resources that entrepreneurs need to access in order to compete in free markets. The banking literature pioneered research on the factors that kill businesses at early stages such as credit scoring. The first empirical investigations focused on the use of financial ratios to forecast the failure of businesses (Beaver, 1966). Later Reynolds (1987) employed data about sales to demonstrate potential value as predictors of failure. Lussier (1995) synthesized the literature developing a model of 15 variables that predict survival and performance: access and control of scant resources, level of competition, effective uses of resources, networks, access to finance, infrastructure, clear regulations, governmental bureaucracy, and availability of human capital.

The Case of Chile

Chile has the lowest level of poverty in Latin America. Chilean performance is due in part to the implementation of various government policies and programs funded by sustained economic growth, which has occurred in recent decades. This sustained economic growth has created new jobs and has resulted in higher wages for workers. In spite of the economic stability and growth, Chile is similar to other Latin American countries in terms of wealth inequalities and firms controlled by a small number of large shareholders (Gallego & Larrain 2012; Lefort & Walker 2000). The distribution of wealth is one of the most disparate in the world and 15 percent of the population lives below the poverty line (Cobham & Sumner, 2013). Earners in the top 10 percent of the income distribution in Chile account for 42.9 percent of all income, compared to 29.9 percent in the United States and approximately 25 percent in Poland and Slovenia (Zimmermann, 2013).

Among the countries with more unequal income distributions in the world are France (7th place), the UK (3rd), and Chile (2nd). But after taking taxes and transfers into account, Chile becomes first (Desilver, 2013). With such income inequality, social classes barely mix in Chile (Redondo, 2009).

The Chilean Educational System

The Chilean secondary school system mixes three types of schools: (a) private not-subsidized schools, (b) public schools, and (c) private subsidized schools. Private subsidized schools have tuition paid by parents and also receive a public subsidy. Most private subsidized schools are for-profit although not-for-profit institutions, such as those run by the Catholic Church, offer a good not-for-profit education.

Two decades of this mixed system have yielded profound segregation of students (Redondo, 2009; Valenzuela, Bellei, & De Los Ríos, 2013; Zimmerman, 2013). Families choose their children's school according to their capacity to pay (Redondo, 2009). People who can pay $50USD monthly will most likely attend different schools than those who can pay $80USD. Two families may live next door to each other, and their children will attend different schools. The poorest children attend a free public school, and the richest attend a private school. Middle-class families can find schools with tuition ranging from $60 to $300 dollars a month. The loss of middle-class families from the public education system implies that social networks are not available for children of poor families (Brunner & Elacqua, 2003). The networks and social capital inherited from educational institutions affect social position, access to the labor market, and opportunities for work of subsequent generations (Valenzuela et al., 2013).

In Chile, 38 percent of the population attend public schools; this is the lowest number in the OECD countries (Mineduc, 2012). Most people educated in the public school system navigate the job market with the inferior skills and knowledge received from the public school system (see figure 8.1). Figure 8.1 presents standardized scores in math according to household income of Chilean families. Average scores range from 200 points to 310. Each line represents the scores in math for the poorest and the richest segments of the population. Each line represents 20% of the population. The higher scores represent the richer, and the lower, the poorer. Middle classes are in between. Note that scores are clearly segregated between rich and poor. The richer the segment of the population, the better the scores. Similar figures can be observed in language and sciences.

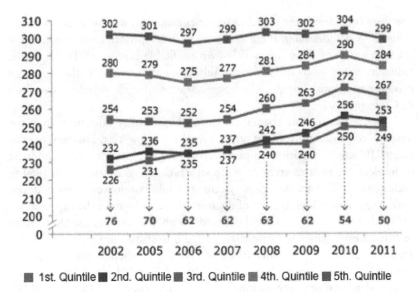

Figure 8.1. Scores in math standardized tests from year 2002 to year 2011 according family income.

Higher Education

In 2010, 38 percent of adults between 25 and 34 years of age had obtained a tertiary degree compared to 42 percent in the United States, 22 percent in Mexico, and 12 percent in Brazil (Zimmerman, 2013). But public universities are expensive in Chile. Universities establish fees that match the willingness of customers to pay. The richest segment of the population goes to public universities because public universities are better, expensive, and receive the best people from the best schools. High-income students enrolled in public universities come from private schools because private schools achieve higher scores on standardized tests and the best public universities are highly selective. People with college degrees earn, on average, five times the income of those who never went to college. The educational system plays an important role in reproducing class structure.

The market-oriented reforms implemented in Chile in the early 1990s profoundly affected the higher education system. In 1989, a law was approved to allow for the creation of private universities. There were private universities before 1989 but those were created by invitation only and were considered traditional universities owned by not-for-profit corporations. Two decades later, there are more than 80 private universities in the country, many of them are well known profitable businesses. For example, Laureate, a well-known American multinational corporation that manages private educational institutions, bought the two largest private universities in Chile in 2001.

Some private universities provide a high-quality education, but the majority of private universities target a market for low-cost, low-quality education. Private universities can profit by offering degrees that are economical to implement, such as secondary school education, business, or hospitality management. The accreditation system in Chile is not well enough developed to guarantee high quality of degrees offered or to meet the expectations for quality in other parts of the world. With few exceptions, the quality of private universities is worse than public universities in Chile. Except for graduates of the top ten universities in Chile, professionals and technicians trained by Chilean universities exhibit skill and knowledge deficiencies when measured against any international benchmark (Brunner & Elacqua, 2003).

After 25 years of market-driven policies, in the Chilean system there is little relationship between the degrees offered by private colleges and the productive needs of the country. Even though the need for technicians is increasing, the ratio of professionals to technicians is three to one. Experts suggest that the productive structure of Chile needs the opposite ratio (one professional per three technicians). The mismatch between the higher education system and the job market makes many students with college degrees pursue professional careers that are not related to their educational background and do not generate enough income to pay back the loans that financed college.

The Job Market

The unemployment rate in Chile has hovered around 6 percent for the last decade (Economic Commission for Latin America, 2012). However, this rate is much higher for young people and women, that is, 30 percent and 18 percent, respectively (Fundación Sol, 2013). If income distribution and level of education are considered, the figures also change. In the poorest 20 percent of the population only 43 percent of women reported holding a job, while in the richer 20 percent, 85 percent of the women have jobs (Medina & Paredes, 2013). For workers with less than 8 years of schooling, the difference between males and females is 35 percent contrasting with workers with more than 12 years of schooling where the difference is 12 percent. In the richer segment of the population the female unemployment rate is 5 percent and in the poorest segment female unemployment is 25 percent (Medina & Paredes, 2013).

The main reason why women do not get jobs is because somebody has to do the domestic work and/or to take care of the children (Medina & Paredes, 2013). Fifty percent of women who are unemployed reported that domestic work and children are the main reason to stay at home (Medina & Paredes, 2013). Figure 8.2 shows participation in the labor market for men and women divided by years of schooling.

With a Gini coefficient (measure of income distribution) of 0.50 (OECD, 2011), 38 percent of Chilean families have difficulties living on their current income (Merco Press, 2013). The average income of people who have completed high school in Chile is USD $612 and full time female workers receive in average 36 percent less than men (Medina & Paredes, 2013). Minimum wage in Chile is about USD $2.30 per hour (OECD, 2013b). The minimum wage in Chile is not enough to make a living. In fact, Argentina, Panama, Brazil, and Paraguay have higher minimum wages than Chile, even though the cost of living in Chile is more expensive (OECD, 2013b).

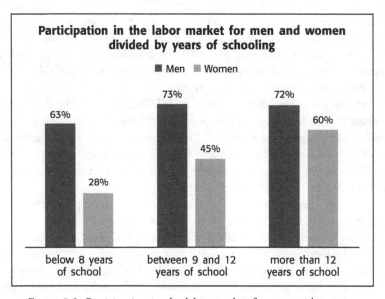

Figure 8.2. Participation in the labor market for men and women.

In order to get a better pay people need to demonstrate valuable skills. But valuable skills are expensive to get outside the formal market. According the National Service of Training and Employment only 75 percent of workers learned their skills through formal education (SENCE, 2009). To develop valuable skills either people need to receive a high-quality education or they need to enter the formal job market.

Access to a salary in Chile depends on the educational level and possession of social capital (Valenzuela, Bellei, & de los Ríos, 2013; Zimmerman, 2013). Individuals with limited access to the job market cope with poverty in Chile. Difficulties accessing the formal labor market force people to generate income by running their own businesses.

Microenterprise in Chile: The Role of the Government

According to the official estimations of 2006 within the poorest 20 percent, 88 percent of household income was generated independently, that is, generated from an activity where there was not an employer (Sol, 2013). In Chile, a country of 17 million people, 14.9 percent of the economically active people are considered active entrepreneurs, and 31 percent of those declared that they started a business because they had no other way of making a living (Amorós, Fernández & Tapia, 2011). There are one million of informal entrepreneurs in Chile, 80 percent of them are micro-entrepreneurs (MINECON, 2012). Only 50 percent of informal entrepreneurs have finished elementary school, 40 percent have finished high school, and 10 perceent reported some college or technical education (MINECON, 2012).

Most entrepreneurs in the informal economy exist at the level of subsistence; only 9 percent create jobs (MINECON, 2012). These entrepreneurs can be found in commerce and restaurants (34%), fishing (24%), industry (13%), personal services (11%), construction (9%), and other services (9%). To be considered a micro-firm, annual sales cannot overpass US $100,000 dollars but micro-entrepreneurs in Chile have average sales of US $10,000 dollars a year (SENCE, 2010).

One of the authors of this article has taught entrepreneurship in a different context in Chile since 1998. Typical micro-businesses in Chile are barbershops, mechanics, gambling machines, greengroceries, seamstresses, homemade food, etc. All these services are provided from home or the provider visits the customers' houses. This implies low overhead costs such as rent, taxes, and administration that would be transferred to the client. In these stores, people usually pay at the end of the month or the day after they receive their salary. Storeowners usually divide bigger containers of something (i.e., soap, sugar, cooking oil) and sell to their clients by cups. Local groceries sell products through their home windows to make a living. Neighbors are accustomed to purchasing from neighbors because visiting the supermarket is something they cannot afford. They may not have the money for a bus fare or a budget to make a monthly or weekly purchase. Instead, they buy on a daily basis from the neighborhood grocery.

The Role of Adult Education

Governments support entrepreneurs by helping them to adapt to the global economy. Eighty-eight percent of micro-entrepreneurs have received some type of training on how to run a business (Minecon, 2012). However, the promise of integration into the global market has to be analyzed with care. In spite of governments allocating resources to help micro-entrepreneurs to compete better, people who received a poor education do not know how to do simple calculations of profit or break-even points (Bravo, 2013). The national survey of microenterprise showed that 95 percent of micro-entrepreneurs did not know how to use a computer and 60 percent could not answer mathematical questions (e.g., how much is 2% of 100?). The promise that everyone can enjoy the benefits of a global market seems to have a major structural problem in Chile because most micro-entrepreneurs received a poor education (SENCE, 2009). People do not have the minimum levels of human or social capital to engage in globalization.

On the other hand, as long as Chile increases its Gross Domestic Product (GDP), the country continues to modernize and the economy is opened to the global market. The Chilean modernizing process has influenced people's ways of living. One way is the development of a retail industry that is growing quickly. The retail industry is competing aggressively to access the different segments of Chilean society. For instance, in 2009 Wal-Mart closed a deal to acquire the control of a major Chilean-based grocery chain. Considering the lower prices and the access to credit Wal-Mart will offer to the lower classes, the micro-entrepreneurs that coexisted with large supermarkets are under threat. Unless entrepreneurs succeed in integrating themselves into the value chain lead by Wal-Mart, their fate will be similar to what happened in Brazil and Mexico. In those countries, small businesses around Wal-Mart facilities disappeared once Wal-Mart opened its doors.

In order to prepare the population to cope with competition and globalization, the Chilean government aggressively fosters entrepreneurship. Each year, more than ten thousand Chileans receive training in how to run a business. However, the impact of those educational programs is insignificant (Bonilla & Cancino, 2011). One of the reasons is that the curriculum is not targeted for an audience having significant skill deficits in math and reading, who lack experience with the labor market, and who have limited social mobility. Still, fostering entrepreneurial skills among the Chilean population has been a major public policy in the last 20 years. For instance, President Piñera declared 2012 as the year of entrepreneurship. The public budget allocated to train entrepreneurs and to provide small seed capital to the low-income population grew ten times in the last two decades (Minecon, 2012b).

Two public agencies work directly with micro-entrepreneurs: FOSIS (Solidarity and Social Investment Fund) and SERCOTEC (Service for Technical Cooperation). FOSIS works with the poorest 20 percent of the population. SERCOTEC emphasizes viable businesses no matter the income of the applicants. FOSIS is a government body that is part of the Ministry of Planning in Chile. It is the main provider of social protection and poverty alleviation programs in Chile. FOSIS works with other government institutions such as SENCE (National Service of Training and Labor), which is part of the Ministry of Labor, providing training to vulnerable populations. FOSIS has implemented training for micro-entrepreneurs since 2006 and has approximately 24,000 beneficiaries each year. The program includes training in business planning, marketing and administration, and funding for entrepreneurship. FOSIS had a budget of US $21 million for 2011.

SERCOTEC assisted 4,830 beneficiaries allocating a total budget of US $40 million dollars in 2012. In 2013, the budget increased 43 percent reaching more than 6,000 beneficiaries (Minecon, 2012b). To receive a subsidy by SERCOTEC, entrepreneurs must undergo an intense selection process that lasts approximately twelve months. Applicants submit a business plan and attend face-to-face interviews. If selected, an entrepreneur can receive up to US $6,000 to start his or her business. If not selected, entrepreneurs receive a scholarship to participate in entrepreneurship education. FOSIS and SERCOTEC provide funds to people to start a business, the amount can be up to US $12,000. Beneficiaries do not pay the money back.

The discourse about the wide range of opportunities that globalization can bring to small towns and less developed nations does not say anything about the inequalities globalization exacerbates. These inequalities include global enterprise with goods priced so low that small businesses and microenterprise cannot compete and the owners do not have the knowledge or skills to compete for jobs in the formal labor market. Several nations, including Chile, attempt to foster entrepreneurship as an important venue for people to overcome poverty.

Among the lower classes, entrepreneurship sharpens the inequalities created by globalization because entrepreneurs who received a low-quality education barely know how to use a computer; most of them have never traveled and cannot compete globally. Meanwhile those who received a good education can take advantage of a huge global market, and those with little education have to watch how international corporations make business in their town and defeat them.

Even though multinational corporations are not responsible for the unfair game that local government implements, adult educators should consider the question of why entrepreneurship training programs are spreading so fast in Latin America and why politicians include them as an important component in their agendas.

Why is microentrepreneurship seen as the panacea for the poor and illiterate? While adult educators are sought to conduct training for entrepreneurs without questioning the usefulness of these activities in preparing the poor to compete in a global marketplace, educators become part of the problem rather than the solution. Many scholars and instructors in the business community make good money by delivering training programs for micro-entrepreneurs. Participants in these training programs have their expectations raised in terms of their employability or entrepreneurial prospects. These expectations cannot be met when the learning needs are not well identified. Entrepreneurial training targeted to the lower segment of the population in Chile is having no effect in terms of survival, employability, or growth of microenterprise. These programs may have an effect in terms of self-esteem of participants or as a political instrument of governments, but not in terms of business performance (Bonilla & Cancino, 2011). Without effect on business performance, assisting people to become entrepreneurs and giving them seed capital only helps to hide unemployment and keep people in the loop of poverty. Perhaps, it is more effective and transparent to transform the curriculum of micro-entrepreneurship into education that will help adults to develop the basic skills in math, reading, and writing necessary to get a job and operate in a global economy. The policy that promotes entrepreneurship could be expanded to provide educational programs which address skill deficits in math, reading, and language; increase employability; and provide access to social networks and the formal labor market. Special programs for women should be implemented that take into account knowledge and skill deficits and childcare needs. Policies and programs will also be needed that target employers in order to eliminate gender inequality in hiring. As globalization of markets and corporations increases, citizens with the least amount of social capital, education, and other resources risk becoming poorer. On the other hand, governments must be careful in their approach to facilitating the arrival of mega-corporations; providing tax relief may decrease available funds for education. Recognizing the basic right of being able to earn a living and maintain one's family should be a concern for educators and politicians.

References

Amorós, J. E., Fernández, C., & Tapia, J. (2011). Quantifying the relationship between entrepreneurship and competitiveness development stages in Latin America. *International Entrepreneurship and Management Journal, 8*(3), 1–22. doi:10.1007/s11365-010-0165-9.

Beaver, W. H. (1966). Financial ratios as predictors of failure. *Journal of Accounting Research, 4*, 71–111.

Bravo, D. (2013). *Segundo Estudio de Competencias Básicas de la Población Adulta 2013 y Comparación Chile 1998–2013* (pp. 1–18). Santiago, Chile. Retrieved from http://www.microdatos.cl/doctos_noticias/Estudio Competencias Final_diseno.pdf.

Brunner, J. J., & Elacqua, G. (2003). Capital humano en Chile. *Universidad adolfo ibáñez, santiago, Chile.* Retrieved from http://200.6.99.248/~bru487cl/files/CapitalHumano_breve.pdf.

Bonilla, C., & Cancino, C. (2011). *El impacto del Programa de Capital Semilla del Sercotec en Chile.* Interamerican Development Bank. Santiago. Retrieved from http://idbdocs.iadb.org/wsdocs/getdocument.aspx?docnum=36501104.

Bosma, N., Jones, K., Autio, E., & Levie, J. (2008). *Global entrepreneurship monitor: 2007 executive report.* Wellesley, MA; Babson Park, MA; and London, UK: Babson College and London Business School. Retrieved from http://www.gemconsortium.org/docs/download/263.

Carter, N., Gartner, W., Shaver K., & Gatewood, E. (2003). The career reasons of nascent entrepreneurs. *Journal of Business Venturing, 18*(1), 13–39.

Cobham, A., & Sumner, A. (2013). *Putting the gini back in the bottle?* London, UK. Retrieved from http://www.kcl.ac.uk/aboutkings/worldwide/initiatives/global/intdev/people/Sumner/Cobham-Sumner-15March2013.pdf.

Davidson, P., & Honig, B. (2003). The role of social and human capital among nascent entrepreneurs. *Journal of Business Venturing, 18*, 301–331.

Desilver, D. (2013) *Global inequality: How the U.S. compares.* Pew Research Center Fact Tank. Retrieved from http://www.pewresearch.org/fact-tank/2013/12/19/global-inequality-how-the-u-s-compares/.

Economic Commission for Latin America. (2012). Macroeconomic report: Chile. *Naciones Unidas.* Retrieved from http://www.eclac.org/publicaciones/xml/6/46986/Chile-completo-web-ing.pdf.

Fundacion Sol. (2013). *Panorama General de los Trabajadores Dependientes que ganan el Salario Mínimo usando la Encuesta Casen 2011* (pp. 1–8). Santiago, Chile. Retrieved from http://www.fundacionsol.cl/wp-content/uploads/2013/03/Panorama-Salario-M%C3%ADnimo-2013-Final.pdf.

Gans, J. (2005). *Citizenship in the context of globalization immigration.* Policy Working Papers. Udall Center for Studies in Public Policy, The University of Arizona. Retrieved from http://udallcenter.arizona.edu/programs/immigration/publications/Citizenship%20and%20Globalization.pdf.

Gallego, F., & Larrain, B. (2014) *CEO* compensation and large shareholders: Evidence from emerging markets. *Journal of Comparative Economics, 40*(4), 621–642.

International Labor Office. (2002). *Women and men in the informal economy: A statistical picture.* Geneva, Switzerland: International Labor Office.

Lefort, F., & Walker, E. (2000) Ownership and capital structure of Chilean conglomerate: Facts and hypotheses for governance. *ABANTE, 3,* 3–27.

Lussier, R. N. (1995). A nonfinancial business success versus failure prediction model for young firms. *Journal of Small Business Management, 33*(1), 8–20.

Medina F., & Paredes P. (2013). *Radiografia del Mercado Laboral Femenino Chileno. Santiago de Chile: Fundación Horizontal.* Retrieved from http://www.horizontalchile.cl/wp-content/uploads/2013/04/Estudio-Mercado-Laboral-Femenino.pdf.

Minecon. (2012). *Encuesta Nacional de Micro Emprendimiento.* Ministerio de Economía Gobierno de Chile: Departamento de Estudios. Retrieved from http://www.economia.gob.cl/estudios-y-encuestas/encuestas/encuestas-de-emprendimiento-y-empresas/segunda-encuesta-de-microemprendimiento/.

———. (2012b). *Proyecto de Presupuesto 2013. Ministerio de Economía Gobierno de Chile: Departamento de Estudios.* Retrieved from http://www.economia.gob.cl/wp-content/uploads/2012/10/PRESUPUESTO-2013.pdf.

Mineduc. (2012). *La Educación en Chile.* Ministry of Education, Chile. Retrieved from http://www.belenuc.cl/sitio/wp-content/uploads/2012/10/Charla-Matias-Lira.pdf.

Merco Press. (2013). *Chile with some of the worst social indicators among the 34 OECD members.* Retrieved from http://en.mercopress.com/2011/04/13/chile-with-some-of-the-worst-social-indicators-among-the-34-oecd-members.

Morisset, J., Pirnia, N., Allen, N., & Wells, L. (2000). *How tax policy and incentives affect foreign direct investment.* World Bank and International Finance Corporation, Foreign Investment Advisory Service.

Naudé, W. A. (2009). Entrepreneurship, developing countries, and development economics: New approaches and insights. *Small Business Economics, 34*(1), 1–12.

OECD. (2011). *6. Equity Indicators. 1. Income Inequality.* Retrieved from http://www.oecd.org/berlin/47570121.pdf.

———. (2013a). *Chile: Education at a glance.* Retrieved from http://www.oecd.org/edu/Chile_EAG2013%20Country%20Note.pdf.

———. (2013b). *Real minimum wages.* Retrieved from http://stats.oecd.org/Index.aspx?DataSetCode=RMW.

Redondo, J. (2009). La educación chilena en una encrucijada histórica. *CIDPA Valparaíso, 1,* 13–39.

Reynolds, P. (1987). New firms: societal contribution versus potential. *Journal of Business Venturing, 3,* 231–246.

Reynolds, P., Bosma, N., Autio, E., Hunt, S., De Bono, N., Servais, I., & Chin, N. (2005). Global entrepreneurship monitor: Data collection design and implementation 1998. *Small Business Economics, 24*(3), 205–231. doi:10.1007/s11187-005-1980-1.

Schumpeter, J. A. (1912/1934). *The theory of economic development.* Cambridge, MA. Harvard University Press.

SENCE. (2009). *La Capacitación y Formación para el empleo en Chile.* Servicio Nacional de Capacitación y Empleo. Retrieved from http://www.sence.cl/sence/wpcontent/uploads/2011/02/NotaTecnica12_2009_CapacitacionparaEmpleo.pdf.

———. (2010). *La Capacitación y Formación para el empleo en Chile.* Servicio Nacional de Capacitación y Empleo. Retrieved from http://www.sence.cl/sence/wpcontent/uploads/2011/03/NotaTecnica7_2010_MicroempresasCapacitacion.pdf.

Valenzuela, J. P., Bellei, C., & de los Ríos, D. (2013). Socioeconomic school segregation in a market-oriented educational system. The case of Chile. *Journal of Education Policy,* 1–25. doi:10.1080/02680939.2013.806995.

Williams, C., & Round, J. (2009). Evaluating informal entrepreneurs' motives: evidence from Moscow. *International Journal of Entrepreneurial Behaviour & Research, 15*(1), 94–107. doi:10.1108/13552550910934477.

Zimmerman, S. (2013). *Making top managers: The role of elite universities and elite peers.* Retrieved from http://pantheon.yale.edu/~sdz3/Zimmerman_JMP.pdf.

9

Shopping at Pine Creek

Rethinking Both-Ways Education through the Context of Remote Aboriginal Australian Ranger Training

Matthew Campbell
Michael Christie

The notion of both-ways education has been part of an Australian Indigenous philosophical tradition for many years now (for example, Marika-Mununggiritj & Muller, 2009). Both-ways education requires all parties to be contributors and learners in educational settings, recognizing that there are different knowledge traditions coming together. It requires the working together of divergent epistemologies—for example the Western objectivist tradition, and Aboriginal understandings of the world, which sees time and space as emerging from collective action. It entails the working together of divergent evidential and ethical systems in a "strategic cross-cultural knowledge community" (Ayre & Verran, 2010). We work in a regional university in northern Australia—Charles Darwin University (CDU)—which has worked with a range of Aboriginal people across the Northern Territory (NT) over many years to implement both-ways approaches and to document the epistemologies and practices that underpin them. In this paper we discuss our efforts to work through what enacting both-ways education means and how it can resist the ongoing suite of practices that marginalize Aboriginal ways of knowing. We will approach our discussion from the perspective of teachers and researchers interested in doing "morally responsible" work, cognizant that we are, by virtue of our positions "cognitive authorities" (Addelson, 1994). This perspective recognizes that the teacher/researcher is a participant, yet is also an agent of governance, working within institutions that make, transmit, and legitimate knowledge in our society. As we attempt to do morally responsible work we endeavor to deliberately undermine the privileging that goes along with occupying the traditional position of the researcher as a "judging observer" (Addelson, 1993, p. xi).

In order to highlight the localized and personal nature of doing both-ways education, and as a way of situating ourselves as participants, we will tell a story from a field experience to draw out some of the tensions of doing both-ways work and the ontological foundations that create them. We will show that the positioning of Aboriginal people and their knowledge as peripheral continues in the present, and that there are alternatives for practitioners that enable resisting locating Aboriginal people in the periphery. Importantly, these alternatives find their expression in the day-to-day life of doing teaching and research, rather than in changing the structures and processes of organizations. We will use stories to show how we are attempting to foreground respect for "Indigenous values, attitudes and practices" (Smith, 1999, p. 125) in our work. We argue that centering our attention on grounded and localized practice is essential for us to collectively address the ongoing marginalization of Aboriginal voices and perspectives about the role, practices, and place of education in the NT today.

Aboriginal people have lived in what we now call the NT for tens of thousands of years (Flood, 1983). Over the vast bulk of this time they have managed their affairs and the land according to their own knowledge practices. In the mid-nineteenth century Europeans started coming overland into the NT, first as explorers, and then as settlers and missionaries. Many Aboriginal groups would have first experienced sustained incursion into their land when the Overland Telegraph line was built in the early 1870s. Following this, the Pine Creek gold rush brought thousands of people south from Darwin into the interior at the same time as cattle were being walked westward from Queensland. These times saw much frontier violence, with many Aboriginal people murdered in punitive expeditions, many of which had official sanction (Aboriginal Land Commissioner, 1991; Roberts, 2009). Given that much of the country in the tropical savannah is attractive for pastoralists, more and more land was taken over for cattle rearing. These changes forced Aboriginal people to change the ways they managed their affairs and their country. For them there were no easy options, to remain on their land they had to deal with a new set of unpalatable realities. On the one hand, Aboriginal people were being killed across the frontier in retribution for acts that they may not have committed (Cribbin, 1984). On the other hand, their capacity to partake in their traditional food gathering practices was severely curtailed as their land was occupied by cattle, which fouled waterholes and damaged the habitats on which their traditional food sources depended. As a result, Aboriginal people had to find ways to survive that entailed radical change to the lives that they had been leading only a few years before.

The colonization process is predicated on moving Aboriginal people to the periphery. This "placement" is a key aspect of what Dussel (1993) calls the ongoing project of modernity, in which Europeans colonized parts of the world, justified through an expansionary myth that characterizes colonization as a service to the other. A central element of (or the myth of) modernity is the creation of a center (Europe) and a periphery (everywhere else), which, in turn, justifies colonial settlement, and the violence that goes along with it as "inevitable and necessary" aspects of development (Dussel, 1993, p. 75). The normalizing of the European perspective, and the associated displacement of Aboriginal perspectives to the periphery, has had grave impacts on Aboriginal people, their knowledge-making practices, and their ability to have their views and aspirations taken seriously. This is not an historical issue, the problems associated with the center/periphery dichotomy still afflict the NT today. In common Australian discourse the NT is still regarded as a frontier, implying that the center lies elsewhere (in this case south-eastern Australia).

In being positioned on the periphery the ongoing presence of Aboriginal people has been constructed as a problem: getting in the way of progress, without reference to the fact that they were invaded and without seeing the possibilities for creating futures in which divergent knowledge systems can function productively side by side. Of course Aboriginal people would have experienced it differently and sought to maintain connections to their land in a number of ways. They worked on the cattle stations that were built on their traditional land. They moved into the missions or compounds set up for Aboriginal people in or on the periphery of their lands or sought to retreat into marginal areas, safe from the depredations of the invaders.

Today the Northern Territory still carries the memories of the "early" days and ancestral times. The sometimes violent history of invasion and subsequent settlement still lives in the stories that people tell about themselves (Bird-Rose, 2004; Lewis, 2012; Roberts, 2009; Verran, 2013). And yet, despite the undoubted impacts of invasion, many Aboriginal people still live lives informed by their ancestral understandings of the world and continue to aspire to maintain their knowledge and practices in the present and into the future (Marika-Mununggiritj, 1999). It is in this space that we find the rationale for taking both-ways education seriously: it actively resists the practices that continue to marginalize Aboriginal perspectives. We see learning as a fundamental part of human experience, and as educators our role is to prepare ourselves and others to perform and fulfill our potential in a range of situations and a future which is uncertain. Further, following American pragmatist philosopher John Dewey, we see education as "the supreme human interest in which . . . other problems, cosmological, moral, logical, come to a head" (quoted in Hildebrand, 2008, p. 124). Education, according to this view, is a key site for the production and reproduction of culture, and thus is a site of great power in terms of creating the change we would like to see in the world. We will return to how we might understand this "we" and its role in creating change later in the chapter.

CDU is one of five Australian universities that call itself dual sector, meaning that it provides Vocational Education and Training (VET) as well as Higher Education (HE). These dual-sector universities have emerged in Australia in response to specific and local conditions; in the case of CDU it was primarily because the population within the NT at the time was not sufficient to support a stand-alone university and so offering VET enabled the university to access a larger student population (Berzins & Loveday, 1999). The training we discuss in this chapter is primarily VET (formerly known as Technical and Further Education (TAFE)), often referred to as technical training. This training operates under a competency based (CB) framework, introduced nationally in the early 1990s (Goozee, 2001), which sees the task of training as developing the competence of individuals to do particular tasks. Competence under this model is defined as "the knowledge and skill, and applications of that knowledge and skill to a standard of performance required in employment" (National Training Board, 1991, p. 7). In Australia VET training has always had a strong industry focus: training is to equip people to participate effectively in the workforce. In relation to the educational setting we discuss this is one of a number of structures that marginalize Aboriginal knowledge and practices. The VET training courses CDU conducts operate under a system of National regulation, which ensures that the courses and qualifications we provide are of equivalent quality and consistent with the same courses run elsewhere in Australia.

The national oversight that the regulator provides is designed so that potential employers can have "greater confidence in the skills and abilities of VET graduates" (Australian Skills Quality Authority, 2013). However it is acknowledged that for training to be most effective, it must be customized and contextualized for the situation and the learners who are to be engaged (Training Packages at Work, 2007). This can provide challenges for individual lecturers at an institution like CDU, which provide courses to students from diverse knowledge contexts, including Aboriginal students, many of whom speak Aboriginal languages.

The courses we focus on here are conducted off campus with Aboriginal people who are working as rangers in natural and cultural resource management on their own ancestral lands. This training takes place with numerous ranger groups who collectively are implementing a relatively new approach to managing the lands of Australia's north. This system, of Aboriginal people working in formalized groups managing their ancestral lands through using both Aboriginal and Western scientific land management strategies, began in the NT in the early 1990s. Since then it has expanded and there are now more than 90 Aboriginal ranger groups across Australia. Their success in completing qualifications and documenting their work has contributed to making the case for expanded support for this form of activity and employment.

We are thus operating at the juncture of three systems. One is the nationally accredited training system that facilitates our presence, a second is a Western system of land management based on scientific understandings of the world, and the third is an Aboriginal system of land management that has its origins in the day-to-day practices of people who have belonged to this country for thousands of years. It is our role, as professional educators, to find a way to bring these systems, and the people who inhabit them, together. As we do so we are managing a set of tensions that the interface between these systems produces. We have to be accountable to the university in terms of the rules that govern the delivery of training from the national perspective, we must seek to ensure that the training we deliver is grounded scientifically, and, we must ensure that it respects and incorporates local land management practice. We have a responsibility to contextualize the course so that it makes sense for both the audience and the location, while ensuring that it meets the national standards. The particular course we are delivering is the Certificate 2 in Conservation and Land Management. It contains more than 50 elective units covering areas such as recording and reporting information, weed identification and control, feral animal management, the operation of vehicles and tools, maintaining cultural places, and working in remote areas. Our first task is to customize the course for the needs of the group. To do this effectively requires an understanding of the aspirations, existing knowledge, and local issues of the student group, something which takes time. With this established, the lecturer and the group choose the units from the training package that address the group's needs. Having done this, the next task is to contextualize the units so that they are adapted to the group's particular circumstances. It is in this process that our both-ways process comes to life. However it is often in the process of delivery that some of the tensions associated with doing both-ways teaching are revealed.

In order to understand the nature of some of these tensions and what they mean for both-ways methodologies and practices, we will tell a story to help to tease out the different and often hidden agendas that accompany intercultural work. This is our method. We will follow the lead of Jerome Bruner (1986), who in his book, *Actual Minds Possible Worlds*, points out the critical role of narrative in world making. We will use our own version of narrative inquiry focusing on ethnography (Winthereick & Verran, 2012) and specifically ethnographies of disconcertment (Verran & Christie, 2013). Disconcertments are the places where the easy assumptions we carry around with us, hidden in the institutional structures and practices of our work, rub up against, abrade, and spark off Indigenous systems of governance and engagement alive and vibrant on the ground where we work. Our method entails using stories to open up space for dialogues around meaning, a critical focus in respectful intercultural work. As we tell this story we focus upon those moments when we were learning, in good faith, some sometimes painful lessons of engagement from our Aboriginal colleagues.

In the story that follows the lead author (using pseudonyms) tells of a bush trip to deliver some training. We then describe the ways in which working openly with Aboriginal students and their elders, we came to discern some of the hidden assumptions in the ways that we approach our work, and how bringing them to life enables us to learn more about what it means to do both-ways education.

> I'm heading south down the Stuart Highway for the week to deliver training to the relatively new Aboriginal Ranger group, the Wagiman Rangers, on their land out on the upper Daly River, about 250km south of Darwin. The university vehicle is loaded up with enrolment forms, course documents, GPS units and maps, my swag, tent, esky and a bag of clothes.
>
> After picking people up in Pine Creek, one of the early settlements in the NT, and a site of frontier violence, we drive through to the Daly. We arrive at Claravale Crossing in the late afternoon, and I approach Left-hand, the old man coordinating the group (and father or uncle to most of them). He has a few things he wants to get done this week. It is my practice, when working with people on their own country, to fit my teaching in

with the on-ground work that people are doing. Left-hand says that one of the things he'd like us all to do is to travel north through country still under a land claim to check out a story he's heard about clearing that might be taking place. Being a traditional owner for this country means that he feels a sense of responsibility to understand what is going on as he may be 'called into action' should he feel that his country is being damaged. The other is to continue with burning around the Ah San block, where we are currently staying. This is a traditional land management activity that 'cleans up the country' following the monsoon as well as creating 'green pick' for animals to graze upon. Tuesday morning, after breakfast we head off to do some burning. We light a series of small fires on the side of a track which burn their way slowly back to it before going out. It is the perfect weather for it: the grass is dry, but not too dry, the wind is light and the day is warm. As we go along I ask questions related to the curriculum content when they seem relevant. In doing this we learn from each other as we build an intercultural picture of burning and its role in managing the landscape. Back at camp I pull out my curriculum documents and go through them. I am making connections between what we have done, and the elements of competency contained in the curriculum. I tick off those we have covered. One of my ongoing tasks is to talk about what the curriculum says we are "supposed" to do, and show back at the uni [university] how what we've done meets the criteria. Upon returning to the camp we talk as a group with Left-hand about what we've done and what we should do tomorrow. Everyone is keen on heading up to the north a little way where we could do some more burning while also looking for the land clearing that Left-hand had heard about. We decide that heading north is what we'll do. Wednesday morning is cool and crisp. I sit back in my camping chair and look over some of the elements of competency for the unit 'Undertake traditional burning practices.' As I drink my coffee I look over at the main camp and expect to see everyone doing what they always do: drinking tea, moseying about, talking with each other. And they sort of are, though I have a sense that something is going on which is out of the ordinary. It is not that they are not doing these things, it is just that they are somehow doing them differently; rather than talking as they normally do they seem to be hanging about, looking into the distance or into their cup of tea. Whatever it is it doesn't seem like it is serious, but it is out of the ordinary.

All of a sudden it starts to make some kind of sense as Samuel comes over. He is a young man, one of Left-hand and Doris's sons. He explains that Doris needs to go into Pine Creek to get some more food, and that as I have the only vehicle I am the one who needs to take her. But, I think to myself, 'if we do this we can't go up north like we'd planned.' I do not know what to say; to go on a shop run would be so clearly not part of university business. Thoughts run through my mind: shop runs are not part of my work program; it will cost another $100 in fuel; taking Doris means I won't be doing what I should be doing; but there is no way I can refuse to take Doris because no-one will do anything until this problem is satisfactorily dealt with (which means taking her to Pine Creek); Doris should not be going in the university vehicle as she is not a student and therefore may not be covered by the university's insurance policy.

'I'll have to think about it,' I say, and with that Samuel walks away to report back to the group. I stand in a state of suspended animation. I feel like I don't have much time to for-mulate a response. Yet I know that I need some time. I know I am being watched and my not answering is being observed and reflected upon. Looking at them makes me think they are uncomfortable too. They know I could say no, but they must also realise that I'd have to break some rules to say yes. Either way I have to make a choice, and break some rules, and I have a sense that the choice I make will determine to a huge degree the nature of our ongoing training relationship.

On the surface this story looks like it is about an incident that intrudes into the otherwise relatively smooth running of a training program. And it is, however this "otherwise smooth running" depends on the pedagogical choices that allow the training to fit in the ongoing life of the community in which it finds itself. Further, the disconcerting incident, which enables even deeper analysis of both-ways education, may have been produced by the success of this approach. In the following paragraphs we will outline two of these pedagogical choices and the reasons behind them. This analysis allows us to read this story as one not simply about the delivery of training, but of how training becomes useful to us, both individually and collectively.

Finally, in analyzing the incident we can start to see what it takes to really center Aboriginal ways of knowing and doing in our pedagogy, and the reasons for doing so. We see this process of working collaboratively examining the disconcertments in our everyday cross-cultural engagements as a move toward the decolonization of academic research in Northern Australia (see Verran & Christie, 2013).

The first pedagogical choice that is made is the deliberate negotiation with the community elder. There are a couple of reasons why such a process is important. The first is that presenting training as the delivery of pre-packaged goods, the form and content of which is decided off site, would be at odds with how Aboriginal people conceptualize knowledge making (Campbell, 2007). This point is articulated by Marika, Yunupingu, Marika-Mununggiritj & Muller (2009): "when people come to our community to work with us they often come with ready-made ideas. These ideas may have valuable nourishing components in them but we need time, as a community, to mould these ideas into our own context" (p. 407). Respectful negotiation is critical to working productively with Aboriginal people in knowledge-making contexts. It is important to place oneself in such a context as a participant, with an agenda, but not as the sole arbiter of what counts. Recognizing our own agenda, and positioning it as one ingredient among many in the knowledge making process can be difficult for educators, who see their role as to teach those who need to know. Indeed it is difficult to reconcile this position with that required by the university that permits our presence as educators in the first place. If we are not there to teach the units from the curriculum to enrolled students, then why are we being paid? We would argue that we are seeking to do what Marika et al. (2009) implore us to do: to contribute our knowledge in such a way that it supports community life. To work in such a way is difficult, as it belies our Western ways of understanding how knowledge is produced. For the purposes of this context though, it is a necessity that allows us to work together effectively and without which an ongoing and deepening relationship would not be able to occur.

Approaching community elders with the specific intention of negotiating also demonstrates respect for the ongoing work and traditional authority that surrounds the training program. Any community in which training or research is undertaken has an ongoing life that exists outside of that teaching or research. To show respect for that life, by seeking to understand it and to connect to it, is seen by Aboriginal cultural authorities as respectful and appropriate practice (Gaykamaŋu et al., 2008). In this particular case it is even more important, given that the work that we seek to do is built on the fact that they and their ancestors have been living on and caring for this country using their own knowledge and practices for tens of thousands of years. Indeed, scientists have more to learn from Aboriginal authorities about fire ecology than vice versa.

The second pedagogical choice is to let the work lead the training. Rather than laying out training content as like a recipe, we deliberately let the work take precedence. Our role then is not to say "you need to know this, this and this" but to connect their ongoing work with the curriculum. Our experience has shown us that this is a much more effective way of approaching training, not just in terms of covering content, but also in terms of making the training relevant in the ongoing work that people are involved in. Letting the work lead the training is a way of enacting both-ways education, in that it asks us (and the tools and concepts we use) to arrange ourselves around the ongoing production of Aboriginal knowledge in place. As we develop pedagogical practices that respect Aboriginal knowledge making we must take on board all that it entails—ethics, cognitive authority, evidential practices, and the assessments of truth claims. In this way we are actively resisting those centering/normalizing processes which relegate Aboriginal ways of knowing and doing to the periphery. This resistance is, however, characterized by privileging the present moment, acknowledging the unique constellation of the participants assembled, rather than the more common understanding of resistance against the structures of (in this case) the university. As a result each training episode is an opportunity for us to rethink the work that we do. Centering ourselves on Aboriginal ways of knowing and doing however is not a move to simple relativism. Rather we see the activities, in this particular case burning, acting as "boundary objects" (Star & Griesemer, 1989) allowing us to create new, situated knowledge together that is not reductive or assimilative.

We now want to move to the disconcerting incident and reflect on what it means to do both-ways education. The request to transport a non-student to town (a round trip of 150km) was thoroughly discomfiting. In terms of our professional practice, we had already made a series of changes to accommodate and integrate the alternative knowledge production practices of the people we were working with. We assumed that as we were doing this work in good faith we would not be thrown by the things that emerged. What this incident made us see is that we had still been carrying a range of assumptions about the work that we were doing together. We assumed that there was a neat and uncomplicated separation between us (as members of the university) and them (as members of their own Aboriginal group). The incident revealed that they did not see us as we saw ourselves.

To us there was university business and other business, to them there was just the business of getting on with what needed to be done in the here-and-now. In addition it helped us to see that the categories that we were working with, and which allowed us to make sense of what we were doing, were not shared categories. We are thus awakened to the possibility of seeing the work we do together differently through engaging more deeply in the meaning of our collective work.

Part of our disconcertment had to do with a conflict around what it means to do the job "properly." As indicated at the beginning of this chapter there are a range of tensions inherent in the context in which we work. It is in the sorting through these tensions that doing the job "properly" comes to life. As noted previously, one of the assumptions we had carried with us was that we (as educators) were separate entities from the Aboriginal group we were working with. All of a sudden we were being cast in a different light by the people we were with. We and our university vehicle were participants in the life of the place; the separations that we had assumed were not shared. As a result, we began to see that, therefore, what the job entailed could equally be renegotiated on the basis of our situation together. Entities such as the university and systems of national regulation were still critical participants, but their role needed to be negotiated in the here-and-now if we were able to create ongoing viability. We have no doubt that had we said "no" to the request that our training relationship would have changed considerably, and not for the better. Each of the young students would have felt a moral conflict, and a need to reconsider their commitment to the training. As it was we chose to position ourselves as participants in the group, and not as outsiders coming in as judging observers. This changed the nature of our work together. As a result we are led to see doing both-ways education in a new light. Developing appropriate pedagogical practices collaboratively is critical for the conduct of respectful and productive training. This requires reconceptualizing how curriculum materials and ideas from outside are made useful in training contexts. It also requires rethinking how educators and students relate to each other. The notion of the teacher as the one who knows and the students as those who need to know must be replaced— a difficult process in light of how teachers are trained and curricula are developed and disseminated. Second, it requires a fundamental shift in how we envision ourselves. Rather than seeing ourselves as standing outside the groups we come to work with, we need to see ourselves as participants in collective action, in which our identities, the meaning of our work, and the meanings of the entities which participate, emerge. In this way we can rethink what it means to do our work responsibly. As cognitive authorities

working in knowledge making institutions we have a vital role in addressing the marginalization of Indigenous ways of knowing and being in the
day-to-day acts in which we participate.

In the end I do say yes and a group of us, including Doris,
drive into Pine Creek. We gain some flour and lamb chops, and
through it all learn a little more about what it takes to go on
with each other respectfully and productively.

References

Aboriginal Land Commissioner. (1991). *Aboriginal Land Rights (Northern Territory)
Act 1976 UPPER DALY LAND CLAIM.* Canberra, ACT: Commonwealth
of Australia.

Addelson, K. P. (1993). Knowers/Doers and their moral problems. In L. Alcoff
& E. Potter (Eds.), *Feminist epistemologies* (pp. 265–301). New York, NY:
Routledge.

———. (1994). *Moral passages: Toward a collectivist moral theory.* New York, NY:
Routledge.

Australian Skills Quality Authority. (2013). *National VET regulation.* Retrieved on
26/05/2013 from http://www.asqa.gov.au/about-asqa/national-vet-regulation/
national-vet-regulation.html.

Ayre, M., & Verran, H. (2010). Managing ontological tensions in learning to be
an Aboriginal Ranger: inductions into a strategic cross-cultural knowledge
community. *Learning Communities: International Journal of Learning in Social
Contexts, 1,* 2–18.

Berzins, B., & Loveday, P. (1999) *A University for the Territory: The Northern Territory
University and preceding institutions 1949–1999.* Darwin, NT: Northern
Territory University Press.

Bird-Rose, D. (2004). *Reports from a wild country: Ethics for decolonisation.* Sydney,
NSW: UNSW Press.

Bruner, J. (1986). *Actual minds, possible worlds.* Boston, MA: Harvard University
Press.

Campbell, M. (2007). Process and accountability in University engagement with
Indigenous communities. *Australasian Journal of University Community
Engagement, 2*(1), 166–173.

Cribbin, J. (1984). *The killing times.* Sydney, NSW: Fontana/Collins.

Dussel, E. (1993). Eurocentrism and Modernity (Introduction to the Frankfurt
Lectures). *Boundary 2, 20*(3), 65–76. doi: 10.2307/303341.

Flood, J. (1983). *Archaeology of the dreamtime.* Sydney, NSW: Collins.

Gaykamaŋu, W., Guthadjaka, K., Gurruwiwi, D., Lawurrpa, E., Garŋgulkpuy,
J., Dunbar, T., & Gumbula, M. (2008). Respect. In M. Campbell &

M. Christie (Eds.), *Indigenous community engagement at Charles Darwin University* (pp. 28–30). Darwin, NT: Uniprint NT.

Goozee, G. (2001). *The development of TAFE in Australia*. Leabrook, SA: National Centre for Vocational Education Research.

Hildebrand, D. L. (2008). *Dewey: A beginners guide*. Oxford: Oneworld Publications.

Lewis, D. (2012). *A wild history*. Clayton, VIC: Monash University Publishing.

Marika-Mununggiritj, R. (1999). The 1998 Wentworth Lecture. *Australian Aboriginal Studies, 1*, 3–9.

Marika, R., Yunupingu, Y., Marika-Mununggiritj, R., & Muller, S. (2009). Leaching the poison: The importance of process and partnership in working with Yolngu. *Journal of Rural Studies, 25*(4), 404–413.

National Training Board. (1991). *National competency standards—Policy and guidelines*. Fyshwick, ACT: National Training Board.

Roberts, T. (2009). The brutal truth: What happened in the Gulf country. *The Monthly* Retrieved from http://www.themonthly.com.au/files/Roberts-References.pdf.

Winthereick, B. R., & Verran, H. (2012). Ethnographic stories as generalizations that intervene. *Science Studies, 25*(1), 37–51.

Smith, L. T. (1999). *Decolonising methodologies: Research and Indigenous peoples*. Dunedin: University of Otago Press.

Star, S. L., & Griesemer, J. R. (1989). Institutional ecology, 'translations' and boundary objects: Amateurs and professionals in Berkeley's museum of vertebrate zoology, 1907–39. *Social Studies of Science, 19*(3), 387–420. doi: 10.2307/285080.

Training Packages at Work. (2007). *Contextualisation and packaging of training packages*. Retrieved from http://www.ymcatraining.org.au/coursedocs/training/back2basics/db2_contextualisati.htm.

Verran, H. (2013). The dead as participants: Challenged by the Yolŋu Aboriginal child learner at Gäŋgaŋ. *Learning Communities: International Journal of Learning in Social Contexts, 12*(April 2013), 35–39.

Verran, H., & Christie, M. (2013). The generative role of narrative in ethnographies of disconcernment: social scientists participating in the public problems of north Australia. *Learning Communities: International Journal of Learning in Social Contexts, 12*(April 2013), 51–57.

10

Vocational Teacher Education in Australia and the Problem of Racialized Hope

Sue Shore

Cultural studies and critical race theorists, as well as feminist, postcolonial, and Indigenous scholars provide compelling evidence that workplaces are imbued with normative assumptions of whiteness (Larkin, 2013; Morrison, 1992; Shore, 2010). Nevertheless, vocational education and training (VET) systems around the world continue to promote the view that disadvantaged young people, displaced workers, refugees, women returning to work after a period of childbirth, and stigmatized minorities, should sign up for training as an investment in their own and their family's future. The underlying logic is that training will provide a way out of the hand-to-mouth existence many marginalized people experience. Such thinking has some basis in evidence, yet it also reinforces the idea that training will overcome proven barriers to gaining and retaining employment—institutionalized bigotry, prejudice, stereotyping, and intolerance. From this perspective, more complex under-standings of the concept of hope are important for contemporary educators if they are to engage the normative assumptions about racialized difference and productivity underpinning Australia's national training system.

Following Frankenberg (1993) this chapter approaches the process of knowing a training system, and therefore being in a position to disrupt it, by "thinking through race": a "conscious process" that occurs within an "already constituted field of racialized relations, material and conceptual" and begins from the premise that we are all "racially positioned in society" (p. 142). I draw on a body of literature that understands whiteness as a transnational racial identification (Lake & Reynolds, 2008) and which has been central to, but not explicitly articulated in, theory-building practices about education over time (Said, 1993; Stoler, 1995). This literature offers theoretical tools that unsettle the notion of target groups and minority categories as the only reference points for funding decisions about improved economic and social opportunity (Shore, 2001). The discussion in this chapter is focused on the experiences of *educators* who design and facilitate programs to improve social and economic opportunity. I provide the background to a course (hereafter called EDUC3043) and an investigation of the participants' responses to a collection of readings about whiteness and diversity designed to prompt a rethinking of the relations between the mundane and everyday practices of learning and work and the re-invigoration of colonial norms of protean white capability (Shore, 2010; Stoler, 1995). While many argue that these norms have long since disappeared from contemporary workplaces, it is the argument of this chapter that those norms still form the primary reference points for present-day VET provision.

Tackling Whiteness Head On

Over the past 25 years as elsewhere, the Australian VET system has been progressively restructured from a diverse conglomerate of public and private training organizations and varied non-government organization (NGO) and social movement endeavors to a highly regulated system of registered public and private enterprises that provide nationally accredited training. Sector funding and training priorities are linked to "preparation for work" schemes designed to reduce government welfare expenditure for the unemployed, those on disability allowances, and single-parent payments. Program funding priorities and student targets can change in an instant in response to reforms addressing events as diverse as car industry closures (Kelton & Henderson, 2008; Martin & King, 2013), environmental havoc and subsequent destabilization of whole industries (housing, retail, tourism, and hospitality) in places like New Orleans and Queensland (Australia), and the financial crisis known as "the GFC," which impacted millions around the world. In these circumstances Hage (in Zournazi with Hage, 2002) reminds us that VET acts as a source of (dishonest) hope intimately linked to the enduring "logic of capitalism" underpinning western notions of work: "you suffer now in the hope you might enjoy later without this enjoyment ever really arriving" (p. 151). While "suffering" through training programs might generate employment opportunities, the implicit articulations between hope perseverance and secured economic stability are rarely interrogated in the context of ingrained racialized and gendered practices in education and at work. This is an issue particularly relevant to this chapter given that white capability has historically underpinned notions of productive workers and employable citizens (Stoler, 1995).

Such issues present myriad challenges for VET educators and teacher educators, made more complex by the ever-present restructuring and review associated with the Australian VET system. For example, Australian researchers acknowledge the dearth of research available to theorize even the most fundamental of concepts associated with vocational pedagogy and curriculum knowledge (Wheelahan & Curtin, 2010). Nevertheless, the national system has long resisted any substantive role for university qualifications in preparing vocational trainers. Contemporary research has begun to address the tendencies to reproduce whiteness through employment and training structures and processes (Larkin 2013; Shore, 2010), yet these ideas are far from having a substantive influence on policy. As Edward Said (2005, p. 223) argues, "[t]he great problem in essentially administered societies, the Western democracies, is precisely the drowning out of the critical sense."

In the context of this chapter and its aim of knowing a training system in order to engage in disrupting it, suppression of critical contestation converges with two aspects of adult learning that have become second nature in describing appropriate conduct for this field. First, normative theories of adult learning manifest in a set of reference points that define best practice and simultaneously authorize the theories and pedagogical practices most relevant to training. This is achieved by grounding adult learning practices in the following reference points: promoting transparent self-awareness and self-direction; emphasizing individual experience, indeed often valorizing that at the expense of the collective; focusing on immediate and everyday situations in which adults find themselves and a corresponding tendency to sideline the role of history in constituting the present; validating reflection as a process which produces transparent knowledge about the self and one's experiences; demanding clear accessible writing as the default position for any useful knowledge and theory; and endorsing perseverance as a requirement for progress (Shore, 2004). These reference points have some merit, but they sit uneasily with the naming practices that organize responses to disadvantage within VET (minority categories and target groups), while remaining largely silent on the assumptions about whiteness that circumscribe corresponding ideals of productive citizenry (Shore, 2010; Stoler, 1995).

In this chapter the counterhegemonic activism in which educators might engage has a particular focus: how they navigate ostensibly invisible acts of racialized amnesia that may implicate them in the dominating practices they seek to unsettle. The argument underpinning this chapter is that such acts are *not* invisible, *not* hard to trace, *not* hard to access at all if one has access to theoretical tools that disrupt the normative reference points that define what counts as adult learning. The challenge is in engaging with this supposed invisibility in ways that support educators while being simultaneously aware of the potential for complicity with the racializing practices one intends to disrupt.

The pedagogy I invoked in EDUC3043 was premised on learning to recognize writing and speaking patterns that appeared, on the surface at least, to operate in racially neutral zones. Informed by Said's (1993) notion of contrapuntal readings, the course aimed not only to bring into focus the comprehensively racialized social structure of work and training (Larkin, 2013; Morrison, 1992; Shore, 2010) but also to provide a "toolkit" of theoretical ideas to assist educators in that work. A contrapuntal approach includes examining research texts, policy, and curriculum documents and teaching resources for traces that constitute VET as we know it (Shore & Butler, 2012) and simultaneously highlighting instances of the selective forgetting embedded in educational theory building. This approach differs from pedagogies that "read against the grain" of the mainstream project of VET (for example critical pedagogy) or one that focuses on the experiences of marginalized groups within a training system. Rather, one function of contrapuntal pedagogy is "bibliographical": "to provide alternatives: alternative sources, alternative readings, alternative presentation of evidence" (Said, 2005, 222). This "polyphony" of perspectives fosters an understanding of the racialized intertwining of past, present, and future relations of knowing and being. When one reads VET contrapuntally it is difficult to deny the historical conflation of "being human" and "being white" (Morrison, 1992; Shore, 2010; Stoler, 1995) which has been illustrated in a range of other disciplines.

In the remaining sections of this chapter I briefly outline the decisions involved in designing the course and the data collection strategies I used to access educators' responses to tackling whiteness head on. I then offer a reading of their responses in the context of tensions the educators faced as they engaged with ideas that were often at odds with reference points they encountered in other parts of their university program as well as in their professional and personal lives.

Assembling Alternative Readings and Producing Data with Participants

EDUC3043 was a required course in a 3-year teacher education program for Australian VET educators. As the Course Coordinator I chose readings that prompted students to think about the theory-building practices underpinning their vocational work. Students were introduced to a conceptual toolkit that unsettled the above noted reference points that marked adult education and hence VET as a knowable field of practice (Shore & Butler, 2012). The toolkit drew on Raymond William's (1977, p. 132) notion of "structures of feeling" and Mansfield's (2000) discussion of theories of the self, including understanding *sociality* beyond the fixed identity categories commonly used to name the target groups and structures that addressed disadvantage or promoted equity in VET. The toolkit included an introduction to the notion of whiteness in education (Durie, 1999; McKinney, 2004) and the manifestation of educational sites as "white public spaces" (Hartigan, 1997). Second, the course encouraged students to *explore* what was going on in their education settings in local and specific ways. Rather than use the above concepts to *specify* the impact of whiteness in an organization or program, students were encouraged to think contextually about the contours of whiteness at work—in Australia, in the VET system, within their particular occupational field in that system, within the context of their role in an organization—as they also learned to look for enduring similarities and differences with overseas studies. Third, students were encouraged to try out selected concepts from their growing toolkit, not with their students, but in relation to their particular politics of transformation when working with marginalized workers and learners.

While enrolment in the course was a required part of their program, participation in the research about their learning was voluntary. Students were contacted about the research project via a generic letter of invitation from the Head of School, at least one semester or more after receiving their final results for the unit (Ethics Protocol P147/06). If they wanted to participate they contacted me direct. I negotiated use of their data including: anonymous URL responses canvassing thoughts at the beginning and mid-point of the course; course evaluation surveys; case studies produced for assignments and transcripts of semi-structured interviews conducted after they had completed the course. The purpose of this array of data was to access both self-identified and anonymous responses about a course that, in essence, challenged the reference points of adult learning presented in other courses in the program. Any student who had failed the course was not eligible to participate in the project until he or she had completed all requirements in a subsequent enrolment.

Learning to See Whiteness

For many students, this was their first attempt to explicitly articulate the racialized character of their Australian lives, so it was not surprising that some experienced it as something of an epiphany (McKinney, 2004). Reflections on childhood played a significant part in how and at which point in their lives students reflected on their lives as racialized.

> When I was younger I really did not think about whiteness very much but as I have got older and have been mostly teaching [I]ndigenous students and found out how 'white' all teaching textbooks and reading material are I have had to think about this subject a lot.

Despite enduring commentary in research literature that whiteness is invisible, the above survey response illustrates whiteness at work in some Australian childhoods. For one of the students, thinking through childhood via contrapuntal readings linked an "absent presence," blackness (Morrison, 1992)—discussed in the course and presented as an exemplar of the default category of the white citizen informing Australian VET policy—with the absent presence of Indigenous voices in school texts and curriculum texts that selectively exclude the details of Australia's violent settler history. For another student, looking back through a contrapuntal lens prompted memories of friendships and the presence of Aboriginal friends in his early life.

> Growing up in [X] . . . I was shielded from the [I]ndigenous community at a young age. Once I got [to] high school and started playing football and associating with many Aboriginal boys I made friends with them easily.

The above excerpt positions as normative, parenting practices designed to control and shield (white) children from influences deemed undesirable. Students in the course could often recognize the contradictions in the contrapuntal readings through which they were reading their personal and professional lives but were often stuck when they thought they had to reconcile these incommensurable logics. "Being white" meant, as one survey respondent suggested, "a particular emphasis on Anglo English, not so much in skin color but in social, political, and legal viewpoints of the world." Another also remarked on the connection with Anglo practices, but also noted the disconnect they experienced between knowing that notions of whiteness extended beyond surface connections to British heritage or skin color but reverting to skin as the default option despite knowing differently: "[it] seems crazy and not logical at all but this is the first picture in my head when faced with 'being white.'" What *seems* crazy, "not logical," is in part the whole purpose of reading contrapuntally, not simply for the purpose of being exposed to alternative readings and resources, but also to experience the dissonance that exposure creates in the natural order of (logical) thought.

While a number of students were unsettled but persevered with the alternatives, there were ample times when students rejected outright the theoretical toolkit provided in the course. When asked what whiteness meant, one common line of response was that these alternative sources, readings, and presentations of evidence (cf Said 2005) were "irrelevant" to their work, or in another student's words not meriting a stand-alone course: "I did not think it needed to be its own course—just on whiteness." This latter line of responses is important to address as it aligns with the reference points of relevance and immediacy promoted as important pedagogical principles in adult learning literature. But these responses also reflect the agentic force of whiteness on curriculum decisions that determine what counts as relevant and how much time should be spent on that across the curriculum.

Rather than pursue this explicit issue of resistance, I now want to direct attention to an issue more closely aligned with the challenge of supporting educators to disrupt certain racialized logics in everyday practice, even as they may also be unwittingly involved in the re-invigoration of colonial norms of protean white capability.

Alternative Reading: Alternative Listening

While many of the VET educators in this study *could* see whiteness at work in their childhood, it was nevertheless challenging to deploy the theoretical tools they encountered in EDUC3043 although some writers were helpful in this regard. As one student reflected, reading McKinney (2004) "was probably my first experience where I became conscious of whiteness. It was at this moment that I gained a new understanding of race." For another it was reading Ruth Frankenberg via Australian researcher Jane Durie's (1999) work:

Ruth Frankenberg's quote in Durie provides [my] epiphany—'as a white person I needed only to write about racism, rather than experiencing it in any other way. And even if I could not do that I would not die of that failure.'

EDUC3043 was not intended as (racial) therapy for white folk. I actively discouraged personal storytelling, primarily because I considered that students had ample opportunities to experience those pedagogies in other units. In addition, I had seen firsthand how the sharing of personally challenging events experienced by self-identified white folk often triggered expressions of sympathy (or empathy) within a group, precipitating a range of strategies designed to reduce discomfort for the (often but not always white) storyteller and simultaneously stall the momentum to confront the effects of whiteness head on. I found the storytelling genre tended to reinforce the reference points of adult learning noted previously and, in so doing, placed primary emphasis on the alleviation of discomfort at the expense of how a periphery is constituted as always and already requiring help, support, guidance, and transformation.

As is often the case though, educators and researchers can be tripped up by our pre-existing beliefs when we least expect it. And this was what happened to me when I read the following excerpt from a case study prepared for a course assignment by "Alana" (pseudonym), a self-identified white woman:

As a single parent I felt isolated and disadvantaged. . . . I enrolled in personal development classes that focused on relationships with others, particularly on communication skills, parenting skills, conflict resolution and team building. I ran with this newfound knowledge and felt more confident with my new skills. I felt as though I was equipped to face the world with a language that many people spoke but had somehow evaded me, my own working class 'communities of practice' [cf Paechter, 2003] did not include this systematic way of relating and communicating with others. I set out then to broaden my horizons and enroll in TAFE and then University. My focus and intention was to learn the skills I needed to be an adult educator so I too could 'make a difference' and support other single parents to find their voice and give them the opportunities to 'fit' in the world, so they too could feel as empowered as I had felt.

What I realize now is that I was being primed and empowered into a possessive investment in whiteness. I was learning to 'whitespeak' (Moon, 1999) learning the 'nice' middle class skills of being white, these skills giving me a language and position in society that I had never had before. I had always been told I was a bright kid, but University was never a topic discussed in my family as I am the first to go to university and have found the process very difficult at times. I was not privy to the social norms that many of my middle class peers had experienced. I was becoming empowered into 'whiteness,' I could pass as white, I was smart and keen to make a future for my children and myself, I no longer wanted to survive on the 'welfare merry go round' for the rest of my life. I was aspiring to the middle classes without being aware or conscious of the process.

Paradoxically, this case study exemplifies the personally empowering storytelling I sought to avoid. Yet the assignment provided precisely the opportunity for Alana to think through her entry into VET employment in a way that surfaced the racialized character of her "second chance" at education and the contribution whiteness made to activating that pathway to her empowerment.

Other students expressed similar experiences with respect to what VET employment had made available to them. Rick, Jessica, Chris, Jenny, and Ken (all pseudonyms) never expected to find themselves at university. They had enrolled after many years of employment in industries as diverse as hospitality, business studies, manufacturing, or time as a social movement activist. If in recognized occupations such as the former, they wanted to continue passing on their occupational knowledge to others. If involved in social movement activism, for the most part they intended to continue their activist work.

Their employment conditions within the VET sector were often aligned with casual and noncontinuing contracts, yet also caught up in the mandatory certification requirements of the sector and the corresponding fee payments. It should be noted that maintaining certification was no guarantee of employment security, nor was completing the degree for which they were enrolled since the sector remained ambivalent about the value of university qualifications (cf Wheelahan & Curtin 2010).

Each participant in his or her own way also expressed the associated pressures adult learners experience: family responsibilities; casual and unpredictable employment; underemployed or in contrast expected to work far beyond the allocated hours of their weekly contracts with few opportunities for time in lieu. Few participants had a prior degree, however, following a longstanding Australian practice, each could access generous prior learning arrangements that recognized their occupational experience (Shore, 1998). Paradoxically, this simultaneously hampered their preparation for university by granting credit for prerequisite courses which may have explicitly developed the academic skills they required in the later years of the program.

As mature-aged educators with responsibilities, the participants in this study were very "time poor," they struggled with online learning and experienced dissonance between the academic expectations of their occupation and the contrapuntal "thinking" required by EDUC3043. For many their employment required wholesale acceptance of market forces as the primary driver for "delivering" learning. In this industrial and professional milieu students remarked in surveys and evaluations that the readings were difficult.

> There were just too many difficult concepts to get your head around too quickly. I don't think that this course should be run offline—it is too hard to monitor your progress.

> The readings are heavy, and I needed more time to process this invaluable theory. Workload exceptionally high for a 4.5 subject. Needs to be run over 2 semesters so as to process the concepts and it NEEDS to be a 9 point subject. Many of the readings needed to be re-read many times due to their 'heavy nature.'

> I appreciated having my eyes opened to this topic, but it is so huge that the amount of time given didn't equate to 4.5 units. The readings were often difficult to understand until read and re-read many many times.

Besides the discomfort and the sheer challenge of time available to do the work, some students wanted to remind me that they did not belong to the imaginary well-resourced, stable, financially secure, well skilled, employed center.

> Don't assume that we all have easy and free access to the internet—yes we could use the computer pool at the uni but we are externals for a reason and may have difficulty accessing this resource. For example my employer although [with] a strong

> computer focus does not supply internet access to staff and once
> I have worked 8–10 hours a day driving for an hour to get to
> the Uni pods is just too too hard.

Students reiterated that "thinking" was not part of their daily work and that this feature of the course, combined with its emphasis on racialized lives was unreasonably arduous. They felt like they, too, were on the periphery of Australia's economic system and white privilege did not always seem to accurately describe their experiences as VET educators and as adult learners. In survey responses and course evaluations a particular form of justification for not engaging emerged. At first glance it was not apparent that there was a link to the work of this chapter: understanding the responses educators have to a collection of readings that brings into sharp focus their profession's culpability in remaining largely silent about racialized manifestations of structural and systemic inequality at play in employment and training practices. The pedagogical approach adopted in this course provided a space for students to read their life through the overlapping and interdependent histories that constituted their VET pedagogies. In turn this prompted some to see how they might unwittingly be involved in distributing uneven discourses of hope that further reinscribed long-standing employment disparities. Others, though, were clear that this was not their responsibility or that it was difficult to take up these issues because they had more pressing and immediate concerns. Not many actually saw the paradox associated with how they positioned themselves in order to make the choice to *not* address the inequalities present in the training system—inequalities they may also be unwittingly perpetuating—by *not* reading their way through these more arduous and confronting bibliographical resources.

No Neat Closure

The assumption running across the work of researchers such as Aileen Moreton-Robinson, Edward Said, Ann Stoler, Ghassan Hage, and my own studies of vocational education and training is that storytelling practices, if they are to avoid a self-indulgent practice of how difficult it is to be white these days, must come to terms with the intertwining of economic and social hope as racialized constructs in those storytelling texts.

EDUC3043 did not offer one way of engaging with these issues, nor did it offer specific solutions to intractable pedagogical moments in vocational classrooms or at family dinner tables. In fact, one aim was to disrupt the belief that such courses would provide students with a readymade skills package to deliver learning in the complicated circumstances in which they taught. In addition, the course promoted the idea of thinking VET *through* the lens of racialized theory building in order to see how ostensibly intangible and invisible practices of racialization continue to produce VET literature and experiences that deny the effects of whiteness in the making of VET. The contrapuntal pedagogy adopted in EDUC3043 should not be misconstrued as a pedagogy that offered no answers, no solutions, no options, no closure. It was premised on the view that whiteness, as an enduring and visible discourse associated with work, employability, and civil society, has much to say about the kind of teacher education required to prepare people for a world of work and life that is always-already racialized (Larkin, 2013; Morrison, 1992; Shore, 2010). Such a pedagogy has no neat closure. Nor should it if it is to also grapple with the dynamics of protean whiteness as it manifests in the gendered, sexualized, able-ist, and classed sites of production of occupational knowledge.

In this course some of the VET educators, as students, felt "released to explore" while others felt "shut down," coerced into a course not of their own making or drawn down a path that was irrelevant to *their* occupational needs. The contrapuntal pedagogy underpinning EDUC3043 involved foregrounding the racialized repertoires that shape how marginalized workers and learners hope for and achieve a secure future, given the racialized logics of capitalism within which they work, and what educators might need to do to respond to their complicity with those repertoires and logics.

Acknowledgments

My thanks to the students who took the course and to those who participated in the study. It is a rare gift to be able to learn with educators who engage (albeit not always happily or easily) in university study and then have them return to participate in a research project about that learning.

References

Durie, J. (1999). Naming whiteness in different locations. In B. McKay (Ed.), *Unmasking whiteness: Race relations and reconciliation* (pp. 147–160). Griffith University, Queensland: The Queensland Studies Centre.

Frankenberg, R. (1993). *The social construction of whiteness: White women, race matters*. London, UK and New York, NY: Routledge.

Hartigan, J. (1997). Establishing the fact of whiteness. *American Anthropologist, 99*(3), 495–505.

Kelton, G., & Henderson, N. (2008, February 05). $50m Mitsubishi support package as Adelaide management shuts factory. *The Advertiser Adelaide Now.* Retrieved from http://www.adelaidenow.com.au/news/our-decision-to-close/story-e6freo8c-1111115472177.

Lake, M., & Reynolds, H. (2008). *Drawing the global colour line: White men's countries and the question of racial equality.* Carlton, VIC: Melbourne University Press.

Larkin, S. L. (2013) *Race matters: Indigenous employment in the Australian Public Service* (Doctoral Dissertation). Queensland University of Technology, Brisbane, Australia.

Mansfield, N. (2000). *Subjectivity: Theories of the self from Freud to Haraway.* St. Leonards, NSW: Allen & Unwin.

Martin, S., & King, P. (2013, December 07). Detroit decides: Holden will close. *The Australian.* Retrieved from http://www.theaustralian.com.au/business/detroit-decides-holden-will-close/story.

Moon, D. (1999). White enculturation and bourgeois ideology: The discursive production of "good (white) girls." In T. K. Nakayama & J. N. Martin (Eds.), *Whiteness: The communication of social identity* (pp. 177–197). London, UK: Sage.

McKinney, K. D. (2004). *Being white: stories of race and racism.* New York, NY: Routledge.

Moreton-Robinson, A. (2000). *Talkin' up to the white woman: Indigenous women and feminism.* St. Lucia, Queensland: University of Queensland Press.

Morrison, T. (1992). *Playing in the dark: Whiteness and the literary imagination.* Cambridge, MA: Harvard University Press.

Paechter, C. (2003). Masculinities and femininities as communities of practice. *Women's Studies International Forum, 26*(1), 69–77. doi 10.1016/S0277-5395(02)00356-4.

Preston, J. (2003). White trash vocationalism?: Formations of class and race in an Essex Further Education College. *Widening participation and lifelong learning, 5*(2), 6–17.

Said, E. W. (1993). *Culture and imperialism.* London, UK: Vintage.

———. (2005). *Power, politics, and culture: Interviews with Edward W. Said.* London, UK: Bloomsbury.

Shore, S. (1998). On the ground: Weaving theory and practice in an adult education degree. *Australian Journal of Adult and Community Education, 38*(3), 89–97.

———. (2001) Talking about whiteness: 'Adult learning principles' and the 'invisible norm.' In V. Sheared & P. Sissel (Eds.), *Making space: Merging theory to practice in adult education* (pp. 42–56). Westport, CT: Bergin and Garvey.

———. (2004). Destabilising or recuperating Whiteness?—(un)mapping 'the self' of agentic learning discourses. In A. Moreton-Robinson (Ed.), *Whitening the race: Essays in social and cultural criticism* (pp. 89–103). Canberra, ACT: Aboriginal Studies Press.

———. (2010). Whiteness at work in vocational training in Australia. *New Directions for Adult and Continuing Education, 125*(Spring), 41–51. doi: 10.1002/ace.361.

Shore, S., & Butler, E. (2012). Missing things and methodological swerves: Unsettling the it-ness of VET. *International Journal of Training Research, 10*(3), 204–218.

Stoler, A. L. (1995). *Race and the education of desire: Foucault's history of sexuality and the colonial order of things.* Durham, NC, and London, UK: Duke University Press.

Wheelahan, L., & Curtin, E. (2010). *The quality of teaching in VET: Overview.* Melbourne, VIC: LH Martin Institute.

Williams, R. (1977). *Marxism and literature.* New York, NY: Oxford University Press.

Zournazi, M., with Hage, G. (2002). 'On the side of life'—Joy and the capacity of being: A conversation with Ghassan Hage. In M. Zournazi (Eds.), *Hope: New philosophies for change* (pp. 150–171). Annandale, NSW: Pluto Press.

IMMIGRANT EXPERIENCES OF WORK AND LEARNING IN THE NEW WORLD ORDER

11

Unauthorized Migrant Workers

(L)Earning a Life in Canada

Susan M. Brigham

Rapid economic, political, social, and cultural changes are occurring globally, including a rise in transnational migration, the development of new diasporas, increasingly fractured labor markets, widening gaps between people who can access formal education and those who cannot, greater social and economic exclusions of unskilled laborers, and a deepening divide between the people deemed valuable and those who are not (Johnston, 2003). Overlaying these global changes is a neoliberal ideology that emphasizes individualization and individualism with less importance placed on state provision of social welfare which is contributing to a vulnerable populace (Davies, 2005). Counted in this vulnerable populace is a diverse group of workers, specifically migrants, authorized and unauthorized, who have played valuable roles in economies around the world. High-income nations have witnessed a dramatic increase in the use of migrant workers (UFCW Canada, 2011). With the power to repatriate migrant workers at will, some employers may extort low wages from such workers and provide them few benefits and deplorable work conditions (UFCW Canada, 2011). While authorized migrant workers face exploitation, unauthorized migrant workers, including Black women, face unique pressures and have an even more fragile claim on belonging in Canadian society. Marginalizing policies and practices position unauthorized Black women migrant workers at the periphery of the economy in both their host and home countries. Indeed, "the creation and maintenance of well-policed borders has been long understood as an essential ingredient in the creation of the marginalized identities, in keeping them contained and controlled . . . positioning subjects in a way that ensures their continued marginalization" (Massaquoi, 2007, p.88). How have adult education practitioners and researchers in North America responded to the persistent peripherality and marginalization experienced by migrant workers? Although there has been some attention paid to (im)migration issues in workplace studies, the focus has tended to be on credentializing and language learning. As yet, the experiences of unauthorized female migrant workers including their gendered roles in the family and workplace have not received critical uptake in the field of adult education.

In this chapter I center on the economic and social margins where a heterogeneous group of unauthorized migrant women locate themselves. I refer to a qualitative study that involved in-depth one-to-one interviews with Black Jamaican women in their forties and fifties, all mothers of between one and three children who had worked unauthorized (i.e., without a work visa) in Toronto and Montreal as caregivers, and had since returned to Jamaica. Each interview lasted between two and three hours and was audio recorded. All interviews were transcribed. In this chapter I draw on the transcripts of five participants. At the request of the participants their quotes were altered to reflect Standard English even if it was not used in the interviews. Each participant is assigned a pseudonym to protect her confidentiality. I highlight the complex constellation of economic, political, social, cultural, and affective forces that impact the research participants' gendered work experiences in their home and host countries. The chapter is organized this way: first, I provide a background to this study. I then focus on themes found in the research data, namely vulnerabilities, regrets, and resistance. Following that, I conclude with recommendations for adult educators.

The Research Context

Adult educators, scholars, students, and practitioners have a rich history of working with community groups, organizations, and social movements, providing educational activities, and rallying for improved economic and social change for marginalized populations. Lessons from the past are reminders that charges of illegality did not dampen the enthusiastic dedication of adult educators who worked toward social justice, even (and at times, especially) for those deemed illegal or criminal when they were trying to live, study, work, and/or vote, including women, and sexual and racial minorities.

A migrant who resides in Canada, is not Canadian, and does not have authorization to work in Canada (i.e., work visa) is referred to as "unauthorized." I use this term as opposed to illegal, or non-status in agreement with Simmons (2010, p. 104) who asserts, "the advantage of the term unauthorized is that it is more general and covers most circumstances that lead to unauthorized presence without implying any criminality." It is difficult to know the number of unauthorized migrants mainly because they are undocumented and hence un-countable and also because there are several diverse categories which migrants may move between over a period of time. For example, a migrant may have entered the host country legally and is residing legally but working illegally, or s/he may have entered legally but is illegally residing and working, or s/he may have entered illegally and is residing illegally but not working (Tapinos, 1999). Further, a migrant may be authorized, become unauthorized, and then become authorized again. Although the number of illegal migrants around the world can only be estimated, it is "quite high and rising" and public concern about this phenomenon is growing (Entorf, 2002, p. 28). In the United States (U.S.), the estimate is between 11.5 and 12 million or 4 percent of the total population (Passell, 2005) and in Canada it is estimated to be between 100,000 and 200,000, which is less than one percent of the total population (Simmons, 2010), up to 500,000 plus (UFCW Canada, 2011). The comparatively lower number of unauthorized workers in Canada can be attributed, in part, to geography (Canada borders on only one country, the U.S., and is surrounded by oceans on the east, west, and north coasts) and Canadian humanitarian responses to unauthorized migrants (Simmons, 2010).

The reasons migrants work unauthorized around the world are wide-ranging, though the motive is often based on economics, specifically the availability of employment, differences in the quality and remuneration of employment between migrants' home and the host countries, and migrants' hopes to improve the material lives of their families. Migrants' decisions, especially women's, mothers in particular, are impacted by their transnational networks and the availability of "Other mothers" (women who may or may not be related who take on mothering responsibilities) in their home country who can be counted on to care for their children (Brigham, 2015). Also, as alluded to above, some authorized temporary migrant workers whose work permits are tied to a single employer may not choose to become unauthorized; rather, they are put into circumstances where they "are forced into illegality when they are laid off or leave the job" (UFCW Canada, 2011, p. 20). For example, while trying to secure employment with a new employer, laid off/unemployed migrant workers may not have the financial means to pay for room and board, recruitment fees to find another job, and/or be able to send remittances to his/her dependents. During the time the worker is without a sponsoring employer s/he is unauthorized, yet s/he may have to find immediate (read: unauthorized) employment in the interim in order to meet his/her basic living needs.

The destination and number of unauthorized migrants are determined by the interplay between the migrants' decisions, public policy, and public perceptions (i.e., attitudes and perceptions of citizens in the host country) (Entorf, 2002). With regard to the latter, public attitudes toward migrants have shifted and "states [are] turning inward to protect their national security interests" (Crocker, Dobrowolsky, Keeble, Moncayo & Tastsoglou, 2007, p. 9). The securitization of migration has increased since the events of 9/11 (Dauvergne, 2007). While the recent intensification of control over people entering Canada is creating a risk to civil liberties, human rights, and protection under international law (Dauvergne, 2008), some migrant workers take the risk of working unauthorized because the regular migration process is out of their reach due to a lack of qualifications and/or financial means to pay the various fees required for legal documents that are increasingly complicated, bureaucratized, and expensive.

Jamaica has an extensive historical connection with Canada through trade in commodities and migration. Indeed, "the earliest bonds between Canada and Jamaica were a product of each region's role in the British imperial world built in large part on the backs of African descended people" (Walker, 2012, p. 23). These connections have shaped both countries. Canada has been a destination for Jamaican migrant workers for centuries beginning with the first group in 1796, the 550 Jamaican Maroons, who came to Halifax at the behest of the British who had sought unsuccessfully to control them in Jamaica. Although immigration policy has continually sought to exclude and control the movement of Black migrants from the Caribbean (Bashi, 2004), Jamaicans have worked in many occupations in Canada from coal miners in the late 1800s, to black smiths, train porters, live-in caregivers/domestic workers, and teachers in the 1950s (Brigham, 1995; Calliste, 2000; Kelly & Cui, 2010). They have also worked as seasonal agricultural workers hired under the federal Seasonal Agricultural Worker Program, which was established in 1966, and as temporary foreign workers in a range of occupations. Currently, Jamaica continues to be a top source country for caregivers under the federal Live-in Caregiver Program (CIC, 2010).

Migration is part of Jamaican identity, as Senior (2012, pp. 18, 19) illuminates:

> From birth we know personally the dislocations brought about by our family structures, which to a great extent are based on the widespread displacement of children and the absence of parents; the requirements of schooling, which usually takes us away from home; the movement demanded by work opportunities; and possibilities for upward social mobility. Moving upward socially and economically usually implies moving away . . . away is programmed into our hopes, expectations and ambitions.

With a 13.4 percent unemployment rate for people aged 14 to 65 years and over (10.1% for men and 17.4% for women in 2014 [Statistical Institute of Jamaica, 2015]), rising poverty, limited expansion of economic opportunities for career development, low wages, and high cost of living, many Jamaicans seek opportunities for employment and education in other countries.

In the present-day securitization climate, immigration legislation has become tighter, while the demand for both live-in and live-out caregiving continues to rise as many working families struggle to balance household labor and caregiving, particularly when women in the household are working outside the home; men do not contribute to an equal share of the household labor; and generally, the state does not sufficiently support the provision of affordable quality care for children, the elderly, and disabled persons. Middle- and upper-class families may hire domestic workers to avoid conflicts about how to delegate household work, to service a particular lifestyle, or to demonstrate "a form of social plumage" with domestic workers representing status symbols (Anderson, 2002, p. 104). This has set the scene for a vibrant unauthorized caregiver/domestic work market supported by organized transnational systems and networks. For many unauthorized female migrants, live-in caregiving is one of the easiest jobs to find, especially in urban centers. The predominantly white Canadian society has traditionally viewed Blacks and other racialized people as ideally suited for unskilled laboring jobs and women specifically for domestic work/caregiving. Such assumptions have relied on representations that involve a "complex range of political, economic, cultural and social constructs that divide people" by attributing to them varying degrees of power and privilege (Stiell & England, 2003, p. 45). Representations of the racialized domestic worker as "naturally nurturing, docile and good with children" (Brigham, 2002, p. 228) is a social construction. Such a construction involves "an on-going constitutive process [that] mediates between people, their identities and their relationships" (Brigham & Walsh, 2011, p. 228). Hence the social construction will continually shift. For example, Black Jamaican caregivers are often constructed as hard working, having come from a long line of hard workers traced back to slavery, "mammy-ish," firm but good-humored, caring and asexual, independent, reliable, and hardy. Yet, such constructions have and will continue to change. A case in point is offered by Bakan and Stasiulus (1997) who noted a shift in representations of Jamaican caregivers in Toronto in the 1990s from submissive and good with children to assertive, selfish, and prone to lying, a construction still ascribed by placement agency personnel in the early 2000s (Stiell & England, 2003). Such a shift was attributed to the increased involvement of Jamaican caregivers in an organization that led a push for changes in the federal domestic work schemes (Bakan & Stasiulus, 1997). The research participants in my study trouble representations of a composite, singular "Black Jamaican domestic worker" by situating themselves in a multifaceted context that takes into consideration transmigration, gendered experiences, and the global economy, coupled with the legacy of Jamaica's colonial past, slavery, imperialism, and present day neo-colonialism.

According to the most recent national household survey, there is an estimated 256,915 Canadians in private households whose ethnic origin is Jamaican. Jamaica is also one of the top 10 source countries for temporary foreign workers (CIC, 2010). The women's choice of work in Canada, caregiving/domestic work, underscores a complex relationship with unauthorized labor migration. Caregiving/domestic work, especially live-in, is often deemed low skilled, highly flexible (e.g., hours, tasks and salary are variable) and informal since it is confined to the employers' private homes. It entails close proximity, and complex personal and emotional power relations, which are full of contradictions (Brigham, 2013). This work, often involving demeaning tasks, is described as undesirable and largely performed by women, many of whom are racialized migrants. Caregiving/domestic work intersects race, class, gender, and citizenship and therefore offers a rich and unique context for analysis. While the experiences of the women in this case study do not reflect the experiences of all unauthorized migrants, it casts light on what neoliberal discourse attempts to place beyond question, namely the inequalities the women experience, both in their home and host countries, and it raises questions about the role of adult education in relation to migration.

Research Study Themes

The research participants' knowledge of Canada came from their social/familial networks in Jamaica. Based on this knowledge they chose to migrate to Canada to work unauthorized primarily for employment, for the sake of their families, especially to ensure their children's health and well-being including providing them access to educational opportunities that they themselves could not access growing up as well as material resources; in the hope of breaking a cycle of poverty. Shortly after they arrived all the women found work as caregivers in private homes.

Vulnerabilities

The research participants' work varied in terms of conditions, hours, pay, and responsibilities although mainly their work involved home-based tasks, such as caring for people who are either very young, elderly, infirm, or disabled; as well as cleaning; cooking; laundry; and grocery shopping. A common denominator was the varying degree of exploitation, which some employers supported if they knew their workers were unauthorized as this participant explains: "My employers knew I didn't have [authorization] to work in Canada. They hired me anyway but they knew I couldn't complain about my salary or about the job." One participant asserted that some employers, like hers, hire unauthorized workers with a genuine wish to help them, although even with good intentions the working conditions remained exploitative. She described her duties as risky to her health because she was required to lift and carry a paralyzed adult several times throughout the day. So, in addition to the fear of being reported or deported, the worry about one day requiring medical attention was constant, as reflected by this participant who had injured her back when lifting an elderly woman in a wheelchair up a set of stairs: "[My employer] couldn't help me with my [medical] issues. I couldn't go to the hospital because I didn't have [health insurance]. I couldn't work, I couldn't stand. I had to go to the dollar store to buy something to help and I had to lay down for my back." Research shows that newcomers to Canada are more likely to take jobs that are physically demanding and riskier than Canadian-born workers (Smith, Chen, & Mustard, 2009) while unauthorized workers specifically are more likely than authorized workers to be forced to perform risky jobs and take longer work shifts and are more likely to be injured on the job (Mastrangelo et al., 2010). This is attributed to lower levels of education, low proficiency in English, and a lack of access to occupational health and safety training (Orrenius & Zavodry, 2009), exacerbated by limited access to appropriate health care, disability and compensation benefits (de la Hoz et al., 2008).

With regards to differences living in or living out, participants explain that living in offers at least some temporary relief from housing concerns but it invariably leaves migrant workers at the beck and call of employers 24 hours a day and often seven days a week, as this participant describes: "the disadvantage of when you live in is that you don't have any hours when you should stop working. It is like going back into slavery." Living out provides a little more freedom and independence but, as this participant explains, it may leave the worker at risk for living in poverty and poor housing conditions:

> I had three jobs for the day. Three different people I work for in one day. So sometimes in the winter it is really difficult. I had nowhere to go between jobs so I was walking on the sidewalks and sitting on a bench. I was so cold. It would take a long time to travel by bus to another job. In the neighborhood where rich people live, the public transit does not go. I wondered why I have to work so hard. . . . I couldn't buy anything for myself until after the bills were paid. . . . I would just keep working just to pay bills and send back [home] something . . . I needed a job that was going to pay me a decent salary.

Regrets

The participants' greatest regret was being away from their children for long periods of time, between five to ten years. Their children were left in the care of female relatives since men were, as one participant put it, "out of the picture." For the women, returning home for visits was not an option if they wanted to continue working in Canada. Their absence from home caused emotional stress for the women, their children, and the family members caring for the children in Jamaica; and to add insult to injury, none of the participants' children's educational opportunities improved and in some cases their children's academic success slipped further behind over the years and in a few cases their children's health and well-being suffered for lack of a parental figure in their lives. Participants offered these examples:

> I do have regrets for leaving him because before I left . . . [his] reading and writing was way advanced for his age and [when I returned] all that was gone. He could not read any more stuff that he used to read. . . . My mother and sisters just let him go. I would say he was neglected.

***

What my daughter went through, she got pregnant at 14 and I was not there for her. She was raped, she became suicidal and the family . . . [did] not want to call because they know your papers are not okay. . . . Mummy was not there that she could not talk to mummy. I spent many nights crying.

The emotional impact of living for years in a state of exile away from their children, while never feeling fully established or free to move back and forth across the border, took a toll on the participants' sense of self-worth and level of stress as this participant describes:

Your life is put on hold, my self-esteem was plunged. I could never trust. I was living alone and I was scared, so reserved. I'd bolt when people ask, "You got your landing [status]? You got your papers?" . . . Lying became a part of my life. I forgot what the truth is.

Resistance

The regrets, guilt, and fear the research participants experienced could well have been debilitating yet, as much as the women felt overwhelmed and were made vulnerable by various mechanisms, they also spoke of ways they resisted oppressive conditions. For instance, participants drew on the strength of their Jamaican identity to set boundaries around what employers could expect, as these participants explain:

Jamaican women are good workers but we have limits. When [employers] tell us that, "you have to walk this dog and pick up after the dog" a Jamaican woman will not do it. And when they will tell you to wear a uniform and walk in the park with babies, a Jamaican woman will not do it. We will not wear a uniform. A Filipino would but not a Jamaican. We know what slavery is. We will never bend back.

***

Jamaicans, if we don't like the work we can leave it and leave it good. We sometimes have a bad name, but if you stay in a job you don't like or if it doesn't pay anything people will think "she is not landed," so you got to leave the job, don't stay.

Additionally, participants found support in transnational networks and social spaces, which included fellow caregivers, religious groups, and Othermothers (a term used in some Black communities to describe women who provide strong social support, including nurturing, imparting values, culture, traditions, and wisdom as well as occasional economic support to other women and their families) which allowed them to "pull through," share resources, bolster their resilience, and strengthen their ability to resist. For example, these participants explain: "In Canada I gave my life to the Lord. The Church gave me support in my times of need."

> You become friends with people in the same [situation] because you work in the same thing, you are in the same place, so you form a bond with others who are illegal so when one cries all cries. I cried but the people around me they were supportive. It has made a difference even though you have the hopes, the downs and the hurts. You can only hurt for so long, not for the rest of your life.

With regard to their hopes and plans for the future some of the participants expressed their wish to have taken formal education while in Canada that could have made them more competitive in the job market both in Jamaica and Canada, such as accounting, and basic literacy, yet none of the participants enrolled in nonformal or formal programs during their years in Canada, mainly due to the cost, lack of time and energy, and fear of being found out they were unauthorized. Most of the learning the women gained during their time in Canada was informal, through personal experience, the media, stories and advice from other unauthorized workers, and/or involvement in a church community. Participants stated their desire for more "spaces where people that are not getting their connections to other people can go for help, to learn about their rights, and connect with each other and with Canadian people." One participant suggested that the Canadian government has a role to play "in making it easier for us to get work whether we are legal or illegal." Being stereotyped and misunderstood by people who did not know them and their stories were identified as limiting factors to the possibility of building relationships based on respect in Canada, of working in solidarity toward a more just work and learning environment. Such is the call for action for adult educators and practitioners.

Recommendations for Adult Education

Through migration, unauthorized workers are finding ways to redress the shortfalls of their home country, such as an economy that does not appear to have sufficient opportunities for them, poor working conditions and low salaries in the limited number of jobs that exist for semi- and unskilled workers, inadequate and often inaccessible formal education for themselves and their children, and a system that generally does not support low-income families. Sending countries, like Jamaica, may be perceived as benefitting from having their unemployed and underemployed citizens go abroad and remit what savings they can in order to support their families in Jamaica, yet the long-term social and economic consequences on the families and communities left behind are often not figured into the equation. The toll on health and well-being and the general lower quality of life of some migrant workers and their families are often immeasurable, their hidden costs unacknowledged. Carens (2013, p. 157) reminds us that "over time an irregular migration status becomes morally less relevant while the harm suffered by the person in that status grows." In Canada, migrants have played and continue to play a role in nation building. Unauthorized migrant caregivers, such as the research participants are making up for inadequacies in child-care and elder-care provisions in Canada while being exploited as cheap and disposable labor, and often made the scapegoats for all manner of social, economic, and political ills. It is clear that in a professional field such as adult education, which has historically been committed to social justice, there are inequalities that must be confronted within the growing phenomenon of precarious work through labor migration.

Community organizations, such as non-profits, women's groups, and faith-based associations are spaces of possibility for the involvement of migrant workers, authorized and unauthorized. In such spaces Black women migrant workers have a platform to speak and be heard; they are not assumed to be passive victims of systems, rather as active agents who have resisted borders and dis-locations and worked for survival for themselves and their families. As Massaquoi (2007, p. 88) suggests, "The process of displacement, movement, and re-placement to a new locality facilitates the opportunity for a unique form of political consciousness to arise and be spoken." Interrogating these processes alongside issues such as labor migration can expose links with various social and economic issues, at the micro, meso, and macro levels, including healthcare, homelessness, exploitative working conditions, policy, gender issues, racism, global structural

inequities, neo-colonialism, debt, and so on. Recognizing and understanding these links can lead to action, such as advocating for individual and
collective change in work conditions, national immigration policies, and
international relations. In these spaces of possibility, adult educators must be
committed to active listening, democratic practices, self-reflexivity, and the
on-going development of the ability to critically analyze (Coare & Johnston,
2003). An example of mobilizing adult education that seeks "to change the
destructive dynamics of individual isolation, economic marginality and the
resulting political disenfranchisement" is offered by De Rienzo (2008, p.
245) who suggests that house meetings can become places of educational
campaigns, where neighborhood groups can informally gather to discuss
challenges faced by migrants.

A challenge for adult educators is to reach those "hidden" learners
(i.e., live-in caregivers who are on duty 24/7) in private homes and those
who do not have the opportunities, time, energy, or access to a physical
space in which to engage in learning opportunities and group activities.
This challenge demands a variety of imaginative ways to create new spaces
for learning possibilities and take advantage of existing social spaces (i.e.,
church groups, sports activities, musical events, skills development events,
food courts in shopping centers, fashion shows, etc.).

Adult education researchers need to contribute to migration policymaking processes not only through quantitative studies but also through
participatory, collaborative, and action-based research methodologies that
involve diverse migrant communities and center their voices and research
agendas. Research findings about, for example, work conditions including
workplace injuries, mental health and well-being, personal and family kinship circumstances, as well as factors that contribute to resilience and the
social capital of migrants need to be disseminated creatively and broadly,
possibly through arts-informed methods, such as plays, poetry, photography,
and art installations to inform and engage adult educators and practitioners,
policymakers, and the general public.

Migrants' issues must not be assumed to be solely migrants' issues but
as human rights concerns that require more than the attention of migrants.
A political adult education approach that challenges the status quo and
brings about significant change "requires the support and solidarity of those
within community, labour, women's, and faith-based groups, adult education
movements, NGOs, and government organizations at the local and international levels" (Brigham, 2013, p. 171). There are several examples of how
this has been done by groups, such as labor unions, which have worked
in solidarity to mobilized support and advocate for programs of regulation

that have authorized previously unauthorized migrant workers (such as those who for years have contributed in numerous ways to Canadian society) (Simmons, 2010).

Finally, it is apparent that caregiving/domestic work lacks dignity, respect, and a living wage. Worthy of continued discussion among adult education circles is: Why is such work devalued and how can its value be raised? Hochschild (2002, p. 29) suggests that the declining value of care/domestic work "results from a cultural politics of inequality . . . the low market of care keeps the status of women who do it—and ultimately of all women—low." Hochschild recommends we examine the role of men in families for it is "with them that the 'care drain' truly begins" (p. 29), while Ehrenreich (2002) declares the moral challenge is to make work visible again, including the ghostly pursuits of the affluent like "stock-trading, image making and opinion polling" (p. 103). Ehrenreich concludes that unless men voluntarily take on a greater share of the care/domestic work burden and young people in the growing middle class who take their families' caregivers/domestic workers for granted learn how to do such work without constant assistance, there is every reason that families will continue to rely on paid caregivers/domestic workers and this will continue to be outsourced predominantly to migrant women from countries of the global South, including unauthorized workers.

In conclusion, this chapter sheds light on a group often made invisible and silent in the socioeconomic margins, yet who are also ironically often centered (albeit temporarily and precariously) in the private homes as caregivers, entrusted with the well-being of some of the most vulnerable Canadians (e.g. the elderly, infirm, disabled, and children). Further illumination is required on this group of migrant workers, for as Massaquoi (2007) states, within the broader context of "a transnational world where cultural asymmetries and linkages continue to be influenced by economic and political interest at multiple levels we need detailed, historicized, geopolitical mappings of the circuits of power in relation to black womanhood" (p. 80).

References

Anderson, B. (2002). Just another job? The commodification of domestic labour. In B. Ehrenreich & A. Hochschild (Eds.), *Global woman: Nannies, maids, and sex workers in the new economy* (pp. 104–114). New York, NY: Henry Holt & Co.

Bakan, A., & Stasiulis, D. (1997). *Not one of the family foreign domestic workers in Canada*. Toronto, ON: University of Toronto Press.

Bashi, A. (2004). Globalized anti-blackness: Transnationalizing Western immigration law, policy, and practice. *Ethnic and Racial Studies 27*(4), 584–606.

Brigham, S. (1995). *The perceptions and experiences of immigrant Filipino caregivers: A study of their integration into Canadian society.* Unpublished master's thesis, University of Alberta, Edmonton, AB.

———. (2002). *Women migrant workers in a global economy: The role of critical feminist pedagogy for Filipino domestic workers.* Unpublished doctoral dissertation, University of Alberta, Edmonton, AB.

———. (2013). Filipino overseas domestic workers: Contradictions, resistance and implications for change. In R. Brickner (Ed.), *Migration, globalization and the state* (pp. 142–178). Basingstoke, Hampshire, UK: Palgrave.

———. (2015). Mothers without borders: Undocumented Jamaican domestic workers in Canada and transnational kinship networks. In G. C. Man & R. Cohen (Eds.), *Transnational voices: Global migration and the experiences of women, youth and children.* Waterloo, ON: Wilfrid Laurier University Press.

Brigham, S., & Walsh, S. (2011). Having voice, being heard, and being silent: Internationally educated teachers' representations of "immigrant women" in an arts-informed research study in Nova Scotia. In E. Tastsoglou & P. S. Jaya (Eds.) *Immigrant women in Atlantic Canada: Challenges, negotiations and re-constructions* (pp. 209–234). Toronto, ON: Canadian Scholars/Women's Press.

Calliste, A. (2000). Nurses and porters: Racism, sexism and resistance in segmented labour markets. In A. Calliste & G. Dei (Eds.), *Anti-racist feminism: Critical reader, race and gender studies* (pp. 143–164). Halifax, NS: Fernwood.

Carens, J. (2013). *The ethics of immigration.* New York, NY: Oxford Press.

Citizenship and Immigration Canada (CIC). (2010). *Canada: Facts and figures: Immigrant overview permanent and temporary residents.* Research and Evaluation Branch, Citizenship and Immigration Canada: Ottawa, ON. Available at: http://www.cic.gc.ca/english/resources/statistics/facts2010/index.asp.

Coare, P., & Johnston, R. (2003). The role of the adult educator. In P. Coare & R. Johnston (Eds.), *Adult learning, citizenship and community voices: Exploring community-based practice* (pp. 205–223). Leicester, UK: NIACE.

Crocker, D., Dobrowolsky, A., Keeble, E., Moncayo, C. C., & Tastsoglou, E. (2007). *Security and immigration, changes and challenges: Immigrant and ethnic communities in Atlantic Canada, presumed guilty?.* Ottawa, ON: Status of Women Canada.

Dauvergne, C. (2007). Security and migration law in the less brave new world. *Social & Legal Studies, 16*(4), 533–549.

———. (2008). *Making people illegal: What globalization means for migration and law.* New York, NY: Cambridge University Press.

Davies, B. (2005). The (im)possibility of intellectual work in neoliberal regimes. *Discourse: Studies in the Cultural Politics of Education, 26*(1), 1–14.

de la Hoz, R., Hill, S., Chasan, R., Bienenfeld, L., Afilaka, A., Wilk-Rivard, E., & Herbert, R. (2008). Health care and social issues of immigrant rescue and recovery workers at the World Trade Center site. *Journal of Occupation and Environment, 50*(12), 1329–1334. doi: 10.1097/JOM.0b013e31818ff6fd.

De Rienzo, H. (2012). Community organizing for power and democracy: Lessons learned from a life in the trenches. In J. DeFilippis & S. Saegert, (Eds.), *The community development reader* (2nd ed.) (pp. 244–250). New York, NY: Routledge.

Ehrenreich, B. (2002). Maid to order. In B. Ehrenreich & A. Hochschild (Eds.), *Global woman: Nannies, maids, and sex workers in the new economy* (pp. 85–103). New York, NY: Henry Holt & Co.

Entorf, H. (2002). Rational migration policy should tolerate non-zero illegal migration flows: Lessons from modelling the market for illegal migration. *International Migration, 40*(1), 27–43.

Hochschild, A. (2002). Love and gold. In B. Ehrenreich & A. Hochschild (Eds.), *Global woman: Nannies, maids, and sex workers in the new economy* (pp. 15–30). New York, NY: Henry Holt & Co.

Johnston, R. (2003). Adult learning and citizenship: Clearing the ground. In P. Coare & R. Johnston (Eds.), *Adult learning, citizenship and community voices: Exploring community-based practice* (pp. 3–21). Leicester, UK: NIACE.

Kelly, J., & Cui, D. (2010). A historical exploration of internationally educated teachers: Jamaican teachers in 1960s Alberta. *Canadian Journal of Educational Administration and Policy, 100,* 1–22. Retrieved Jan. 31, 2015 from http://www.umanitoba.ca/publications/cjeap/.

Mastrangelo, G., Rylander, R. Marangi, G., Fadda, E., Fedeli, U., & Cegolon, L. (2010). Work related injuries: Estimating the incidence among illegally employed immigrants. *BMC Research Notes, 3,* 331. doi: 10.1186/1756-0500-3-331.

Massaquoi, N. (2007). An unsettled feminist discourse. In N. Massaquoi & N. Wane (Eds.), *Theorizing empowerment: Canadian perspectives in Black feminist thought* (pp. 75–94). Toronto, ON: Inana.

Orrenius, P., & Zavodny, M. (2009). Do immigrants work in riskier jobs? *Demography, 46*(3), 535–551.

Passell, G. (2005). *Unauthorized migrants: Numbers and characteristics.* Background briefing paper prepared for task force on immigration and America's future. Washington, DC: Pew Hispanic Center.

Senior, O. (2012). Crossing borders and negotiating boundaries. In C. James & A. Davis (Eds.), *Jamaica in the Canadian experience: A multiculturalizing presence* (pp. 14–22). Halifax, NS: Fernwood.

Simmons, A. (2010). *Immigration and Canada: Global and transnational perspectives.* Toronto, ON: Canadian Scholar's Press.

Smith, P., Chen, C., & Mustard, C. (2009). Differential risk of employment in more physically demanding jobs among a recent cohort of immigrants to Canada. *Injury Prevention, 15*(4), 252–258. doi: 10.1136/ip.2008.021451.

Statistics Canada (2011). *National household survey.* Retrieved Jan. 31, 2015 from http://www12.statcan.gc.ca/nhs-enm/2011/dp-pd/prof/details/page.cfm?.

Statistical Institute of Jamaica. (2015). *Labour market and earnings: Labour force. Unemployment rates.* Retrieved March 27, 2015 from http://statinja.gov.jm/LabourForce/UnemploymentRatesByAgeGroup.aspx.

Stiell, B., & England, K. (2003). Jamaican domestics, Filipina housekeepers and English nannies: Representations of Toronto's foreign domestic workers. In J. Momsen (Ed.), *Gender, migration and domestic service* (rev. ed.) (pp. 43–60). London, UK: Routledge.

Tapinos, G. (1999). Illegal immigrants and the labour market. *OECD Observer.* Retrieved July 20, 2013 from http://oecdobserver.org/news/archivestory.php/aid/190/Illegal_immigrants_and_the_labour_market.html.

UFCW Canada (2011). *Report on the status of migrant workers in Canada.* Prepared by the Human rights, equity and diversity department. Toronto, ON: UFCW Canada.

UNICEF (2013). *Parenting in Jamaica.* Retrieved October 15, 2013 from http://www.unicef.org/jamaica/parenting_corner.html.

Walker, B. (2012). Jamaicans and the making of modern Canada. In C. James & A. Davis. (Eds.), *Jamaica in the Canadian experience: A multiculturalizing presence* (pp. 23–34). Halifax, NS: Fernwood.

12

Shifting the Margins

Learning, Knowledge Production, and Social Action in Migrant and Immigrant Worker Organizing

Aziz Choudry

This chapter explores the relations between knowledge production, activist research, informal learning, and action, highlighting the importance of the intellectual and conceptual resources produced in the course of migrant and immigrant labor organizing in Montreal. Concurring with radical adult education scholars Griff Foley (1999) and John Holst (2002, 2011), I suggest that the significance of incidental learning and informal education in activist milieus is frequently overlooked by social movement activists and scholars alike. Such learning in social action is crucial not only to inform strategies to create counter-power and contribute toward the formulation of radical alternatives to the prevailing world order, but can also inform scholarship about social movements, and therein the relationship between critical adult education and social change. I argue that these forms of social movement learning—"learning from the ground up" (Choudry & Kapoor, 2010)—are also important factors in producing conceptual resources for longer-term struggles for social change. Alongside this, and in critical dialogue with this collection's theme of lives on the periphery, the chapter problematizes dominant understandings of "margin" and "center" in relation to Canada's labor market, given that the conditions of precarious work and vulnerability are now impacting across society rather than being seen as lurking at the margins. I discuss the context for, and processes surrounding learning and knowledge production in the course of campaigns and organizing to defend immigrant and migrant workers' rights, especially the ongoing work of the Immigrant Workers Centre (IWC) in Montreal on temporary labor agencies.

This chapter draws from my engagement with research, learning, and activism with im/migrant worker organizing in Quebec/Canada (particularly the IWC), and transnational migrant labor justice networks (Choudry, Hanley, Jordan, Shragge & Stiegman, 2009; Choudry & Henaway, 2012, 2014; Choudry & Thomas, 2012; Henaway, 2012; Rodriguez, 2010a, 2010b). Located in a tradition of engaged scholarship which builds upon knowledge production and learning in social movements, I illustrate how knowledge produced by agency workers themselves is a vital resource for analysis, education, and action against the multiple levels of exploitation that they often face. Such knowledge is key to mapping the extent of labor precarity and documenting the particular practices of agencies and the businesses which use them to hire temporary staff and circumvent labor standards.

Kinsman (2006) contends that research and theorizing is a broader everyday/everynight part of the life of social movements whether explicitly recognized or not:

> Activists are thinking, talking about, researching and theorizing about what is going on, what they are going to do next and how to analyze the situations they face, whether in relation to attending a demonstration, a meeting, a confrontation with institutional forces or planning the next action or campaign. (p. 134)

Similarly, Jennifer Chun (2012) argues that it is

> at the outer edges of existing union tactics and strategies that we observe examples of innovation and dynamism. What we find is a concerted effort by a relatively small group of unions and labour activists to expand the conception of labour politics beyond the workplace and beyond narrowly defined labour-management struggles. (p. 40)

This, as Chun argues, is part of a growing effort to prioritize the struggles of workers at what has tended to be seen as the margins of the economy and society and transform understandings of who makes up today's working class and how unions should organize them.

On Knowledge Production and Learning in Struggle

In thinking through the forms of significant learning and knowledge production taking place in these struggles, Church's (2008) notion of solidarity learning, Foley's (1999) "learning in social action" and the significance of incidental and informal learning, and Holst's (2002) pedagogy of mobilization are helpful. For Church (2008), solidarity learning happens not according to an explicit curriculum but spontaneously and unpredictably through social interaction in situations that foster people's participation. Often, the learning that takes place is both individual and collective. In coining the term "pedagogy of mobilization," Holst writes that "there is much educational work internal to social movements, in which organizational skills, ideology, and lifestyle choices are passed from one member to the next informally through mentoring and modelling or formally through workshops, seminars, lectures, and so forth" (p. 81). Mario Novelli's (2010) thoughts on the dialectics of strategic learning through struggle and contestation—which includes incidental, formal, informal, and nonformal education—are particularly salient to the learning and knowledge production discussed in this chapter:

> "[P]opular education" needs to be seen as not only involving formal educational events, but is part of much bigger processes which, though appearing "informal" and "arbitrary," are very deliberate. In this definition, both the "popular education" events that take place, and the actual practice of "strategy development" and "protest actions" can be seen as examples of popular education whereby the "school" (the social movement) learns. (p. 124)

Foley (1999) emphasizes the importance of "developing an understanding of learning in popular struggle" (p.140). His attention to documenting, making explicit, and valuing incidental forms of learning and knowledge production in social action is consistent with others who understand that critical consciousness and theory emerge from engagement in action and organizing contexts, rather than ideas developed elsewhere being imposed on "the people" (Bevington & Dixon, 2005; Choudry & Kapoor, 2010; Kelley, 2002; Kinsman, 2006; Smith, 1999). Scandrett's (2012) characterization of the common terrains and dynamics of learning within social movements is also insightful:

> [L]earning may take place as a dialectical interrogation of knowledge from the perspective of struggle, and may occur through

structured popular education or incidental learning, and in a complex relationship between the two as values and knowledge interact. Incidental learning occurs prior to and as a result of structured popular education, but is affected by such experience through dialogue with knowledge to discern what is 'really useful.' At the same time, incidental learning, even in the absence of structured popular (or indeed didactic) education, can take place through alternative processes, such as in discursive encounters with other movements, in which the methodology, if not the method of popular education occurs. (p. 52)

This captures well the dynamic relations between more structured forms and processes of popular education/nonformal learning in social movements and the more informal and incidental learning and knowledge production that takes place. Moreover, a Marxist theory of praxis which insists upon the unity of thought and action necessitates a dialectical theory of consciousness in which thought, action, and social relations are inseparable (Allman, 2001).

Global Capitalism and Neoliberal Immigration

McNally (2002) contends that "the fundamental truth about globalization—that it represents freedom for capital and unfreedom for labour—is especially clear where global migrants are concerned" (p. 137). In addition to the neoliberal underpinning of domestic policy, in international forums such as the Organization for Economic Cooperation and Development (OECD) and the World Trade Organization (WTO), Canada actively supports the expansion of freemarket capitalist policies—not least in agriculture—which have destroyed or eroded traditional societies and livelihood opportunities in the name of a model of development through export-driven, market-oriented growth.

Migration continues to be shaped by interconnected economic, political, and social push and pull factors. As Razack (2004), Thobani (2007) and others contend, Canada's role in creating or exacerbating these push factors needs close scrutiny. Push factors include structural adjustment programs imposed in the global South by the World Bank, the International Monetary Fund, and other financial institutions, and often supported through bilateral official aid, "development" projects, restructuring of economies along neoliberal lines through trade and aid arrangements in which Canadian international aid and development, trade, and economic policies play roles. Neoliberal policies force people from their farms, jobs, families, and communities and into exploitation and precarity as migrant workers in other countries. Deindustrialization and the downsizing and privatization of essential services—accompanied by increasing user fees—are other push factors, forcing growing numbers to seek work abroad (Mathew, 2005; McNally, 2002; Stasiulis & Bakan, 2003).

The material conditions in workers' countries of origin, as well as the structure of labor markets in the migrant-receiving countries shape the place of migrant workers. Free trade and investment agreements such as the North American Free Trade Agreement (NAFTA) and structural adjustment programs push farmers off their land as common lands are privatized—often to facilitate corporate export-based agricultural production. This forces people into low wage labor in *maquiladora* assembly plants or to find ways to migrate north across an increasingly dangerous and militarized U.S.-Mexico border. Likewise, Canadian corporations operating in countries such as the Philippines, India, and Colombia have both shaped and benefited from deregulated natural resources policy regimes, which have led to the impoverishment of communities and subsequent displacement as they are forced to migrate to seek livelihoods elsewhere. Akers Chacón (2006) describes such dynamics as "neoliberal immigration"—"displacement accompanied by disenfranchisement and often internal segregation in host countries" (p. 90).

The economies of Mexico, the Philippines, Pakistan, and Bangladesh, for example, have become increasingly dependent on remittances in the wake of loss of foreign exchange earning capacity, takeovers by privatization, and massive public sector cuts. Sutcliffe (2004) observes that "the individual decisions of individual migrant workers lead to considerably more money being transferred to poorer countries than all the development aid provided by the world's richest countries (including the multilateral agencies)" (p. 273). Migrant workers and remittances are a key area of interest to the World Bank, the European Commission, the International Organization for Migration (IOM), and other international agencies, which increasingly promote the concept of migrant workers' family remittances to keep their countries of origin from collapsing. Remittances are what Kapur (2004), calls "the new development mantra." The growing dependence on remittances from migrant workers puts many countries at the mercy of vagaries of anti-immigrant sentiment and immigration (and other) policies of other countries, not least in times of economic crisis and uncertainty. Kurmanaev (2011), for example, suggests that U.S. anti-immigration laws have negatively impacted remittance flows to Mexico. Yet overall, growth of remittances has outpaced that of private capital flows and Official Development Assistance (ODA) during the last fifteen years. A recent World Bank (2013) report on migration and development found that remittance flows to the global south totalled $401 billion in 2012, an increase of 5.3 percent over the previous year.

Locked into a neoliberal model, countries that have grown dependent on exporting workers often have shrinking policy space to pursue other options for economic development. Rodriguez (2010b) contends that migration-as-development approaches, through the promotion of temporary labor migration programs by the World Bank, IOM, and others "allow employers to exploit foreign workers, absolve developing states from introducing truly redistributive developmental policies and relieve states from extending the full benefits of citizenship to immigrants" (p.55). Remittances have been a way of downloading state responsibility to individual workers, as well as a social safety valve for masses of unemployed or underemployed workers in many countries. In both migrant-worker sending and receiving countries, a more general trend of state withdrawal for responsibility for provision of social services impacts local and migrant workers alike.

Abu-Laban and Gabriel (2002) and Arat-Koç (1999) draw attention to the way in which the increasing neoliberalism underpinning Canadian government policy has impacted immigration policy. Under a neoliberal regime, the state role in regulating the labor market is changing; so too with the restructuring of the state and the economy. As temporary foreign worker programs expand their intake on the one hand, on the other, new immigrants to Canada are increasingly viewed through a lens of how they might benefit Canada's "global competitiveness"; and in a time of fiscal restraint, new immigrants are expected to be self-sufficient and shoulder increased responsibilities for adaptation and integration. By 2008, the number of workers entering Canada under temporary foreign worker programs outnumbered those arriving through the traditional immigration system to become permanent residents: 370,000 temporary foreign workers were admitted, while 250,000 people were granted permanent residence—the first time that the numbers of temporary foreign workers arriving in Canada exceeded those arriving as landed immigrants (Office of the Auditor-General of Canada, 2009). These programs are predicated on maintaining qualitatively different sets of rights and status for citizens, permanent residents, and temporary workers respectively.

Built around labor flexibilization, Ottawa has responded to business demands to make the use of temporary foreign workers more friendly to employers, while critics, including trade union and immigration justice groups (e.g. Alberta Federation of Labour, 2009; Choudry, Hanley, Jordan, Shragge & Stiegman, 2009; United Food and Commercial Workers, 2010) and a strongly worded report by the Auditor-General's Office (2009) have charged that these programs have few real safeguards, and lead to much actual and potential abuse of workers. To extend Panitch and Swartz's (2003) concept beyond unionized (primarily public sector) workers, agency workers and migrant workers experience a generally similar form of "permanent exceptionalism" or permanent temporariness, in the service of capital accumulation. As Bauder (2006) notes, the presence and proliferation of precarious and vulnerable migrant and immigrant workers acts as a deregulatory force in labor markets. Agencies often justify practices such as paying low wages and providing no benefits, arguing that recent immigrants receive valuable "Canadian experience" (Vosko, 2000). Yet Vosko (2000) claims that

> just as officials argued that the industry represented an ideal labour force re-entry vehicle for women absent from the labour force while raising children in the late 1960s and early 1970s, they now claim that temporary help work is a suitable means for immigrants to gain experience and exposure in the Canadian market. (p. 190)

While those newly arrived in Canada are often under pressure to find a way to make ends meet, the claim that working through a temporary agency can help someone gain a foothold in the labor market and stable permanent work is questionable. The temp agency industry has continued to move away from a reactive use of temps (temporary workers) as replacements for absent employees, or as purely supplemental staff during peak periods of demand, to the "systematic" use of temps, in which entire job clusters and industries are staffed with agency workers indefinitely. Vosko (2000) warns of the potential of the temporary employment relationship to become the norm for a wider segment of the population. Thus, at the same time as migrant and immigrant workers employed through temp agencies have often been viewed as working at the periphery of the labor market, where it is assumed that full-time, permanent employment is the norm, increasingly the margins have moved to the center, as more and more workers experience conditions of greater labor precarity.

Migrant and Immigrant Worker Organizing in Montreal

Montreal's Immigrant Workers' Centre (IWC) was founded in 2000 as a community-based workers' organization in the diverse, working-class neighborhood of Côte-des-Neiges by some Filipino-Canadian union and former union organizers, and other activist and academic allies. The IWC engages in individual-rights counseling and casework, as well as popular education and political campaigns that reflect the general issues facing immigrant and temporary foreign workers—dismissal, problems with employers, wage theft, and sometimes inadequate representation by their unions. Often the issues which arise from individual cases form the basis for campaigns and demands which are expressed collectively. DeFilippis, Fisher, and Shragge (2010) argue that for community organizations to be part of a broader longer-term movement for social change, social analysis, and political education are vital. They write that "both contribute to understanding that the specific gains made and the struggles organizations undertake are part of something larger, but so is the broader political economy that structures organizational choices" (p. 177). It should be emphasized that this model of organizing is not being romanticized, nor the knowledge and learning that takes place therein. There are many challenges for workers centers and migrant and immigrant worker organizing. Indeed, as Chun (2012) notes: "the struggles of workers at the margins have the potential to create new horizons of organizational and structural transformation. However, how do we evaluate this potential without exaggerating its broader impact?" (p. 41). While it is outside the scope of this chapter to answer this question, we are aware of the dangers of false optimism about new modes of labor organizing.

For the IWC, labor education is a priority, targeting organizations in the community and increasing workers' skills and social, political, and economic analysis. Workshops on themes such as the history of the labor movement, the Labour Standards Act, and collective organizing processes have been presented in many organizations that work with immigrants as well as at the IWC itself. For example, the "Skills for Change" program run by the Centre teaches basic computer literacy, while incorporating workplace analysis and information on labor rights and supporting individuals in becoming more active in defending those rights in their workplaces. Language classes teach workers French through engaging with the labor code. But labor education also happens in the course of outreach work—notably while distributing flyers at work locations to connect with migrant and immigrant workers involved in precarious work such as that often associated with temporary labor agencies (Choudry & Henaway, 2014). Formal and informal learning and knowledge production also occur in meetings, workshops, and worker assemblies. The IWC strives to develop leadership among immigrant workers in order to take action on their own behalf. Support for self-organizing, direct action, coalition-building, and campaigning are used to win gains for workers and to build broader awareness of, and support for, systemic change in relation to their working conditions and, often, immigration status. As IWC organizer Mostafa Henaway (2012) states, the Centre:

> tries to build from an organizing model that incorporates radical traditions, going back to basics, focusing on outreach, collective organizing, casework, and education. At times, there are many challenges faced in balancing all of these facets in the organization; but each facet has proven to be critically important to the political work of the centre, such as weekly outreach outside Metro [subway] stations, building relationships with both communities and individual immigrant workers, or attempts to collectivize the casework and individual issues faced by workers, and to respond in a politicized way. The foundation of this organizing has come from these principal organizing methods, in addition to a flexibility in tactics and strategy, due to ever-changing economic conditions in Montreal, and globally. (p.146)

Significantly, organizations such as the IWC and the workers' struggles that they support can be key sites of informal and nonformal learning and knowledge production for labor justice organizing. This process occurs through workers' struggles and contestation of their conditions and rights and is important in winning gains for workers. A recent study on immigrant workers' struggles in Quebec, which conducted extensive interviews (Choudry et al., 2009, p. 112) notes:

> Individuals that did eventually take action always did so with the support of others, who provided information and other resources to help them in a dispute with an employer. These others can be unions, community organizations or co-workers or friends with whom they have informal relationships. 'Street smarts' and small victories are shared between people: this in turn encourages others to take action. Such learning most often grows out of pre-existing relations with other individuals, peers or friends. However, organizations play a key role.

This study found that learning to question or to resist exists in tension with learning to cope, adapt or "get by"—as indeed it does in workplace industrial relations since the emergence of capitalism. Sometimes, as Rodriguez (2010b) notes, such knowledge forms contest not only the power (and knowledge) produced by governments, but also that of professionalized non-governmental organizations (NGOs) which purport to speak on behalf of migrant workers. But building alliances with trade unions, through education and supporting internal debates occurring within organized labor to encourage unions to more meaningfully represent the needs and concerns of immigrant and migrant workers, is an important aspect of these local and global struggles for justice. As Mathew (2005) notes, migrant and immigrant workers can and do bring their own histories of struggle and organizing strategies from their countries of origin to the new countries in which they labor.

Mobilizing Workers' Knowledge to Build Strategy and Action

Paula Allman (2001) suggests that "authentic and lasting transformation in consciousness can occur only when alternative understandings and values are actually experienced 'in depth'—that is, when they are experienced sensuously and subjectively as well as cognitively, or intellectually" (p. 170). Knowledge produced by workers themselves has been key to building the organizing, strategy, and broader campaign work on temp agencies around the IWC and the newly formed Temporary Agency Workers Association (TAWA, see Choudry & Henaway, 2012; 2014). Besides workers' own experiences of exploitation, they are often positioned to be able to shed light on the identities and (mal)practices of the agencies, for example, in a sector which is notoriously difficult to document and map, let alone organize. Such knowledge is evident in the course of outreach to agency workers at various sites, and at meetings of agency workers where they can pool their experiences and discuss the conditions and possibilities for action. This is also key to mapping the sector in Quebec, especially given the "fly-by-night" nature of some temp agencies, and informing the direction of campaigns.

Another major challenge is the ability to create effective outreach strategies and target sites of companies that contract out agency workers. The ability to effectively learn and understand the political economy and geography of the agencies could only happen through contacts in different immigrant communities, and with agency workers, especially through assemblies and organizing meetings. For example, at one meeting, an agency worker working for one food processing company, discussed how many of the agencies operate through financial services offices clustered in neighborhoods with sizeable immigrant communities. Other workers shared that some agencies did not pay workers directly but rather they received their weekly pay from these businesses that service working immigrants. Similarly, in the course of outreach at such locations, through building a wider contact base, agency workers told organizers that to find out which employers use agencies one must go to various metro stations at 6 a.m. where workers are picked up for work. This has helped locate more companies, especially in the agricultural sector that use agency workers, and paved the way for bringing these workers into contact with organizers and the TAWA.

One instance of agency worker exploitation which IWC has confronted concerns Dollarama, Canada's fastest growing chain of dollar stores (whose CEO, Larry Rossy, is one of Canada's wealthiest people). Dollarama's major Montreal distribution warehouses are staffed by hundreds of mainly immigrant workers, many of whom are from North Africa. From this company comes an example of the significance of worker knowledge about agency work: the existence of a second Dollarama warehouse was only made known to IWC organizers through a contact who came to an organizing meeting as a result of ongoing outreach to agency workers. This process of outreach and organizing meetings has enabled IWC and TAWA to begin to map the web of agencies in multiple sectors such as healthcare, food processing, warehouse work, cleaning, and hospitality. This has contributed to a clearer picture of the structure of temp work in Montreal and aided in compiling a list of abusive and exploitative agencies: a challenge made more difficult precisely because there is no organized existing body of knowledge that has systematically mapped the political economy of Montreal's temp agencies and the added logistical difficulties of mapping fly-by-night operations.

Another strategy for mapping the temp agency industry involves two other forms of coalition building. The first is a collaboration between IWC and several unions in order to discuss temp agencies and acquire the knowledge they have from organizing workplaces with agencies, or share resources on broader issues of precarious work which the unions are currently engaged in such as a process to put forth a series of demands around temp agencies in Quebec. The second initiative has been to try to transform and build upon the knowledge presented by workers to create a coherent critical narrative by forming a temp agency research committee in collaboration with engaged academics based on the experiences of the organizers. This is a more critical and organic attempt to facilitate research combining the real experiences and knowledge of workers/organizers with the tools and resources available to academics to develop research that is relevant to organizing/campaigns.

New organizing strategies also emerge from agency workers' knowledge, which in turn is connected to learning in their own struggles for justice and dignity. One issue that the TAWA has taken up is that of holiday pay.

This demand is a strategic way to ensure a living wage, without confronting the employer directly. In Quebec, all workers are entitled to statutory holiday pay for holidays such as Christmas and Thanksgiving. But agency workers are usually left out of this scheme and do not receive this pay. An agency worker originally from Colombia suggested that if the fight is for agency workers to have equal rights with other workers, they should therefore be entitled to holiday pay. So he put forward a strategy to fight for this by posting complaints and educating workers about their entitlements. In turn, the TAWA has produced flyers and framed outreach based on what the workers themselves see as being strategic demands, and effective locations and times to communicate with other agency workers. Further demands came from workers and reflected a shift in strategy and the political demands itself. In 2013 in an open letter to Quebec's Minister of Labour, many Dollarama workers demanded the right to be made permanent after three months of work at the same workplace, arguing that merely making agencies co-responsible for the treatment of temp workers was not enough. This was critical because agency workers themselves are directly articulating proposals about creating a healthy labor market and workplace conditions.

Labor Organizing: From the Expanding Margins to a Contracting Center

Such strategies of worker self-organization described above highlight community responses to labor issues through organizations in which workers themselves would drive the agenda. IWC support for building a worker-led campaign and organization to change the structural issues of agency work has enabled the TAWA to address the implications of agency workers coming from a wide variety of experiences and ethnicities. The TAWA grapples with challenges faced by mainly newer immigrants and migrant workers in more exploitative conditions, contending with both labor problems and the regularization of status. Alongside this are workers in factories and manufacturing mainly seeking temporary work hoping to improve their skills and education. This organizing approach allows the IWC to build a more comprehensive organizing strategy, and a sense of solidarity across communities, immigration status, and other experiences. Leadership development and education are central to the IWC hybrid model of organizing through labor rights workshops, media training and opening up of leadership roles to workers. This hybrid model is characterized by three features: firstly, via an organization or association that can have a broad membership; second, through capacity to deal with policy issues at the provincial level; and third, working directly to solve workers' grievances with agencies and employers around wage theft, health and safety, and other industrial violations.

Workers' centers like the IWC and new workers' groups like the TAWA are testing grounds for new or alternative approaches or models of collective organization, and in a sense, are grounded attempts to work through some of the issues, debates, and tensions around the shifting centers and margins of labor market regulation and workers' struggles in Canada today. The expansion of agency work enhances employers' ability to create a sense of fear, austerity, and denial of decent work with job security in order to generate profits. So organizing amongst a changing working class and their daily struggles arising from precarious work is a key way to highlight local impacts of capitalist globalization and is critical at fighting for public services and against privatization and outsourcing. There are challenges in the political coordination of organizing for precarious workers and their conditions across Canada. This kind of precarious worker organizing is a relatively new phenomenon in Canada, by comparison with more established networks in the United States. Organizers are beginning to facilitate a conversation that could allow organizing experiences to be a way of building more effective campaigns and synergies, yet due to the relatively young nature of this organizing it will take some time and resources to achieve this. The need for coordination will be crucial between the mainstream labor movement/ trade unions, community-based labor organizations, and other community organizations to build a broader movement against exploitation by the agencies and workplaces that exist transnationally and within Canada.

For those of us located in universities and engaged in research on im/migrant workers this work requires some careful reflection and political commitment to this cause. Rodriguez (2010b) argues that it is vital to pay attention to the knowledge production of those excluded from official venues and who cannot participate in the networks, virtual and otherwise, frequented by others in the "global justice movement" and many international forums on migration and development.

> In order to be able to document the kinds of struggles engaged in by migrant worker activists . . . requires some level of political investment on our part as scholars, for it is in spaces outside of the seats of power, like the space of the street, where migrants can come together not only to narrate their experiences, but

also to articulate radical alternatives to the contemporary global order. (p. 67)

More broadly, we must also be aware of the politics of which campaigns, organizations, and movements are documented, and which are not. Indeed, for engaged academics working on immigration and labor issues, and for organizers on the frontlines of struggles for social justice, the analyses, activist learning, and knowledge produced in the course of such struggles can be seen as not only important intellectual contributions, but also as rich conceptual resources for understanding and challenging the continued exploitation and commodification of migrant workers and immigrants, locally and internationally.

Finally, the significance of the work done by activists on temp agencies and with agency workers in the TAWA lies not simply in organizing a smaller vulnerable marginal workforce. Rather, this organizing should be seen in the larger context of the fightback against the on-the-ground impacts, and the economic crises wrought by global capitalism which include the spread of precarious working conditions and increased dependence on contingent labor on an ongoing basis through contracting out, casualization, the rolling back of the welfare state and sustained attacks on trade unions. As such, we need to rethink standard core-periphery ideas about contingent workers. This struggle is critical in holding the line against declining wages and working conditions for all workers, and in extending understandings of who and where the working class is in the twenty-first century—and how to rebuild a working-class movement. Indeed, it may well be that the struggles of workers held to be at the margins of society are crucial for this work. Knowledge and learning which arises in the context of such struggles is key to acting to win gains for workers. Perhaps, as Julie Hearn and Monica Bergos (2010) contend,

> organized migrant workers pose two of the greatest threats to employers and the hierarchical and divisive way in which the segmented labour-market has been constructed and accepted. Their low wages and working conditions 'offer the greatest potential for worker dissatisfaction and protest' (Strikwerda and Guerin-Gonzales 1998: 20). In addition, if they become integrated into the indigenous union structure, in the process radicalizing it by bringing their raw experiences of exploitation and marginalization, they realize the capitalists' worst nightmare, a united working class. (p. 13)

References

Abu-Laban, Y., & Gabriel, C. (2002). *Selling diversity: Immigration, multiculturalism, employment equity and globalization.* Peterborough, ON: Broadview Press.

Akers Chacón, J. (2006). Introduction. In J. Akers Chacón & M. Davis (Eds.), *No one is illegal: Fighting racism and state violence on the US-Mexico border* (pp. 90–100). Chicago, IL: Haymarket Books.

Alberta Federation of Labour. (2009). *Entrenching exploitation.* http://www.afl.org/index.php/View-document/123-Entrenching-Exploitation-Second-Rept-of-AFL-Temporary-Foreign-Worker-Advocate.html. Accessed 2 May 2013.

Allman, P. (2001). *Critical education against global capitalism: Karl Marx and revolutionary critical education.* Westport, CT: Bergin and Garvey.

Arat-Koç, S. (1999). Neo-liberalism, state restructuring and immigration: Changes in Canadian policies in the 1990s. *Journal of Canadian Studies, 34*(2), 31–56.

Bauder, H. (2006). *Labor movement: How migration regulates labor markets.* New York, NY: Oxford University Press.

Bevington, D., & Dixon, C. (2005). Movement-relevant theory: Rethinking social movement scholarship and activism. *Social Movement Studies, 4*(3), 185–208.

Choudry, A., Hanley, J., Jordan, S., Shragge, E., & Stiegman, M. (2009). *Fight back: Workplace justice for immigrants.* Halifax, NS: Fernwood Press.

Choudry, A., & Henaway, M. (2014). Temporary agency worker organizing in an era of contingent employment. *Global Labour Journal, 5*(1), 1–22.

———. (2012). Agents of misfortune: Contextualizing im/migrant workers' struggles against temporary labour recruitment agencies. *Labour, Capital and Society, 45*(1), 36–64.

Choudry, A., & Kapoor, D. (Eds.). (2010). *Learning from the ground up: Global perspectives on knowledge production in social movements.* New York, NY: Palgrave MacMillan.

Choudry, A., & Thomas, M. (2012). Organizing migrant and immigrant workers in Canada. In Ross, S, and Savage, L. (Eds.), *Rethinking the politics of labour in Canada* (pp. 171–183). Halifax, NS and Winnipeg, MB: Fernwood Press.

Chun, J. J. (2012). The power of the powerless: New schemas and resources for organizing workers in neoliberal times. In A. Suzuki (Ed.), *Cross-national comparisons of social movement unionism: Diversities of labour movement revitalization in Japan, Korea and the United States* (pp.37–59). Bern: Peter Lang.

Church, K. (2008). While no one is watching: Learning in social action among people who are excluded from the labour market. In K. Church, N. Bascia, & E. Shragge (Eds.), *Learning through community: Exploring participatory practices* (pp. 97–116). Dordrecht, The Netherlands: Springer.

DeFilippis, J., Fisher, R., & Shragge, E. (2010). *Contesting community: The limits and potential of local organizing.* New Brunswick, NJ: Rutgers University Press.

Foley, G. (1999). *Learning in social action: A contribution to understanding informal education*. London, UK and New York, NY: Zed Books.

Hearn, J., & Bergos, M. (2010). *Learning from the cleaners? Trade union activism among low paid Latin American migrant workers at the University of London*. Identity, Citizenship and Migration Centre, Working Paper No. 7, University of Nottingham. WP 10-07.

Henaway, M. (2012). Immigrant worker organizing in a time of crisis: Adapting to the new realities of class and resistance. In A. Choudry, J. Hanley & E. Shragge (Eds.), *Organize!: Building from the local for global justice* (pp. 144–155). Oakland, CA: PM Press.

Holst, J. D. (2011). Frameworks for understanding the politics of social movements. *Studies in the Education of Adults, 43*, 117–127.

———. (2002). *Social movements, civil society, and radical adult education*. Westport, CT: Bergin and Garvey.

Kapur, D. (2004). "Remittances: The new development mantra? G-24 Discussion Paper No. 29." Retrieved from http://www.cities-localgovernments.org/committees/fccd/Upload/library/gdsmdpbg2420045_en_en.pdf. Accessed 24 March 2015.

Kelley, R. D. G. (2002). *Freedom dreams: The Black radical imagination*. Boston, MA: Beacon Press.

Kinsman, G. (2006). Mapping social relations of struggle: Activism, ethnography, social organization. In C. Frampton, G. Kinsman, A. K. Thompson, and K. Tilleczek (Eds.), *Sociology for changing the world: Social movements/social research* (pp. 133–156). Black Point, NS: Fernwood.

Kurmanaev, A. (September 2, 2011). Remittance growth loses dynamism as anti-immigration laws bite—Bancomer. *BNamericas*. Retrieved from http://www.bnamericas.com/news/banking/remittance-growth-loses-dynamism-as-us-anti-immigration-laws-bite-bancomer. Accessed 24 March 2015.

Mathew, B. (2005). *Taxi! Cabs and capitalism in New York City*. New York, NY: New Press.

McNally, D. (2002). *Another world is possible: Globalization and anti-capitalism*. Winnipeg, MB: Arbeiter Ring.

Novelli, M. (2010). Learning to win: Exploring knowledge and strategy development in anti-privatization struggles in Colombia. In A. Choudry & D. Kapoor (Eds.), *Learning from the ground up: Global perspectives on social movements and knowledge production* (pp. 121–138). New York, NY: Palgrave Macmillan.

Office of the Auditor-General of Canada. (2009). *2009 Fall Report of the Auditor General of Canada*. Retrieved from http://www.oag-bvg.gc.ca/internet/English/parl_oag_200911_02_e_33203.html. Accessed 24 March 2015.

Panitch, L., & D. Swartz. (2003). *From consent to coercion: The assault on trade union freedoms*. (3rd Edition). Aurora, ON: Garamond.

Razack, S. H. (2004). *Dark threats and white knights: The Somalia affair, peacekeeping and the new imperialism*. Toronto, ON: University of Toronto Press.

Rodriguez, R. M. (2010a). *Migrants for export: How the Philippine state brokers labor to the world.* Minneapolis, MN: University of Minnesota Press.

Rodriguez, R. M. (2010b). On the question of expertise: A critical reflection on "civil society" processes. In A. Choudry & D. Kapoor (Eds.), *Learning from the ground up: Global perspectives on social movements and knowledge production* (pp. 53–68). New York, NY: Palgrave Macmillan.

Scandrett, E. (2012). Social learning in environmental justice struggles: Political ecology of knowledge. In B. L. Hall, D. E. Clover, J. Crowther, & E. Scandrett (Eds.), *Learning and education for a better world: The role of social movements* (pp. 41–55). Rotterdam, The Netherlands: Sense.

Smith, L. T. (1999). *Decolonizing methodologies: Research and Indigenous Peoples.* Dunedin, New Zealand: University of Otago Press, and London, UK: Zed Books.

Stasiulis, D. K., & A. B. Bakan. (2003). *Negotiating citizenship: Migrant women in Canada & the global system.* New York, NY: Palgrave Macmillan.

Strikwerda, C., & Guerin-Gonzales, C. (1998). Labor, migration and politics. In C. Guerin-Gonzales, C. & C. Strikwerda, C. (Eds.), *The politics of immigrant workers: Labor activism and migration in the world economy since 1830* (pp. 3–55). New York, NY: Holmes & Meier.

Sutcliffe, B. (2004). Crossing borders in the new imperialism. In L. Panitch & C. Leys (Eds.), *The new imperial challenge: Socialist register 2004* (pp. 261–280). London, UK: Merlin Press.

Thobani, S. (2007). *Exalted subjects: Studies in the making of race and nation in Canada.* Toronto, ON: University of Toronto Press.

United Food and Commercial Workers. (2010). *UFCW Canada union victory for Quebec farm workers.* Press release, 21 April 2010. Retrieved from http://www.ufcw.ca/index.php?option=com_content&view=article&id=690&catid=5&lang=en. Accessed 24 March 2015.

Vosko, L. F. (2000). *Temporary work: The gendered rise of a precarious employment relationship.* Toronto, ON: University of Toronto Press.

World Bank (2013, April). *Migration and development brief, 20.* Retrieved from http://siteresources.worldbank.org/INTPROSPECTS/Resources/334934-1288990760745/MigrationDevelopmentBrief20.pdf. Accessed 24 March 2015.

13

Making the Invisible Visible

The Politics of Recognition in Recognizing Immigrant's International Credentials and Work Experience

Shibao Guo

As the globalization of migration intensifies, Canada has joined an international competition for the most talented, skillful, and resourceful workers. Immigrants are admitted into Canada under four major categories: family class, economic immigrants, refugees, and other immigrants (CIC, 2014). Family class is comprised of foreign nationals sponsored by close relatives or family members in Canada. Economic immigrants are people selected for their skills and ability to contribute to Canada's economy, including skilled workers, business immigrants, provincial and territorial nominees, and live-in caregivers. Skilled workers are those who meet education, language, and work experience criteria. Canada has three classes of business immigrants: investors, entrepreneurs, and self-employed persons, each with separate eligibility criteria. In 2008, Canada introduced the Canadian experience class which allows temporary foreign workers and international students who graduated in Canada to apply for permanent residence. Refugee protection is usually offered to those who fear returning to their country of nationality or habitual residence because of war, or due to fear of persecution, torture, or cruel and unusual treatment or punishment. Since the mid-1990s, Canada has shifted to a knowledge-based economy and subsequently its immigrant selection practices have placed more weight on education and skills, favoring economic immigrants over family-class immigrants and refugees. As Li (2003) notes, this new shift was based on the assumption that economic immigrants bring more human capital than family-class immigrants and refugees, and are therefore more valuable and desirable.

Despite Canada's preference for highly skilled immigrants and despite the fact that immigrant professionals bring significant human capital resources to Canada, the international credentials and work experiences of recent immigrants are often invisible. Upon arriving in Canada, many immigrants find their prior learning and work experiences undervalued or unrecognized because their real and alleged differences are claimed to be incompatible with the cultural and social fabric of traditional Canada (Andersson & Guo, 2009; Basran & Zong, 1998; Guo, 2009, 2013a, 2013b; Shan, 2009). As a consequence, many of them experienced downward social and occupation mobility, which adversely hindered their integration process. This chapter examines some of these challenges facing immigrants, as a group often marginalized due to social and structural disenfranchisement, and how these challenges affect their transitions to a new living and working environment. The findings raise important questions about the marginalized experiences of adult immigrants and I discuss implications for adult education with regard to disrupting the boundaries around prior learning assessment and recognition.

Mapping the Process of Foreign Credential Recognition

Foreign credentials can be defined as any formal education higher than a high school diploma, including professional or technical qualifications and any other degrees, diplomas, or certificates received outside Canada (Statistics Canada, 2003). Foreign credential recognition (FCR) is often referred to as "the process of verifying that the education, training and job experience [immigrants] obtained in another country are equivalent to the standards established for Canadian workers" (FCRO, n.d.). The notion of credential recognition is closely linked to the adult education tradition of Prior Learning Assessment and Recognition (PLAR). PLAR emerged in the 1980s in Canada following the introduction of Prior Learning Assessment in the 1970s in the United States as part of the effort to broaden access to higher education (Van Kleef, 2011). In 1997, the Canadian Association for Prior Learning Assessment was established as a national forum to advocate for continuous learning opportunities and formal acknowledgment of past learning experiences, or prior learning in the traditional sense. At present, PLAR involves "the recognition of informal learning acquired through various means: employment, volunteer work, military training, hobbies, personal reading, and other significant life experiences" (Simosko, 2012, p. 5).

Canada's immigrant selection system awards points to applicants with advanced educational qualifications. Prior to landing in Canada, immigrants normally receive no reliable information about the process of foreign credentials recognition. Upon arrival, they need to navigate through "a complex and possibly a lengthy, costly, and frustrating process on their own" (Guo, 2009, p. 41). According to an overview conducted by The Alliance of Sector Councils, FCR in Canada involves 13 jurisdictions, 55 ministries, more than 50 regulated occupations, more than 400 regulatory bodies, 5 assessment agencies, more than 240 post-secondary institutions, a large community of immigrant service agencies, not to mention numerous employers (TASC, 2010). Such institutional complexity means that the field comprises a multitude of authorities and myriad policies and practices, all of which are undergoing changes as this chapter is being written.

Unfortunately, there is no centralized office responsible for the evaluation of foreign credentials in Canada. Depending on the nature of the evaluation, immigrants may need to approach one or all of the following organizations: (1) provincial and territorial credential assessment services, (2) regulatory or professional bodies, (3) educational institutions, and (4) employers. The outcomes of the evaluation may serve one or more of the following purposes: general employment, studying in Canada, and professional certification or licensing in Canada. Since professional associations set their own standards of certification, no generalizations can be made regarding the national criteria for evaluating foreign qualifications. Reviewing the requirements of a number of assessment and licensing bodies in Canada, the evaluation of foreign credentials usually considers the following criteria: level and type of learning; duration of study program; status of issuing institutions; the education system of the country concerned; and authenticity, currency, relevance, trustworthiness, and transferability of the credential. Document verification does not guarantee that those who are found to have equivalent education will be licensed. Furthermore, successful immigrant professionals will obtain a certificate or license to practice their profession. Nonetheless, employment is not guaranteed in spite of shortages in the labor force since each professional immigrant needs to find a willing employer, not an easy task.

Given the national divergence, it is almost impossible to capture the complexity of the FCR process. The next section will provide a review of the role of major players in the recognition of foreign credentials for immigrants in Canada.

Multiple Authorities and Players

Federal, Provincial/Territorial, and Municipal Governments

Immigration falls under the jurisdiction of the federal government which is also responsible for national labor market policies as well as for maintaining occupational competency standards for certain regulated occupations. FCR did not make it onto the federal policy agenda until 2001, when the Throne Speech (to open the Parliament and outline the government's agenda) mentioned it for the first time. Currently, three federal departments are involved in the FCR process, including the Foreign Credentials Referral Office (FCRO) at Citizenship and Immigration Canada, the Foreign Credential Recognition Program (FCRP) at Human Resources and Skills Development Canada (HRSDC), and the Internationally Educated Health Professionals Initiative at Health Canada. FCRP is the main source of federal funding for FQR initiatives, which supports provinces, territories, and other stakeholders, such as national associations and regulatory bodies, to undertake projects that lead to better FCR outcomes.

The provincial and territorial governments have jurisdiction over skilled trades and professions and higher education. With respect to FCR, provincial governments have provided both policy frameworks and funding to coordinate and support initiatives that enhance immigrants' access to the labor market. Administratively, at least four ministries are involved in immigrants' adaptation at the provincial level: education, immigration, labor market, and health (TASC, 2010). TASC (2010) provides a map of the various institutional arrangements and ministries responsible for FCR in different provinces and territories. Yet, given the continuous restructuring of the governments and institutional reorganization, in the last few years there has been some juggling around in some provinces as to who is responsible for FCR. For instance, in the past, British Columbia's (BC) Ministry of the Attorney General housed Multiculturalism and Immigration Branch that dealt with immigration issues, including those associated with FCR (TASC, 2010). A ministerial reorganization in March 2011 saw the creation of the new Ministry of Jobs, Tourism, and Innovation, which now deals with FCR issues in BC.

In recent years, municipal governments have played a more important role in immigrant settlement and services. They address issues of immigration and access to trades and profession, often through collaboration and partnerships. For instance, in 2003 the city of Toronto established the Toronto Region Immigrant Employment Council (TRIEC), a multi-stakeholder council that brings together employers, regulatory bodies, professional associations, educators, labor, community groups, government, and immigrants. Its mentoring program in particular has been emulated by other cities. As of 2011, over 5,600 people had been mentored through the program (TRIEC, 2011). TRIEC was initially funded by the Maytree Foundation and the Greater Toronto Civic Action Alliance, the former a private foundation that promotes equity and prosperity through leadership building, the latter an organization that focuses on social, economic, and environmental issues in the Greater Toronto Area.

Regulatory Bodies

Regulatory bodies are an important stakeholder group in FCR. Canada is certainly not the only country that regulates trades and professions. Yet it differs from other countries "in the extent of its legislation, the number of occupations covered and the number of professions granted self-regulation" (Adams, 2007, p. 14). In Canada, the regulation of skilled trades and most professions falls under provincial and territorial jurisdiction, much of which is delegated to professional bodies (Adams, 2007). Currently, there are more than 400 occupational regulatory bodies and professional associations that establish standards of entry for 15 percent of Canada's professions. These regulatory bodies all belong to the Canadian Network of National Associations of Regulators, which serves as a clearinghouse for information on issues of common concern and develops and shares resources. Still, notable inconsistencies persist between provinces in terms of regulatory practices. Each regulatory body has discretion over its own policies and procedures. Further, some occupations that are regulated in some provinces may not be regulated in others. For instance, audiologists and speech-language pathologists are regulated in Alberta, British Columbia, Manitoba, New Brunswick, Ontario, Quebec, and Saskatchewan, but not in the rest of the country (Canadian Information Centre for International Credentials, 2012). It is also important to note that although decisions on entry into professional practice are made by professional regulatory bodies, national associations often play a role in developing standards and negotiating mutual agreements on behalf of the professions.

To get licensed, foreign-trained professionals typically need to get their degrees and diploma verified. In engineering, for example, those from non-MRA (mutual recognition agreements) countries are often assigned with an examination program to confirm to the licensure bodies of their educational backgrounds. They also need a minimum of four years' work experience, including one year in Canada. The ways that different regulatory programs administer confirmatory exams are not consistent. For instance, for the regulatory body in Alberta, in some cases applicants need 10 years' work experience in order to be exempted from confirmatory exams. In Ontario, people with five years' work experience get an interview opportunity to demonstrate their professional knowledge and skills. Despite these differences, there have been some positive changes in the regulatory practices in different engineering associations. For instance, in Ontario, the *Professional Engineers Act* was amended in October 2010 to eliminate the requirement that an applicant be a Canadian citizen or permanent resident in order to be licensed as a professional engineer in Canada (PEO, n.d.). Yet, this change appears to have had limited effects in practice.

Post-Secondary Institutions

Post-secondary institutions are increasingly becoming a labor market access point for immigrants who wish to receive training in order to enter the Canadian labor market. According to Statistics Canada (2003), two-thirds of new immigrants plan to pursue further education or training upon arrival in Canada. Post-secondary institutions in Canada facilitate credentialing processes through accessing credential assessment services (see the section below) and by providing their own Prior Learning Assessment and Recognition (PLAR) services. In addition to FCR, post-secondary institutions also deliver language training, career programs, and workplace and community-based training, which may help bridge immigrants to the host labor market.

The following organizations of post-secondary institutions are also involved in addressing FCR: the Association of Universities and Colleges of Canada (AUCC), the Association of Canadian Community Colleges (ACCC), the Association of Registrars of Universities and Colleges of Canada (ARUCC), the Canadian Bureau for International Education (CBIE), the Canadian Alliance of Education and Training Organizations (CAETO), the Canadian Federation of Students (CFS), the Canadian Association of University Teachers (CAUT), and the Canadian Commission for UNESCO (CCU). For instance, supported by the Government of Canada funds, ACCC developed and implemented the Canadian Immigrant Integration Program (CIIP), which prepares newcomers for economic integration, including credential recognition, while still in their country of origin. The CIIP operates regional offices in China, India, the Philippines, and the United Kingdom, and offers itinerant services in Bahrain, Bangladesh, and other countries on demand (ACCC, 2011).

Credential Assessment Services Agencies

Five provincial and territorial credential assessment agencies provide foreign credential assessment services to immigrants. These agencies are: International Qualifications Assessment Service (Alberta), International Credential Evaluation Service (British Columbia), Academic Credentials Assessment Service (Manitoba), World Education Services (Ontario), and Education Credential Evaluation (Quebec). The five agencies formed the Alliance of Credential Evaluation Services of Canada (ACESC), which facilitates the dissemination and exchange of information regarding international education. Small licensing bodies may need help from these organizations to determine the equivalency of an immigrant's foreign credentials. As mentioned earlier, large professional associations (e.g., the College of Physicians and Surgeons) usually conduct their own assessment and determine whether the applicants need further training or tests in order to re-enter their professions in Canada.

Furthermore, the process of recertification varies for each profession and each subspecialty. Based on licensing regulations, professions can be categorized as "protected" and "unprotected" (Salaff & Greve, 2003). Different occupational subgroups face different challenges, depending on the degree of control by Canadian professions. Generally, the protected occupations require professional certification in addition to a bachelor's or higher degree, including architectural designers, engineers, doctors, teachers, just to name a few. To practice in the protected professions, however, immigrants must also pass Canadian courses and examinations and acquire a stint of supervised employment in Canada. For example, medicine requires foreign-trained professionals to take a certification examination in combination with language testing, and/or to undertake a period of internship or practicum in Canada. Thus, with multiple barriers in the protected professions, former professionals in these areas have the most trouble getting back to their original professions. By comparison, the unprotected professions may require a bachelor's degree or diploma but do not require certification, such as computer programmers, delivery coordinators, sales persons, and construction site supervisors. The unprotected professions provide greater access and opportunities because their fields are less institutionalized. This comparison reveals the complexity involved in the process of devaluation of immigrants' credentials. In addition, immigrant-serving agencies, some not-for-profit organizations, and employers are also closely involved in the issue of FCR.

The above discussion clearly demonstrates that the foreign credential recognition process is an extraordinary complex system. As Hawthorne

(2007) notes, "the legacy of [the] Canadian history is a credential assessment maze involving an extraordinary array of stakeholders" (p. 9).

Furthermore, very often assessment of the same credentials by different institutions can be inconsistent. It is clear however that the process of foreign credential recognition is hampered by three major barriers: poor information on the accreditation process; lack of a responsible, coordinated approach for the evaluation of foreign credentials; and lack of agreed-upon national standards. These barriers mean that seeking accreditation in Canada requires undertaking a personal journey involving complex interactions with multiple authorities and players.

Recent FCR Initiatives

Given the mounting criticisms toward the FCR process, various initiatives have emerged in recent years with claimed goals to facilitate the recognition of international education and qualifications. At the federal level, Citizenship and Immigration Canada started a Foreign Credential Referral Office in 2007 to provide information, path-finding and referral services on foreign credential recognition for foreign-trained workers. An international qualifications network was also launched by the office for practitioners to showcase initiatives and events, network with others, and build knowledge on international qualification assessment and recognition. In 2009, the Forum of Labour Ministers was tasked to compile a Pan-Canadian Framework for the Assessment and Recognition of Foreign Qualifications. This framework lays out the pathways to recognition in Canada. The first step is for immigrants to get accurate information both overseas and in Canada. The second step is for immigrants to go through the assessment process. Those who fully demonstrate the required qualifications should be supported to employment. Applicants who need to obtain additional requirements in order to practice in their profession should be directed to the skill-upgrading pathways. Although it is not a law, the framework has provided a guide for federal, provincial, and territorial governments to work collaboratively to enhance the foreign qualifications recognition process.

At the provincial level, a notable move is initiatives taken by some provincial governments to legislate fair registration practices. Ontario is the province that first passed the Fair Access to Regulated Professions and Compulsory Trades Act in 2006 to hold licensure bodies responsible for making their assessment processes transparent and fair. A Fair Access commissioner was appointed shortly after to monitor the compliance of different regulatory bodies in Ontario. Nova Scotia and Manitoba passed Fair Access Act[s] in 2008 and 2009, respectively. In Quebec, a similar bill was passed in 2009 by the National Assembly of Quebec. In some provinces where fair access is not legalized, alternative policy frameworks have been established. In Alberta, for instance, A Foreign Qualification Recognition Plan for Alberta (FQR Plan) was announced in November 2008. There has been no systematic evaluation of the impact of the Fair Access Act on immigrants' access to professions. But from the available reports submitted to the Fairness Commissioner's Office in Ontario, for instance, regulatory bodies have at least met the timeliness requirements in assessing immigrants' credentials. Many regulatory bodies have also changed their assessment procedures to make processes more easily negotiable. Some have allowed immigrants to apply for licensure before permanent residence status has been granted.

In addition to the abovementioned national and provincial initiatives, professional bodies have been negotiating mutual recognition agreements with professional regulatory bodies in other countries. For example, Engineers Canada negotiates education-based international mutual recognition agreements (MRA) on behalf of Canada's engineering profession. These agreements recognize the equivalence of the accreditation systems (engineering education) of other countries and those of Canada. An applicant who is a graduate of an accredited or recognized engineering program offered in a country that has an agreement with Engineers Canada is generally considered to have met the academic requirements to be licensed as a professional engineer in Canada. Currently, Engineers Canada is also experimenting with alternative methods of licensure (Engineers Canada, 2010). The Alternative Methods of Licensure project was launched in December 2008 to study alternative methods that would clarify the process of licensing professional engineers in Canada, making it more consistent and objective. With funding obtained through FCRP at HRSDC, the Competency-Based Assessment of Engineering Work Experience project started in January 2011. This project aims to develop and pilot competency-based assessment tools and processes to assess engineering work experience. During this project, a framework for a competency-based assessment of engineering work experience and an initial set of core engineering competencies were defined and accepted by all 12 constituent associations. So far, the project has validated the initial set of competencies.

We have also witnessed more partnerships among non-governmental organizations, employers, and various levels of government. One example of such initiative is employment bridging programs. Skills for Change, one of the well-known immigrant serving agencies in Toronto, has about 30 years' experience delivering employment programs and professional development courses. These programs are often designed to address the specific needs of job seekers, while targeting particular professional and occupational fields. Of note, these programs and services are often project based, depending on the availability of funding opportunities as well as the ability of different agencies to acquire funding. A review of the annual report of Skills for Change shows that the agency has acquired funding from both the provincial governments and community-based foundations and were able to launch a number of new projects to enhance immigrants' access to the labor market (Skills for Change, 2011). In the meantime, some projects have also closed down, presumably due to short-term funding.

There is no doubt that the abovementioned programs are important and long overdue initiatives in attempting to solve issues pertaining to devaluation of immigrant' foreign credentials. Despite the promising prospects of these initiatives, we need to be wary that they were introduced with the hope to maximize immigrant professionals' potentials. What is reinforced in these practices is the neoliberal managerialism that reinforces the ideals of market individualism and procedural fairness that are discursively situated within the economic interests of the Canadian state to increase its global competiveness (Guo & Shan, 2013a). In this view, immigrants are objectified as "valuable" human resources with the potential to contribute to the knowledge bases in Canada. As such, immigrants are not only left out of the process to decide on the value of their qualifications, they have also been further objectified vis-à-vis universal Canadian occupational standards.

Making the Invisible Visible: The Politics of Recognition

Despite recent policy attempts to address the issue of FCR facing immigrant professionals, a number of studies have consistently shown that as a result of devaluation and denigration of immigrants' prior learning and work experiences, recent immigrants have experienced unemployment and underemployment, downward social mobility, and poor economic performance in Canada (Guo, 2009, 2013a, 2013b; Li, 2008; Plante, 2011; Shan, 2009). The 2006 census of Canada shows that recent immigrants continued to have lower employment rates (67%) and higher unemployment rates than the Canadian-born, this despite the fact that Canada led Group of Seven (G7) nations in creating jobs at an annual average rate of 1.7 percent (Statistics Canada, 2008a). For those who are employed, they are less likely than Canadian-born paid workers to be employed in their field of study or in an equivalent occupation, particularly for members of visible minority (Plante, 2011). Furthermore, the earnings gap between recent immigrants and the Canadian-born widened significantly over the past quarter century (Statistics Canada, 2008b). In 1980, recent immigrant men who had some employment income earned 85 cents for each dollar received by Canadian-born men. By 2005, this figure had dropped to 63 cents. The situation for immigrant women was even worse. The corresponding numbers for that group were 85 cents and 56 cents, respectively. It is worth noting that among recent immigrants aged 25 to 64, many held doctoral (49%) and master's (40%) degrees (Statistics Canada, 2008c). That said, however, not all foreign credentials are devalued in Canada (Li, 2008). According to Li, foreign credentials held by majority member immigrants bring a net earning advantage; only those held by visible minority suffer an earnings penalty. Li's study suggests that foreign credentials of immigrants are racialized since the local market rewards credentials differentially depending on the racial background of the immigrants.

Guo (2013a) uses *the triple glass effect* to illustrate the multiple layers of barriers facing immigrant professionals as a result of devaluation of their prior learning and work experiences, including *a glass gate*, *a glass door*, and *a glass ceiling*. The concept of *the triple glass effect* was developed out of a study of the integration experience of recent Chinese immigrants in Canada with a goal to determine the extent to which glass ceiling and related effects may apply to this group in the process of economic integration. The findings demonstrate that Chinese immigrants hit glass ceilings in the process of transferring their human capital to Canada. Despite the fact that many immigrant professionals came with masters' and doctoral degrees, they faced serious barriers in their transition to the Canadian labor market. Because the glass ceiling concept is primarily concerned with the ability to rise to management positions in the corporate hierarchy, Guo (2013a) argues that it alone cannot fully explain immigrants' experience because the main issue for immigrants lies in entering the corporate hierarchy in the first place. Hence, *the triple glass effect* was developed to interpret the experience of Chinese immigrant professionals, a framework which can be used to understand other visible minority groups in Canada.

Guo maintains that immigrant professionals potentially face three layers of glass in their integration process. The first layer, *the glass gate*, denies immigrants' entrance to guarded professional communities. Among the number of players and institutions that may be blamed for the devaluation of immigrants' foreign credentials and prior work experiences are professional associations and prior learning assessment agencies, which often function as gatekeepers by restricting immigrants' access to high-paying professional jobs. Immigrants' knowledge and experiences are often deemed deficient and devalued simply because they are different. At the same time, successful licensure does not automatically guarantee a professional job, and immigrant professionals need a professional company to house them. According to Guo, in their attempts to secure a professional job, many immigrants hit the second layer of glass—*the glass door*, which blocks immigrants' access to professional employment at high-wage firms. At this level, employers are the key players. Employers may refuse to offer immigrants professional jobs because they do not have Canadian work experience, or their prior work experience is devalued because it is seen as inferior to the Canadian experience. Alternatively, immigrants may not secure a professional job because of their skin color or their "non-standard" English accents. The third glass is *the glass ceiling* that prevents immigrants from moving into management positions, often because of their ethnic and cultural differences. Worse still, some immigrants may work on the same job but be paid less than their white colleagues, creating racialized disparities in earnings. Guo concludes that the *glass gate, glass door,* and *glass ceiling* may converge to produce *a triple glass effect* that creates multiple structural barriers which cause unemployment and underemployment, poor economic performance, and downward social mobility.

At this point, it might be worth asking why such inequities occur in a democratic society like Canada where democratic principles are upheld and where immigrants are "welcome." More importantly, what prevents us from moving forward? Non-recognition of immigrants' foreign credentials and prior work experiences can be attributed to a deficit model of difference which led us to believe that differences are deficiency, that the knowledge of immigrant professionals, particularly for those from the developing countries, is incompatible and inferior, and hence invalid (Guo, 2009). Furthermore, it is important to recognize the politics of recognition embedded in this process with our commitment to an objectivist ontology and liberal universalism. Objectivists believe that if something exists, it can be measured. By adopting a set of "value-free" criteria, it is argued that knowledge can be measured without accounting for the social, political, historical, and cultural context within which it is produced. In a similar vein, Guo continues, by applying a one-size-fits-all criterion to measure immigrants' credentials and experience, liberal universalism denies immigrants opportunities to be successful in a new society. The claimed neutral assessment and measuring usually disguises itself under the cloak of professional standard, quality, and excellence without questioning whose standard is put in place, and whose interests it represents. As such, prior learning assessment and recognition (PLAR) procedures are deployed as technologies of power and a system of governing in discounting and devaluating immigrants' prior learning and work experience (Andersson & Guo, 2009).

Conclusion and Implications for Adult Education

The above discussion has made it clear that the attempt to use the Canadian-centered, objectivist and universal yardstick to evaluate others is essentially problematic. While recent FCR initiatives may have played an instrumental role in bridging some immigrants to the host labor market, unfortunately they do not address the epistemological and ontological root causes of the problem. The discussion also demonstrates that qualification recognition of immigrant professionals in Canada is a much more complex issue than it at first appears to be. To find long-term solutions that are sustainable and equitable, it requires much more than a sole focus on the badly needed harmonization process. Guo and Shan (2013b) suggest a holistic integrated approach which embraces principles of transparency, fairness, and justice with support of a strong political will that uses legislation to make all stakeholders accountable for how they treat immigrants.

More importantly, a holistic integrated approach should combine a revamped qualification recognition with public pedagogy educating the public about the potential contributions that immigrants can bring to the host society as well as raising awareness of barriers facing immigrants' access to the labor market. It is imperative that a holistic integrated approach be introduced, one with the capacity to remove the multiple barriers that work together to constitute the glass gate, the glass door, and the glass ceiling.

This discussion also has important implications for adult and lifelong education. To build a more inclusive and more equitable PLAR system for immigrant professionals, I also suggest a paradigmatic shift toward trans-national adult and lifelong education (Guo, 2010). Informed by notions of recognitive justice and multicultural citizenship (Fraser, 2000, 2008; Kymlicka, 2008; Young, 1995, 2008), this framework simultaneously challenges the culturally neutral premise of distributive justice, which is supported by the liberal-democratic principles of individual freedom and the equal distribution of material and social goods, and problematizes retributive justice, which favors market-individualism. It questions the Eurocentric perspectives, values, and standards and challenges the claims that universal standards transcend cultural difference and particularity. It also rejects the deficit approach in viewing the knowledge and experiences brought in by "the other." Instead, it embraces cultural difference and diversity as positive and desirable assets. More importantly, it balances the freedom of mobility with recognition, inclusive membership and democratic citizenship, where migrant professionals can find a participatory space to decide on the validity and usefulness of their own knowledge and practices. The alignment with recognitive justice will also take us beyond the discourse of righteousness in debating issues of PLAR and disrupting the boundaries around foreign qualifications recognition for immigrant professionals.

References

Adams, T. (2007). Professional regulation in Canada: Past and present. *Canadian Issues*, Spring, 14–16.

Andersson, P., & Guo, S. (2009). Governing through non/recognition: The missing 'R' in the PLAR for immigrant professionals in Canada and Sweden. *International Journal of Lifelong Education, 28*(4), 423–437.

Association of Canadian Community Colleges (ACCC). (2011). *Canadian Colleges and Institutes—Supporting Foreign Credential Recognition and the Labour Market Integration of Immigrants*. Retrieved from http://www.accc.ca/ftp/briefs-memoires/20111130StudyonFCR_LMI.pdf.

Basran, G. S., & Zong, L. (1998). Devaluation of foreign credentials as perceived by visible minority professional immigrants. *Canadian Ethnic Studies, 30*(3), 7–23.

Canadian Information Centre for International Credentials (CICIC). (2012). *Untitled*. Retrieved from http://www.cicic.ca/.

Citizenship and Immigration Canada (CIC). (2014). *Immigrate to Canada*. Retrieved from http://www.cic.gc.ca/english/immigrate/index.asp.

Engineers Canada. (2010). *Annual Report 2010*. Retrieved from http://www.engineerscanada.ca/e/pu_annual.cfm/.

Fraser, N. (2000). Rethinking recognition. *New Left Review, 3*, 107–120.

———. (2008). From redistribution to recognition? Dilemmas of justice in 'postsocialist' age. In S. Seidman & J. Alexander (Eds.), *The new social theory reader* (pp. 188–196). London, UK: Routledge.

Foreign Credential Recognition Office (FCRO). (n.d.). *Untitled*. Retrieved from http://www.credentials.gc.ca/.

Guo, S. (2009). Difference, deficiency, and devaluation: Tracing the roots of non/recognition of foreign credentials for immigrant professionals in Canada. *Canadian Journal for the Study of Adult Education, 22*(1), 37–52.

————. (2010). Toward recognitive justice: Emerging trends and challenges in transnational migration and lifelong learning. *International Journal of Lifelong Education, 29*(2), 149–167.

————. (2013a). Economic integration of recent Chinese immigrants in Canada's second-tier cities: The triple glass effect and immigrants' downward social mobility. *Canadian Ethnic Studies, 45*(3), 95–115.

————. (2013b). The changing face of work and learning in the context of immigration: The Canadian experience. *Journal of Education and Work, 26*(2), 182–186.

Guo, S., & Shan, H. (2013a). The politics of recognition: Critical discourse analysis of recent PLAR policies for immigrant professionals in Canada. *International Journal of Lifelong Education, 32*(4), 464–480.

————. (2013b). Canada. In A. Schuster, M. V. Desiderio, & G. Urso (Eds.), *Recognition of qualifications and competences of migrants* (pp. 229–253). Brussels, Belgium: International Organization for Migration.

Hawthorne, L. (2007). Foreign credential recognition and assessment: An introduction. *Canadian Issues*, Spring, 3–13.

Kymlicka, W. (2008). Multicultural citizenship. In S. Seidman & J. Alexander (Eds.), *The new social theory reader* (pp. 270–280). London, UK: Routledge.

Li, P. S. (2003). *Destination Canada: Immigration debates and issues*. Don Mills, ON: Oxford University Press.

————. (2008). The role of foreign credentials and ethnic ties in immigrants' economic performance. *Canadian Journal of Sociology, 33*(2), 291–310.

Plante, J. (2011). *Integration of internationally-educated immigrants into the Canadian labour market: Determinants of success*. Ottawa, ON: Statistics Canada.

Professional Engineers Ontario (PEO) (n.d.). *Fact sheet*. Retrieved from http://www.peo.on.ca/FactSheets/PEO_IEG_Fact_Sheet%202010.pdf.

Salaff, J., & Greve, A. (2003). Gendered structural barriers to job attainment for skilled Chinese emigrants in Canada. *International Journal of Population Geography, 9*, 443–456.

Shan, H. (2009). Practices on the periphery: Highly educated Chinese immigrant women negotiating occupational settlement in Canada. *Canadian Journal for the Study of Adult Education, 21*(2), 1–18.

Simosko, S. (2012). Assessing the Skills and Competencies of Internationally Trained Immigrants: A manual for regulatory bodies, employers and other stakeholders. Retrieved from http://recognitionforlearning.ca/library/assessing-skills-and-competencies/.

Skills for Change. (2011). *Annual report 2011*. Retrieved from http://www.skillsforchange.org/.

Statistics Canada. (2003). *Longitudinal survey of immigrants to Canada: Process, progress and prospects*. Ottawa, ON: Statistics Canada.

————. (2008a). *Canada's changing labour force, 2006 census*. Ottawa, ON: Statistics Canada.

————. (2008b). *Earnings and incomes of Canadians over the past quarter century, 2006 census*. Ottawa, ON: Statistics Canada.

————. (2008c). *Educational portrait of Canada, 2006 census*. Ottawa, ON: Statistics Canada.

The Alliance of Sector Councils (TASC). (2010). Who does what in foreign credential recognition: An Overview of credentialing programs and services in Canada. Retrieved from http://www.councils.org/gateway/who-does-what/.

Toronto Region Immigrant Employment Council (TRIEC). (2011). *About us.* Retrieved from http://triec.ca/.

Van Kleef, J. (2011). Canada: A typology of prior learning assessment and recognition (PLAR). In J. Harris, M. Breier & C. Wihak (Eds.), *Researching the recognition of prior learning: International perspectives* (pp. 44–84). Leicester, UK: NIACE.

Young, I. M. (1995). Polity and group difference: A critique of the ideal of universal citizenship. In R. Beiner (Ed.), *Theorizing citizenship* (pp. 175–207). Albany, NY: SUNY Press.

————. (2008). Justice and the politics of difference. In S. Seidman & J. Alexander (Eds.), *The new social theory reader* (pp. 261–269). London, UK: Routledge.

14

How Welcome Are We?

Immigrants as Targets of Uncivil Behavior

Fabiana Brunetta
Thomas G. Reio, Jr.

In light of mounting recent economic and competitive pressures world-wide, uncivil workplace behavior has been increasing (Porath & Pearson, 2013). Workplace incivility is defined as "low intensity deviant behavior with ambiguous intent to harm the target, [that is] in violation of workplace norms for mutual respect" (Andersson & Pearson, 1999, p. 457). Workplace incivility contributes to toxic work environments that can harm individuals, teams/groups and the organization as a whole (Andersson & Pearson, 1999; Estes & Wang, 2008; Lim & Cortina, 2005; Johnson & Indvik, 2001; Pearson, Andersson, & Porath, 2000; Pearson & Porath, 2005; Porath & Erez, 2007; Reio & Ghosh, 2009). Incivility tends to have negative influences on not only the targets of uncivil behavior (e.g., dampened satisfaction, greater turnover intent), but also on onlookers (e.g., lost time through avoiding perpetrators) (Montgomery, Kane, & Vance, 2004). As a mild form of deviant behavior that is vague as to intent to harm and of low intensity, workplace incivility can spiral into patterns of intentionally harmful behaviors like bullying and physical violence (Andersson & Pearson, 1999). Of distinct interest is that while there are gender and ethnic differences in being the target of uncivil behavior, the frequency and intensity of these uncivil behaviors may be best understood as a manifestation of racial and gender biases (Cortina, 2008). Thus, workplace incivility is not merely a problem because it is detrimental to job performance, organizational commitment, voluntary turnover, etc.; it can contribute to the establishment of workplace settings that marginalize differences and foster conditions that promote physical forms of aggression and harm.

With the advent of pronounced immigration increases throughout the United States (U.S.), Canada, the European Union, and most developing countries (Ahonen, Benavides & Benach, 2007), the conditions seem ripe for greater conflict, incivility, and the associated negative outcomes. Indeed, Ayoko (2007) and Pelled (1996) posited that the diversity of the work environment is directly related to an increase in interpersonal conflict and rude behaviors. A rude or discourteous act to a member of one culture may be perfectly acceptable to someone from another. Similarly, tried-and-true styles of handling conflict (e.g., taking a "win-lose," dominant-style approach to solving a problem) in one setting may be totally inappropriate in another (Trudel & Reio, 2011). An increase in diversity in the workplace sets the stage for the miscommunication and mistrust that leads to interpersonal conflict, which in turn increases the likelihood of incivility. However, little is known about how incivility relates to group-specific expressions of hostility (Cortina, 2008), or how incivility is linked to power structures found in the typical work environment (Callahan, 2011; Reio & Ghosh, 2009).

Although researchers continue to uncover risk factors associated with workplace incivility, there is little literature on immigrants as incivility targets. There is evidence to suggest that employees who are different from the majority in the workplace have a higher risk of being bullied than the majority (Zapf, Einaresen, Hoel, & Vartia, 2003). Similarly, preliminary research supports the hypothesis that gender, ethnic, and age differences do exist in being an incivility target in a wide range of international settings (Brownridge & Halli, 2002; Fox & Stallworth, 2005; Jones & Lewis, 2011; Montgomery et al., 2004; Power et al., 2013). More work is necessary, however, to open the discourse on workplace diversity in the human resource development (HRD) field by exploring the experiences and perspectives of marginal groups (Mizzi & Rocco, 2013).

Exploring some of the findings in both the workplace and immigrant literature can serve as a starting point to inform our understanding of factors that may influence incivility targeted toward immigrant workers. In this chapter, after presenting incivility theory, we explore risk factors that may influence acts of uncivil behavior targeting immigrants. We organized these risk factors into three broad social dimensions: structural (economy and cultural identity), individual characteristics of the immigrant (race/ethnicity, gender, and social competence), and organizational (industry) factors. The chapter ends with some implications and a summary.

Incivility Theory

Andersson and Pearson (1999) posited "tit-for-tat" incivility theory to explain how incivility can spiral into more serious forms of aggressive behavior that can be detrimental in workplace settings. Examples of incivility include talking behind one's back, giving a supervisee the silent treatment, snapping at a colleague, ignoring a team member's e-mail or call, blatantly disregarding or wasting a coworker's time, ostracizing a fellow group member, and teasing an individual about the way he or she dresses or speaks. When one becomes the target of uncivil behavior, all too often the target responds in kind. In turn, the instigator targets more uncivil acts. This tit-for-tat exchange can escalate from seemingly ambiguous threats of harm to more severe forms of aggression that include patterns of behavior where there is an intent to harm, like bullying and physical violence. Yeung and Griffin (2008) used incivility spiral theory to predict workplace incivility and worker engagement in the context of six Asian countries/regions: China, Hong Kong, India, Japan, Korea, and Singapore. With a sample of almost 117,000 participants, the researchers found that coworkers were the greatest source of incivility, followed by managers and leaders. As predicted, engagement was less among those who had experienced incivility.

Building upon Andersson and Pearson's (1999) pivotal work, Cortina (2008) focuses her work on the different manifestations of incivility and proposed a theory of *selective incivility*, making the argument that incivility is sometimes targeted toward specific individuals as an expression of bias that ostracizes women and ethnic minorities in particular. She adds that selective incivility is a veiled form of sexism and racism in organizations and could serve as a mechanism that perpetuates disparities based on stereotypes that ultimately result in discrimination. Workplace incivility that is targeted toward a specific class of individuals like women, ethnic minorities, or immigrants often persists without challenge and is one means by which disparities persist, despite best efforts to eliminate bias (Kabat-Far & Cortina, 2012). In an empirical test of the theory where women and minorities were predicted to experience the most incivility, Cortina, Kabat-Farr, Leskinen, Huerta, and Magley (2011) found gender and race influenced vulnerability to being treated in an uncivil manner, with women of color reported as experiencing the worst treatment. Although both theories have demonstrated utility in predicting workplace incivility and its outcomes, we use Cortina's (2008) selectivity theory since it is most closely aligned with the aim of the chapter.

Structural Risk Factors

Stephan and Stephan (2000) suggest a classification of the types of threats that cause conflict between groups. These threats can be *realistic threats* or *symbolic threats*, and both types of threats relate to the interest of the groups and how the groups perceive that their interests are being threatened. Realistic threats are concerned with the perception of any threat that may directly affect the welfare of the group (e.g., economy, politics, or well-being). Symbolic threats involve perceived threats to the worldview of the group (e.g., beliefs and attitudes). In this section, we discuss the economy (realistic threat) and cultural identity (symbolic threat) as factors that may contribute to uncivil behavior targeting immigrants.

Economy

Economic uncertainty is a factor that leads to resentment and disparate treatment against immigrants (Dancygier & Donnelly, 2013; Jones, Peddie, Gilrane, King & Gray, 2013; Massey & Sánchez, 2010; McLaren, 2003; Portes, 1997). Fragile economies and economic environments that encourage intense competition for employment create an atmosphere that places greater strain on the relationship between native-born groups and immigrant groups in many countries. Anti-immigrant sentiment tends to escalate in times of economic crisis or stagnation (Massey & Sánchez, 2010), reinforcing public concern that immigrants compete with native workers for employment and public resources (Portes, 1997). Since 2008, millions of workers have been affected by the global economic crisis. Attitudes toward immigration are partly a function of the patterns that non-immigrants experience in their work life (Dancygier & Donnelly, 2013). In the U.S. and Europe, immigrants and members of other minority groups have been hit harder than all other groups, suffering not only being over-represented in the ranks of the unemployed, but often being viewed as the reason why members of the native-born populations are suffering economically (Papademetriou, 2012). A general sentiment among native-born groups is that immigrants contribute to unemployment, take jobs away from native-born employees, reduce wages, and compete with low-skilled native workers (Dancygier & Donnelly, 2013; Hainmueller & Hiscox, 2010).

Anti-immigrant sentiment, often bordering on xenophobia, is often strongest in countries unused to intense immigration flows. Many developed countries have transitioned from being countries of emigration to being countries of immigration (Turton & González, 2003). In the 1990s, for example, Germany was the second largest immigrant receiving country (Thranhardt, 1995), and today ranks third in the world in percentage of foreign-born population (International Labor Organization, 2013). On the other hand, countries like Spain and Italy, with a scarce history of immigration, are just now facing the need to establish immigration policies that will shape the emerging patterns of an immigrant workforce (Lucassen, 2005). In the presence of an unstable economy, conditions are ripe to fuel disparaging immigrant stereotypes and hostility because they are perceived as competing for limited resources (Dancygier & Donnelly, 2013; McLaren, 2003). Thus, as predicted by selective incivility theory (Cortina, 2008), the generalized hostility toward immigrants expressed in national discourses can easily become instances of incivility in the structured daily routines and practices of the workplace (Cortina, 2008).

Cultural Identity

In 2013, 232 million people, or 3.2 percent of the world's population, were international migrants and 74 percent of migrants were of working age (20 to 64 years) (International Labor Organization, 2013). The often daunting challenges faced by immigrants when entering the workforce are well documented. In both Europe and the U.S., for instance, discussions about immigrants are often associated with crime and prevention in ways that suggest immigrants are mostly criminals, resulting in unfavorable views toward immigrants and immigration in general (Angel-Ajani, 2003; Turton & Gonzalez, 2003). Immigrants are all too often viewed as "foreigners" not only in the legal sense, but also in a cultural sense. Group differences in morals, beliefs, values, standards, and attitudes can develop into perceived symbolic threats (Stephan & Stephan, 2000). The current nature of immigration into the U.S. poses a challenge to the major social, political, cultural, and economic institutions of the nation (Huntington, 2004). Similarly, European countries face such an immigration scenario. Immigrants from Northern and Sub-Saharan Africa, along with Eastern Europeans, have established chain migration patterns very similar to those presented as threatening by Huntington (2004) in the U.S. (i.e., Mexican and Latin American migration patterns).

Power et al. (2013) in a large international study found bullying (a more severe form of incivility) to be prevalent on six continents. Parallel to these findings, incidences of bullying and physical violence against immigrants have been widespread in the United States, Canada, and the European Union (Koopmans & Olzak, 2004; Scherr & Larson, 2010). While hypotheses designed to measure incivility targeted toward immigrants are not tested, selective incivility theory posits that incivility directed toward immigrants should increase as immigrants become more numerous in the workplace (Cortina, 2008).

Individual Risk Factors

Minority groups who differ from the majority are at risk of being seen as outsiders and are more likely to be socially excluded in the workplace (Zapf, 1999). Immigrants are considered outsiders along several dimensions in their receiving countries. Even when they are documented, they are most likely considered to be ethnic and cultural minorities in their receiving countries. Immigrants often experience discriminatory attitudes and negative reactions in the workplace (Tran, Lee & Burgess, 2010). In this section, we discuss specific individual characteristics of immigrants that may have an effect on how immigrants are treated in the workplace.

Race and Ethnicity

While immigrants were not investigated in the following studies, related literature on workplace incivility suggests that ascribed individual differences are significant in experiencing incivility. For example, Yeung and Griffin (2008) found that Asian managers were more likely to be the target of incivility than supervisors and workers. Cortina et al. (2011) demonstrated also that women in general and women of color in particular were more likely to be incivility targets. From an instigator perspective, Reio and Ghosh (2009) found that the younger, male, and white workers were more likely to instigate incivility.

Likewise, individual differences in bullying, a closely related construct, have been reported (Fox & Stallworth, 2005). One study of immigrant worker bullying targeting newcomers from North Africa, the Middle East, and the former Yugoslavia revealed that the immigrant group had a higher risk of being a target of bullying behavior compared to the native-born group (Vartia & Giorgiani, 2008). A similar exploration found that immigrant health care workers are more at risk of being bullied at work compared to their non-immigrant counterparts (Hough, Gomes, Giver, & Rugulies, 2010). Ethnic minority workers are more likely to label themselves as suffering from bullying behaviors than their white counterparts (Lewis & Gunn, 2007). Moreover, Zapf (1999) found that bullying at the workplace was more common at the lower levels of the organization, where most ethnic workers labored.

Gender

Globally, women account for 48 percent of all international migrants (International Labor Organization, 2013). Immigrant women face multiple forms of prejudice, such as sexism and racism, across different social contexts (Browne & Misra, 2003; Espin, 1999). Research suggests that women are more likely to be the target of workplace incivility (Cortina et al., 2011). A large Canadian study of 7,115 women found that immigrant women from developing countries were the greatest targets of violence (Brownridge & Halli, 2002). Zapf (1999) demonstrated that, while male workers were bullied more than women at the lower levels of the organization, female senior managers reported more incidences of incivility (categorized as bullying in this study) than male workers.

Social Competence

As the phenomenon of immigration continues to diversify workforces around the world, diversity in cultural norms sets the stage for miscommunication, interpersonal conflict, and uncivil behavior (Power et al., 2013; Reio, 2011). What constitutes mutual respect and acceptable behavior is determined by individual, situational, and cultural variables (Hershcovis et al., 2007; Reio, 2011). Immigrants with poor sociocultural adaptation are more likely to violate social norms and elicit aggressive behavior in others in workplace settings (Jimenez, Moreno, Munos, Garrosa, & Galvez, 2006). Reio and Ghosh (2009) conducted a study in the U.S. and found that the lack of workplace adaptation (i.e., establishing relationships with peers and supervisors) and negative affect were strongly associated with interpersonal (instigated against a coworker or supervisor) and organizational incivility (instigated against teams, groups, and organization). This sociocultural adaptation can be an important precursor to both the likelihood of being a target of uncivil behavior, as well as being an instigator of uncivil behavior. Productive interpersonal relationships with coworkers and management allows for a workplace climate of cooperation and interconnectedness (Reio & Wiswell, 2000).

The emergence of multilingual workplaces poses a challenge to the establishment of a cooperative environment (Cortina, 2008). Language exclusion has been associated with expressed prejudice toward immigrants (Hitlan, Carrillo, Zarare, & Aikman, 2007). In the U.S., "Official English" campaigns have coincided historically with large waves of immigration. For example, in the 1980s the dominance of immigrants in Miami, Florida, fueled anti-bilingual sentiments that resulted in the passing of the first English Only amendment in the U.S. (Dowling, Ellison, & Leal, 2012).

Organizational Risk Factors

Immigrants have a tendency to cluster in specific regional and local job markets where industries are located that require low technical and interpersonal skills (Bauder, 2006). Thus, some companies within an industry can have a strong immigrant presence that may challenge the requisite relationship formation, cooperation, and trust-building required to minimize the likelihood of conflict and incivility among coworkers, supervisors, and managers. In this section we discuss the role of industry in workplace incivility.

Immigrants are contributing more than ever to the creation of multicultural workplaces (Ahonen et al., 2007). Research exploring the settlement patterns of immigrants in the U.S. indicates that national origins and geographic destinations of new immigrants are highly concentrated, creating large foreign language and cultural communities in many areas of the U.S. (Massey, 2004). The industries within such areas are generally those that attract immigrant workers because of the low educational or skill necessities required to perform their jobs (e.g., construction, garment, hotel). In the last two decades, the large majority of immigrants to Western Europe and the U.S. have been low-skilled workers (Hainmueller & Hiscox, 2010; Hanson, 2012). Part of the attraction for these immigrant workers has been the presence of low-skilled jobs that they would be qualified to perform. Interestingly, immigrants with professional occupational skills (e.g., engineers, doctors) have often been unsuccessful in attaining employment in their preferred fields, and are then left to compete also for low-skill jobs with other less skilled immigrants (Iredale, 2004).

Dancygier and Donnelly (2013) found that industry-inflows of immigrant workers in Europe after the 2008 financial crisis had an effect in increasing negative attitudes toward immigrants in the workplace. Even though little research has focused on the frequency or intensity of uncivil behavior in immigrant-dominated industries, these industries present researchers with the rich potential to explore new dimensions of incivility.

Implications

The changing landscape of the workplace has been accompanied by tension both within workplaces and in society at large, at times leading to discrimination directed at the immigrant worker (Koeppel 2008). Better understanding of the factors that are related to acts of incivility in the workplace would be a step forward for multicultural organizations. We have discussed how structural, individual, and organizational risk factors can create a context where immigrant incivility is more likely to occur. In an effort to move forward theoretically, empirically, and practically, there needs to be further research regarding immigrant workplace experiences in general as it compares to majority culture members' experiences (Pasca & Wagner, 2011). Diversity research is still focused on the study of high-skilled immigrant employees (Dietz, 2010), as specific areas of diversity research often do not correspond to the interests and needs of practitioners (Rynes, Giluk, & Brown, 2007). Critical theory and its emphasis on understanding power structures would seem to be a potent lens for undergirding future research (Callahan, 2011). As explicit discrimination is being replaced by more subtle biases (Brief et al., 2000; Cortina, 2008; Petersen & Dietz, 2005), the experiences of the majority of immigrant workers are excluded by diversity research. Given their practical engagements with workers, adult education and HRD scholars are well positioned to explore, understand, and address incivility that selectively marginalizes people.

Clearly, more knowledge about workplace incivility from the perspectives of immigrant women and men is necessary to understand how they experience the workplace. What are the similarities and differences of their work experiences and how they are addressed in the workplace? Diversity initiatives and educational agendas can impact how workers relate to one another and shape productivity (Mizzi & Rocco, 2013). That said, how can we design workplaces where stereotypes, biases, and discrimination and thus the conditions for conflict and incivility are reduced? Unmistakably, if certain groups are being targeted more frequently than others, the practical implications for HRD professionals and adult educators are profound.

Summary

Workplace incivility cannot be explained fully without taking into consideration the possible influence of race, gender, and age biases (Cortina, 2008). Acknowledging that immigrants are at higher risk of being the targets of uncivil workplace behavior can have important utility in unmasking modern forms of discrimination that may be hidden in the informal and subtle nuances of incivility. Both subtle and overt forms of discrimination result in comparable adverse outcomes for the targets of the discrimination (Jones, Peddie, Gilrane, King, & Gray, 2013). Selective incivility (Cortina, 2008) might be a mechanism by which racial and gender disparities persist in the workplace (Kabat-Farr & Cortina, 2012). Research on workplace incivility that targets immigrants may lead us to rethink and expand current thinking about the nature of workplace incivility and its consequences for adult education and human resource development.

References

Ahonen, E. Q., Benavides, F. G., & Benach, J. (2007). Immigrant populations, work and health—a systematic literature review. *Scandinavian Journal of Work Environment and Health, 33*, 96–104.

Andersson, L. M., & Pearson, C. M. (1999). Tit for tat?: The spiraling effect of incivility in the workplace. *Academy of Management Review, 24*, 452–471.

Angel-Ajani, A. (2003). The racial economies of criminalization, immigration, and policing in Italy. *Social Justice, 30*, 48–62.

Ayoko, O. B. (2007). Communication openness, conflict events, and reactions to conflict on culturally diverse workgroups. *Cross Cultural Management, 14*, 105–124.

Bauder, H. (2006). *Labor movement: How migration regulates labor markets.* New York, NY: Oxford University Press.

Brief, A., Dietz, J., Cohen, R., Pugh, S., & Vaslow, J. (2000). Just doing business: Modern racism and obedience to authority as explanations for employment discrimination. *Organizational Behavior and Human Decision Processes, 81*(1), 72–97.

Browne, I., & Misra, J. (2003). The intersection of gender and race in the labor market. *Annual Review of Sociology*, 487–513.

Brownridge, D. A., & Halli, S. S. (2002). Double jeopardy?: Violence against immigrant women in Canada. *Violence and Victims, 17*, 455–471.

Callahan, J. L. (2011). Incivility as an instrument of oppression: Exploring the role of power in constructions of civility. *Advances in Developing Human Resources, 13*(1), 10–21.

Cortina, L. M. (2008). Unseen injustice: Incivility as modern discrimination in organizations. *Academy of Management Review, 33*, 55–76.

Cortina, L. M., Kabat-Farr, D., Leskinen, E. A., Huerta, M., & Magley, V. J. (2011). Selective incivility as modern discrimination in organizations: Evidence and impact. *Journal of Management, 39*, 1579–1605.

Dancygier, R. M., & Donnelly, M. J. (2013). Sectoral economies, economic contexts, and attitudes toward immigration. *The Journal of Politics, 75*(1), 17–35.

Dietz, J. (2010). Introduction to the special issue on employment discrimination against immigrants. *Journal of Managerial Psychology, 25*(2), 104–12.

Dowling, J. A., Ellison, C. G., & Leal, D. L. (2012). Who doesn't value English? Debunking myths about Mexican immigrants' attitudes toward the English language. *Social Science Quarterly, 93*, 356–378.

Espin, O. M. (1999). *Women crossing boundaries: A psychology of immigration and the transformations of sexuality*. New York, NY: Routledge.

Estes, B., & Wang, J. (2008). Integrative literature review: Workplace incivility: Impacts on individual and organizational performance. *Human Resource Development Review, 7*, 218–240.

Fox, S., & Stallworth, L. E. (2005). Racial/ethnic bullying: Exploring links between bullying and racism in the US workplace. *Journal of Vocational Behavior, 66*, 438–456.

Hainmueller, J., & Hiscox, M. J. (2010). Attitudes toward highly skilled and low-skilled immigration: Evidence from a survey experiment. *American Political Science Review, 104*, 61–84.

Hanson, G. H. (2012). Immigration and economic growth. *Cato Journal, 32*, 24–34.

Hershcovis, M. S., Turner, N., Barling, J., Arnold, K., A., Dupré, K. E., Inness, M., LeBlanc, M., & Ivanathan, N. (2007). Predicting workplace aggression: A meta-analysis. *Journal of Applied Psychology, 92*, 228–238.

Hitlan, R. T., Carrillo, K., Zarare, M. A., & Aikman, S. N. (2007). Attitudes toward immigrant groups and the September 11 terrorist attacks. *Peace and Conflict: Journal of Peace Psychology, 13*, 135–152.

Hough, A., Gomes Carneiro, I., Giver, H., & Rugulies, R. (2011). Are immigrants in the nursing industry at increased risk of bullying at work?: A one year follow up study. *Scandanavian Journal of Psychology, 52*, 49–56.

Huntington, S. P. (2004). The Hispanic challenge. *Foreign Policy, 141*, 30–45.

International Labor Organization. (2013, June 3). *World of work report 2013: Repairing the economic and social fabric*. Retrieved from: http://www.ilo.org/global/lang--en/index.htm.

Iredale, R. (2004). Gender, immigration policies and accreditation: Valuing the skills of professional women migrants. *Geoforum, 36*, 155–166.

Jimenez, B. M., Moreno, Y., Munos, A. R., Garrosa, E., & Galvez, M. (2006). Workplace bullying to ethnic minorities: The moderating role of sociocultural adaptation. In M. O'Moore, J. Lynch, & M. Smith (Eds.), *The way forward* (pp. 112–114). Dublin, Ireland: Trinity College.

Johnson, P. R., & Indvik, J. (2001). Rudeness at work: Impulse over restraint. *Public Personnel Management, 30*, 457–466.

Jones, J. R., & Lewis, D. M. H. (2011). Let's not go down that path again: Lessons from the past applied to immigrant-targeted discrimination. *Employee Responsibilities and Rights Journal, 23*(4), 229–247.

Jones, K. P., Peddie, C. I., Gilrane, V. L., King, E. B., & Gray, A. L. (2013). Not so subtle: A meta-analytic investigation of the correlates of subtle and overt discrimination. *Journal of Management.* doi: 0149206313506466.

Kabat-Farr, D., & Cortina, L. M. (2012). Selective incivility: gender, race, and the discriminatory workplace. In Fox, S. & Lituchy, T. R. (Eds.), *Gender and the dysfunctional workplace* (pp. 120–134). Northampton, MA: Edward Elgar Publishing.

Koeppel, P. (2008). The business case for cultural diversity: Satisfaction, market orientation and international success. *International Journal of Diversity in Organizations, Communities and Nations, 7*(6), 311–319

Koopmans, R., & Olzak, S. (2004). Discursive opportunities and the evolution of right-wing violence in Germany. *American Journal of Sociology, 110*(1), 198–230.

Lewis, D., & Gunn, R. (2007). Workplace bullying in the public sector: Understanding the racial dimension. *Public Administration, 85*(3), 641–665.

Lim, S., & Cortina, L. M. (2005). Interpersonal mistreatment in the workplace: The interface and impact of general incivility and sexual harassment. *Journal of Applied Psychology, 90*, 483–493.

Lucassen, L. (2005). *The immigrant threat: The integration of old and new migrants in Western Europe since 1850.* Champaign, IL: University of Illinois Press.

Massey, D. S. (2004). Theories of international migration: A review and appraisal. In Mobasher, M. M., & Sadri, M. (Eds.), *Migration, globalization, and ethnic relations* (pp. 2–28). Saddle River, NJ: Pearson Prentice Hall.

Massey, D. S., & Sánchez, M. (2010). *Brokered boundaries: Creating immigrant identify in anti-immigrant times.* New York, NY: Russell Sage Foundation.

McLaren, L. M. (2003). Anti-immigrant prejudice in Europe: Contact, threat perception, and preferences for the exclusion of migrants. *Social Forces, 81*, 909–936.

Mizzi, R. C., & Rocco, T. R. (2013). Deconstructing dominance: Toward a reconceptualization of the relationship between collective and individual identities, globalization, and learning at work. *Human Resource Development Review, 12*(3), 364–382.

Montgomery, K., Kane, K., & Vance, C. M. (2004). Accounting for differences in norms of respect: A study of assessments of incivility through the lenses of race and gender. *Group & Organization Management, 29*, 248–268.

Papademetriou, D. (2012). Migration meets slow growth. *Finance and Development,* *49*(3). Retrieved from: http://www.imf.org/external/pubs/ft/fandd/2012/09/papademe.htm.

Pasca, R., & Wagner, S. L. (2011). Occupational stress in the multicultural workplace. *Journal of Immigrant and Minority Health, 13,* 697–705.

Pearson, C. M., Andersson, L. M., & Porath, C. L. (2000). Assessing and attacking workplace incivility. *Organizational Dynamics, 29,* 123–137.

Pearson, C. M., & Porath, C. L. (2005). On the nature, consequences and remedies of workplace incivility: No time for "nice"? Think again. *The Academy of Management Executive, 19,* 7–18.

Pelled, L. H. (1996). Relational demography and perceptions of group conflict and performance: A field investigation. *International Journal of Conflict Management, 7,* 230–246.

Petersen, L., & Dietz, J. (2005). Prejudice and enforcement of workforce homogeneity as explanations for employment discrimination. *Journal of Applied Social Psychology, 35*(1), 144–59.

Porath, C. L., & Erez, A. (2007). Does rudeness really matter? The effects of rudeness on task performance and helpfulness. *Academy of Management Journal, 50,* 1181–1197.

Porath, C., & Pearson, C. (2013). The price of incivility: Lack of respect hurts morale—and the bottom line. *Harvard Business Review, 91,* 115–121.

Portes, A. (1997). Immigration theory for a new century: Some problems and opportunities. *International Migration Review, 31*(4), 799–825.

Power, J. L., Brotheridge, C. M., Blenkinsopp, J., Bowes-Sperry, L., Bozionelos, N., Buzády, Z., & Nnedumm, A. U. O. (2013). Acceptability of workplace bullying: A comparative study on six continents. *Journal of Business Research, 66,* 374–380.

Reio, T. G., Jr. (2011). Supervisor and coworker incivility: Testing the work frustration-aggression model. *Advances in Developing Human Resources, 13,* 54–68.

Reio, T. G., Jr., & Ghosh, R. (2009). Antecedents and outcomes of workplace incivility: Implications for human resource development research and practice. *Human Resource Development Quarterly, 20,* 237–264.

Reio, T. G., Jr., & Wiswell, A. K. (2000). Field investigation of the relationship between adult curiosity, workplace learning, and job performance. *Human Resource Development Quarterly, 11,* 1–36.

Rynes, S., Giluk, T., & Brown, K. (2007). The very separate worlds of academic and practitioner periodicals in human resource management: Implications for evidence-based management. *Academy of Management Journal, 50*(5), 987–1008.

Scherr, T. G., & Larson, J. (2010). Bullying dynamics associated with race, ethnicity, and immigration status. In S. Jimerson, S. Swearer, & D. Espelage (Eds.), *Handbook of bullying in schools: An international perspective* (pp. 223–234). New York, NY: Routledge.

Stephan, W. G., & Stephan, C. W. (2000). An integrated threat theory of prejudice. In S. Oskamp (Ed.), *Reducing prejudice and discrimination* (pp. 23–46). Hillsdale, NJ: Lawrence Erlbaum.

Thranhardt, D. (1995). Germany: An undeclared immigration country. *Journal of Ethnic and Migration Studies, 21,* 19–35.

Tran A., Lee, R., & Burgess, D. (2010). Perceived discrimination and substance use is Hispanic/Latino, African-born Black, and Southeast Asian immigrants. *Cultural Diversity Ethnic Minority Psychology, 16,* 226–36.

Trudel, J., & Reio, T. G., Jr. (2011). Managing workplace incivility: The role of conflict management styles—antecedent or antidote? *Human Resource Development Quarterly, 22*(4), 395–423.

Turton, D., & González, J. (2003*). Immigration in Europe: Issues, policies, and case studies.* Bilbao: University of Deusto. Retrieved from http://www.humanitariannet.deusto.es/publica/PUBLICACIONES_PDF/13%20Immigration%20in%20Europe.pdf.

Vartia, M., & Giorgiani, T. (2008). Bullying of immigrant workers. In A. Soares, N. Jeanneau, G. Plante, & G. Hannah (Eds.), *Sharing our knowledge* (pp. 149–150). Montreal, QC: Université du Québec.

Yeung, A., & Griffin, B. (2008). Workplace incivility: Does it matter in Asia? *People and Strategy, 31*(3), 14–19.

Zapf, D. (1999). Organisational, work group related and personal causes of mobbing/bullying at work. *International Journal of Manpower, 20*(1/2), 70–85.

Zapf, D., Einsarsen, S., Hoel, H., & Vartia, M. (2003). Empirical findings on bullying in the workplace. In S. Enarsen, H. Hoel, D. Zapf & C. L. Cooper (Eds.), *Bullying and emotional abuse in the workplace: International perspectives in research and practice* (pp. 103–126). London, UK and New York, NY: Taylor and Francis.

TRANSNATIONAL ADULT EDUCATION AND GLOBAL ENGAGEMENT

15

The Sputnik Moment in the Twenty-First Century

America, China, and the Workforce of the Future

Peter Kell
Marilyn Kell

Never before had so small and so harmless an object created such consternation.

—Daniel J. Boorstin, *The Americans: The Democratic Experience*

Fifty years later our Sputnik moment is back.

—Barack Obama, President of the United States of America

Blip, Blip, Blip: A Space Signal for a New Era in Education

On October 4, 1957, the Soviet Union launched Sputnik 1, the first man-made object to orbit the earth. Sputnik 1 was a small circular steel ball estimated to be the same size as a basketball weighing only 183 pounds, and took about 98 minutes to orbit the earth in an elliptical pattern. It emitted a constant radio signal on 20,007 MHz that was easily received by trackers on the ground including ham radio operators who were able to verify this Soviet achievement of science and engineering (CBS, 2007;

AMSAT, n.d.). As it orbited in the October sky Sputnik was visible to people on the ground, compelling evidence of this scientific achievement by the communist state.

A Sputnik Moment! An Artefact of the Cold War

The term, "Sputnik moment," entered the English language to describe a situation where urgent action results from shocked reaction to a phenomenon. It generally assumes that complacency and incompetence has resulted in a deterioration of standards that require an urgent and dramatic response. Sputnik moments are *wake-up calls*, which subsequently influence the nature of public policy. The current Sputnik moment surrounds education. Justification for dramatic intervention in education is based on the notion that "public schools are . . . broken, lacking, insufficient, and scarce; they operate on a model of deficiency always looking to illuminate what is absent, broken, or needs to be fixed" (Steeves et al., 2009, p. 76). However, more concerning is the manner in which this sense of crisis has been repeatedly used as discourse that opposes progressive education programs. The crisis about falling standards has been manipulated as a way of criticizing programs that specifically address disadvantage or social inequality through customized interventions. Such initiatives are often maligned as being *faddish* and lacking rigor with critics pleading for a *back-to-basics* approach concentrated on improving the reading of printed text, writing skills, pronunciation, and simple arithmetic.

Although the launch of Sputnik 1 did not inflict a physical blow on the United States (U.S.) itself, it was seen as a devastating blow to the U.S. in terms of status and prestige (Finn, 2010). Further it created the perception that the U.S., as a world political leader, had been pushed from the center to the periphery. For the U.S. this was a profound moment of shock and subsequent reflection that created the impetus for educational reform by the U.S. government. This chapter argues that in the intervening years U.S. government policy has failed in both educational reforms designed to shift educational achievement and equality from the periphery to the center *and* in shifting itself politically from the periphery to the center. The inequalities that characterize U.S. society have created a periphery of a permanently marginalized section of society. The cyclic sense of crisis that has pervaded American policy has claimed that the U.S. is moving to a peripheral status, but the authors in the chapter argue that globalization makes much of the rhetoric and viewpoints about the center and the periphery meaningless and redundant. Despite this, much of the discourse of policy is trapped in a cold-war style time warp.

U.S. Response to the First Sputnik Moment

Dwight D. Eisenhower, the U.S. President at the time of the Sputnik launch crisis, attempted to maintain a calm demeanor saying: "that the Sputnik does not raise my apprehensions, not one iota" and dismissed the satellite as a "ball" (CBS, 2007). However, under the pressure of cold war rivalries conservative analysts claimed that Sputnik 1 exposed U.S. vulnerabilities and argued for an urgent and aggressive defense response.

Eisenhower acted on several fronts. Legislatively, he created the National Aero Space Agency (NASA) commonly known as the "space act." Programs developed as a result of this act eventually led to "the space race," between the USSR and the U.S., culminating in the first Apollo mission to the moon in 1969.

Administratively, Eisenhower identified a "scientific gap," resulting in the formation of the National Science Foundation with an appropriation of US $14 million. Here the U.S. President sought to place an emphasis on redressing the imbalance with the Soviets through improvements in science, mathematics, and engineering in schools. This response emerged from a sense of national crisis about the ability of the U.S. to match the achievements of its rivals in science and technology.

In 1958 the National Defense Education Act (NDEA), "couched in terms of catching up with and exceeding the Soviet Union in the Cold War race for military superiority" (Sander, 2010, p. 1) provided education institutions with US $183 million to support students to attend colleges, particularly "to improve teaching in the sciences, foreign languages and mathematics" (p. 1). The effect of the NDEA Act was that by 1960, 3.6 million students were attending college, a sevenfold increase on 1940 attendance.

Senator J. F. Kennedy campaigned on the gap between Soviet and U.S. standards in education during the 1960 Presidential election campaign, emphasizing a "perceived educational crisis" (Bales, 2006, p. 396). But it was President L. B. Johnson who improved funding through the Elementary and Secondary Education Act (ESEA) in 1965 "to augment and enhance the education of poor and minority children" (Sanders, 2010, p. 1). At its heart ESEA aimed to assist special interest groups, such as "women, minorities, young people, old people, farmers, workers" (Chomsky, 2013, n. p.).

Responses by Eisenhower, Kennedy, and Johnson always positioned the United States as lacking skills or being behind the Soviet Union and having to catch up. In reshaping public policy, under the constitutional rider of providing general welfare (Bales, 2006), these presidents oversaw an unprecedented intervention by the federal government that challenged the view that education was a local or state obligation and linked funding to standards.

The sense of crisis around standards also displaced other demands on education. For example, it failed to respond to inequalities in American society for access to quality education through the equal rights movement (Easley, 2011). This meant that the quest for the "great society" where those on the periphery had a chance to move to the center, championed by the democrats, was attacked as undermining the quest for excellence and watering down standards. The school effectiveness movement, which has attacked progressive education and has argued for more "rigorous" curriculum, standardized testing, and greater attention to moral standards and values (Apple, 2001) has become an enduring feature of the politics of American education. Resistance to progressive education is portrayed as a *middle class revolt* and is linked with demands for lower taxes, the deregulation of the economy, and calls for smaller government, principally because middle-class parents are more adept at "exploiting market mechanisms in education and in bringing social, economic, and cultural capital to bear on them" (p. 73).

The dilemma at the mid-point of the twentieth century was that,

> Education was expected to establish an equal society, maintain economic growth and promote national prosperity, while at the same time provide everyone with higher incomes, interesting jobs and a pleasant middle class life. (Bennett, 1982, p. 165 cited in Angus, 1986)

The election of Ronald Regan in 1980 and the introduction of Reaganomics witnessed a revival of neoclassical economics with a commitment to competition and the unfettered power of the market. Under the umbrella of *public choice* the balance shifted from the post-war consensus on the role of the state to a new orthodoxy of reducing the size and the capacity of the state to intervene on behalf of the common good.

Crisis dominated the language of the Education Commission of Excellence 1983 report *Nation at Risk* that attributed the decline of America's industrial capacity to a failure of leadership in education to stimulate competition and facilitate a rise in standards. The assumption of *Nation at Risk* was that competition and leadership are the ingredients for successful reform and renewal. *Nation at Risk* was a withering critique and a retreat from the progressive liberal direction established by Kennedy and Johnson and demanded tighter links between curriculum content and testing. The theory, according to Angus (1986), was that "by teaching what is to be tested and how to go about doing tests, reading and mathematics scores are improved and so demonstrate that schools are effective or excellent" (p. 19). Teaching under this paradigm reoriented teaching practice toward direct methods of instruction and introduced a *test-taking culture* based on a testing methodology that stressed notions of objectivity, prediction, and control, acting as "an instructional blinder" (Easley, 2011, p. 231).

China and American Education: A Sputnik Moment for New Times

The initiatives of the 1960s, championed by the Democratic administration to build the great society, were aimed at improving science and mathematics education and equality of access. However, Michael Apple has argued that the equal rights movement of the 1960s triggered a reaction by the predominantly white majority that compensatory programs actually discriminated "against" them (Apple, 2001). The backlash created by this newly energized right wing was successful in portraying the disadvantaged and poor as having some special and unjust form of elevated and privileged status.

Mirroring the original Sputnik crisis, there is a new sense of crisis surrounding science, engineering, and technology. This is a shift from seeing the Soviets as the prime threat, as was the case in the cold war, to seeing China as the latest threat to the U.S. There is now another contest over global power and influence that sees education as a tussle for global power between the West and Orient (Kell & Kell, 2013). This contest emerges from East Asia where the Asian economic miracle has transformed the region from being the poorest on the globe at the end of the Second World War to being the source of global economic growth at the beginning of the twenty-first century. Unlike the anxieties created by the former Soviet Union, this new tension has not been prompted by any military threat but by the consistent high performance of Asian students in international tests in literacy, mathematics, science, and technology. The tests include the Program of International Students Assessment (PISA), Trends in International Mathematics, Science Survey (TIMSS), and Performance in Reading and Literacy Survey (PIRLS). East Asian countries including Singapore, Hong Kong, South Korea, Japan, and Macau have consistently achieved high scores and rankings in all the international student achievement tests over the last 15 years. In the context of policies designed to improve U.S. educational achievement, all of these countries have consistently out ranked the United States.

TIMSS, an international test of mathematics and science, is administered to grade 8 and 10 students in participating jurisdictions around the world every five years. The rankings are dominated by the East Asian nations such as Hong Kong, Singapore, Japan, and South Korea. They consistently share the top five positions and are viewed as high performing systems (Kell & Kell, 2013, p. 43).

The U.S. also performs poorly in PIRLS, an international test of literacy for grade 4 and 8 students. Like TIMSS the test is administered through jurisdictions every five years and focuses on reading, comprehension, and aspects of grammar and spelling and favors traditional views of literacy. The achievement of U.S. students in 2009 placed them last in a group of 27 nations including Moldova, Morocco, Iran, and Romania (Kell & Kell, 2013, p. 48).

There are many reasons attributed to East Asian success, particularly cultural norms that strongly value educational achievement, a strong test and examination culture, and teaching methodologies that favor recall and memorization. Aligned with the strong social norms about educational achievement is a high level of parental discretionary income allocated to schooling and coaching (Kell & Kell, 2013). However, the success of some Asian nations is attributed to the fact that Asian students achieve in higher numbers in the top bands of achievement and have very low numbers of students in the bottom achievement bands.

International testing results have compounded a sense of failure and inadequacy in Western nations including the U.S. and Australia, where periodic calls for dramatic reform have seen a repeat of the schools effectiveness movement's demand to standardize curriculum, standardize testing, and create greater accountability and monitoring of teaching standards.

Alarm bells rang in the U.S. and other countries with the performance of China, represented by the mega-city of Shanghai, which topped the world in PISA 2009. China's participation was unusual on two counts because, first, it is not member of the Organisation for Economic Cooperation and Development (OECD) and second, participating states are not usually represented by a single jurisdiction. Although Shanghai is larger than many participating states, including many other successful Asian nations such as Singapore and Hong Kong, it is not a sovereign nation and its inclusion represented an important precedent for PISA.

China's success in topping the globe shocked many observers (Zhao, 2012) with some accusing the Chinese of cheating to get such good results. Mark Schneider, the U.S. commissioner of educational research in the Bush administration, refuted these claims and argued that the students' success was more a product of nationalist pride after being informed of the importance of their success for China's image. Schneider suggests a similar reaction could be achieved in the U.S. saying, "can you imagine the reaction if we told the students of Chicago that this was an important international test and that America's reputation depended on them performing well" (Dillon, 2010, n.p.). Schneider also identified Shanghai's success as evidence of China taking education seriously and a work ethic that is "amazingly strong."

President Obama invoked the metaphor of the 1957 Sputnik moment, linking it to America's educational performance stating, "fifty years later our Sputnik moment is back." He invoked the challenge from Asian nations who are "suddenly plugged into the world's economy" with the most educated workers prevailing and cautioned, "as it stands now America is in danger of falling behind" (Dillon, 2010).

In a vein similar to the earlier Sputnik crisis, recent events have been surrounded by dire warnings about a shortage of qualified scientists and workers in science, engineering, and technology (STEM) in the U.S. A 2012 report by The Council of Advisors on Science and Technology noted that in the next ten years an additional one million STEM workers are needed. The U.S. is not alone in facing a shortage with the Royal Academy of Engineering predicting that the UK will require 100,000 STEM majors every year until 2020 (Charette, 2013). Many Western nations are creating a range of programs to boost the numbers of students studying science, mathematics, and engineering and also increasing the number of science and mathematics teachers. President Obama has quantified this as needing to train an additional 10,000 engineers every year and 100,000 STEM teachers by 2020. In response to these shortages American corporations such as IBM and Microsoft and others are lobbying the government for larger intakes of qualified scientists and technology under the H-1B visa category, lifting the numbers of skilled migrants from 65,000 to an estimated 180,000.

The sense of crisis has also been manifested in Australia where a recent paper authored by Australia's Chief Scientist identified (a) a trend where too little teaching time is spent on science in primary school, (b) there is declining interest in STEM disciplines in secondary schools, and (c) there is limited growth and stagnation in information and technology study at the tertiary level. The paper cites an Australian industry study that claims,

> It has been estimated that 75% of the fastest growing occupations require STEM skills and knowledge. Yet . . . young people in schools and universities are not acquiring the STEM skills we need for our future prosperity. (OCS, 2013, p.10)

However, this sense of crisis is contradicted by data that indicate that there are more STEM graduates than there are suitable jobs and that employment conditions and careers for science graduates are poor relative to other occupations. In reality the global financial crisis has seen massive job shedding of science and engineering graduates in corporations, such as Boeing and IBM. There is in fact a growing surplus of qualified workers.

STEM workers' earnings are also stagnating at levels equivalent to those in the year 2000 with few opportunities for permanent careers. Stanley Aronowitz and William Di Fazio, as far back as 1994, identified that shifts in the character of the employment in science and engineering, which has been reshaped by flexible specialization has created more short contracted positions than long-term permanent positions. They stressed that "market principles and profit are increasingly important in the production of scientific knowledge and this presupposes a power relation, a social structure and a labour process" (Aronowitz & Di Fazio, 1994, p.150). Under these conditions they argue that there has been a de-professionalization of science careers where production is increasingly owned and controlled by another. Yet having an oversupply of STEM graduates is seen by Charette (2013) as not being such a bad development, arguing that this gives employers a larger pool from which they can pick the best and brightest. Having choices also suggests that this will likely stop inflated wage levels for scientists.

This perception of a STEM shortage in the U.S. juxtaposed against China's rapid expansion of training in science, engineering, and technology has created another Sputnik moment. It has triggered anxieties that the center of world knowledge production is shifting away from the U.S. and is moving to Asia as the epicenter of scientific and engineering achievement. That is, in moving from the periphery to the center Asia has pushed the U.S. from the center to the periphery.

Commentators, such as Fareed Zakaria (2009), have pondered this impression of a shifting of the balance of power between America and Asia in favor of Asia. Zakaria (2009) describes a shift in America's disposition toward the world after 60 years of the U.S. urging open global markets. He argues that the U.S. has now adopted "an angry defensive crouch" where innovation is looked at fearfully and suspiciously (2013, p. 48). These reflect U.S. behaviors of the cold war where the interests of the U.S. are seen as threatened by "unfriendly" nations that are in competition with the U.S. Viewing the twenty-first century through the prism of the cold war contributes to a retrogressive nationalism and a sense of pessimism about globalization (Kell, Shore, & Singh, 2004). Zakaria argues that while the U.S. globalized the world, it forgot to globalize itself (2009, p. 48). However, the vulnerability and weakness of the U.S., mostly attributed to the decline of the economy during the global financial crisis, is an exaggeration and the frenzied reaction of many conservative commentators, needs to be viewed more critically.

Predictions about the ultimate demise of the U.S. as a global power are justified by the rapid rise of China in particular, where the economy has doubled every year for eight years with growth rates of 9 percent for almost 30 years. The combined effect of this is that China is "the world's largest country, the fastest growing economy, largest manufacturer, second-largest consumer, largest saver" (Proctor & Gamble, 2009, p. 92, cited in Zakaria, 2009).

Zhao (2012) argues that Shanghai's world number-one-status on PISA reflects only the ability of some 15-year-olds in Shanghai to take tests. He contends that this is not sufficient basis to warrant the position of education giant. This is because China has yet to produce thinkers such as Steve Jobs and, until creativity, lateral thinking, and individuality are valued, China will remain "labor-intensive rather than knowledge-intensive" (p. 57).

There is also a frenzied reaction around an impression that India and China are achieving superiority in science and technology and education. Claims that India and China are surpassing the U.S. graduates in science and technology are disputed by Zakaria (2009), who argues that the count of China and India's graduates includes two- and three-year programs and that this artificially inflates their graduate levels (p. 88). However, in the U.S., STEM is America's "biggest business" and a focal point for international education.

Views about the decline of U.S. higher education and a shift toward the periphery, are also contradicted by evidence of the world ranking of universities. U.S. universities consistently rank above Asian universities in several of the global ranking systems that have been recently popularized as a proxy for quality (Altbach, 2004). The Shanghai Jiao Tong University ranking was developed by the Chinese as a way of identifying the salient features of a world-class university for Chinese planners to establish high status local universities. This has since evolved into a global ranking system for potential students to choose a university. In the Shanghai Jiao Tong University rankings for 2013 there are eight U.S. universities in the top ten (ARWU, 2013). In contrast, no Chinese mainland universities feature in the top 150. U.S. universities were in 17 of the top 23 places, indicating that U.S. universities are in a class above those in Asia and suggesting that the prestige of American universities is not diminished.

The best Asian university is University of Tokyo (21st) and seven of the top ten Asian universities from the 2013 Shanghai Jiao Tong rankings are Japanese, not Chinese. Indian and Chinese universities do not appear in the first 150 universities. Mainland Chinese universities make appearances in specialist areas such as the world engineering rankings but not until the 34th spot with Tsinghua University, which ranks below Special Administrative Region universities like the City University of Hong Kong (25th) and the Hong Kong Institute of Technology (26th). The field where Chinese universities feature is computer science where there are 13 Chinese universities in the top 100 world universities (ARWU, 2013).

Popular discourse in the West and the U.S. portrays a virtual conveyor belt of science and technology graduates emerging from Chinese and Indian universities. In fact there are almost 4 million unemployed graduates in China. In Japan one-third of graduates in 2011 had not found work in the following year (Kell & Kell, 2013). In reality, youth in Asia are three times more likely to experience unemployment than youth in other regions despite the much-vaunted Asian economic miracle (Kell & Kell, 2013). In both the U.S. and Asia, graduate employment opportunities are changing and many of the permanent jobs offered in large corporations, or state owned enterprises and government departments, are no longer available (Kell & Kell, 2013, p. 71).

New Paradigms for the Global Moment

Narrow perspectives about national rivalries that characterized the cold war era fail to account for the increased mobility and interdependence that is evident in the post-cold war era of globalization. Rigid boundaries between ideologies and physical boundaries of the cold war that featured in the 1950s at the time of the first Sputnik moment have been all but dissolved. There is now great promise emerging from the notion of the borderless world where there is an increased mobility across the globe.

This global movement saw an estimated 214 million people moving to work and live in new countries during 2010. Migration is now also oriented to those with higher education levels with one-third of migrants (5.2 million people) to the OECD being tertiary educated. There are over 26 million migrants in the OECD nations possessing a higher education degree (OECD, 2012). A total of 16 percent of migrant workers in Europe, Canada, Australia, and New Zealand who are of Asian or Sub-Saharan background, are employed as professionals and 11 percent are employed as technicians. Another source of immigrants is international and foreign students who make up 6 percent of the student population in OECD nations (OECD, 2012).

Skilled migrants benefit their destination in three ways. First, they provide needed skills, different skills, and quality skill sets (Legrain, 2009). Second, talented foreigners boost innovation. A 10 percent rise in immigration in the U.S. has boosted patents by 8 percent and university patent grants by 1.3 percent (Legrain, 2009). Third, there are benefits associated with the clustering of skilled workers that sees centers such as Silicon Valley created (Legrain, 2009).

Rather than seeing competition between Asia and America for global superiority there is increasing evidence of an emergent transnational interdependence through education. One of the most interesting features of American education is the fact that it is the favored destination for international students from China who make up the largest individual country for students going overseas to study (Kell & Vogl, 2012). In the period 2009–2010 there were 127,628 Chinese students in the U.S. This grew from 98,235 in 2008–2009 (Kell & Vogl, 2012). Many of these students offer potential to meet skills shortages in the U.S.

U.S. business estimates that an in-flow of some 200,000 workers annually will be required to meet labor and production needs of the country. Recent attempts to reform U.S. immigration have sought to boost the number of available visas for skilled workers, particularly IT and students who have completed their studies in the U.S.

As the American economy has slowly recovered, the pressure for reform has increased and the need for more flexible visa conditions has been urged as other countries such as those in Latin America compete for highly skilled workers. Many employer groups are arguing for increasing visa options as well as promoting the benefits of temporary workers in the face of growing anti-foreign worker sentiments. In support of broader reforms, Steve Case, the former chief executive officer and chairman of America Online (a multinational mass media corporation) points to the proportion of start-up companies founded by foreigners in Silicon Valley which has dropped from 50 percent ten years ago to 42 percent in 2013. Rather than siphoning off activity and creating competition for local jobs, Case and others argue that many high skilled temporary workers stimulate the economy through creating new businesses to rebuild eroded U.S. infrastructure including roads, bridges, ports, railways, and utilities. The American Society of Civil Engineers has estimated that the U.S. needs to invest in over $3.6 trillion of infrastructure and capital works. The availability of both capital and qualified labor continues to be an impediment to economic recovery in the U.S. (The Economist, 2013).

Rather than see the emergence of China as a threat within the paradigm of the cold war, and re-invent a new crisis that challenges the U.S. status as a global power in the economic, military, or education sphere, the quest is for a new paradigm that stresses interdependence and the integration of national objectives directed toward prosperity and peace. The concerns that the U.S. is being consigned to a global periphery are, according to the authors, a flawed way of interpreting the interdependent features of modern globalization. Establishing a fantasy about a shift in power and a changing of the global balance denies the way in which power and influence are increasingly dispersed in this era of global capitalism. Reproducing the metaphors that invoke the cold war and jingoistic nationalism reinforces negativity toward others and fails to capitalize on the opportunities for peace and prosperity that typify the optimistic potential of globalization. Worse, the authors have highlighted that politicizing education as a race between nations has also done little to promote equality of opportunity and overcome the marginalization of groups in the community. Indeed there is evidence that successive policy frameworks designed to boost the performance of the nation have exacerbated the distance between those wealthy and connected at the center and those who are impoverished, alienated and poor.

References

Altbach, P. (2004). Globalization and the university: Myths and realities in an unequal world. *Territory Education and Management, 1*, 3–25.

AMSAT. (n.d.). *Sounds from the first satellites.* Retrieved from http://www.amsat.org/amsat/features/sounds/.

Angus, L. (1986). *Schooling, the school effectiveness movement and educational reform.* Geelong, VIC: Deakin University.

Apple, M. (2001). *Educating the "right way": Markets, standards and inequality.* London, UK: Routledge Falmer.

Aronowitz, S., & Di Fazio W. (1994). *The jobless future: Sci-Tech and the dogma of work.* Minnesota, MN: University of Minnesota.

ARWU. (2013). *Academic ranking of world universities since 2003.* Retrieved from http://www.shanghairanking.com/ARWU-SUBJECT-Statistics-2013.html.

Bales, B. L. (2006). Teacher education policies in the United States: The accountability shift since 1980. *Teaching and Teacher Education, 22*(4), 395–407. doi:10.1016/j.tate.2005.11.009.

CBS. (2007). *How Sputnik changed America.* Retrieved from http://www.cbsnews.com/8301-3445_162-3312190.html.

Charette, R. N. (2013). *The STEM crisis is a myth: Forget the dire predictions of a looming shortfall of scientists, technologists, engineers, and mathematics.* Retrieved from http://spectrum.ieee.org/at-work/education/the-stem-crisis-is-a-myth.

Chomsky, N. (2013, March 8). Chomsky: The corporate assault on public education. *AlterNet, Education*. Retrieved from http://www.alternet.org/education/chomsky-corporate-assault-public-education.

Dillon, S. (December 7, 2010). Top scores from China stun educators. *New York Times*. Retrieved from http://www.nytimes.com/2010/12/07/education/07education.html?_r=0.

The Economist. (2013). Immigration reform: Getting there. *The Economist*, 6–12th April, 37–38. Retrieved from http://www.economist.com/news/united-states/21575764-progress-last-making-things-easier-immigrants-america-getting-there.

Finn, C. E. (Jr). (December, 8, 2010). A Sputnik moment for U.S. education. *The Wall Street Journal*—Opinion [online]. Retrieved from http://online.wsj.com/news/articles/SB10001424052748704156304576003871654183998.

Kell, M., & Kell, P. (2013). *Literacy in East Asia: Shifting meanings, values and approaches*. Singapore: Springer Publishing.

Kell, P., Shore, S., & Singh, M. (2004). *Adult education@21ˢᵗ century*. New York, NY: Peter Lang.

Kell, P., & Vogl, G. (2012). *International students in the Asia Pacific: Mobility, security and global optimism*. Dordrecht: Springer Publishing.

Legrain, P. (2009). *Immigrant: Your country needs them*. London, UK: Abacus.

OECD. (2012). *Better skills, better jobs, better lives: A strategic approach to skills policies*. Retrieved from http://www.oecd-ilibrary.org/education/better-skills-better-jobs-better-lives_9789264177338-en.

OCS (Office of the Chief Scientist). (2013). *Technology, Engineering and Mathematics in the national interest (STEM): A strategic approach—a position paper*. Canberra, Australia: Australian Government.

Sanders, B. (2010). *School leaders and the challenge of the Elementary and Secondary Education Act, 1960–1968* (Doctoral thesis, University of Michigan, Ann Arbor, MI, USA). Retrieved from http://deepblue.lib.umich.edu/handle/2027.42/77841.

Steeves, K. A., Bernhardt, P. E., & Burns, J. P. (2009). Transforming American educational identity after Sputnik. *American Educational History Journal*, *36*(1), 71–87.

Zakaria, F. (2009). *The post-American world and the rise of the rest*. London, UK: Penguin.

Zhao, Y. (2012). Flunking innovation and creativity. *Phi Delta Kappan*, *94*(1), 56–61.

16

Radical International Adult Education

A Pedagogy of Solidarity

Bob Boughton

Radical adult education has a long and proud history of international-ism. In the late nineteenth and early twentieth centuries, labor colleges, plebs leagues, and popular universities provided a foundation from which hundreds of internationally linked and networked socialist and communist political parties and movements emerged, all committed to educating their members and supporters to change the world. To this end, they established study circles and adult schools which trained a great many leaders and activists of the twentieth century's labor, peace, and women's movements in the North, and the national liberation movements of the Global South (Macintyre, 1980; Gettleman, 1993, 2008; Boughton, 2005). A key lesson this worldwide learning movement taught to those who joined it was that the struggle against capitalist globalization (called imperialism within the movement) would only be won through the practice of international solidar-ity. In this chapter, I invite adult educators from both the North and the South to re-discover and re-ignite this pedagogy of international solidarity, in a coherent socialist challenge to the fundamental contradiction between center and periphery.

This is not about devising new, more militant rhetoric or new forms of action. Rather, as Brookfield and Holst (2011) explain, a genuinely radical adult education must base itself on the needs of the most marginalized, the people who today are deemed surplus to capitalism's requirement for labor, the millions, perhaps billions, of people for whom survival in this century is not possible without revolutionary social transformation (Allman, 2010). This chapter uses Cuba's international adult literacy work as an example of such a commitment. Drawing on my research into radical adult education's history and my recent direct experience of Cuba's role in the national adult literacy campaign in Timor-Leste, I will demonstrate that radical adult education, despite its marginal position with respect to a highly-professionalized "mainstream," is an innovative, relevant, and vibrant practice; as well as the source of some key theoretical insights in our field.

I begin with some personal context and a brief vignette which illustrates the historical and theoretical roots of international radical adult education. Then I introduce Cuba's international work, as both a product of this tradition and a concrete example of "learning (and teaching) from the periphery." The next section describes the involvement of Cuba in the national literacy campaign in Timor-Leste, a small newly independent Asia Pacific island state six hundred kilometers off the northern coastline of my own country, Australia. The foregoing sections lead into a theoretical reflection, on the dialectics of international adult education and development. The conclusion summarizes the major lesson from this analysis, suggesting a renewed international focus on mass literacy campaigns as a concrete expression of the pedagogy of solidarity.

Popular Education Has a Past

Adult education as a field of practice has at least two international connections. The first is the subfield of international and comparative adult education (Reischman, 2009), while the second arises through adult education's association with community development, and through that, with international development studies (Boughton, 2008). Personally, however, I found my way into international adult education through the practice of solidarity activism, with the Aboriginal rights movement in Australia and the movement to support the independence struggle of the East Timorese people. Both forms of activism grew under the umbrella of the international socialist movement, to which I became affiliated as a radical young student at the University of Sydney in the early 1970s.

Two decades later, my doctoral research examined the historical links between adult education and socialist politics (Boughton, 1997). Most accounts of the origin of the field in the English-speaking world acknowledge the importance of the 1840s Chartist movement (Johnson, 1988), and some studies trace that lineage through into contemporary practice (e.g., Welton, 2013). But contemporary adult education texts spend little time interrogating anything but the most recent history of our field, focusing on the late twentieth and early twenty-first century (see Knowles, Holton, & Swanson (2011) and Merriam & Brockett (2007) for examples). This period, which was dominated by increasing professionalization of the field, was also, as Holst (2007) explained, a period during which radical and particularly socialist politics were incorrectly believed to be in decline.

Still, almost every adult educator knows of Paulo Freire, the Brazilian literacy educator and theorist considered to be the founder of modern "popular education," the term used in Latin America to refer to radical adult education undertaken within movements for social and political change (Kane 2001). A decade after his death, Freire's popularity continues unabated, as recent studies by Schugurensky (2011) and Mayo (2013) demonstrate. Freire was heavily influenced by the revolutionary socialist tradition of theory and practice (Lewis, 2012). Following his exile from Brazil in 1967, he became an exemplary internationalist adult educator, travelling the world assisting people to understand the connection between education and politics, a connection he first made explicit through his work in literacy campaigns in northeastern Brazil (Freire, 1972). Freire visited my country, Australia, very briefly in 1974 (Freire, 1975), and his presence helped to launch a radical literacy movement among community educators which survives today.

Few of us knew in Australia at that time, however, that as Freire was leaving Australia for Africa (Freire, 1994), a small group of university students from Portuguese Timor were returning from studies in Portugal to their country, a small island off Australia's northern coastline, to begin a Freirian-inspired literacy campaign as part of a movement for decolonization and independence. The Timorese learned about Freire from fellow students they had met in Lisbon from other anticolonial movements in the Portuguese colonies of Africa, and from Portugal's own antifascist revolutionary movement, which finally overthrew the Portuguese dictatorship in the Carnation Revolution of April 1974 (Da Silva, 2011).

This story illustrates that radical adult education was already a well-developed international practice by the 1970s. Moreover, while Freire has become its best-known representative, his ideas developed inside a movement which spread from Africa through Europe and Asia, and across Latin America and the Caribbean, as ideas and methods developed in one country were learned, adapted, and adopted in other places, but with little recognition in the "official" international adult education literature of the time, or since. One reason was that this was "southern theory" (Connell, 2007), derived from a practice in the peripheral states of global capitalism, not at its centers in North America and Europe. This "social movement learning" predated the popularization of this concept within professional adult education by Finger (1989) and Hall & Clover (2005) and others.

Lessons (and Teaching) from the Periphery

Mass adult literacy campaigns, such as the one Freire initiated in Brazil, were a key strategy of that international movement, and Cuba's 1961 campaign was the most iconic example. Many features of the Cuban campaign replicated earlier campaigns, including in the Soviet Union in the 1920s (Clark 1995), in the Chinese liberation struggle in the 1930s (Boshier & Yan, 2010), and in the Vietnamese war of independence against the French in the 1950s (Bhola, 1984). Three things, however, distinguished the Cuban literacy campaign from earlier examples. The first was its massive mobilization of high school students and teachers, and educated urban workers, to go into the countryside to live and work with the peasants as they taught them how to read and write, a process which built a new social solidarity between the better educated and the less educated (Kozol, 1978). The second was that this campaign was followed by a series of "post-literacy" campaigns, starting with the "Battle for the Sixth Grade," enrolling the newly literate in an ever-expanding system of adult education, which played a major role in breaking the intergenerational transmission of education inequality, and ultimately producing a substantial professionally educated workforce whose roots lay in the villages. Third, and most significant for this chapter, the Cubans took their successful literacy campaign model into other countries and movements that were fighting imperialism and colonialism in the Global South (Abendroth, 2009).

Cuba's massive international adult education efforts over the last half-century are little known outside the field of Latin American studies, because of its status as a peripheral state. Cuba is peripheral, not only because it has attempted to build an independent social and economic system outside the capitalist world-system, but also because it has been deliberately marginalized through a strict regime of international embargo and boycott maintained by the Unites States and its allies. Cuba is therefore a particularly appropriate focus for my contribution to this volume. If international adult education's metropolitan center is North America and Europe, then its periphery certainly includes not only Cuba, but also the many states and movements around the world, and particularly in the Global South, which have enjoyed the benefits of Cuba's commitment to international solidarity.

A comprehensive analysis of Cuba's role in international adult education is beyond the scope of this chapter, but it would include stories from Angola, Mozambique, Guinea Bissau, Namibia and pre- and post-apartheid South Africa, all on the African continent; and from Haiti, Nicaragua, El Salvador, Grenada, Chile, Uruguay, Paraguay and Argentina in Latin America and the Caribbean. As Hickling-Hudson, Gonzalez, and Preston (2012) demonstrate, Cuba's educational "aid" to anticolonial independence movements, to newly independent governments, and to social movements and states trying to resist neoliberalism has given it legendary status among the recipients and almost complete invisibility in the world of mainstream international aid and development. The same is true of its health assistance program through which thousands of Cuba-trained doctors and health professionals have worked all over the world, while nationals from the recipient countries complete their degrees at the Latin American School of Medicine outside Havana (Brower, 2011; Walker & Kirk, 2013).

As a state committed to building socialism, Cuba adopted a development model in which growth and prosperity is driven not by private capital accumulation but by a planned and coordinated development of the country's own resources, of which the most important are its people. Cuba's educational achievements, built from the foundation of the literacy campaign, are now well-documented (Carnoy, Gove, & Marshall, 2007). The focus on education and health makes good sense inside their development model, since unless the maximum number of people are both well-educated and in good health, how can they contribute their best to their country's development as an independent and sovereign nation? Moreover, in Cuba's view of international solidarity, the country also has a duty to share its resources with other countries and movements struggling to find their own alternative development path (Artaraz, 2012). To illustrate this, I return to the story of Timor-Leste.

From *Yo, Sí Puedo!* to *Los Hau Bele*

In January 2006, 11 Cuban educators arrived in Timor-Leste to assist the government to carry out a national literacy campaign. Their leader, José Manuel "Llera" Garcia, was a veteran of Cuban education and internationalism, who had participated as a high school student in the 1961 literacy campaign, and then fought in the Cuban international brigade in Angola.

His Timorese counterpart in the Department of Non-Formal Education, Adalfredo De Almeida, also had an international story. When his country was ruled by Portugal, he was conscripted to fight the national liberation forces in Angola, and when Indonesia invaded his country in 1975, he was forced into exile in Australia, only returning after independence was won in 1999. Between 2006 and 2007, these two men worked together to prepare for the launch of Timor's national literacy campaign in June 2007.

As mentioned above, this was not Timor's first experience of a literacy campaign. In 1974, the Timorese university students who had returned from studying in Portugal organized a high school students' union and trained them to use a simple manual they had developed, called *Timor is Our Country*. This adaptation of Freire's method aimed to conscientize the illiterate rural-dwelling "Maubere," the majority people of Timor-Leste, who had been ruled by Portugal since the seventeenth century. Their work bore fruit and the independence party, FRETILIN, quickly developed a mass following. But this was the 1970s, and radical independence movements conscientizing people about colonization and imperialism were not welcome in the "American Lake," as the Pacific was then known. With the tacit support of the United States, Australia, and their Western allies, Timor's giant neighbor Indonesia invaded the Portuguese half of this tiny island less than a year after the literacy campaign had started. This began a brutal, twenty-four-year military occupation, during which one-third of the local population perished (Dunn, 2003). Slowly, throughout this period, a resistance was built, led in part by the university and high school students and the men and women who had participated in those first classes. They kept alive the idea of popular education, and when independence was finally won and FRETILIN became the government in 2002, they once again resolved to conduct a literacy campaign (Cabral & Martin-Jones, 2008; Da Silva, 2011).

Between 2004 and 2010, I spent several months each year working in-country with the Ministry of Education, the Cuban adviser team, and the Timorese popular education movement. During this period, Timor-Leste was the site of a major international intervention in the name of post-conflict peace building and reconstruction, involving all the United Nations agencies, the World Bank, and many international NGOs (Boughton, 2013). A common question among the English-speaking international adviser community, when we spoke about the national literacy campaign, was: "But why Cuba? Why has the government invited the Cubans to advise them?" The fact that many international development advisers, almost all tertiary-educated, found this so puzzling, is an object lesson in the nature of hegemony, a concept developed by the Italian communist leader Antonio Gramsci, and now regularly used in the adult education literature (Mayo, 1999; 2005). Yet for the Timorese, this was a non-question. For twenty-four years, while the international agencies and donor countries were ignoring their plight, Cuba had remained a steadfast ally of their independence struggle, as it had been of FRETILIN's sister movements in the African Portuguese colonies of Angola, Mozambique, Cape Verde, and Guinea Bissau. After the Indonesians had been expelled and the country was independent, Cuba sent doctors, in 2004, one for every suco, i.e., 450 small administrative clusters of villages—and provided 500 scholarships to the FRETILIN government so young Timorese could travel to Havana to study medicine (Anderson, 2010). When the decision was made in 2005 to re-launch the literacy campaign, Cuba again offered its assistance. The advisers it sent were trained in the "Yes I Can" (Yo, Sí Puedo!, or YSP) model which the Institute of Pedagogy for Latin America and the Caribbean (IPLAC) in Havana had developed in 2000, and which was already, in 2005, operating in 15 other countries (Boughton, 2010).

As a review by UNESCO explains:

> [T]he *YSP* method is in fact more than a method. It would be more appropriate to understand it as a literacy training model that goes beyond processes, materials, strategies etc., as it includes, both explicitly and implicitly, concepts of literacy training, learning, life skills and social mobilization, and involves a wide range of actors with varied roles from the beneficiaries of the literacy training to other stakeholders such as state entities and other concerned institutions. (UNESCO, 2006, p. 4)

While UNESCO does not explicitly say so, YSP uses the campaign model (Bhola, 1984) for developing literacy on a mass scale (Bhola, 1984), a model from the Global South with which Western readers may have little familiarity. According to this model a campaign has three elements. The first is a phase of socialization and mobilization, where the aim is to encourage as many people as possible to take part, as learners, teachers, organizers, and supporters, and at the same time to enhance the understanding of society as a whole of the importance of literacy to wider social and economic development goals. During this phase, organizations are created at national, regional, and local levels to lead the campaign, widening responsibility for raising literacy levels beyond the government education authority, enlisting support and commitment from all government agencies, from non-government organizations and from the community as a whole. Phase

Two consists of 64 basic literacy lessons, run over a short period, usually three months, in which nonliterate and low-literate members of the community are encouraged to enroll and supported to complete. These lessons are nonformal, nonaccredited, and taught by nonprofessional local facilitators in the community, with the assistance of professional advisers and materials provided by the central campaign authority. Each set of classes ends with a local ceremony, honoring the people who have completed and welcoming the next group into the classes. The final element, Phase Three of the campaign, is for "post-literacy." This consists of activities to help the newly literate participants continue building their literacy, and to create a more literate culture in the community. Throughout the process, the central authority maintains a close oversight of progress, to ensure that targets for literacy improvement are met at a sufficiently rapid rate. All three phases continue until everyone has achieved a basic level of literacy, as defined in "Education for All": "the capacity of young people and adults aged fifteen and over to read and write, with understanding, a simple sentence about their own life" (UNESCO, 2005, p. 29).

The Cuban model uses prerecorded audio-visual lessons on DVD to provide the basic literacy tuition in Phase Two. During each lesson, the class watches on TV a group of actors/students being taught by an actor/teacher, utilizing the same tasks, discussion points, and practice exercises as the "live" students must complete, using their own workbooks. Lessons are led by local facilitators trained in a relatively short time—a matter of weeks—by the Cuban advisers, and then supported with ongoing training in lesson preparation and evaluation, and regular monitoring visits to the classes. Initially, the Cubans brought a set of lessons on DVD developed for Brazil. These were in Portuguese, one of the two official languages of Timor-Leste, the other being Tetum, an Indigenous lingua-franca spoken in many of the country's 13 districts. After piloting the model in two districts, they developed a handbook in Tetum to assist the facilitators who were less familiar with Portuguese. They also began work on a new set of lessons in Tetum. The adaptation of *Yo, Sí Puedo!* to *Los Hau Bele* was finalized in Havana, with the Timorese medical students studying there becoming the actors for the new DVD lessons (Boughton, 2010; 2012).

The first classes opened in Dili, the capital, in June 2006. By the end of 2012, all 13 districts and 65 subdistricts of Timor-Leste had taken part in the campaign, and had been declared "free of illiteracy." This meant that over 95 percent of the individuals identified as illiterate had successfully completed YSP, and demonstrated their new found skills through writing a simple letter in either Tetum or Portuguese. The total number of participants was over 200,000, and the campaign had reached virtually every one of over 12,000 small hamlets (called *aldeias*) where the majority of the population live.

Despite this achievement, significant problems remained. A rebellion in the Timorese security forces occurred less than 12 months before the campaign began, causing massive disruption to the lives of the people in the capital, the re-entry of an international peacekeeping force, and a significant increase in donor and multilateral agency intervention in the country's governance. A major objective of this intervention was to re-orient the country's radical social democratic development strategy, and to this end, it fostered the creation of many more small political parties and civil society organizations (Boughton, 2013). This was done in the name of valuing diversity and local autonomy over "centralized authority"; but its effect was to undermine national support for the historic party of independence. FRETILIN subsequently lost the 2007 election, and has not been returned to power since. The new alliance government, supported by an increased international adviser presence, agreed to complete the literacy campaign's second phase, but it also took the advice of the World Bank, UNICEF, and other international agencies, and re-focused its post-literacy work, not on the population as a whole, but on the development of "functional literacy" among out-of-school youth, especially in the cities and large towns. It also closed down the National Literacy Commission, returning control of the campaign to the Education Ministry. There remains a real risk that many of the poorest and most isolated adults will lose the literacy they gained from the YSP classes, and the intergenerational reduction in educational inequality will be much less pronounced.

The Dialectics of International Adult Education and Development

The Cuban *Yo Si Puedo* literacy campaign model has, since 2000, been utilized in more than 25 countries, reaching over six million learners (Boughton & Durnan 2014). This work has been described by some Latin American Studies scholars (e.g., Artaraz, 2012; Muhr, 2013), but has received almost no attention in the English-language adult education or literacy studies journals. Herein lies a contradiction. How can an international adult education phenomenon of such magnitude be considered peripheral? For an answer, we must return to Freire and Gramsci, whose work exposes the dialectical nature of the relationship between metropole and periphery, and between civil society and the state (Holst 1999).

Within the "liberal" tradition of adult education, democracy is safeguarded when citizens are sufficiently educated to be able to understand and demand accountability for the actions of the state and its rulers. Thus, in the United States, John Dewey argued that adult education was a necessary adjunct to democracy because it gave to the people the knowledge and understanding they required to exercise wisely their democratic rights. But as Gramsci, Freire, and others in the radical tradition discovered, this way of thinking relies on an unsustainable separation between individuals, who are more or less educated, and the society as a whole, from which both spring. Freire critiqued the notion of "illiterates" as marginal in these words:

> The social structure as a whole does not 'expel,' nor is marginal man (sic) a 'being outside of.' He is, on the contrary, a 'being inside of,' within the social structure, and in a dependent relationship to those we falsely call autonomous beings. . . . These men . . . are not marginal to the structure, but *oppressed men within it*. Alienated, they cannot overcome their dependency by 'incorporation' into the very structure responsible for their dependency. (Freire, 1972, pp. 27–28; emphasis added)

It was no accident that this insight originated on the "periphery" of the adult education world, far enough from the centers of imperial power to reveal the fallacy of thinking it was simply a matter of bringing everyone, including over 800 million people lacking basic literacy, "inside" a just, but mythical, social whole.

The radical perspective requires us to think about society, the social whole, from the point of view of an alternative; that is, we have to learn to envision a society which does not generate such inequalities in the first place, while, at the same time, taking action to create that alternative. As Miles Horton and Paulo Freire argued "we make the road by walking," (Horton & Freire, c. 1990) and education is one moment in the dialectical processes of revolutionary social change. Individuals learn in order to change the world, and, in the act of trying to change it, they learn more about its true nature and how to construct something quite different, something which does not yet exist. Reflecting this popular education vision, the Argentinian NGO, which since 2003 has been sponsoring the spread of *Yo, Sí Puedo!* across that country, is called *A Better World is Possible* (UMMEP, n.d.).

In this dialectical mode of analysis (Allman, 2010), the periphery is constructed by the mainstream, as it simultaneously marginalizes ideas and practices which might contradict its own survival and reproduction. The mainstream is only possible for as long as the periphery remains peripheral. Cuba with its literacy model is peripheral, *because* it is not mainstream; it exists on the periphery, and will remain there, for as long as the mainstream decrees that it will. This is the true nature of hegemony, the capacity to authorize some practices and theories as legitimate, and others as not. By the same token, it is also why the YSP model has become so popular, changing the lives of millions of people in illiterate and marginalized communities the world over. Its popularity among the poor, and its invisibility in the academic journals of the Global North, are two sides of the same dialectical coin.

This brings us back to civil society. When Cuba mounted its own national literacy campaign in 1961, sponsored by the new revolutionary state brought into being by Castro's 26 July Movement, its achievements were noted throughout the Third World. This helped to begin a process in which many other countries embarked on similar campaigns over the next two decades, often with Cuban support (Perez Cruz, 2007). In this period, the concept of the Tricontinental emerged, linking Africa, South America, and Asia in a worldwide movement whose most eloquent spokesperson until his death in Bolivia was Ernesto Ché" Guevara (Holst, 2009a). This was the era of the Cold War, but for the people of many countries in the Global South the war was not "cold" at all. In many national liberation struggles, and in many newly independent states which emerged from those struggles, mass literacy campaigns became an integral part of the politicization of the people (e.g., Hammond, 1998). The response of the West was to insist in international forums like UNESCO and UNICEF that such campaigns were both ineffective and too expensive, and that comprehensive education in newly independent states—Education for All, as it became known—could best be built if the focus was on primary basic schooling, that is schooling for children. Adult literacy should be the work of non-government organizations, and it should focus on "functional literacy" for youth and young adults, since they were the only ones for whom additional education would bring the quickest return in economic productivity (Abadzi, 1994; Jones, 1990).

These arguments were backed by the weight of World Bank funding, held out as an inducement to countries which complied. Some resisted, like President Nyere of Tanzania, one country whose national literacy campaign was maintained. Other countries where the campaign model survived included Mozambique and Guinea Bissau, and some countries in Latin America and the Caribbean, including Grenada. However, the last great national literacy campaign outside Asia, great in the sense that it broke through into the imagination and the writing of the mainstream adult education world, was the Nicaraguan Literacy Crusade (Arnove, 1986). By 1984, although the International Council of Adult Education was still calling for a global literacy campaign (Bhola, 1984), the movement had been turned.

In its place, small-scale localized literacy projects, undertaken by donor-funded NGOs proliferated. Rather than recognize this for the defeat it was, the academic world of literacy studies (e.g., Street, 2001) celebrated the spread of localism as an invigoration of civil society, a concept which became popular in the 1980s as a way of theorizing social movement opposition to authoritarian dictatorships of the right (e.g., in Latin America) or of the left (e.g., in pre-1989 Eastern Europe) (Buttigieg, 2005). However, when the civil society-state relationship is understood dialectically, to be contained within "civil society" is in fact *not* to exercise state power; and the only point of working within civil society is, as Gramsci always understood, to prepare through a war of position for the eventual winning of state power (Holst, 2009b). So it is, that in Venezuela and Bolivia, where progressive governments were in power in the 2000s, the mass literacy campaign spread quickly (Artaraz, 2012), as it did in Timor-Leste, under FRETILIN's leadership. In such situations, it is not a matter of civil society NGOs working against the state, but in partnership with it. However, as Timor-Leste's experience shows, once the state loses a coherent progressive development vision, international agencies will advise a return to their default neoliberal position. The role of the state in leading such campaigns is deemed unnecessary, while NGOs are encouraged and funded to take over, but with one proviso: the NGO must eschew all connection with politics, including any direct association with political parties of the left (Choudry & Kapoor, 2013).

Conclusion

As the Global Financial Crisis creates more and larger surplus populations, not only in the Global South but increasingly in the North, the objective basis emerges for a return to notions of international solidarity, which some late twentieth-century social theorists considered passé. Leading adult education theorists, including Sharzad Mojab, Sarah Carpenter, Aziz Choudry, and Dip Kapoor (Choudry, 2010; Mojab & Carpenter, 2011), have shown that this does not mean turning our back on the insights of feminist and postcolonial theorizing, but it does require a re-discovery of older traditions of political economy and historical materialism, and re-readings, such as Paula Allman (2010), Peter Mayo (2005) and John Holst (2002; 2009b) have done, of Marx, Gramsci, and Freire.

This chapter has also demonstrated the importance of an historical analysis of our ideas and the practices from which they emerged. We only learn, as Myles Horton famously put it, from the experiences we learn from. Most importantly, new theory is unlikely to emerge without a new practice; and the search is now on to discover new forms of international coalitions which can unite adult educators working across the very different contexts of the north and south. Such alliances are emerging in the global environmental movement, the antiglobalization movement and the antiwar movement, and in the "movement of movements" around the World Social Forum. My intention in writing this chapter has been to show that it is possible, as Cuba has done, to include in this process the people who have most to lose if the world continues on its current course, the 800 million people who lack basic literacy. The next instalment in this story will, I hope, be about the way progressive social movements in the North have learned to embrace this strategy, joining with the Cuban state and its many allies in the international popular education movement to keep alive the vision of a global literacy campaign.

References

Abadzi, H. (1994). *What we know about the acquisition of adult literacy: Is there hope?* World Bank Discussion Papers, No. 245. Washington, DC: World Bank.

Abendroth, M. (2009). *Rebel literacy: Cuba's national literacy campaign and critical global citizenship*. Duluth, MN: Litwin Books.

Allman, P. (2010). *Critical education against global capitalism: Karl Marx and revolutionary critical education*. Rotterdam, The Netherlands: Sense Publishers.

Anderson, T. (2010). Cuban health cooperation in Timor Leste and the south west pacific. In Reality of Aid Management Committee (Eds.) *South-South cooperation: A challenge to the aid System?* (pp. 77–86). Quezon City, The Philippines: IBON Foundation.

Arnove, R. (1986). *Education and revolution in Nicaragua*. New York, Westport, CT, and London: Praeger.

Artaraz, K. (2012). Cuba's internationalism revisited: Exporting Literacy, ALBA, and a New Paradigm for South–South Collaboration. *Bulletin of Latin American Research, 31*, 22–37.

Bhola, H. S. (1984). *Campaigns for literacy: Eight national experiences of the twenti-eth century, with a memorandum to decision-makers.* Paris, France: UNESCO.

Boshier, R., & Yan, H. (2010). More important than guns: Chinese adult education after the Long March. *Adult Education Quarterly, 60* (3), 284–302.

Boughton, B. (1997). Does popular education have a past? In B. Boughton, T. Brown, & G. Foley (Eds.), *New Directions in Australian Adult Education* (pp. 1–27). Sydney, Australia: University of Technology Sydney (UTS) Centre for Popular Education.

———. (2005). "The Workers' University": Australia's Marx Schools and the International Communist Movement's contribution to popular education. In J. Crowther, V. Galloway, & I. Martin (Eds.), *Popular Education: Engaging the Academy* (pp. 100–109). Leicester, UK: NIACE.

———. (2008). Adult education and development. In J. Athanasou (Ed.), *Adult Education and Training* (pp. 119–133). Sydney, Australia: James Barlow Publishing.

———. (2010). Back to the future? Timor-Leste, Cuba and the return of the mass literacy campaign. *Literacy and Numeracy Studies, 18* (2), pp. 23–40.

———. (2012). Adult literacy, popular education and Cuban educational aid in Timor-Leste. In A. Hickling-Hudson, J. C. Gonzalez, & R. Preston (Eds.), *The capacity to share: A study of Cuba's international cooperation in educational development* (pp. 197–216). New York, NY: Palgrave Macmillan.

———. (2013). Timor-Leste: Education, decolonisation and development. In L. Symaco (Ed.), *Education in South East Asia* (pp. 299–321). London, UK: Continuum.

Boughton, B., & Durnan, D. (2014). Cuba's Yo, Sí Puedo. A Global Literacy Movement? *Postcolonial Directions in Education. Special Issue: Adult Literacy and Adult Education, 3*(2), 325–359.

Brower, S. (2011). *Revolutionary doctors: How Venezuela and Cuba are changing the world's conception of health care.* New York, NY: Monthly Review Press.

Buttigieg, J. A. (2005). The contemporary discourse on civil society: A Gramscian critique. *Boundary, 2*(Summer), 31–52.

Cabral, E., & Martin-Jones, M. (2008). Writing the resistance: Literacy in East Timor 1975–1999. *International Journal of Bilingual Education and Bilingualism, 11* (2), 149–169.

Carnoy, M., Gove, A. K., & Marshall, J. (2007). *Cuba's academic advantage: Why students in Cuba do better in school.* Stanford, CA, USA: Stanford University Press.

Choudry, A., & Kapoor, D. (Eds.). (2013). *NGOization: Complicity, contradictions and prospects.* London & New York: Zed Books.

Clark, C. E. (1995). Literacy and labour: The Russian literacy campaign within the trade unions, 1923–27. *Europe-Asia Studies, 47* (8), 1327–1341.

Connell, R. (2007). *Southern Theory: The global dynamics of knowledge in social science.* Sydney: Allen & Unwin.

Choudry, A. (2010). Global Justice? Contesting NGOization: Knowledge politics and containment in antiglobalization networks In A. Choudry & D. Kapoor. (Eds.), *Learning from the ground up: Global perspectives on social movements and knowledge production* (pp. 17–34). New York, NY: Palgrave Macmillan.

Da Silva, A. B. (2011). *FRETILIN Popular Education 1973–78 and its relevance to Timor-Leste today.* Unpublished PhD Thesis, University of New England: Armidale, Australia.

Dunn, J. (2003). *East Timor: a rough passage to independence* (3rd ed.). Double Bay, NSW: Longueville Books.

Finger, M. (1989). New social movements and their implications for adult education. *Adult Education Quarterly, 40,* 15–21.

Freire, P. (1972). *Pedagogy of the oppressed.* Harmondsworth, UK: Penguin Education.

———. (1975). *Education for liberation and community: Two articles and reports arising from his 1974 Visit.* Melbourne, Australia: Australian Council of Churches.

———. (1994). *Pedagogy of hope: Reliving pedagogy of the oppressed.* New York, NY: Continuum.

Gettleman, M. (1993). The New York Workers School, 1923–1944: Communist Education in American Society. In M. Brown, R. Martin, F. Rosengarten, & G. Snedeker (Eds.), *New studies in the politics and culture of U.S. Communism* (pp. 261–280). New York, NY: Monthly Review Press.

Gettleman, M. (2008). Defending left pedagogy: U.S. communist schools fight back against the SACB (Subversive Activities Control Board) . . . and lose (1953–1957). *Convergence, 41,* (2/3), 193–209.

Hall, B., & Clover, D. (2005). Social movement learning. In L. English (Ed.), *International Encyclopedia of Adult Education* (pp. 584–589). London, UK: Palgrave Macmillian.

Hammond, J. L. (1998). *Fighting to learn: Popular education and guerrilla war in El Salvador.* New Brunswick, New Jersey, and London: Rutgers University Press.

Hickling-Hudson, A., Gonzalez, J. C., & Preston, R. (Eds.). (2012). *The capacity to share. A study of Cuba's international cooperation in educational development.* New York, NY: Palgrave Macmillan.

Horton, M., & Freire, P. (c1990). *We make the road by walking. Conversations on education and social change.* Philadelphia, PA: Temple University Press.

Holst, J. D. (1999). The affinities of Lenin and Gramsci: Implications for radical adult education theory and practice. *International Journal of Lifelong Education, 18*(5), 407–421.

———. (2002). *Social movements, civil society and radical adult education.* Westport, CT: Bergin & Garvey.

———. (2007). The politics and economics of globalization and social change in radical adult education: A critical review of recent literature. *Journal for Critical Education Policy Studies, 5*(1).

———. (2009a). The pedagogy of Ernesto Ché Guevara. *International Journal of Lifelong Education, 28*(2), 149–173.

————. (2009b). The revolutionary party in Gramsci's pre-prison educational and political theory and practice. *Educational Philosophy and Theory, 41*(6), 622–639.

Kane, L. (2001). *Popular education and social change in Latin America.* London, UK: Latin America Bureau.

Kozol, J. (1978). A new look at the literacy campaign in Cuba. *Harvard Educational Review, 48* (Summer), 341–377.

Knowles, M. S., Holton, E. F., & Swanson, R. A. (2011). *The adult learner: The definitive classic in adult education and human resource development.* Hoboken, NJ: Taylor & Francis.

Johnson, R. (1988). 'Really useful knowledge' 1790–1850: Memories for education in the 1980s. In T. Lovett (Ed.), *Radical Approaches to Adult Education: A Reader* (pp. 3–34). London and New York: Routledge.

Jones, P. W. (1990). UNESCO and the politics of global literacy. *Comparative Education Review, 34*(1), 41–60.

Lewis, T. (2012). Mapping the constellation of educational Marxism(s). *Educational Philosophy and Theory, 44* (S1), 98–114.

Mayo, P. (1999). *Gramsci, Freire and adult education: Possibilities for transformative action.* London and New York: Zed Books.

————. (2005). "In and against the state": Gramsci, war of position, and adult education. *Journal for Critical Education Policy Studies, 3*(2). Accessed 19/8/08, from http://www.jceps.com/?pageID=article&articleID=49.

————. (2013). *Echoes from Freire for a critically engaged pedagogy.* New York, NY: Bloomsbury.

Macintyre, S. (1980). *A proletarian science: Marxism in Britain, 1917–1933.* Cambridge and New York: Cambridge University Press.

Merriam, S. B., & Brockett, R. G. (2007). *The profession and practice of adult education: An Introduction.* San Francisco, CA: Jossey-Bass.

Mojab, S., & Carpenter, S. (Eds.). (2011). *Educating from Marx: Race, gender, and learning.* New York, NY: Palgrave MacMillan.

Muhr, T. (2013). Optimism reborn: Nicaragua's participative education revolution, the citizen power development model and the construction of '21st century socialism.' *Globalisation, Societies and Education, 11*(2), 276–295.

Perez Cruz, F. (2007). *Paulo Freire and the Cuban Revolution.* Proceedings of the joint international conference of the Adult Education Research Conference (AERC) (48th National Conference) and the Canadian Association for the Study of Adult Education (CASAE)/l'Association Canadienne pour l'Étude de l'Éducation des Adultes (ACÉÉA) (26th National Conference).

Schugurensky, D. (2011). *Paulo Freire.* London, UK: Continuum.

Street, B. (Ed.). (2001). *Literacy and development. Ethnographic perspectives.* London, UK: Routledge.

UMMEP (n.d.) *Fundación UMMEP "Un Mundo Mejor es Posible"* (Trans. Another World is Possible). Retrieved 20 June 2013, from http://fundacionummep.blogspot.com/.

Walker, C., & Kirk, J. M. (2013). From cooperation to capacitation: Cuban medical internationalism in the South Pacific. *International Journal of Cuban Studies, 5*(1), 10–25.

Welton, M. (2013). *Unearthing Canada's hidden past. A short history of adult education.* Toronto, ON: Thompson Publishing.

17

From Generation to Generation

Teaching Adults to Teach about the Holocaust

Mark J. Webber
with Michael Brown

The Holocaust occurred just over three generations ago and hovers on the periphery of lived experience and first-hand memory. In the tension between the Holocaust's perceived centrality and peripherality, generational succession and the intergenerational transmission of memory (and trauma) play a significant role. A key element here is recursivity. The recursive approach resists a "final word" and acknowledges the necessity of continuously interrogating one's own assumptions, conceptual framework, and terminology.

From the start, the Holocaust involved generations and generativity (cf. Kay, 1998). The perpetrators' final goal was not only to prevent Jewish adults from contaminating the putative "racial purity" of a German-"Aryan" *Volk*, but also to murder children to ensure that Jewish life, lineage, and culture could never be regenerated (Wildt, 2003, pp. 574–576). The term *gen*ocide, coined in response to this human catastrophe, is etymologically related to the concepts of *gen*eration and *gen*erativity discussed below (Power, 2002, p. 42). The perpetrators sought to destroy that Jewish intergenerational physical, religious, and cultural transmission captured in the Hebrew liturgical refrain, *mi dor ledor*, "from generation to generation."

For those who teach about the Holocaust, other aspects and implications of intergenerational relations are also relevant. These include issues of recollecting as child and adult; constraints on presenting horrific material to younger learners, including differences in how specific age cohorts experience traumatic sites (Timm, 2010, p. 76); the transmission of knowledge, empathy, and skills from one generation of teachers to the next; and consideration of the lessons of the Holocaust for future generations and in other contexts.

This chapter investigates issues of teaching adults to teach about the Holocaust and related issues in the context of The Mark and Gail Appel Program in Holocaust and Antiracism Education, an initiative of the Canadian Centre for German and European Studies and the Israel and Golda Koschitzky Centre for Jewish Studies (both at York University in Toronto) in cooperation with universities and governmental and civic institutions in Canada, Germany, and Poland. This program incorporates important aspects of teaching and learning across generations, including a key discursive aspect: the conversations and debates within the program, given additional emphasis and urgency by the interaction of varied cultural, linguistic, and disciplinary perspectives, require and motivate recursivity. In practice this means that wherever we begin, we have not begun early enough, nor are our conclusions ever final. In this chapter we argue that this practice represents the discursive equivalent of intergenerationality and decentering.

Framework Issues

At the outset we want to explain our conceptual and pedagogical understanding of three key points: (a) the Holocaust and Holocaust education, (b) generations and generationality, and (c) our own program.

The Holocaust and Holocaust Education

The Holocaust and associated phenomena—aspects of National Socialist pseudo-scientific racism, repression, terror, and mass murder; the continuities of Jewish life in Europe and elsewhere; the presence of racism, discrimination, and genocide today; the pedagogies of "difficult subjects"; how and why individuals, groups, and states perpetrate, allow, facilitate, resist, or counter genocide and terror—provide an unusually complex framework that implicates and illuminates other questions. These include, for example, the incongruous pair of practices and effects of social marginalization on the one hand and conceptual decentering on the other.

We understand the Holocaust as the genocide against European Jewry by National Socialist Germany and its allies and supporters (Webber &

Brown, 2001). Two points deserve elaboration here. First, defining the Holocaust in this way is not a form of "Holocaust-centricity." Specifically, it does not preclude links with, and comparisons to, other genocides and atrocities, prior, contemporaneous, or subsequent. In fact, understanding the singularity of each of these phenomena by studying their particularities is the precondition for seeing them in relation to one another. But synchronically and diachronically, extrapolations from the particular to the particular and from the particular to the universal are valid and useful only if we understand the particularities in question (Bartov, 2003; Brown, 2011).

Second, what happened 70 years ago continues to resonate today. The Holocaust is used (and abused) in contemporary debates. This projection of the past onto the present involves a kind of intergenerational transference whose mechanisms and trajectories are not always easy to discern. The study of the Holocaust in its relevance for today is also a recurring study of how these arguments are constructed and deconstructed (Webber, 2011).

Our program's title links Holocaust education with antiracism education. Here, too, we are conscious of the role played by (pseudo-)scientific notions of race as the basis of societal exclusion developed in the nineteenth century, aspects of which the Nazis used, and some of which persist to this day (Schwarz-Friesel & Reinharz, 2013, pp. 397–398). Remarkably, some antiracist theory and practice excludes antisemitism, on the grounds that, as "White folks," Jews are ineligible for "victim status" (Brodkin, 1998; Gutman, 1994). Some of our (non-Jewish) participants have encountered skepticism, marginalization, and even hostility for taking part in a project that ostensibly privileges "the Jews." Ongoing discussions of race and racism, therefore, are relevant to historically contextualized considerations of the Holocaust and its reception (Webber & Brown, 2001).

Pointing out the potential for abuse, while trying to avoid it, is a means for understanding what happened in the Holocaust and modeling how to teach it and comparable events. We thus operate on multiple levels, asking: (a) What happened then and why? (b) How is what happened then understood today from various perspectives and to what ends? and (c) How does our meta-tracking of analytical and interpretational processes recursively feed into an enriched reception and augmented transmission of, and engagement with, knowledge?

Generational Change: Holocaust Education as Adult Education

Notions of generativity, generations, and intergenerationality inform the program both implicitly and explicitly. The authors have long-since entered that adult phase of the human life cycle in which, according to Erik Erikson, we confront the conflict of "generativity versus stagnation." In introducing the concept of generativity to the literature of psychology, Erikson explained that he wanted to highlight "primarily the concern in establishing and guiding the next generation" (Erikson, 1950, p. 267; cf. Slater, 2003, pp. 55–57; McAdams & de St. Aubin, 1998).

In Erikson's later thinking, adult generativity was seen as an "investment" in the younger generation that went beyond literal parenthood. Hoare explains this as follows:

> [T]he adult is defined as one who is integral to the cycle of generations. Here there is an interlocking reciprocity. . . . In this view, adults' lives and those of their children are tightly interdependent, for "the generational cycle links life cycles together by confronting the older generation's generativity with the younger one's readiness to grow." (Hoare, 2002, p. 191)

Generativity is thus bound up with intergenerationality. It enacts reciprocal connections between those in various stages of life in a way that relativizes or calls into question concepts of hierarchy or centricity.

Belonging to a generation (whether by self-ascription or assignment by others) signifies not only a certain commonality of birthdate, but a shared set of experiences and presumably of perspective (so-called "cohort generations"). In addition, the experiences and perspectives of certain "typological" generations take on ascribed symbolic ("stereotypical") significance within society and may feature in processes of societal change (Becker, 2008). Understanding generational belonging is useful in coming to terms with the perpetrators and their offspring, as well as with victims and survivors; and in an extended sense, with Holocaust educators.

The Appel Program

The Appel Program's subtitle "Learning from the Past—Teaching for the Future" situated the program as an educational enterprise whose reflexive and recursive practice resisted reenacting the dialectic of centralization and exclusion that lay at the heart of National Socialist oppression and murder.

The program operated with academic and experiential modules in Europe and Canada. In each cycle, preparatory workshops took place in late spring in all three countries. The European field study, lasting almost four full weeks, followed later in the summer. Apportioned roughly equally between Germany and Poland, the field study included workshops on group dynamics and key concepts such as stereotyping (Lawler, 2003) and victimhood; visits to historical sites, museums, sites of memory, and ethnic and religious sites; and lectures by and discussions with experts from academe, civil society, and government.

When the group members returned home (and to university) in the late summer, they worked on individual and group projects. The full group then reconvened in Canada for a ten-day symposium in February. The time in Canada featured follow-up workshops flowing from the field study, public lectures by invited speakers, visits to Canadian institutions of interest and relevance to our topic, and a closed mini-conference at which all students presented their projects. The rest of the academic year provided time for students to complete written versions of those projects, taking into account the feedback received.

The program's first phase encompassed five cycles (2001–2002, 2003–2004, 2005–2006, 2007–2008, 2009–2010), each approximately coterminous with one academic year. Phase 1, the focus of this study, concluded in 2011 with a retrospective-prospective symposium in Poland, Germany, and Israel, to which all past participants were invited.

Of the 142 students in Phase 1, 35 were from Polish universities; 33 from German universities (with one further participant from Sri Lanka nominated by a German institution); and 73 from Canadian universities. Thus, there was rough numerical parity between North American and European participants in each group.

Involving students drawn from diverse disciplines, across three national university systems, with four official languages (French and English for Canada) and multiple cultures of teaching and learning, productively complicated the teaching and learning environment more than a visit to Europe by a Canadian group or a classical bilateral exchange would have done. Nor is the program's decentered demography adequately captured by the term tri-national. Particularly for Canadian participants, but also increasingly for those studying in Europe, place of birth, self-identified ethnicity, language of the home, and religion (or lack of it) made the putatively national groups diverse and the plenary group even more so.

There were also the usual differences of gender and sexual orientation, as well as age, level of study, and academic major. Undergraduates far outnumbered graduate students, though graduate numbers increased during the course of Phase 1 (national differences in the structure of academic programs preclude any systematic analysis of participants' levels of study). Upon completing the program, some 70 percent were between 21 and 25 years old, and just under 30 percent were 26 or older; only one student was under 21 when she completed the cycle. Fields of study (including many multiple majors) spanned history (42%); languages and literatures, including humanities and cultural studies (37%); the social sciences, including law (27%); religious studies (including Protestant and Catholic theology and Jewish /Judaic Studies) (13%); sciences, including psychology, biology, kinesiology and mathematics (10%); philosophy and the fine arts (each 8%); and journalism (4%). Balancing the diversity of the students' backgrounds and academic focus was their shared interest in becoming educators (broadly defined), including classroom teachers at the primary, secondary, and post-secondary levels; but also journalists, archivists, museum/memorial site professionals, and adult educators.

Although an applicant's creed or religious affiliation did not affect the application process, and although we did not ask participants about their religious affiliation, we did provide access to Christian, Jewish, and Muslim services in both Europe and Canada. Most participants had been brought up in a Christian tradition (Roman Catholic, Protestant, Greek Orthodox). Approximately 10 percent were Jewish. There were also Muslim, Hindu, and Wiccan participants and others who did not identify with any religious community.

APPLICATION

The program was inspired by, and partly responded to, a program for practicing teachers operated by B'nai Brith Canada's League for Human Rights (cf. Frede-Wenger & Trummer, 2005; Mock, 2000). In contrast, our program focused on pre-service education, and hence *future* educators, for strategic and practical reasons. Strategically, we wanted to embed our program in a university setting with its academic standards of research and teaching, to maximize the potential for learning and teaching prior to our students' embarking on their professional careers in education. In practical terms, working with current students provided us and them access to expertise and logistical and financial support.

HOLOCAUST EDUCATION AND GENERATIONAL STATUS

In the context of teaching and learning about the Holocaust, generational status (and the Eriksonian idea of adult generativity) was implicated in multiple and sometimes contradictory ways. We can distinguish at least three kinds of generational belonging, pertaining to (1) those who experienced the events at the time, in whichever capacity; (2) accounts (including those by contemporaneous witnesses) about the different generations as subjects in the Holocaust; and (3) members of generational cohorts today who visit memorial sites and museums, or who learn about and/or respond to accounts and representations of the Holocaust.

In addition, generationality is relevant to pre-service and in-service Holocaust educators, and specifically to the Appel Program. We initially excluded future primary teachers, partly because the school systems in Poland and Germany seemed skeptical about teaching about the Holocaust at the lower level (Deckert-Peaceman, 2002). In the course of the program, however, interested students in the "Junior/Intermediate" stream of York's Faculty of Education, as well as students preparing for equivalent teaching careers in Germany at pedagogical universities (*pädagogische Hochschulen*), argued persuasively that, particularly in diverse societies, it was possible and important to find age-appropriate ways to teach younger students about the Holocaust and other genocides (see Totten & Feinberg, 2001).

The issue of age-appropriateness arose repeatedly, most often after visits to memorial sites. Our students were troubled by the presence of very young children at particular sites of memory, such as Auschwitz. Their concerns are also reflected in the literature on museums and memorial sites (Anderson, 2007; Linenthal, 1995). The Auschwitz-Birkenau State Museum discusses the "problem of age and coping with emotion as a visitor to Auschwitz" in a volume for educators who are planning group visits. Although allowing for exceptions, these guidelines recommend that visits to the full site and exhibits with graphic photographs and personal items (including victims' ashes, hair, and personal effects) be reserved for students at least in their mid-teens (Białecka, Oleksy, Regard, & Trojański, 2010, pp. 27–31). The Auschwitz-Birkenau guidelines also shed light on another set of pedagogical and ethical considerations, Holocaust education's focus on children in the Holocaust, noting that:

> the children of former times can "speak" to the children of today. . . . Giving these people a voice once again—and the right to a voice—does not diminish the horror of what happened to them. On the contrary, it highlights the violence that was done to ordinary life. (2010, p. 27)

Both the Swedish government's "Living History" project (Bruchfeld & Levine, 1998) and the Anne Frank House in the Netherlands have produced expertly researched and pedagogically attractive projects that speak directly to younger readers. The graphic novels of the Anne Frank House, while aimed at younger readers, are consciously and explicitly intergenerational, linking multiple generations by exploring family and societal history (Heuvel, van der Rol, & Schippers, 2007).

Relying on "child witnesses" such as Anne Frank to make the Holocaust accessible, though effective in reaching a larger public, carries risks and limitations. In this connection, Mark Anderson (2007) criticizes the emotionalization and infantilization of the Holocaust, whereby children as victims are disproportionately represented as foci and vehicles for adult empathy and as accessible identification points for children. The problem stems, according to Anderson, from an intention to "touch" audiences as opposed to informing them. This is valid criticism. Centering notions of victimhood and witnessing on children's experiences distorts the Holocaust through the very process of rendering it immediate. To reduce the Holocaust to an atrocity against children is comparable to reducing the complex sequencing as well as simultaneity of genocidal measures against the Jews to one symbolic place and mode: death by prussic acid (Zyklon B) in the gas chambers of Auschwitz-Birkenau (Webber, 2011).

In contrast, our program placed considerable emphasis on preserving and illuminating the complexity of the Holocaust. As such it was designed for adult learners who were intellectually and emotionally capable of tolerating complexity and ambiguity. At the same time, our approach emphasized the *mediacy* of research and analysis over the *immediacy* of emotion.

This tension between mediacy and immediacy was evident in the question of whether and how to use Holocaust survivors as presenters. Survivors do add a firsthand authentic voice that many pre-service professionals, active teachers, and their students find moving. Survivors have lived the history we are studying. Survivors' stories, like their authors, are individual and particular. That is their strength and validity. Discussions with survivors have an important role as long as they are not mistaken for objective lessons on the entire scope of the Holocaust. Nevertheless, challenging accepted wisdom lies at the heart of ethical curiosity and critical inquiry. Yet the position of survivors is such that one cannot easily challenge possible factual inaccuracies or deeply felt convictions on how things were and/or are.

A further issue concerns the role and status of memory in re-telling experience. Those who experienced the events of the Holocaust, in whichever capacity, and who are still alive, will have been children at the time. No matter how accurate their memory, how well informed or even learned they have become about what took place some 70 years ago, their experience was that of a child or adolescent. In an intergenerational act within one person, survivors recount their experiences from the split perspective of old age and youth. This split perspective is susceptible to distortion, both conscious and unconscious (Anderson, 2007). The ability to experience and learn from the affective immediacy of the survivor's presence, but simultaneously to maintain an appropriate intellectual distance from the narrative as a memory mediated in words through time and space—in other words, to balance emotion and analysis—is a high-level competence that not even all adults possess. Like other forms of critical thinking, it must be fostered explicitly and purposefully (Meyers, 1986).

We therefore adopted an approach that appreciated survivors and their stories for the opportunity they presented to learn about Holocaust experiences, and afterwards subjected the interview to ethical and critical scrutiny in terms of the pedagogical practices that best suited the educational settings in which our future colleagues would act. Similarly, we positioned visits to memorial sites such as Ravensbrück (the former concentration camp for women), as visits to a memorial museum, rather than a concentration camp. The site, with its own pre-Nazi, Nazi, and post-Nazi history, may now have multiple societal functions; its narrative must, like that of a survivor or other contemporaneous witness, be analyzed carefully (Webber, 2014). The high emotional expectations invested in both conversations with survivors and visits to sites of atrocity can also act as barriers to the examination of pedagogical practice.

Holocaust Education as Adult Education (but also for Children)

Balancing immediacy and mediacy requires consciousness of one's own perspective. Empathy, as the ability to see oneself in another's situation, while not mistaking oneself for that other person, is a quintessentially ethical capacity that makes connections while maintaining critical distance, including the distance that allows self-knowledge (LaCapra, 1998). As Levinas points out, recognizing and respecting others is the reciprocal of (and possibly the prerequisite for), self-respect (Levinas, 2003, 2006 [1972]).

We have been illustrating some of the ways in which generationality is implicated in the Holocaust and in Holocaust education. In doing so, we have been insisting on the importance of recognizing one's own and others' perspectivity. For example, as educators educating educators, we tried to make explicit the ways in which the educational system in Germany was complicit in justifying, supporting, and extending the reach of National

Socialism. The complicity of learnedness is part of the history of almost every discipline that we and our colleagues and students pursued and pursue (cf. Wildt, 2003).

As recent research on the response of Canadian academic institutions to the rise of fascism and National Socialism demonstrates, learnedness is not always the same thing as wisdom and courage (Brown, 2012). Before the war, the post-secondary systems in both Canada and Poland perpetuated prejudices about Jews and discriminated against them. These practices reinforced the Nazis' resolve and their sense of "being right" (cf. Abella & Troper, 1983; Rudnicki, 2005; Norwood, 2009; Brown 2012). At the same time, we believe in the power of education to create enlightenment as well as pleasure, and to provide the means to resist oppression. This was evident even as the events in question unfolded (cf. Kleßmann & Długoborski [1997]; Cochavi [1988]).

The awareness that teaching and learning can be and have been perverted to serve racism and mass murder places a special obligation on those who teach and learn about the Holocaust. By modeling awareness of the contingency, historicity, and potential for abuse of the very tools used to understand abuse, one wants not only to shed light on the Holocaust, but also to demonstrate how future educators, in their own research and teaching, might approach the issue.

The Appel Program sought to foster tolerance for ambiguity with a view to enhancing student teachers' critical competence and their pedagogical capacity to promote a more fitting understanding of the Holocaust with their own future students. The broad range of academic majors among our participants helped to illuminate the understanding of the Holocaust, and ways to teach about it, from a variety of perspectives. Similarly, the influence of different university systems helped to expand the groups' understanding of learning. Our rather subjective way of "jumping into" a text—by going around the room and asking for spontaneous responses—was initially jarring to Polish students, and we found we had to draw attention to the apparent mismatch of expectations in order to negotiate a productive way forward. Discussions of films and literary texts often featured marked disagreements among the faculty members. For students expecting knowledge (primarily in the form of "facts") to be dispensed by an authoritative teacher at the front of the room, it was at times disconcerting to be confronted by a circle of professorial voices that expressed self-doubt and dissent. Fostering tolerance for ambiguity, in part by providing the vocabularies and modeling the processes for doing so, is part of what we wanted to achieve in the project—in support of a more fitting understanding of the Holocaust, our students' overall critical competence, and their pedagogical toolkit.

The ethnic diversity of our groups was also both a reality to be acknowledged and a pedagogical boon. The changing demographies in Europe and North America prompted a rethinking of traditional and assumed distinctions between societies of "perpetrators," "victims," "bystanders," or "victors." Because some of our participants (and the publics with whom they do and will work) came from societies and families that directly experienced National Socialism and the Holocaust, sensitivity and openness were required from all concerned. In some families, complicated intergenerational processes of memory, repression, and rewriting were still being worked out (Hilmar, 2010; Welzer, 2008). This combination of coexisting personal, familial, and other group narratives retrospectively rejected Nazi theory and practice that sought to exclude, repress, incarcerate, and even murder those whom its totalizing and mono-perspectival worldview construed as alien.

To de-center conventional understandings of victimhood, our first visit to a memorial site focused on the murder of those deemed "unworthy of life" by virtue of their ascribed physical, cognitive, or social status. The so-called "euthanasia" program, almost all of whose victims were German Christians, was the forerunner of the mass murder of European Jewry (Friedlander, 2001), which itself coincided with the repression and often murder of other stigmatized groups (Gellately & Stoltzfus, 2001). Antisemitism and other forms of racism and group-focused enmity persist to this day (Küpper, Wolf, & Zick, 2010), and some participants came to the program precisely because they wished to counter the antisemitism that they sensed in their own families.

At the same time, the increasing presence in Europe and Canada of immigrant families with no ties to this history means that educators must develop new approaches to teaching about National Socialism and the Holocaust (Gryglewski, 2013). Revised pedagogies must connect students' own stories (and intergenerational trajectories) while resisting the temptation to co-opt the Holocaust for other agendas by projecting it in irresponsible and historically unfounded ways onto other events (Georgi & Ohliger, 2009).

The informal discussions, debates, and personal and intellectual encounters among our group, often turning on issues of family tradition, were at least as crucial to the learning that took place as the formal academic sessions. The strains of dealing with a complex, controversial, and emotionally charged topic during a demanding four-week itinerary and often in languages other than one's first language not infrequently led to intense and emotional exchanges.

In this context it proved crucial to model and foster ways in which controversial opinions could be exchanged openly, respectfully, and with increasing self-awareness. A safe space and sense of trust were essential in allowing the sensitivities, when they arose, to be registered and thrashed out without automatically assuming ill intentions. We found that, no matter where one started a particular discussion, it turned out that it should have begun earlier. Hence our emphasis on recursive consideration, (re-) definition, discussion.

One key vehicle was the journal that all York students presented and was recommended for other students and faculty alike (cf. Lawler, 2003). As we explained in our instructions, the journal was not the same as the diary or daily record of the trip:

> The word that recurs repeatedly in attempts to explain what a journal is to students is "reflection." The process of reflection inserts time and distance between the events themselves and the response to them. Reflection implies high-level analysis, including self-analysis. Reflection simultaneously requires and leads to greater clarity—for the writer and the reader. (Webber & Brown, 2011)

The process of revision that transforms a diary into a journal adds, through distance and reflection, a revisioning of the experience. It is thus a form of the recursive and distinctive revisiting of experience and knowledge that we advocated and tried to practice.

Conclusion

The Appel Program incorporated at least five types of teaching and learning. It was simultaneously:

1. An example of Holocaust education in the contextualized, critical sense that we have explained above and that reflected, but that also went beyond, previous approaches (e.g., Totten and Feinberg, 2001; Totten, 2002; Totten, Jacobs, and Bartrop, 2004);

2. A teacher-education course that, by example as well as precept, (re)presented education more broadly than as "just" classroom pedagogy (cf. Lindquist, 2007);

3. A team-taught, interdisciplinary course that featured polyperspectivity and polyvocality;

4. A course in international and intercultural studies that included features of experiential education and the exploration of the self and others (cf. Howden, 2012);

5. An adult education course in which the educative force was multidirectional, de-centering, and recursive, and in which the teachers, themselves adults, learned from their students, thus practicing a reciprocal form of Erikson's notion of generativity.

Throughout this account we have paid considerable attention to "family matters," including issues of intergenerational transmission of experience, framing, and interpretation. It is probably no accident that the metaphor that came to characterize the relationship among the participants (students and faculty) in the Appel Program was one of family. The program's subtitle, "Learning from the Past—Teaching for the Future," was programmatic also in the sense of generations and generativity.

In this family there was reciprocal influence among the generations, as well as an eventual succession of one generation by another. The true test of our approach resided and will reside in its generativity and sustainability. As we take stock of developments so far, we are heartened by the number of our former students, now colleagues, who continue, in diverse ways and settings, and from diverse perspectives, to work on important issues related to our program. They have initiated and sustained their projects as well as nominating their own students to participate in ours. Past participants are also contributing to the literature on the program and its foci (e.g., Frede-Wenger & Trummer, 2005; Dufour & Roy, 2007).

In 2001, two students proposed an intergenerational project that utilized creative writing as a way for contemporaneous witnesses and younger Germans to reflect together on aspects of National Socialism. Skeptical, we advised the students to seek another project. Happily, they resisted our advice and carried out several workshops whose results are embodied in the volume *Gegen das Vergessen* (*Against Forgetting*). When these former students, now colleague teacher-trainers in Germany, honored us by asking us to provide an introduction to their volume, we wrote the following words that apply to the entire Appel Program:

> *Rabi said: "Much have I learned from my teachers and even more from my colleagues. But I have learned most from my students."* (Babylonian Talmud, Tractate Makot, 10a)

***

That one learns most from one's students sounds odd at first. What kind of a teacher sits at the feet of his students? In fact, however, the notion is not odd at all. Every good teacher is stimulated to rethink his approach and to rework his analyses by students' probing questions and creative responses. And for teachers, there is no greater reward than being taught by their students. (Brown & Webber, 2006)

We taught our adult students about the Holocaust, primarily through trying to model how to think and teach about it, and that has meant that "learning for the future" was also learning from our students. In this sense, too, the project was a form of adult education in which recursivity was both a methodology and a form of self-sustaining teaching and learning.

Acknowledgments

We are grateful to our former student Robert Mizzi for the opportunity to learn from and contribute to his area of expertise—adult education; to the German Academic Exchange Service (DAAD) for a grant supporting our research; and to Mark and Gail Appel of Toronto for their generous support. This chapter also draws on unpublished presentations discussing the project (Brown & Webber [2007]; Webber [2009]).

References

Abella, I., & Troper, H. (1983). *None is too many: Canada and the Jews of Europe 1933–1948*. Toronto, ON: University of Toronto Press.

Anderson, M. (Fall 2007). The child victim as witness to the Holocaust: An American story? *Jewish Social Studies: History, Culture, Society, n.s. 14*(1), 1–22. Retrieved from http://www.jstor.org/stable/40207081.

Bartov, O. (2003). Seeking the roots of modern genocide: On the macro- and microhistory of mass murder. In R. Gellately & B. Kiernan (Eds.), *The specter of genocide: Mass murder in historical perspective* (pp. 75–96). Cambridge, UK: Cambridge University Press.

Becker, H. A. (2008). Karl Mannheims "Problem der Generationen"—80 Jahre danach. *Zeitschrift für Familienforschung/Journal of Family Research, 20*(2), 203–221. Retrieved from http://www.zeitschrift-fuer-familienforschung.de/pdf/2008-2-becker.pdf.

Białecka, A., Oleksy, K., Regard, F., & Trojański, P. (Eds.). (2010). *European pack for visiting Auschwitz-Birkenau memorial and museum: Guidelines for teachers and educators.* Strasbourg, France: Polish Ministry of Education, Auschwitz-Birkenau State Museum and Council of Europe Publishing.

Brodkin, K. (1998). *How Jews became white folks and what that says about race in America.* New Brunswick, NJ, and London, UK: Rutgers University Press.

Brown, M. (2011). The universal and the particular: Twin foci in Holocaust education. *Images: The International Journal of European Film, Performing Arts and Audiovisual Communication, 8*(15–16), 31–48.

———. (2012). On campus in the thirties: Antipathy, support and indifference. In R. L. Klein (Ed.), *Nazi Germany, Canadian responses: Confronting antisemitism in the shadow of war* (pp. 144–182). Montreal, QC, and Kingston, ON: McGill-Queen's University Press.

Brown, M., & Webber, M. (2006). Vorwort. In P. I. Trummer, J. Heger, & J. Ehrnsberger (Eds.), *Wider das Vergessen. Schreibend zwischen Vergangenheit und Gegenwart* (pp. 7–9). Waldburg, Germany: Demand.

———. (2007). *Equipping future educators from Canada, Germany and Poland to teach for and in diversity.* Paper presented at the International Conference on Tolerance and Education, Gdańsk, Poland, November 16, 2007 (unpublished).

Bruchfeld, S., & Levine, P. A. (1998). *Tell ye your children . . . A book about the Holocaust in Europe 1933–1945* (Gothia, Trans.). Stockholm, Sweden: Regerungskansliet.

Cochavi, Y. (1988). Arming for survival: Martin Buber and Jewish adult education in Nazi Germany. *Holocaust and Genocide Studies, 3*(1), 55–67. Retrieved from http://hgs.oxfordjournals.org.ezproxy.library.yorku.ca/content/3/1/55.full.pdf. doi:10.1093/hgs/3.1.55.

Deckert-Peaceman, H. (2002). *Holocaust als Thema für Grundschulkinder? Ethnographische Feldforschung zur Holocaust Education am Beispiel einer Fallstudie aus dem amerikanischen Grundschulunterricht und ihre Relevanz für die Grundschulpädagogik in Deutschland.* Europäische Hochschulschriften,

Reihe XI Pädagogik, Bd 862. Frankfurt/Main: Peter Lang Europäischer Verlag der Wissenschaften.

Dufour, F. G., & Roy, M. (2007). L'Éducation de l'Holocauste et d'antiracisme face au défi de l'hétérogénéité: analyse d'une formation pédagogique tri-nationale. *Canadian Jewish Studies/Études juives canadiennes, 15*, 53–74. Retrieved from https://pi.library.yorku.ca/ojs/index.php/cjs/article/viewPDF Interstitial/22609/21080.

Erikson, E. H. (1950, 1963). *Childhood and society.* New York, NY, and London, UK: W. W. Norton.

Frede-Wenger, B., & Trummer, P. (2005). "Learning from the past—teaching for the future": Ein kanadisch-deutsch-polnisches Universitätsprojekt mit Lehramtsstudierenden. In H.-F. Rathenow & N. H. Weber (Eds.), *Nationalsozialismus und Holocaust. Historisch-politisches Lernen in der Lehrerbildung* (pp. 297–315). Hamburg, Germany: Krämer-Verlag.

Friedlander, H. (2001) The exclusion and murder of the disabled. In Robert Gellately and Nathan Stoltzfus (Eds.). *Social outsiders in Nazi Germany* (pp. 145–165). Princeton, NJ: Princeton University Press.

Gellately, R., & Stoltzfus, N. (Eds.). (2001). *Social outsiders in Nazi Germany.* Princeton, NJ: Princeton University Press.

Georgi, V. B., & Ohliger, R. (Eds.). (2009). *Crossover Geschichte. Historisches Bewusstsein Jugendlicher in der Einwanderungsgesellschaft.* Hamburg, Germany: Körber-Stiftung.

Gryglewski, E. (2013). *Anerkennung und Erinnerung: Zugänge arabisch-palästinensischer und türkischer Berliner Jugendlicher zum Holocaust.* Berlin, Germany: Metropol.

Gutman, S. J. (1994). The marginalization of antisemitism in multicultural curricula. In M. Brown (Ed.), *Approaches to antisemitism: Context and curriculum* (pp. 178–192). New York and Jerusalem: The American Jewish Commitee and The International Center for University Teaching of Jewish Civilization.

Heuvel, E., van der Rol, R., & Schippers, L. (Eds.). (2007). *De Soektocht* [English: *The Search*]. Amsterdam: Anne Frank Stichting.

Hilmar, T. (Ed.). (2010). *Ort, Subjekt, Verbrechen. Koordinaten historisch-politischer Bildungsarbeit zum Nationalsozialismus.* Wien, Austria: Czernin Verlag.

Hoare, C. H. (2002). *Erikson on development in adulthood: New insights from the unpublished papers.* New York, NY, and Cary, NC: Oxford University Press. Retrieved from http://site.ebrary.com.ezproxy.library.yorku.ca/lib/oculyork/docDetail.action?docID=10084777.

Howden, E. (2012). Outdoor experiential education: Learning through the body. *New Directions for Adult and Continuing Education, 134*(Summer 2012), 43–51. Retrieved from http://onlinelibrary.wiley.com.ezproxy.library.yorku.ca/doi/10.1002/ace.20015/pdf. doi:10.1002/ace.20015.

Kay, A. (1998). Generativity in the shadow of genocide: The Holocaust experience and generativity. In D. P. McAdams & E. de St. Aubin (Eds.), *Generativity and adult development: How and why we care for the next generation* (pp.

335–359). Washington, DC: American Psychological Association. Retrieved from http://books.scholarsportal.info/viewdoc.html?id=242492.

Kleßmann, C., & Długoborski, W. (1997). Nationalsozialistische Bildungspolitik und polnische Hochschulen 1939–1945. *Geschichte und Gesellschaft, 23*(4), 535–559.

Küpper, B., Wolf, C., & Zick, A. (2010). Social status and anti-immigrant attitudes in Europe: An examination from the perspective of social dominance theory. *International Journal of Conflict and Violence, 4*(2), 205–219. http://www.ijcv.org/index.php/ijcv/article/view/85/pdf_4.

LaCapra, D. (1998). *History and memory after Auschwitz*. Ithaca, NY: Cornell University Press.

Lawler, P. W. (2003). Teachers as adult learners: A new perspective. *New Directions for Adult and Continuing Education, 98*(Summer 2003), 15–22. Retrieved from http://dx.doi.org/10.1002/ace.95 doi:10.1002/ace.95.

Levinas, E. (2003, 2006 [1972]). Without identity (N. Poller, Trans.). In R. A. Cohen (Ed.), *Humanism of the other* (pp. 58–69). Urbana, IL, and Chicago, IL: University of Illinois Press.

Lindquist, D. H. (2007, Spring). A necessary Holocaust pedagogy: Teaching the teachers. *Issues in Teacher Education, 16*(1), 21–36. Retrieved from http://go.galegroup.com/ps/i.do?id=GALE%7CA169960706&v=2.1&u=yorku_main&it=r&p=EAIM&sw=w.

Linenthal, E. T. (1995). *Preserving memory: The struggle to create America's Holocaust museum*. New York, NY: Penguin.

McAdams, D. P., & de St. Aubin, E. (Eds.). (1998). *Generativity and adult development: How and why we care for the next generation*. Washington, DC: American Psychological Association. Retrieved from http://books.scholarsportal.info/viewdoc.html?id=242492.

Meyers, C. (1986). *Teaching students to think critically: A guide for faculty in all disciplines*. San Francisco, CA, and London, UK: Jossey-Bass.

Mock, K. S. (2000). Holocaust and hope: Holocaust education in the context of anti-racist education in Canada. In F. C. Decoste & B. Schwartz (Eds.), *The Holocaust's ghost: Writings on art, politics, law and education* (pp. 465–482). Edmonton, AB: University of Alberta Press.

Norwood, S. H. (2009). *The Third Reich in the ivory tower: Complicity and conflict on American campuses*. New York, NY: Cambridge University Press.

Power, S. (2002). *"A problem from hell": America and the age of genocide*. New York, NY: Perennial [HarperCollins].

Rudnicki, S. (2005). Anti-Jewish legislation in interwar Poland. In R. Blobaum (Ed.), *Antisemitism and its opponents in modern Poland* (pp. 148–170). Ithaca, NY: Cornell University Press.

Schwarz-Friesel, M., & Reinharz, J. (2013). *Die Sprache der Judenfeindschaft im 21. Jahrhundert*. Berlin, Germany, and Boston, MA: Walter de Gruyter.

Slater, C. L. (2003). Generativity versus stagnation: An elaboration of Erikson's adult stage of human development. *Journal of Adult Development, 10*(1),

53–65. Retrieved from http://link.springer.com.ezproxy.library.yorku.ca/content/pdf/10.1023%2FA%3A1020790820868.pdf.

Timm, B. (2010). *Verunsichernde Orte. Selbstverständnis und Weiterbildung in der Gedenkstättenpädagogik.* Frankfurt, Germany: Brandes & Apsel.

Totten, S. (Ed.). (2002). *Remembering the past, educating for the present and the future: Personal and pedagogical stories of Holocaust educators.* Westport, CT: Praeger.

Totten, S., & Feinberg, S. (Eds.). (2001). *Teaching and studying the Holocaust.* Boston, MA: Allyn and Bacon.

Totten, S., Jacobs, S. L., & Bartrop, P. R. (Eds.). (2004). *Teaching about the Holocaust: Essays by college and university teachers.* Westport, CT: Praeger.

Webber, M. (2009). *Collaboration: A double-edged sword.* Paper presented at the conference The St. Louis era: Looking back, moving forward, Toronto, June 1, 2009 (unpublished).

———. (2011). Metaphorizing the Holocaust: The ethics of comparison. *Images: The International Journal of European Film, Performing Arts and Audiovisual Communication, 8*(15–16), 5–30.

Webber, M. J. (2014). Memorial sites as educational sites: An ethical-rhetorical approach. In J. Roche & J. Röhling (Eds.), *Erinnerungsorte und Erinnerungskulturen. Konzepte und Perspektiven für die Sprach- und Kulturvermittlung* (pp. 59–72). Baltmannsweiler, Germany: Schneider Verlag Hogengehren.

Webber, M., & Brown, M. (2001). Ist Holocaust-Unterricht mit antirassistischem Unterricht vereinbar? Eine kanadische Perspektive. In O. Fuchs, R. Boschki, & B. Frede-Wenger (Eds.), *Zugänge zur Erinnerung. Bedingungen anamnetischer Erfahrung. Studien zur subjektorienten Erinnerungsarbeit* (pp. 249–268). Münster: Lit Verlag.

Webber, M., & Brown, M. (2011, July 02). Explanation: Journal of the summer field trip 2011. *Mark and Gail Appel (TftF) project 2011.* Retrieved from https://learn.yorku.ca/moodle/mod/resource/view.php?id=10568.

Welzer, H. (2008). Collateral damage of history education: National socialism and the Holocaust in German family memory. *Social Research, 75*(1), 287–314. Retrieved from http://search.proquest.com.ezproxy.library.yorku.ca/docview/2 09670550?accountid=15182.

Wildt, M. (2003). *Generation des Unbedingten. Das Führungskorps des Reichssicherheitshauptamtes.* Hamburg, Germany: Hamburger Edition HIS Verlagsgesellschaft.

18

Study Abroad Programs, International Students, and Global Citizenship

Colonial-Colonizer Relations in Global Higher Education

Korbla P. Puplampu
Lindsay Wodinski

The significance of education to individuals and society at large has almost become a universal statement of faith. Higher educational institutions, the focus of this study, have and continue to occupy a central role in society because they provide the framework for creating knowledge for both human and social development (Barnet, 2012; Rhoads & Szelényi, 2011; Thorp & Goldstein, 2010; Watson et al., 2011). Universities, like other social institutions, have been caught up in globalization, a theoretical and policy concept that has captured the attention and imagination of educators, educational policy analysts, the state, and broader society for more than three decades (Bok, 2003; Puplampu, 2004; Rhoads & Torres, 2006; Slaughter & Rhoades, 2004). One effect of globalization, among other things, is state cutbacks to university funding (Bok, 2003; Burbules & Torres, 2000). In response, universities have embarked upon several initiatives and programs, ostensibly to cope with the shortfalls in funding in order to continue providing quality teaching, research, and service to the community. These initiatives and programs range from program reviews that aim at eliminating some departments or amalgamating others, internationalizing student and faculty recruitment, restructuring research and teaching, intensifying industry partnerships, and promoting study abroad programs. Another significant issue is the emerging notion of global universities and how these universities present a unique opportunity to deepen the discourse on global citizenship (Khoo, 2011; Rhoads & Szelényi, 2011).

The above responses are not without problems, nor are all universities able to pursue them without difficulty. For example, with respect to global citizenship, both the university and the concept of citizenship, traditionally, have been defined in a national context. Second, placing the university and citizenship in a global framework reveals the nature of global inequality and how universities, especially the historically old ones, have occupied a legitimated and privileged position in the production of knowledge about societies both at home and abroad (Hayhoe, 1993; Smith, 2006). Hence, the knowledge universities produce has to be situated in a context of power (Forstorp, 2008; Joseph, 2008; Puplampu, 2008).

This chapter interrogates the relationship between universities and global citizenship, focusing on two specific activities in this linkage: study abroad programs and the recruitment of international students (Jefferess, 2008; Khoo, 2011; McCowan, 2012; Wynveen, Kyle & Tarrant, 2012). Study abroad programs and enrolment of international students offer opportunities for continuous dialogue and debate about experiential learning and its impact on knowledge legitimation and utilization. The chapter argues that the role of universities in education for global citizenship has to be grounded in reflexive and participatory practices. Consequently, international students, specifically students who have enrolled in a study abroad program or have moved away from their country of origin and thus domiciled in a new educational environment must be able to challenge and resist the prevalent assumptions that protect the privileged status of the knowledge claims. In the first section, this argument will be substantiated against a background of globalization of higher education by examining the literature on study abroad programs, international students, and global citizenship, while paying attention to the nature of knowledge and positionality inherent in these programs. The second section discusses the challenges of study abroad programs and international students with respect to global citizenship, and the final section identifies some transformative possibilities and offers concluding remarks.

Study Abroad Programs, International Students, and Global Citizenship: An Overview

At the heart of contemporary globalization are dramatic breakthroughs in communication and information technologies as well as the consequent compression in time and space (Held & McGrew, 2004). The compression of time and space has significance for political, economic, and sociocultural relations (Scholte, 2005; Steger, 2009). Briefly stated, political globalization revolves around changes in the role of the state in the economic and social spheres leading to the emergence of non-state actors. The economic aspects of globalization include the increasing emphasis on market forces and an unfettered mobility of financial capital relative to labor, while sociocultural globalization engages with the role of language and the homogeneity versus diversity debate. The implications of globalization for higher education in particular and educational policy in general has been the subject of several studies (Abdi & Kapoor, 2009; Burbules & Torres, 2000; Maringe & Fosket, 2010; Puplampu, 2004; Torres, 2009).

Higher education systems have become, within the context of the market model, another site for consumers or clients of knowledge (learners) to be satisfied at all cost. Academic knowledge laborers are differentiated as continuing or part-time laborers and the significance of knowledge-producing activity is interpreted through the lens of its market value and not its social relevance per se. Successful universities within this context are portrayed as global, innovative, and entrepreneurial and with teaching research and service activity aligned with flexible new models of industrial production (Altmann & Ebersberger, 2013; Thorp & Goldstein, 2010). One aspect of this entrepreneurial ethos is to initiate study abroad programs, expand student enrollments by recruiting from abroad, and simultaneously promote the notion that these programs graduate global citizens (Khoo, 2011; Matthews & Sidhu, 2005; Rhoads & Szelényi, 2011; Suárez-Orozco & Sattin, 2007).

Student recruitment or mobility can be categorized into two major forms: study abroad programs and the international recruitment of students, particularly for graduate education. Study abroad programs are generally short in duration and tend to originate mainly in the Global North and end in the Global South, while international recruitment of students (longer duration) have the reverse flow—from the Global South to the Global North (Knight, 2012; Woodfield, 2010). Study abroad programs have become an integral aspect of the expected learning experiences of several undergraduate programs in the Global North. These programs are premised on the idea of offering students a holistic education by extending their understanding beyond their national or local context and ultimately rendering them as global citizens (Dolby, 2008; Green, 2012; Killick, 2012; Roman, 2003; Sison & Brennan, 2012). By engaging students with knowledge systems and educational practices in other parts of the world, students are expected to be better educated and prepared for a globalized world. Bok (1986) and others have argued that the program, in the context of American students, helps students to be less "parochial" and better prepared for living and working in a global age (American Council on Education, 2003; Falk & Kanach, 2000).

The implicit assumption is that study abroad is an indispensable aspect in the quest for global citizenship (Lewin, 2009; Sison & Brennan, 2012). Perhaps, that is why nearly 250,000 American college students study abroad each year. It further explains the desire of some legislators in the United States "to facilitate study abroad for one million [American] undergraduate students per year by 2017" (Lantis & DuPlaga, 2010, p. 1). This action aligns with the argument that, "international knowledge and skills are imperative for the future security and competiveness of the United States" (Association of International Educators, as cited in Szelényi & Rhoads, 2007, p. 25). Study abroad programs therefore seek to improve intercultural understanding and mindfulness, as well as foster partnerships, pragmatic hope, and social entrepreneurship (Bellamy & Weinberg, 2006).

Another aspect of student mobility is the recruitment of international students. According to the UNESCO Institute of Statistics (UIS) (2013), the number of students enrolled in higher or tertiary education abroad increased from 2 million to 3.6 million in 2000 and 2010, respectively. The international mobility of students, consistent with trends in global migration flows, has a north-south axis, where the former serves as magnet and destination for the latter. The same UNESCO source notes that East Asia and the Pacific region constitute the largest source of international students representing 28 percent of the global total, with students from China accounting for 17 percent of the total. Meanwhile, North America and Western Europe account for 15 percent of international students. In relative terms, students from Central Asia and Sub-Saharan Africa are the most mobile in the world, even though the Arab States have been the site of a steady increase of students leaving to study abroad. The top destination countries for international students are: United States of America, United Kingdom, Australia, France, Germany, and Japan. In Canada, international students represent about 8 percent of the undergraduate population and close to 20 percent of the graduate student population (Association of Universities and Colleges of Canada (AUCC), 2010). Through intense marketing programs, the United Kingdom and Australia have increased their proportion of international students, hence the argument that Canada can only increase its share by investing in an international student recruitment strategy and building a relationship with emerging societies of strategic significance such as China, India, and Brazil (AUCC, 2010). The foregoing trends are indications of the market-driven aspects of the restructuring of higher education.

Underpinning the study abroad program and the recruitment of international students is the view that "the world is our oyster, or perhaps, our garden, in which we sow the seeds from the fruits of our academic labours: powerful knowledges, proven (best) practices, and established systems of scholarship, administration and inquiry" (Ninnes & Hellstén, 2005, p. 1). Knowledge refers to the ideas, beliefs and value systems and how these elements interact with the larger society, specifically the political, economic, and social conditions (Mannheim, 1952). An analysis of the role of knowledge entails an interpretation of "ideas or intellectual phenomena in general" (Ritzer, 2000, p. 24; See also Banks, 1993).

As centers of knowledge production, the state and society have conferred on universities and academic knowledge producers a certain degree of credibility and legitimacy in knowledge production and utilization (Puplampu, 2008). Knowledge, however, is not produced in a vacuum, and its emergence and subsequent validation are essential aspects of positionality. Positionality "reveals the importance of identifying the positions and frames of reference from which scholars and writers present their data, interpretations, analyses, and instruction" (Banks, 1993, p. 5). This means that to understand how knowledge is constructed, "we must not only be aware of the knowledge produced, but must also understand that the knowledge producer is located within a particular social, economic, and political context of society" (Banks, 1995, p.15). Universities, as an integral component of the global and national social structure, are structured in such a way that privileges certain values and ways of knowing. Such knowledge hierarchies that exist in study abroad programs and the recruitment practices of international students undoubtedly shape the learning process and understandings of global citizenship.

Citizenship has multiple meanings (Cabrera, 2010; Heater, 2004). However, Marshall's (1950) seminal work, *Citizenship and Social Class*, provides a useful point of departure. Citizenship, according to Marshall (1950), has three main components: civil, political, and social. Civic citizenship includes individual liberty, freedom of speech and thought, while a key aspect of the political citizen is the right to vote and contest for political office. Finally, social citizenship calls for economic welfare and security against the background of the prevailing social norms of society. The state, through citizenship, confers rights and privileges on people within its territorial boundaries and space as it also imposes some responsibilities. Since the 1980s, there has been a renewed interest in citizenship (Kivisto & Faist, 2007). Citizenship has therefore transcended Marshall's (1950) three elements to a plethora of citizenships, including global, dual, multicultural, nested, and transnational citizenship (Falk, 1994; Miller, 1991).

As the main focus of this chapter, global citizenship "challenges the conventional meaning of citizenship as exclusive membership and participation within a territorially bounded political community" (Gaventa & Tandon, 2010, p. 9). The state's role in citizenship has been "further deepened in recent years due to trends towards 'globalization,' which has weakened [static notions of] national boundaries" (Gülalp, 2006, p. 2). Global citizenship ranges from an internalized sense of belonging, to a global community, to a more specific global polity that collectively enforces legal and human rights and responsibilities within the context of international law (Schattle, 2008; Stromquist, 2009). There is an indirect understanding that it operates at the global and national levels and affects people's abilities to address their common interests. The contemporary emphasis on global citizenship demonstrates the challenges confronting the ethics-driven nature of global higher education. Due to differences in logic, market-driven and ethics-driven global higher education do not align comfortably with each other, but rather reveal tensions and contradictions (Khoo, 2011).

Global Higher Education and Global Citizenship: Unravelling the Ambiguities

The extent to which study abroad programs and international students can educate for global citizenship calls for transformations in curriculum, teaching styles, and other forms of pedagogy, as well as a renewed interest in critical learning. Most study abroad programs are crafted on the curriculum needs of the sending institution in the Global North. While the sending institution makes every attempt to verify and certify the curriculum of the receiving institutions, and rightfully so, many, if not all, higher educational institutions in the Global South are developed within the colonial framework and modeled on universities in the colonizer's country (Daza, 2006; Lavia & Moore, 2010; Neave & van Vught, 1994). Even though universities in the Global South continue to experience dramatic change, most of their practices mirror that of their counterparts in the Global North. Attempts at institutional renewal and the development of an indigenous capacity have not attained the desired results, largely because of the changing role of the state in the funding of higher education (Abdi, Puplampu, & Dei, 2006; Altbach & Balan, 2007). Therefore, students from the Global North study abroad in institutions that are similar to their own, as Sison & Brennan (2012) document in the case of students in Australia. Furthermore, most study abroad programs are for language-training purposes and given their short duration, offer a limited exposure to the nuances of the local environment (Chieffo & Griffiths, 2007; Wanner, 2007). Consequently, learning in these programs is more likely to be fleeting while reinforcing stereotypes rather than offering an opportunity for meaningful intercultural education as the basis for global citizenship.

At the same time that Australian students want to pursue study abroad programs in similar situated institutions, Australian universities, like others in the Global North, are at the forefront in the recruitment of international students from the Global South. The result is that they now have to rethink the forms of engagement with students from diverse cultural and political backgrounds (Harman, 2005; Joseph, 2008; Singh, 2005). In Australia, and in other countries in the Global North, there is a hostile attitude and challenges to multicultural education and educating for global citizenship (Mitchell, 2001; Stearns, 2009).

Thus, the question is the extent to which international students will be exposed to tenets of global citizenship. International students in graduate education have a longer period of study. Graduate education, given its nature, purpose, and organization, offers an appropriate, but problematic context to reposition global citizenship (Green, 2012; Zahabioun, et al., 2013). Foreign students from Brazil, China, and Italy studying in the United States did not necessarily become global citizens as a result of their graduate education. Rather, their notions of global citizenship were mediated by "cross-national tensions and the significant imbalances in power and economic development among nation-states" (Szelényi & Rhoads, 2007, p. 42). This is because the market-driven and ethics-driven processes are not the same when study abroad programs and international students are presented as the springboard for forging global citizenship (Khoo, 2011).

The overarching issue is the status of knowledge. Education in the Global North (particularly North America and Europe) has, for several years, coalesced around the so-called Western canon (Banks, 1993; Connell, 2007; Cope and Kalantzis, 1997). To adherents of the Western canon, it is privileged knowledge that "produced not only terrestrial empires and colonies but also an intellectual empire in which it alone exemplified the proper meaning and use of reason, objectivity, and adherence to universal concepts and principles, the routine procedures of its disciplines of knowledge" (Sardar & Davies, 2002, p.141). This is akin to Said's (1978) notion of "positional superiority" where anything associated with the Western canon is presented as superior and definite. This assigns proponents of such knowledge the right to construct the other and its knowledge systems.

An intriguing phenomenon emerges when graduate students from the South complete their studies in the Global North, acquire citizenship and, potentially, gain employment in the same academy (Rhee, 2006; Rhee & Subreenduth, 2006; Subedi, 2006). Two main concerns emerge from this situation. The first issue is the extent to which their training within the Eurocentric curriculum will undermine their understanding of the real issues that affect their communities, especially in the Global South or as diasporic denizens in the Global North. Second, would they be "legitimized as intellectuals in the [Global North] or . . . ever be seen as legitimate in mainstream academe?" (Rhee & Subreenduth, 2006, p. 545).

Transformative Possibilities and Conclusion

The transformative possibilities of study abroad programs and international studies for global citizenship flow from the intersections of student interactions, student-faculty relations, and underlying knowledge claims and pedagogical practices. Freire (1993) reminded us years ago that learners do not come to the classroom as blank vessels waiting to be filled with the wisdom of their educators. Rather, they possess and bring to the classroom experiential or primary knowledge. This knowledge and its multiple forms of existence and political implications have to be acknowledged and validated in the learning process. Educating for global citizenship necessitates forms of pedagogy "that inform or challenge the precepts of contemporary life" (Aronowitz, 2000, p. 169). Pedagogy for transformative learning involves a counter-hegemonic narrative, similarly counter-hegemonic work calls for allies. The two main allies are educators and learners studying abroad.

For educators, a key requirement is to ensure that the knowledge they bring to the classroom relates to diverse student experiences and breaks away from "knowledge forms that tend to denigrate one group, especially when there is considerable evidence to show that such knowledge forms (e.g., those on human classification) flow more from myth than from systematic evidence" (Puplampu, 2008, p. 139). A change is required because learners are resistant to knowledge that does not reflect their lived experiences (Codjoe, 2006, 2005; Singh, 2005; Subreenduth, 2006). Former international students who now find themselves in the Euro-American academe can provide a different lens, but not without an awareness and a resolve to directly address their contradictory location (Rhee & Subreenduth, 2006; Subedi, 2006). For learners in study abroad programs, Metzler (2000) reports that faculty members in several African universities acknowledged how American students brought "to the university classroom a healthy 'disrespect' for the dominant 'culture of silence' [of not speaking out in class] by asking questions and respectfully challenging the perspective presented, international students encourage African students to be less 'passive'" [in the learning process] (p. 16).

Since global citizens need to understand and relate beyond the local, interactions between study abroad and international students have the potential to bring about positive changes in learning, attitudes, and perceptions about the "strangers among us." However, as Puplampu (2006) argues with respect to African universities, if "year abroad" programs are geared to meet the "financial shortfalls in African universities, then a critical opportunity for genuine intercultural understanding might have been lost on the altar of the market god" (p. 46). A similar argument applies to universities in the Global North who pursue international students through a market-driven logic to make up for shortfalls in funding, rather than an ethics-driven focus that builds notions of global citizenship. In view of global inequality and the general state of universities, the impact of globalization on higher education will give rise to differential outcomes. As such, the impact of study abroad programs and the recruitment of international students with respect to global citizenship education are going to be contingent on broader social forces in the global community.

References

Abdi, A. A., & Kapoor, D. (Eds.). (2009). *Global perspectives on adult education.* New York, NY: Palgrave Macmillan.

Abdi, A. A., Puplampu, K. P., & Dei, S. (Eds.). (2006). *African education and globalization: Critical perspectives.* Lanham, MD: Lexington Books.

Altbach, P., & Balan, J. (Eds.). (2007). *World class worldwide: Transforming research universities in Asia and Latin America.* Baltimore, MD: Johns Hopkins University Press.

Altmann, A., & Ebersberger, B. (Eds.). (2013). *Universities in change: Managing higher education institutions in the age of globalization.* New York, NY: Springer.

American Council on Education. (2003). *Mapping internationalization on US campuses.* Washington, DC: American Council on Education.

Aronowitz, S. (2000). *The knowledge factory: Dismantling the corporate university and creating true higher learning.* Boston, MA: Beacon Press.

Association of Universities and Colleges of Canada (AUCC). (2010). *Value of a degree in a global marketplace.* Ottawa, ON: Association of Universities and Colleges of Canada.

Banks, J. A. (1993). The canon debate, knowledge construction, and multicultural education. *Education Researcher, 22*(5), 4–14.

———. (1995). The historical reconstruction of knowledge about race: Implications for transformative teaching. *Education Researcher, 24*(2), 15–25.

Barnet, R. (2012). (Ed.). *The future university: Ideas and possibilities.* New York, NY: Routledge.

Bellamy, C., & Weinberg, A. (2006). Creating global citizens through study abroad. *Connection: The Journal of the New England Board of Higher Education, 21*(2), 20–21.

Bok, D. (1986). *Higher Learning.* Cambridge, MA: Harvard University.

———. (2003). *Universities in the marketplace: The commercialization of higher education.* Princeton, NJ: Princeton University Press.

Burbules, N. C., & Torres, C. A. (Eds.). (2000). *Globalization and education: Critical perspectives.* New York, NY: Routledge.

Cabrera, L. (2010). *The practice of global citizenship.* Cambridge, MA: Cambridge University Press.

Chieffo, L., & Griffiths, L. (2007). Here to stay: Increasing acceptance of short-term study abroad programs. In R. Lewin (Ed.). *The handbook of practice and research in study abroad: Higher Education and the quest for global citizenship* (pp. 365–380). New York, NY, and London, UK: Routledge for Association of American Colleges and Universities.

Codjoe, H. M. (2005). Africa(ns) in the Canadian educational system: An analysis of positionality and knowledge construction. In W. J. Tettey & K. P. Puplampu (Eds.), *The African diaspora in Canada: Negotiating identity and belonging* (pp. 63–91). Calgary, AB: University of Calgary Press.

Codjoe, H. M. (2006). The role of an affirmed black cultural identity and heritage in the academic achievement of African-Canadian students. *Intercultural Education, 17*(1), 33–54.

Connell, R. (2007) *Southern theory: The global dynamics of knowledge in social science.* Cambridge, UK: Polity Press.

Cope, B., & Kalantzis, M. (1997). White noise: The attack on political correctness and the struggle for the Western canon. *Interchange, 28*(4), 283–329.

Daza, S. L. (2006). Local responses to globalizing trends: Student-produced materials at a Colombian public university. *International Journal of Qualitative Studies in Education, 19*(5), 553–571.

Dolby, N. (2008). Global citizenship and study abroad: A comparative study of American and Australian undergraduates. *Frontiers: The Interdisciplinary Journal of Study Abroad, 17,* 51–67.

Falk, R. (1994). The making of citizenship. In B. Van Steenbergen (Ed.), *The condition of citizenship* (pp. 42–61). London, UK: Sage.

Falk, R., & Kanach, N. (2000). Globalization and study abroad: An illusion of paradox. *Frontiers: The Interdisciplinary Journal Study Abroad, 6,* 155–168.

Forstorp, P. (2008). Who's colonizing who? The knowledge society thesis and the global challenges in higher education. *Studies in Philosophy & Education, 27*(4), 227–236.

Freire, P. (1993). *Pedagogy of the oppressed* (20th Anniversary Edition). New York, NY: Continuum.

Gaventa, J., & Tandon, R. (2010). Citizen engagements in a globalizing world. In J. Gaventa & R. Tandon. (Eds.). *Globalizing citizens: New dynamics of inclusion and exclusion* (pp. 3–30). London, UK: Zed Books.

Green, M. (2012, February/March). What is global citizenship and why does it matter? *IAU Horizons, 17*(3) & *18*(1), 27–28.

Gülalp, H. (2006). Introduction: Citizenship vs nationality? In H. Gülalp (Ed.). *Citizenship and ethnic conflict: Challenging the nation-state* (pp. 1–18). New York, NY: Routledge.

Harman, G. (2005). Internationalization of Australian higher education: A critical review of literature and research. In P. Ninnes & M. Hellstén (Eds.), *Internationalizing higher education: Critical explorations of pedagogy and policy* (pp. 119–140). Hong Kong: Springer.

Hayhoe, R. (Ed.). (1993). *Knowledge across cultures: Universities east and west.* Wuhan, China and Toronto, ON: Hubei Education and Ontario Institute for Studies in Education Presses.

Heater, D. (2004). *A brief history of citizenship.* New York, NY: New York University Press.

Held, D., & McGrew, A. (Eds.). (2004). *The global transformations reader: An introduction to the globalization debate.* Cambridge, MA: Polity Press.

Jefferess, D. (2008). Global citizenship and the cultural politics of benevolence. *Critical Literacy: Theories and Practices, 2*(1), 27–36.

Joseph, C. (2008). Difference, subjectivities and power: (De)colonizing practices in internationalizing the curriculum. *Intercultural Education, 19*(1), 29–39.

Killick, D. (2012). Seeing-ourselves-in-the-world: Developing global citizenship through international mobility and campus community. *Journal of Studies in International Education, 16*(4), 372–389.

Kivisto, P., & Faist, T. (2007). *Citizenship: Discourse, theory and transnational prospects.* Oxford, UK. Blackwell Publishing.

Knight, J. (2012). Student mobility and internationalization: Trends and tribulations. *Research in Comparative and International Education, 7*(1), 20–33.

Khoo, S. (2011). Ethical globalisation or privileged internationalisation? Exploring global citizenship and internationalisation in Irish and Canadian universities. *Globalisation, Societies and Education, 9*(3–4), 337–353.

Lantis, J. S., & DuPlaga, J. (2010). *The global classroom: An essential guide to study abroad.* Boulder, CO: Paradigm Publishers.

Lavia, J., & Moore, M. (Eds.) (2010). *Cross-cultural perspectives on policy and practice: decolonizing community contexts.* New York, NY: Routledge.

Lewin, R. (Ed.). (2009). *The handbook of practice and research in study abroad: Higher Education and the quest for global citizenship.* New York, NY, and London, UK: Routledge for Association of American Colleges and Universities.

Mannheim, K. (1952). *Essays on the sociology of knowledge.* London, UK: Routledge and Kegan Paul.

Marshall, T. H. (1950). *Citizenship and social class, and other essays.* Cambridge, MA: Cambridge University Press.

Maringe, F., & Fosket, N. (Eds.). (2010). *Globalization and internationalization in higher education: Theoretical, strategic and management perspectives.* London, UK: Continuum International.

Matthews, J., & Sidhu, R. (2005). Desperately seeking the global subject: International education, citizenship and cosmopolitanism. *Globalisation, Societies and Education, 3*(1), 49–66.

McCowan, T. (2012). Opening spaces for citizenship in higher education: Three initiatives in English universities. *Studies in Higher Education, 37*(1), 51–67.

Metzler, J. (2000). Strengthening reciprocity in study-abroad programs. *African Issues, 28* (1&2), 13–19.

Miller, M. J. (1991). Dual citizenship: A European norm. *International Migration Review, 33*(4), 945–950.

Mitchell, K. (2001). Education for democratic citizenship: Transnationalism, multiculturalism, and the limits of liberalism. *Harvard Educational Review, 71*(1), 51–79.

Neave, G., & van Vught, F. (Eds.). (1994). *Government and higher education relationships across three continents: The winds of change.* Oxford, UK: Pergamon Press.

Ninnes, P., & Hellstén, M. (2005). Introduction: Critical engagements with the internationalization of higher education. In P. Ninnes & M. Hellstén (Eds.), *Internationalizing higher education: Critical explorations of pedagogy and policy* (pp. 1–8). Hong Kong: Springer.

Puplampu, K. P. (2004). The restructuring of higher education and part-time instructors: A theoretical and political analysis of undergraduate teaching in Canada. *Teaching in Higher Education, 9*(2), 171–182.

———. (2006). Critical perspectives on higher education and globalization in Africa. In A. Abdi, K. P. Puplampu & S. Dei (Eds.), *African education and globalization: Critical perspectives* (pp. 34–52). Lanham, MD: Lexington Books.

———. (2008). Knowledge, power and social policy: John M. MacEachran and Alberta's 1928 Sexual Sterilization Act. *Alberta Journal of Educational Research, 54*(2), 129–146.

Rhee, J. (2006). Re/membering (to) shifting alignments: Korean women's transnational narratives in US higher education. *International Journal of Qualitative Studies in Education, 19*(5), 595–615.

Rhee, J., & Subreenduth, S. (2006). De/colonizing education: Examining transnational localities. *International Journal of Qualitative Studies in Education, 19*(5), 545–548.

Rhoads, R. A., & Szelényi, K. (2011). *Global citizenship and the university: Advancing social life and relations in an interdependent world.* Stanford, CA: Stanford University Press.

Rhoads, R. A., & Torres, C. A. (2006). (Eds.). *The university, state and market: The political economy of globalization in the Americas.* Stanford, CA: Stanford University Press.

Roman, L. G. (2003). Education and the contested meanings of 'Global citizenship.' *Journal of Educational Change, 4*(3), 269–293.

Ritzer, G. (2000). *Sociological theory* (5th ed.). New York, NY: McGraw Hill.

Said, E. (1978). *Orientalism*. New York, NY: Vintage Books.

Sardar, Z., & Davies, M. W. (2002). *Why do people hate America?* New York, NY: Disinformation Company.

Schattle, H. (2008). *The practices of global citizenship*. Lanham, MD: Rowman and Littlefield.

Scholte, J. (2005). *Globalization: A critical introduction* (2nd ed.). New York, NY: Palgrave.

Singh, M. (2005). Enabling transnational learning communities: Policies, pedagogies and politics of educational power. In P. Ninnes & M. Hellstén (Eds.), *Internationalizing higher education: Critical explorations of pedagogy and policy* (pp. 9–36). Hong Kong: Springer.

Sison, M. D., & Brennan, L. (2012). Students as global citizens: Strategies for mobilizing studies abroad. *Journal of Marketing for Higher Education, 22*(2), 167–181.

Slaughter, S., & Rhoades, G. (2004). *Academic capitalism and the new economy: Markets, state and higher education*. Baltimore, MD: Johns Hopkins University Press.

Smith, L. T. (2006). Colonizing knowledges. In H. Lauder, P. Brown, J. Dillabough, & A. H. Halsey (Eds.), *Education, globalization, and social change* (pp. 557–569). Oxford, UK: Oxford University Press.

Stearns, P. N. (2009). *Educating global citizens in colleges and universities: Challenges and opportunities*. New York, NY: Routledge.

Suárez-Orozco, M. M., & Sattin, C. (2007). Wanted: Global citizens. *Educational Leadership, 64*(7), 58–62.

Steger, M. B. (2009). *Globalization: A very short introduction*. Oxford, UK: Oxford University Press.

Stromquist, N. P. (2009). Theorizing global citizenship: Discourses, challenges, and implications for education. *Interamerican Journal of Education for Democracy, 2*(1), 6–29.

Subedi, B. (2006). Theorizing a 'halfie' researcher's identity in transnational fieldwork. *International Journal of Qualitative Studies in Education, 19*(5), 573–593.

Subreenduth, S. (2006). 'Why, why are we not allowed even . . . ?': A de/colonizing narrative of complicity and resistance in post/apartheid South Africa. *International Journal of Qualitative Studies in Education, 19*(5), 617–638.

Szelényi, K., & Rhoads, R. A. (2007). Citizenship in a global context: The perspectives of international graduate students in the United States. *Comparative Education Review, 51*(1), 25–47.

Thorp, H., & Goldstein, B. (2010). *Engines of innovation: The entrepreneurial university in the twenty-first century*. Chapel Hill, NC: University of North Carolina Press.

Torres, C. A. (2009). *Education and neoliberal globalization*. New York, NY: Routledge.

UNESCO UIS (2013). Global Flow of Tertiary-Level Students. Retrieved from http://www.uis.unesco.org/Education/Pages/international-student-flow-viz. aspx.

Wanner, D. (2007). Study abroad and language: From maximal to realistic models. In R. Lewin (Ed.), *The handbook of practice and research in study abroad: Higher Education and the quest for global citizenship* (pp. 81–98). New York, NY, and London, UK: Routledge for Association of American Colleges and Universities.

Watson, D., Stroud, S. E., Hollister, R., & Babcock, E. (2011). (Eds.). *The engaged university: International perspectives on civic engagement*. New York, NY: Routledge.

Woodfield, S. (2010). Key trends and emerging issues in international student mobility (ISM). In F. Maringe & N. Fosket (Eds.), *Globalization and internationalization in higher education: Theoretical, strategic and management perspectives* (pp. 109–123). London, UK: Continuum International.

Wynveen, C. J., Kyle, G. T., & Tarrant, M. A. (2012). Study abroad experiences and global citizenship: Fostering proenviromental behavior. *Journal of Studies in International Education, 16*(4), 334–352.

Zahabioun, S., Yousefy, A., Yarmohammadian, M. H., & Keshtiaray, N. (2013). Global citizenship education and its implications for curriculum goals at the age of globalization. *International Education Studies, 6*(1), 195–206.

19

Teaching, Learning, and Working in the Periphery

Provocations for Researchers and Practitioners

Sue Shore
Robert C. Mizzi
Tonette S. Rocco

Jane Thompson writes (2000a), "Education—*on its own*—cannot change societies in which there are economic and class systems which encourage vast discrepancies of wealth and access to resources, including access to information" (p. 4; italics added). This means that the analysis of education and its inequalities must occur in the context of broader discrepancies in order to achieve social change (Thompson, p. 4). Unfortunately, a substantial amount of literature on adult, community, and workplace learning and teaching reinscribes the invisibility of social class and economic systems. Yet, there is a substantial strand of scholarly adult education literature that links concerns for social inclusion, justice, equity, and opportunities for learners. Herein lies the conundrum of adult and community education; while it is a platform known for social emancipation, its current deployment continues to reflect many exclusionary practices evidenced in schooling and higher education sectors. In Raymond Williams's words (1977, p. 132), these gestures to progressive social change are an exemplar of the "affective elements of consciousness and relationship"—the "structures of feeling"—that repeatedly surface in policy texts, institutional visions and mission statements, and edited collections such as this book. These structures of feeling are integral to understanding something named variously as a social movement, a professional discipline, a social institution, or simply "a practice." Perhaps, in light of Thompson's caution, analyses of social justice work and those realms where social injustice occurs could use this idea of structures of feeling to explore such dichotomies and why they continue to exist.

Frank Youngman (2000) linked the contemporary genesis of historical discourses that "approve" of certain groups and their contemporary genesis to development narratives driven by First World articulations of "the problem" and associated solutions to be implemented residing in Second- and Third-World sites. Notably, solutions which maintained a distance from assigning any responsibility for emergency of the problem to the First World. Youngman questions the development narrative driving adult education. In recent times the development narrative's hold over adult education's purpose has been mirrored in educational sites around the globe—schooling, vocational training colleges, workplace learning units, community centers, non-governmental organizations (NGO) amongst others—and the extent education has been held hostage by the three major producers of governing or "boss texts" (Smith & Turner, 2014)—UNESCO, the World Bank, and the OECD. The influence of these texts has varied over decades. A major UNESCO document—The Delors Report (1996)—posits a framework for a "utopian" vision of a politically aware community activating the premise of "living together" (ibid. 22), a premise which The Delors Report views as one of the foundational pillars for peaceful citizenship in contemporary times. The hinge between knowledge and power in this and similar documents is framed as a seemingly instrumental relationship of "trust," a relationship which ignores the complexity of struggles between individuals, communities, and nations, over knowledge about the self and how it is that we come to know our selves and others differently. Delors and other UNESCO texts posit a particular role for adult education in addressing many of the social *and* economic challenges facing people around the world. As exemplified in the chapters in this collection, such trust must be repeatedly renegotiated.

Fast forward into the twenty-first century and Grace (2013) claims the "OECD, in tandem with multinational corporate interests, national governments, and an array of educational interests, has ardently linked lifelong learning to the demands of neoliberalism, globalization, individualism, privatization, corporatism, competition, and progress as it is defined within a burgeoning knowledge economy" (n.p.). Over decades *adult learning* has been increasingly positioned as integral to the economy, for the good of the nation, and the benefit of "the people," and individuals. The alignment with policies and funding mechanisms that shape Western country economies has not gone unnoticed and their effects have been felt.

The goal of policy documents produced by these transnational agencies, explicit or otherwise, has included merging the unruly boundaries of "adult education" into a seamless system of productive training for working life. Thrift (2006, p. 191) helps us understand how national training systems for example have been constituted through "more and more things . . . being tagged and integrated into metasystems which are part and parcel of those things' existence. Then, these metasystems themselves become new ways of categorizing this augmented existence." The tagging and integration of all things associated with work and learning into a metasystem geared to productivity in service of corporations simultaneously shrinks the space for *collective* activity—community and neighborhood housing programs, home-less shelter programs, prisoner education, adult literacy programs, and other learning activities. Activity in these spaces cannot necessarily be tracked and counted according to metasystem requirements (see, for example, Collins, Pettaway, Whitehead, & Rios, this volume) yet this learning also fosters the capacity of adults to better their lives. In practice the manifestation of vocational education and training (VET) in Australia is a good example of this metasystem demonstrated by

> its goals, its benchmarks and points of attachment/detachment vis-a-vis entering the workforce for the first time, re-entering the workforce, retraining for a new job, upgrading skills for an exist-ing job, and learning throughout life (DEEWR, 2012). When spoken, the word VET does particular epistemological work. It collects up multiple worlds and homogenises this heterogeneous messy complexity, to render it knowable, knowing and known as 'itself.' (Shore & Butler, 2012, p. 209)

"Adult education" in this guise is big business—a complex and diverse one—with associated sectors (university, vocational education and training, international education, higher education) combining with fields of prac-tice as diverse as community education, union worker training, corporate human resource development, and international NGO work in the service of bettering lives. Little wonder then that while our concerns in this book range across continents and draw on studies from countries which have starkly different views on gun control, child soldiers, hate speech, legislated homophobia, and sanctioned violence toward women by people known to them, it is possible to say there are still certain recognizable "structures of feeling" circulating in institutions providing adult education across all of these locations.

One tangible feature of metasystems is the extent to which the historical trajectories and complexities of those spaces are repeatedly and neatly aligned with "economic growth." Albornoz and Rocco (this volume) leave no doubt that capacity for economic interdependence is critical in nations and communities caught up in the dynamics of turbo-capitalism. However, Thompson (2000a), along with others in this volume (Campbell & Christie; Deer & Chlup; Webber & Brown), demonstrates that in working toward a secure financial future there are many constitutive structures of feeling—family heritage, working-class traditions, and racialized and gendered histories—that play a part in bettering lives.

Another tangible feature involves the textually mediated regulatory environments in which providers now operate. In these environments new boss texts shape funding and resource practices with very real consequences for those who contest the power of the center to define the participation of those who inhabit the "learner fringe" (Brigham; Grace; Guo; Nichols, this volume) and their capacity to gain access to social, cultural and economic resources for their decision making. The coordinating capacity of these boss texts (Smith & Turner, 2014) is facilitated by global resource allocations regulated by World Bank and International Monetary Fund decisions and associated benchmarks of employability and adult skills competence constituted through OECD surveys of population competence. At the national level the coordination of productive citizenry is captured by national quality assurance frameworks and assessment grids that supplant the complex articulations of "knowledges, capabilities, capacities and values—the very 'things' around which the global trade in knowledges operates" (Shore & Butler, 2012, p. 209). In regional locations such coordination occurs via "strategic" grant priorities and project management practices that reframe regional economic priorities through metrocentric notions of community and industry. At the level of individual engagement the coordination of productive citizenry is manifest in curriculum outcomes that design agentic productive citizenship through their activities and assessment practices. When most effective, these coordinating practices constitute the conditions for a nationally engaged citizen whose likeness is filtered through a homogeneous metropolitan imaginary, despite cultural and regional variety in dispositions, orientations, and geographic features. These coordinating practices are now recognizable as a metasystem for managing learning and learners around the globe.

Vigilance as Starting Point

The circulation of ostensibly benign and well-intentioned metanarratives within adult education, such as those presented for contestation within this collection, resonates with Spivak's exhortation that we think carefully about our starting points and what our moves to reposition those with whom we work, with or without their agreement, might "say about the margin being constituted to suit the institutional convenience of the colonizer/[us]?" (1993, p. 58). Taking responsibility for a starting point therefore requires one to be particularly vigilant about one's role in how living, learning, and working spaces are portrayed, for example, as peripheral spaces of "drudgery," inhabited by people who are not deserving of conditions that might enable them to enjoy life and grow their personal and community satisfaction. How does such positioning happen? What does taking responsibility for disrupting these practices look like? What kind of practical scholarly vigilance is required to do this work?

Examples abound of scholars who have traced the influence of contemporary discourses of the market on lifelong learning. Patricia Gouthro (2002) argues we need to be vigilant about the extent to which discourses of cooperation and team action are taken up as the contemporary "logic of the market place," yet simultaneously, suppress histories of collective action anchored in the tensions of profit and analysis of workers conditions. Similarly, Nichols (this volume) demonstrates how drawing on the principles of institutional ethnography can transform a conventional ethnography of homelessness into a methodological tracing of the linear logic in developmental assumptions that underpin community development and homelessness programs to support youth. In the field of human resource development, Mizzi and Rocco (2013) have argued for vigilance in tracking how non-Western identities are pushed into Western understandings of identity in "HR land" (see also Brunetta & Reio, this volume). In these diverse research engagements, identities are not static categories but locations inhabited, institutionally created, and navigated *and* contested (see Kell & Kell, this volume). While some research aligned with adult education goals might promote theorizing that is certain, confident in its assumptions, and assertive in its categorizing, other scholars argue it is important to reflect the blurry, complex, and complicated processes of becoming evident in many communities and learning locations.

We also note the effect of the opening up of higher education to minorities, women, young people living in families with histories of financial insecurity, and the global flows of students arising from increasing mobility of people around the world. Each of these groups of people has prompted a range of initiatives in universities to address an imbalance in university knowledge practices and the perceived and real gaps associated with their preparation for higher education study. International university exchanges and skilled worker programs promote the benefits of such "international-ization" while simultaneously navigating the negative assumptions about non-English speaking, not white, students and workers who are portrayed as lacking in Western theoretical expertise and industrial work practices, and simultaneously penalized for their ostensibly weak claims for indigenous theorizing and local knowledge practices that challenge hegemonic Northern theorizing (Connell, 2007; see also Landorf & Feldman, this volume, for an example of disruption). Disrupting well-entrenched Western assumptions about learning, working, and living requires a reflexive ethic of theory build-ing that renders visible and calls to account our roles as authors (Shore & Butler, 2012). This is not a negation of theorizing. Rather it is recognition that reflexivity involves constant self-engagement as an "author-in-the-mak-ing" (after Wilson 2009, in Shore & Butler, 2012, p. 2009). This is not a practice of superficial, self-indulgent, affirmation of social positioning—I am a white, financially secure, able-bodied, heterosexual, fe/male. Rather it is a starting point for unpacking what one thinks one knows about oneself as an author. Educators and researchers must therefore also practice vigi-lance within a broader set of paradoxical pressures that demand we activate empowering, entrepreneurial, globally mobile knowledge networks as we also reshape some not so global knowledge frames about adult education.

One goal of developing this book has been to position the theory-building practices of adult education within a "trialectics of space-power-knowledge" (Soja, 1996, p. 122) that recognizes the power of binaries in shaping social action: theory and practice; raced and unraced/white peoples; North and South, East and West; schooling and everything else; child and adult; citizens and immigrants. In calling up these preexisting conceptual frames we call forth particular ontologies—a practice Dorothy Smith (2005, p. 56) pointedly describes as "blob-ontology"—to do our thinking work for us:

> [F]or every such concept, there is taken to be a something out there corresponding to it. The disappearance of people and activities is striking once we attend to it. Agency is assigned to conceptually constructed entities that lack determinate references. (Smith, p. 56)

A number of chapters in this collection argue that the theory-building practices available in adult education have much to answer for in reinforcing many of these counterproductive categories of knowing noted above and rushing too quickly to decide which issues are relevant and which are "peripheral" to conversations about lifelong learning (see Boughton; Choudry; Grace; Mizzi, Hill & Vance; Puplampu & Wodinski, this volume). These are indeed provocative challenges for researchers and practitioners who have always imagined being on the "right side" of struggles against neoliberal conservative values that so readily define a mainstream as competent, productive, useful and proactive; and a periphery as idle, dependent, ignorant, and a drain on the public purse.

Troubling Periphery: Three Provocations

Through the main title of this collection—*Disrupting Adult and Community Education*—we have focused on a number of sites and practices that "trouble" teaching, learning, and working in the periphery and draw together issues that have surfaced in working with each other and the authors in this collection. These take the form of provocations to those of us who write of adult education in contemporary times and the responsibilities involved in that writing.

Our *first provocation* is associated with the notion of "invisibility" and poses a challenge to the classificatory practices that define a center and therefore also a periphery. In this collection, authors argue that the classificatory practices of homophobia, whiteness, ableism, ageism, and financial exclusion accompany a range of more traditional understandings of unequal distribution of educational outcomes by class and gender; and that the inequalities produced are both anticipated and unexpectedly nuanced. Within this literature there is a recurring view that "invisibility" accounts for much of the difficulty practitioners and researchers have in naming, tracking, and disrupting educational practices and our complicity in reproducing inequality. In contrast, Brigham; Grace; Karim; Mizzi, Hill and Vance, and Shore (this volume) challenge the default orientations of invisibility and trace a range of dispositions, discourses, and practices that are presumed as central to the reproduction of effective, efficient, proper, citizenship. These authors argue that a discourse of "invisibility" has become acceptable as a replacement discourse for ignorance when engaging with racism or ableism, or reinscribing heteronormativity. Unsettling dominant markers is counter-hegemonic work which holds the potential to activate anger, resentment, and discomfort, and hence is not always "safe" work to undertake as a practice on one self or with others. Here, we argue for the need to understand when clandestine learning is necessary in caring for oneself as a strategic health and safety requirement—to use the audit discourse of contemporary institutions—and when clandestine learning simply consolidates neoconservative attempts to suppress the necessary exploration of tactics that unsettle dominant storylines of exclusion. Activism is an inherent part of clandestine learning as is scholarly writing to create the conditions to imagine that work; both involve language practices for leaders and policy makers which can be used to reshape systems with a goal that such work might no longer need to be clandestine.

Similarly, invisibility is relevant to the epistemologies of ignorance and forgetting that circulate in adult education and training discourses. Boughton (this volume) reminds us of the forgetting of large-scale global movements. Thompson (2000b) reminds similarly of the elision of women in some larger scale movements of radical adult education. Shore (this volume) calls attention to repeated incantations of the "invisibility" of whiteness, which is not so invisible to those who acquire the tools and dispositions to look for whiteness at work in our education and training systems (Shore, 2010).

Our first provocation therefore challenges researchers, practitioners, and policymakers to ask how governing texts, the "boss texts" of our field—and their associated curriculum development and quality assurance processes—re-anchor contemporary adult education in those problematic development roots charted by Youngman (2000) some time ago. What conceptual and activist tools are required to navigate these powerful and not so invisible steering practices and yet remain constantly vigilant to their effects?

Our *second provocation* posits that adult education—a professional field within post-secondary education and a practical field within community development—is inescapably caught up in Western notions of children, their location within Western concepts of the family and schooling as primary vehicles for socialization and self-determination, and transformation of children into "productive adults" and "active citizens." This almost perpetual reference point back to schooling and what adult education is not, draws experienced researchers, policymakers, and those new to the field into repeated engagement with a twentieth-century adult/child Western binary held hostage by Malcolm Knowles's self-determining agentic adult. This collection illustrates the tensions practitioners and researchers experience as they navigate the explicit and implicit manifestations of this adult/child within "adult education" theory building. Chapters have demonstrated that adults and children do not experience the distinct community, family, life, and work experiences invoked by this simple binary: underage sex workers in Asia, child laborers in India, the "forgetting" associated with girls with disabilities who grow to be women workers with disabilities in Bangladesh, university educators navigating whiteness through racialized childhood memories that are far from invisible, sexual and gender minority identities not *discovered* as adult identities but *formed* through childhood and through heteronormative experiences actively negotiated with adult families. Childhood and adulthood are interconnected, and yet, this notion is largely forgotten in dominant, Western framings of institutional adult education.

These two provocations prompt us to offer a *third provocation*: the importance of a particular kind of reflexivity—an inner pause—not intended to paralyze, but rather a pause that activates a new relationship to theory building for social transformation in increasingly conservative times. *Stop . . . pause . . . what is this thing called "adult education"?* Adult education, as with so many professions, has been caught in a pincer movement between the demand for and refinement of textually mediated tools to document, retag, and steer provision towards a metasystem of profit and productivity (cf Thrift, 2006) and a disruption of the ignorance sustained by purportedly rock solid academic concepts as diverse as empowerment, national productivity, collective voice, and quality.

This edited volume conjures up an understanding of collective to be fought for and at the same time learned, a collective-in-the-making (after Wilson in Shore & Butler, 2012), that surfaces "those erasures and moments of amnesia" (p. 210) that are evident in accounts of adult education if we can quarantine some time to look for them. This is somewhat confrontational for educators and researchers who have accrued substantial capital from working and learning in education institutions and *not* positioned precariously at the social, cultural, and financial margins. Some of the chapters in this collection propose that adult education theory building per se has much to answer for in being complicit with the consolidating practices that create a robust and healthy center and its "opposite," a periphery in need of transformation (Campbell & Christie; Grace; Mizzi, Hill & Vance; and Shore, this volume). As noted, adult education as a social institution is caught in a web of development explanations of sociality (cf Youngman 2000) more akin to system-tuning than collective action for social change (Collins, 1991). Inevitably these theoretical explanations charge those who inhabit the socially constructed space of the margins with the burden of redeeming their supposed failure. They are drawn into a set of social relations which is not of their making and not able to facilitate the understandability of that space as the available language cannot begin to portray the polyphony of economic, social, cultural, historical, and political influences that constitute the spaces they inhabit. Moreover, transformation for those from the margins—personal, physical, and collective—often times assumes leaving a family home, community *and* elements of one's "self" behind, as these are the relational practices that the center deems dangerous, debilitating, dysfunctional, and counterproductive to the national imaginary of the productive citizen.

In this collection we have attempted to disrupt certain assumptions when engaging with sites of practice captured by normative ontologies of "the periphery." In this respect we call for an approach which includes exploration and interrogation of questions not yet asked about adult and community education and lifelong learning as these concepts sweep around the globe picking up lives and transforming them in ways that are neither imagined, planned, nor necessarily desired by many practitioners, learners, researchers, and workers. This must invoke multivocality (Mizzi, 2010) to bring into view the arrogance underpinning some approaches to transforming the periphery. There is much work ahead.

References

Collins, M. (1991). *Adult education as vocation: A critical role for the adult educator.* London, UK: Routledge.

Connell, R. (2007). *Southern theory: The global dynamics of knowledge in social science.* Cambridge, UK: Polity.

Delors, J. (1996). *Learning: The treasure within: Report to UNESCO of the International Commission on Education for the Twenty-First Century.* Paris, France: UNESCO.

Gouthro, P. A. (2002). Education for sale: at what cost? Lifelong learning and the marketplace, *International Journal of Lifelong Education, 21*(4), 334–346. http://dx.doi.org/10.1080/02601370210140995.

Grace, A. (2013). On writing, with André P. Grace. *Open Book Toronto.* Retrieved from: http://www.openbooktoronto.com/news/writing_with_andr%C3%A9_p_grace.

Mizzi, R. (2010). Unravelling researcher subjectivity through multivocality in autoethnography [Special Issue]. *Journal of Research Practice, 6*(1), Article M3. Retrieved from http://jrp.icaap.org/index.php/jrp/article/view/201/185.

Mizzi, R., & Rocco, T. (2013). Deconstructing dominance: Towards a reconceptualization of the relationship between collective and individual identities, globalization and learning at work. *Human Resource Development Review, 12*(3), 364–382.

Shore, S. (2010). Whiteness at work in vocational training in Australia. *New Directions for Adult and Continuing Education, 125*(Spring), 41–51.

Shore, S., & Butler, E (2012) Missing things and methodological swerves: Unsettling the it-ness of VET. *International Journal of Training Research, 10*(3): 204–218.

Soja, E. W. (1996). *Thirdspace: Journeys to Los Angeles and other real and imagined places.* Cambridge, MA: Blackwell.

Smith, D. E. (2005). *Institutional ethnography: A sociology for people.* Lantham, CA: Altamira Press.

Smith, D. E., & Turner, S. M. (2014). *Incorporating texts into institutional ethnographies.* Toronto, ON: University of Toronto Press.

Spivak, G. C. (1993). *Outside in the teaching machine.* New York, NY, and London, UK: Routledge.

Thrift, N. (2006). Donna Haraway's dreams. *Theory, Culture & Society, 23*(7–8), 189–195.

Thompson, J. (2000a). *Emancipatory learning.* NIACE Briefing Sheet, Leicester: NIACE Library and Information Service. http://www.aughty.org/pdf/emancipatory_learning.pdf.

Thompson, J. (2000b). *Women, class and education.* London, UK: Routledge.

Williams, R. (1977). *Marxism and literature.* New York, NY: Oxford University Press.

Youngman, F. (2000). *The political economy of adult education and development.* London and New York, NY: Zed Books.

Contributors

Robert C. Mizzi is an Assistant Professor at the University of Manitoba, Winnipeg, Canada. He currently has approximately 50 chapters, articles, and reviews in books, journals, conference proceedings and reports. His work has appeared in several journals, namely *Human Resources Development International*, the *New Horizons in Adult Education and Human Resource Development*, and the *Journal of Homosexuality*. He has co-edited books on teacher education in post-conflict Kosovo and has written several book chapters in the field of international education and queer studies in education. His most recent edited book project was *Breaking Free: Sexual Diversity and Change in Emerging Nations*. Besides his SSHRC postdoctoral fellowship, he has also won numerous awards, including the Ontario Graduate Scholarship and the Stong Estate Education Award. In 2011, Robert was an invited Visiting Professor for the University of Pristina in Mitrovica (Kosovo). Robert is Perspectives Editor (Adult Education) for the journal *New Horizons in Adult Education and Human Resource Development*. His research on the work, welfare, and well-being of educators is situated in the fields of educational administration and adult education, and often within diverse contexts.

Tonette S. Rocco is a professor in adult education and human resource development at Florida International University in Miami, Florida, USA. She has published work on continuing professional education, equity and privilege (specifically in terms of race/critical race theory, sexual minorities/ LGBT, disability, and age), employability/career development, and fostering student research and professional writing in *International Journal of Disability Studies, Human Resource Development Quarterly, Adult Learning, Teacher Education Quarterly* and other journals. She has over 200 publications in journals, books, and proceedings. She is a Houle Scholar and winner of the Elwood F. Holton, III Research Excellence Award 2008 for the article

Towards the Employability-Link Model: Current Employment Transition to Future Employment Perspectives published in *Human Resource Development Review* with Jo Thijssen and Beatrice Van der Heijden. The book *Challenging the Parameters of Adult Education: John Ohliger and the Quest for Social Democracy* (with Andre Grace, Jossey-Bass, 2009) won the 2009 University Continuing Education Association Frandson Book Award. Her other books include the *Handbook of Scholarly Writing and Publishing* (with Tim Hatcher, Jossey-Bass, 2011), and two books each won the 2014 AHRD Forward Publishing Award, the *Routledge Companion to HRD* (Rob Poell & Gene Roth, Routledge) and the *Handbook of Human Resource Development: The Discipline and the Field* (with Neal Chalofsky and Lane Morris, Wiley). She is lead editor of *New Horizons in Adult Education and Human Resource Development*, published by Wiley and serves on a dozen editorial boards.

Sue Shore is Professor of Education at Charles Darwin University and Director of the International Graduate Centre of Education. Since 1979 Sue has worked, taught, and researched issues associated with vocational, post-compulsory, and higher education. Her research program addresses the ways in which education reform agendas shape educational knowledge practices and the dimensions of racialized theory building embedded in those reforms. In recent times Sue has deployed these ideas in rethinking national regulation of teacher education as a metrocentric project and the extent to which recognition of prior learning practices in the academy can be freed from the conventions of disciplinary knowledge practices so central to professional identities.

Information about the Authors

Carlos A. Albornoz, Universidad del Desarrollo, Chile

Dr. Carlos A. Albornoz received a bachelor's degree in psychology and a professional degree in organizational psychology from the Pontificia Universidad Católica de Valparaiso, Chile. He holds a Diploma in Management from the Industrial Engineering Department of the University of Chile, a Master in Business from Florida International University (FIU), and a Doctor of Education from FIU as well. His doctoral dissertation about entrepreneurship teaching received the Pino Center Kauffman Award for his contribution to the field of entrepreneurship education. Currently he is assistant professor at the School of Business of Universidad del Desarrollo, Chile. His research interests are related to entrepreneurship teaching, entrepreneurial self efficacy, and entrepreneurial skills assessment.

Bob Boughton, University of New England, Australia
Dr. Bob Boughton teaches adult education at the University of New England, a small rural university in New South Wales, Australia. His main research interest is in social movement learning, in particular the theory and history of radical popular education. He has a long association in Australia with the peace movement and the Aboriginal Rights movement, and has recently worked with Cuban and Timorese adult educators on the national adult literacy campaign in post-independence Timor-Leste. He is a passionate advocate for the educative role of international solidarity.

Susan M. Brigham, Mount Saint Vincent University, Canada
Susan (Susie) M. Brigham is Associate Professor of Lifelong Learning at Mount Saint Vincent University. Her areas of research interests are international/intercultural adult education, transformative learning, critical race theory, and migration. She has published numerous peer reviewed journal articles and books chapters and is the co-editor of two recent books on adult education. She is Director of the Alexa McDonough Institute for Women, Gender and Social Justice and Associate Editor of the Canadian Journal for the Study of Adult Education.

Michael Brown, York University, Canada
Dr. Michael Brown is Professor Emeritus and Senior Scholar at York University, where he has taught since 1968. He holds degrees from Harvard, Columbia, the Jewish Theological Seminary, and the State University of New York at Buffalo, and has taught for short periods at the Hebrew University of Jerusalem, the University of California at San Diego, and the University of Toronto. He teaches and publishes in the area of Jewish Studies, mostly on topics related to contemporary Jewry, North American Jews, and the Holocaust. A former director of York's Centre for Jewish Studies, Brown was co-founder with Prof. Mark Webber and co-director with Webber and then Prof. Sara Horowitz of the Mark and Gail Appel Holocaust Field Study for Canadian, Polish, and German Students, "Learning from the Past, Teaching for the Future." Webber and Brown were given a medal of commendation by the senate of Adam Mickiewicz University in Poznan for their work in that program.

Fabiana Brunetta, Florida International University, USA
Fabiana Brunetta is a doctoral candidate in the Adult Education and Human Resources program at Florida International University in Miami, Florida. She is currently a Graduate Assistant working as an education and social science research consultant and data analyst. She has published textbooks

for the social sciences and is a contracted author with The History Press. Her research interests include conflict in the workplace, cross-cultural communication in the workplace, and Cuba/U.S. work relations.

Matthew Campbell, Tangentyere Council, Australia

Matthew Campbell is the coordinator of a Research Hub located within Tangentyere Council, the Aboriginal Council for Alice Springs Town Camps. Formerly a researcher at Charles Darwin University, his principal research interest is intercultural community engagement, with a focus on collective action, generative methodologies, and research accountability. In his work at Tangentyere, he, along with his Aboriginal colleagues, undertakes research projects which focus on making a tangible difference in the lives of Alice Springs Town Camp residents while strengthening Aboriginal knowledge production, governance, and leadership.

Dominique T. Chlup, Texas A&M University & Inspiring the Creative Within™, LLC, USA

Dr. Dominique T. Chlup is the President and Founder of Inspiring the Creative Within™, LLC. An Associate Professor of Adult Education at Texas A&M University turned professional Creativity and Writing Coach, she now spends her time offering workshops and coaching her clients in how to recover their creative academic souls and helping them to develop stress-free habits of writing. Her research interests focus on the creative/artistic abilities of adult learners. Additionally, she has a special interest in gender and education and how the areas of social justice and diversity relate to Adult Education and HRD.

Aziz Choudry, McGill University, Canada

Aziz Choudry is associate professor in the Department of Integrated Studies in Education at McGill University and visiting professor at the Centre for Education Rights and Transformation at the University of Johannesburg. He is author of *Learning Activism: The Intellectual Life of Contemporary Social Movements* (University of Toronto Press, 2015), co-author of *Fight Back: Workplace Justice for Immigrants* (Fernwood, 2009), and co-editor of *Learning from the Ground Up: Global Perspectives on Social Movements and Knowledge Production* (Palgrave Macmillan, 2010), *Organize! Building from the local for Global Justice*, (PM Press/Between the Lines, 2012), and *NGOization: Complicity, Contradictions and Prospects* (Zed Books, 2013), and *Just Work? Migrant Workers' Struggles Today* (Pluto, 2015). With a long history as a social and political activist, educator, and researcher, he serves on the boards of the Immigrant Workers Centre, Montreal, and the Global Justice Ecology Project.

Michael Christie, Charles Darwin University, Australia

Dr. Michael Christie worked as a teacher linguist in Yolŋu communities in Arnhem Land for over 20 years before moving to Darwin to set up the Yolŋu Studies program at Charles Darwin University in 1994. He is currently Professor in the Northern Insistute, working on collaborative research and consultancies in a number of areas including health communication and literacy, water management, Yolŋu epistemology and schooling, Indigenous and transdisciplinary methodologies, and knowledge work in a postcolonial institution.

Joshua C. Collins, University of Minnesota–Twin Cities, USA

Dr. Joshua C. Collins is an Assistant Professor of Human Resource Development at the University of Minnesota–Twin Cities in Minneapolis, MN. His research focuses on aspects of critical human resource development and adult education, with an emphasis on advocating for social change through careful examinations of identity, privilege, and development. Recently, he has taken specific interest in how identity and privilege influence the experience of engagement at work and in learning environments.

Shannon Deer, Texas A&M University, USA

Shannon Deer started her career in public accounting before returning to Texas A&M University to teach. She currently teaches a variety of undergraduate and graduate business courses for the Mays Business School, primarily in accounting. Shannon also teaches an energy finance course for the Professional MBA program. Along with teaching, Shannon is currently pursuing a PhD in adult education at Texas A&M University. Shannon received her BBA in accounting and MS in finance from Texas A&M University.

Eric Feldman, Florida International University, USA

Eric M. Feldman, MS, is the Coordinator in the Office of Global Learning Initiatives at Florida International University, where he manages high impact programs, which extend the global learning experience beyond the classroom, including internships. Eric is working on his doctorate in adult education and human resource development and is interested in how social media impacts the public's understanding of the role of justice in society. Eric teaches a first-year Honors course on research, writing, and civic engagement, and holds a consulting role at FIU's Kimberly Green Latin American and Caribbean Center.

John Field, University of Stirling, United Kingdom

John Field is an Emeritus Professor at the University of Stirling and Honorary Professor at the University of Warwick. He chairs Scotland's Learning Partnership, the national organization representing the interests of learners and providers in Scotland. His research interests include social, historical, and policy studies of further, higher, vocational, and adult education. He has authored seven books, edited ten books, and published many papers in scholarly journals. His most recent book is *Working Men's Bodies*, a study of British work camp systems before 1939.

André P. Grace, University of Alberta, Canada

André P. Grace, PhD, is Canada Research Chair in Sexual and Gender Minority Studies and Professor and Director of Research at the Institute for Sexual Minority Studies and Services in the Faculty of Education, University of Alberta, Canada. He received the 2014 American Association for Adult and Continuing Education Cyril O. Houle Award for Outstanding Literature in Adult Education for his book *Lifelong Learning as Critical Action: International Perspectives on People, Politics, Policy, and Practice* (Canadian Scholars' Press, Toronto, 2013). With Dr. Tonette S. Rocco, Florida International University, he received the 2009 Phillip E. Frandson Award for Literature in the Field of Continuing Higher Education from the U.S. University Continuing Education Association. The award acknowledged their co-edited book *Challenging the Professionalization of Adult Education: John Ohliger and Contradictions in Modern Practice* (Jossey-Bass, San Francisco, 2009). At the 2010 Standing Conference on University Teaching and Research in the Education of Adults, University of Warwick, UK, Dr. Grace received the Ian Martin Award for Social Justice for his paper entitled "Space Matters: Lifelong Learning, Sexual Minorities, and Realities of Adult Education as Social Education."

Shibao Guo, University of Calgary, Canada

Dr. Shibao Guo is a Professor in the Werklund School of Education at the University of Calgary, Canada. His research interests include citizenship and immigration, Chinese immigrants in Canada, multicultural and anti-racist education, adult education and community development, and comparative and international education. Over the years he has developed research expertise in the areas of work, learning, transnational migration, and knowledge mobility and recognition. Dr. Guo has numerous publications to his credit, including books, journal articles, and book chapters. His recent work appeared in *Journal of Education and Work, International Journal of Lifelong Education, Compare,* and *Comparative Education.*

Robert Hill, Activist-Scholar, USA

Dr. Robert (Bob) Hill is an activist-scholar whose life centers on anti-oppression engagement. Areas of specialty include activism-as-the-practice of adult education; public policy; international adult education; environmental adult education; lesbian, gay, bisexual, transgender and Queer issues in education; Native American studies; arts-based inquiry; and Queer theory. He engages with those on the social margins like sex-workers, sexual minorities, self-identified radical environmentalists, people of color, radical women, and other troublemakers. He has worked with the United Nations Educational, Scientific, and Cultural Organization (UNESCO) as a specialist in the environment, "gay rights," and in democracy and citizenship. He was appointed to the UNESCO's Commission on Prison Education by the Chaire UNESCO de Recherche Appliquée pour l'Éducation en Prison. Bob was formerly an associate professor at the University of Georgia, affiliated with the Institute of Native American Studies, the Institute for African American Studies, and the Institute for Women's Studies. He has been honored as the recipient of the Dr. Martin Luther King Jr. 'Fulfilling the Dream' Presidential Award, received a university Outstanding Teaching award, and was selected one of Georgia's top 40 educators by the GA Safe Schools Coalition. His autobiography, one of only a few, was solicited for the book dedicated to the late adult educator-activist, Dr. Phyllis Cunningham, *Quintessential Adult Educators of the 21ˢᵗ Century.*

Shuchi Karim, BRAC University, Bangladesh

Dr. Shuchi Karim is a Bangladeshi feminist, academic, and researcher. She had her first MA in English Literature and Language from Jawaharlal Nehru University, Delhi, India, and her second MA in Gender and International Development from University of Warwick, UK. She had her PhD from International Institute of Social Study (ISS) at Erasmus University Rotterdam, The Hague, the Netherlands. Her discipline is Women, Gender and Development and her specialization is on sexuality. Dr. Karim started her career with BRAC Education Programme. For the past 12 years her career has shifted to academia and research. She worked at BRAC University as a Senior Lecturer and at the Department of Women and Gender Studies, Dhaka University as an Assistant Professor. Currently she works as a

Gender and Sexual Reproductive Health and Rights (SRHR) Specialist at the Institute of Educational Development (IED), BRAC University. Her research interest areas are sexuality, marginalization, women with disabilities, identity, gender, and education.

Marilyn Kell, Charles Darwin University, Australia
Marilyn Kell is a Research Fellow at the Northern Institute, Charles Darwin University, Australia. Dr Kell has extensive background as an educator and, as an academic, has experience with students from diverse language and cultural backgrounds. Her research interests include literacy pedagogy and assessment, the international student experience and work integrated learning. In 2013 she and Peter Kell published, *Literacy and Language in East Asia; Shifting Meanings, Values and Approaches.* She is currently investigating ways to enhance the work preparation experiences of international students and the experiences of immigrant teachers in Darwin.

Peter Kell, Charles Darwin University, Australia
Peter Kell is the Professor and Head of the School of Education at Charles Darwin University. Professor Kell's research interests include the internationalization of education, literacy and language, and education in the Asia Pacific. Peter Kell's most recent international publication is *Literacy and Language in East Asia; Shifting Meaning, Values and Approaches* co-authored with Dr. Marilyn Kell. Dr. Kell is a member of the Australian College of Education and the Australian Council of Deans of Education. In 2015 Peter Kell completed a Fulbright Fellowship at the University of Illinois (Urbana-Champaign) exploring the internationalization of graduate studies in education using online learning.

Lincoln Pettaway, The American University of Ras Al Khaimah, U.A.E.
For the past twenty years, Dr. Lincoln D. Pettaway has worked in the fields of organizational management, development, marketing, non-profit management, health services administration and human resource development. During this time he has had the privilege of designing various training curriculums for diverse populations in multiple countries. Currently, as an Assistant Professor at the American University of Ras Al Khaimah, in the United Arab Emirates, he has expanded his research areas to include diversity issues and concerns experienced by expatriates residing within the Middle East. Dr. Pettaway's research considers how cultural practices and belief systems informed behaviors in people from various nationalities, geographic regions, and ethnic backgrounds. This work also focuses on the overall effects

of diverse populations on organizations' return on investment (ROI) and productivity through talent and human capital management efforts.

Hilary Landorf, Florida International University, USA
Dr. Hilary Landorf is an associate professor in the College of Education at Florida International University (FIU) in Miami, Florida. She is also the Director of the Office of Global Learning Initiatives, where she oversees FIU's successful university-wide curriculum and co-curriculum internationalization initiative, *Global Learning for Global Citizenship*. Dr. Landorf holds a PhD in International Education from New York University, an MA from the University of Virginia, and a BA in English Literature from Stanford University. Landorf has held educational leadership positions throughout her professional career, which spans a variety of geographical, cultural, socioeconomic, and academic settings. She writes and presents internationally on integrating global learning into higher education, and on the connection between global learning and liberal education. Among her recent publications is a research-based definition of global learning, "Defining global learning at Florida International University," in *Diversity and Democracy*, and a chapter "Global Learning for Global Citizenship," in *Universities and Human Development: A Sustainable Imaginary for the XXI Century*, edited by Melanie Walker and Alejandra Boni.

Naomi Nichols, McGill University, Canada
Naomi Nichols is an Assistant Professor in the Faculty of Education at McGill University. She is also the Principal Investigator for a Social Sciences and Humanities Research Council (SSHRC) project titled, *Schools, Safety, and the Urban Neighbourhood*. Prior to joining the Faculty of Education at McGill, Nichols completed a Post-doctoral Fellowship with the Canadian Observatory on Homelessness at York University. The Fellowship focused on knowledge mobilization, research impact, and cross-sectoral responses to youth homelessness. Since completing her PhD, Nichols has worked as the Applied Social Scientist in the Learning Institute at the Hospital for Sick Children, a Research Associate and Sessional Instructor in the Faculty of Education at York University and an Adjunct Professor in the Queen's-Trent Concurrent Education Program. Her research activities and publications span the areas of youth homelessness; youth justice; alternative education and safe schools; inter-organizational relations in the youth sector; "youth at risk;" and community-academic research collaborations. In 2014, the University of Toronto Press published her first book: *Youth Work: An Institutional Ethnography of Youth Homelessness*.

Korbla Peter Puplampu, Grant MacEwan University, Canada
Dr. Korbla P. Puplampu is in the Department of Sociology at Grant MacEwan University, Edmonton, Canada. He has a PhD in Sociology as well as a MEd in International and Global Education. His research interests are in the politics of knowledge production and propagation as well as the global restructuring of higher education and agriculture. He has published in academic journals such as the *Canadian Journal of Learning and Technology*, *Alberta Journal of Educational Research*, and *Tailoring Biotechnologies*. He has also co-edited or contributed to several books including *The Public Sphere and the Politics of Survival: Voice, Sustainability and Public Policy in Ghana* (with Wisdom Tettey), and *African Education and Globalization* (with Ali Abdi and George Dei).

Thomas G. Reio, Jr., Florida International University, USA
Dr. Thomas G. Reio, Jr., is Professor of Adult Education and Human Resource Development and Associate Dean for Graduate Studies at Florida International University in Miami, Florida. He is immediate past editor of *Human Resource Development Review* and currently serves as co-editor of *New Horizons in Adult Education and Human Resource Development*. His research concerns curiosity and risk-taking motivation, workplace socialization processes, workplace incivility, entrepreneurship, and workplace learning. His work has been published in leading journals in education, business, and psychology. These journals include *Personality and Individual Differences*, *Educational and Psychological Measurement*, *Journal of Business and Psychology*, *Journal of Interpersonal Violence*, *Human Resource Development Quarterly*, *Human Resource Development International*, *Journal of Management Development*, and the *Journal of School Psychology*, He has over 16 years of experience as a training and development director, organizational consultant, and operations manager.

Steve Rios, Florida Atlantic University, USA
Dr. Steve J. Rios, owner of Rios Research & Evaluation, has been an advocate for marginalized young adults for nearly 20 years. Dr. Rios co-founded Florida Reach, a state-wide network of post-secondary and K–12 educators, child welfare professionals and youth advocates focused on increasing academic success among young people from foster care and homeless situations. His research interests include school-university-community partnerships, qualitative research, and education among underprivileged emerging adults and adolescents. He holds a doctorate in Adult Education and

Human Resource Development from Florida International University. Dr. Rios teaches research methodology at Florida Atlantic University.

Kim Vance, ARC International, Canada/Switzerland
Kim Vance is the Co-Director and Co-Founder of ARC International. Founded in 2003, ARC International is an NGO, based in Canada and Switzerland, geared to advancing lesbian, gay, bisexual, and transgender rights. They have played a key role in the application of international human rights law in relation to sexual orientation and gender identity, as well as providing support to NGO's working in countries around the world, and ensuring that the records of all UN States on LGBT issues are subjected to international scrutiny. Before founding ARC International, Vance served as President of Egale Canada and is a seasoned activist within the LGBT communities at the international, national, and local levels. Vance's background and research is in adult education/community development. She also serves on the executive of a five-year Social Sciences & Humanities Research Council of Canada (SSHRC) project entitled *Envisioning Global LGBT Human Rights* based out of York University.

Mark J. Webber, York University, Canada
Dr. Mark J. Webber is Associate Professor Emeritus and Senior Scholar at York University in Toronto. A Germanist with degrees from Harvard (AB) and Yale (MPhil, PhD), he was the founding director of the Canadian Centre for German and European Studies at York, a center of excellence funded by the German Academic Exchange Service. For many years he also served as academic director in Ontario of the Ontario/Baden-Württemberg Student Exchange Program, for which he received the Officer's Cross of the German Federal Order of Merit. Along with Michael Brown, he initiated the trinational Mark and Gail Appel Program in Holocaust and Antiracism Education. Mark Webber's teaching and research focuses on issues of intercultural (mis)understanding and on metaphor theory.

Chaundra Whitehead, Florida International University, USA
Chaundra Whitehead is a doctoral candidate in the Adult Education and Human Resource Development program at Florida International University. She has over 10 years teaching experience in literacy, vocational, and corrections education. Her research interests are corrections, adult education advocacy, adult basic education, and women's issues. She actively volunteers as a literacy tutor with the public library in Miami-Dade County, Florida.

She is also a facilitator of the Alternatives to Violence Project in correctional facilities in South Florida. She has a MS in Adult Education from Florida International University and a BA in English from Florida A&M University.

Lindsay Wodinski, Grant MacEwan University, Canada
Lindsay Wodinski teaches in the Department of Sociology at Grant MacEwan University. She has an MA in Sociology from the University of Alberta and her research examines broader questions of social inequality and specifically public policy interventions for vulnerable children, youth and families, education, and public advocacy. For her MA, she employed a comparative case study analysis of two youth-serving agencies in Edmonton within the context of the changing landscape of the social, economic, and political conditions that frame the work of community-based organizations in Alberta.

Index